P9-DNO-860

P9-DNO-860

Architecture in North America
since 1960

© Joseph Molitor

Architecture in North America

since 1960

ALEXANDER TZONIS LIANE LEFAIVRE RICHARD DIAMOND

A Bulfinch Press Book
LITTLE, BROWN AND COMPANY
BOSTON • NEW YORK • TORONTO • LONDON

Frontispiece: Detail of Paul Rudolph's Yale School of Art and Architecture Building, New Haven (see pp. 82–5).

Copyright © 1995 by Thames and Hudson Ltd., London

All rights reserved. No part of this book may be reproduced in any form or by any electronic or mechanical means, including information storage and retrieval systems, without permission in writing from the publisher, except by a reviewer who may quote brief passages in a review.

First North American Edition

ISBN 0–8212–2228–7

Library of Congress Catalog Card Number 95–76364

Bulfinch Press is an imprint and trademark of Little, Brown and Company (Inc.)
Published simultaneously in Canada by Little, Brown & Company (Canada) Limited

PRINTED IN SINGAPORE

Contents

8   **Preface and acknowledgments**

10   **ARCHITECTURE IN NORTH AMERICA SINCE 1960**

THE PROJECTS

66   **Edward Larrabee Barnes**
HAYSTACK MOUNTAIN SCHOOL OF ARTS AND CRAFTS
Deer Isle, Maine
1959–61

70   **Marquis & Stoller**
ST. FRANCIS SQUARE COOPERATIVE APARTMENTS
San Francisco, California
1960–61

72   **Louis I. Kahn**
ALFRED NEWTON RICHARDS MEDICAL RESEARCH LABORATORY, UNIVERSITY OF PENNSYLVANIA
Philadelphia, Pennsylvania
1957–60

76   **Skidmore Owings and Merrill**
ROBERT R. MCMATH SOLAR TELESCOPE
Kitt Peak, Pima County, Arizona
1962

78   **Eero Saarinen & Associates**
DULLES TERMINAL
Chantilly, Virginia
1958–63

82   **Paul Rudolph Architect**
YALE SCHOOL OF ART AND ARCHITECTURE
New Haven, Connecticut
1958–63

86   **Venturi and Short**
VANNA VENTURI HOUSE
Chestnut Hill, Pennsylvania
1961–63

90   **MLTW (Moore Lyndon Turnbull Whitaker)**
SEA RANCH CONDOMINIUM 1
Sea Ranch, California
1963–65

94   **Louis I. Kahn**
SALK INSTITUTE OF BIOLOGICAL STUDIES
La Jolla, California
1959–65

98   **Venturi and Rauch**
GUILD HOUSE
Philadelphia, Pennsylvania
1961–65

100   **Sert Jackson and Gourley**
FRANCIS GREENWOOD PEABODY TERRACE
Cambridge, Massachusetts
1963–65

102   **Charles Gwathmey**
GWATHMEY RESIDENCE AND STUDIO
Amagansett, New York
1963–65

106   **Marcel Breuer & Associates**
WHITNEY MUSEUM OF AMERICAN ART
New York, New York
1963–66

110   **Cambridge Seven Associates, Inc. with Buckminster Fuller**
UNITED STATES PAVILION EXPO 67
Montreal, Quebec
1964–67

114   **John Portman & Associates**
HYATT REGENCY ATLANTA
Atlanta, Georgia
1964–67

116   **Moshe Safdie and Associates**
HABITAT
Montreal, Quebec
1964–67

120   **Affleck, Desbarats, Dimakopoulos, Lebensold, Sise**
PLACE BONAVENTURE
Montreal, Quebec
1964–67

124   **Kallmann McKinnell & Knowles**
BOSTON CITY HALL
Boston, Massachusetts
1962–68

128   **Kevin Roche John Dinkeloo and Associates**
OAKLAND MUSEUM
Oakland, California
1961–68

130   **Kevin Roche John Dinkeloo and Associates**
FORD FOUNDATION
New York City, New York
1963–68

132   **Cambridge Seven Associates, Inc.**
NEW ENGLAND AQUARIUM
Boston, Massachusetts
1962–69

136   **Paolo Soleri**
ARCOSANTI
Cordes Junction, Arizona
1970–

138   **Johansen and Bhavnani**
MUMMERS THEATER
Oklahoma City, Oklahoma
1964–70

142   **Eisenman Architects**
HOUSE II
Hardwick, Vermont
1969–71

144   **Skidmore Owings and Merrill**
JOHN HANCOCK CENTER
Chicago, Illinois
1965–70

146   **Gunnar Birkerts and Associates**
FEDERAL RESERVE BANK OF MINNEAPOLIS
Minneapolis, Minnesota
1967–72

148 **Louis I. Kahn**
KIMBELL ART MUSEUM
Fort Worth, Texas
1966–72

152 **MLTW (Moore Lyndon Turnbull Whitaker)**
KRESGE COLLEGE, UNIVERSITY OF CALIFORNIA AT SANTA CRUZ
Santa Cruz, California
1970–73

154 **Craig Zeidler Strong**
MCMASTER UNIVERSITY HEALTH SCIENCES CENTRE
Hamilton, Ontario
1967–72

156 **Cesar Pelli & Gruen Associates, Inc.**
PACIFIC DESIGN CENTER
Los Angeles, California
Phase I 1971–75; Phase II, 1984–88

160 **Arthur Erickson Architects**
MUSEUM OF ANTHROPOLOGY, UNIVERSITY OF BRITISH COLUMBIA
Vancouver, British Columbia
1971–76

164 **Robert A. M. Stern Architects**
POINTS OF VIEW
Mount Desert Island, Maine
1975–76

166 **Richard Meier & Associates**
BRONX DEVELOPMENT CENTER
The Bronx, New York
1970–76

168 **Stanley Tigerman and Associates**
ILLINOIS REGIONAL LIBRARY FOR THE BLIND AND PHYSICALLY HANDICAPPED
Chicago, Illinois
1975–78

172 **Hugh Stubbins & Associates, Inc.**
CITICORP
New York City, New York
1970–77

174 **I. M. Pei & Partners**
NATIONAL GALLERY OF ART EAST BUILDING
Washington, D.C.
1968–78

176 **Richard Meier & Partners**
THE ATHENEUM
New Harmony, Indiana
1975–79

178 **Jersey Devil**
HILL HOUSE
La Honda, California
1977–79

180 **Frank O. Gehry & Associates**
FRANK GEHRY HOUSE
Santa Monica, California
1978–79

184 **Kevin Roche John Dinkeloo and Associates**
DEERE & COMPANY HEADQUARTERS WEST OFFICE
Moline, Illinois
1975–78

186 **Arthur Erickson Architects**
ROBSON SQUARE AND PROVINCIAL LAW COURTS
Vancouver, British Columbia
1973–79

188 **Johnson Burgee Architects**
GARDEN GROVE COMMUNITY CHURCH
Garden Grove, California
1976–80

190 **Fay Jones & Maurice Jennings, Architects**
THORNCROWN CHAPEL
Eureka Springs, Arkansas
1979–80

192 **SITE Projects, Inc.**
BEST FOREST BUILDING
Richmond, Virginia
1978–80

194 **Andres Duany, Elizabeth Plater-Zyberk, Architects Inc.**
SEASIDE PLAN
Seaside, Florida
1980–

196 **Bond Ryder James & Associates**
MARTIN LUTHER KING, JR. CENTER FOR NON-VIOLENT SOCIAL CHANGE
Atlanta, Georgia
1976–81

200 **Antoine Predock Architect**
RIO GRANDE NATURE CENTER
Albuquerque, New Mexico
1982

204 **Arquitectonica**
ATLANTIS BUILDING
Miami, Florida
1978–82

208 **Michael Graves Architect**
PORTLAND BUILDING
Portland, Oregon
1980–82

210 **Hellmuth Obata Kassabaum**
LEVI'S PLAZA
San Francisco, California
1977–82

212 **Johnson/Burgee Architects**
AT&T HEADQUARTERS BUILDING
New York City, New York
1978–83

214 **Edward Larrabee Barnes/ John M. Y. Lee, Architects**
IBM BUILDING
New York City, New York
1973–83

218 **Der Scutt Architect**
TRUMP TOWER
New York City, New York
1979–83

220 **Michael Graves Architect**
SAN JUAN CAPISTRANO
LIBRARY
San Juan Capistrano,
California
1981–83

222 **Kelbaugh + Lee**
ROOSEVELT SOLAR VILLAGE
Roosevelt, New Jersey
1981–83

224 **Esherick Homsey Dodge**
and Davis
MONTEREY BAY AQUARIUM
Monterey, California
1978–84

228 **Gatje Papachristou Smith**
RICHARD B. RUSSELL
POWERHOUSE
Savannah River, Georgia
and South Carolina
1978–85

230 **Steven Holl Architects**
BERKOWITZ ODGIS HOUSE
Martha's Vineyard,
Massachusetts
1984

234 **Clark & Menefee Architects**
MIDDLETON INN
Charleston, South Carolina
1978–85

236 **Murphy/Jahn Architects**
STATE OF ILLINOIS CENTER
Chicago, Illinois
1979–85

238 **Murphy/Jahn Architects**
UNITED AIRLINES
TERMINAL 1
Chicago, Illinois
1987

240 **Center for Maximum Potential**
Building Systems
LAREDO DEMONSTRATION
BLUEPRINT FARM
Laredo, Texas
1987–

242 **Carlos Jiménez Architectural**
Design Studio
HOUSTON FINE ARTS PRESS
Houston, Texas
1985–87

246 **Scogin, Elam and Bray Architects**
CLAYTON COUNTY LIBRARY
Jonesboro, Georgia
1986–88

248 **Cesar Pelli & Associates**
WORLD FINANCIAL CENTER
New York City, New York
1980–88

252 **Douglas Cardinal Architects Ltd.**
MUSEUM OF CIVILIZATION
Hull, Canada
1982–89

256 **Eric Owen Moss Architects**
PARAMOUNT LAUNDRY
OFFICE BUILDING
Culver City, California
1987–89

260 **Eisenman Architects**
THE WEXNER CENTER FOR
THE VISUAL ARTS AND FINE
ARTS LIBRARY
Columbus, Ohio
1983–89

264 **Legorreta Arquitectos with**
Mitchell/Giurgola
SOLANA, IBM SOUTHLAKE
AND VILLAGE CENTER WEST
Dallas, Texas
1988–90

268 **Antoine Predock Architect**
LAS VEGAS CENTRAL LIBRARY
AND CHILDREN'S DISCOVERY
MUSEUM
Las Vegas, Nevada
1987–90

272 **Holt Hinshaw Pfau Jones**
PARAMOUNT PICTURES FILM
AND TAPE ARCHIVES
Los Angeles, California
1989–91

274 **Morphosis**
CEDARS-SINAI COMPREHENSIVE
CANCER CENTER
Los Angeles, California
1991

276 **Patkau Architects, Inc.**
SEABIRD ISLAND SCHOOL
Agassiz, British Columbia
1988–91

280 **Venturi, Scott Brown and**
Associates, Inc.
SEATTLE ART MUSEUM
Seattle, Washington
1984–91

282 **Hellmuth Obata Kassabaum**
CAMDEN YARDS AT
ORIOLE FIELDS
Baltimore, Maryland
1988–92

286 **Pei Cobb Freed & Partners**
UNITED STATES HOLOCAUST
MEMORIAL MUSEUM
Washington, D.C.
1986–93

290 **Frank O. Gehry & Associates**
THE FREDERICK R. WEISMAN
ART MUSEUM
Minneapolis, Minnesota
1992–94

292 **James Stewart Polshek and**
Partners
MASHANTUCKET PEQUOT
MUSEUM AND RESEARCH CENTER
Mashantucket Pequot Reservation,
Connecticut
(Begun 1993)

296 Documentation: architects'
biographies, project specifications,
and select bibliographies

310 Acknowledgments

311 Index

Preface

Mass media coverage has elevated current North American architecture into one of the most widely known expressions of contemporary culture. In the press and on television, images of gilded facades and soaring towers compete with pictures of movie stars. While this attention is not necessarily a bad thing for North American architecture, or architecture in general, it gives only a partial idea of what we believe is significant about the period since 1960.

Our period opens with the emergence of an architecture which breaks with the conventionality and conformism of mainstream design during the 1950s. This new architecture of the 1960s, which we identify as an American Renaissance, was driven by technological exploration and the search for urban, social, and environmental quality.

Change came swiftly, however. By the late 1970s and early 1980s these goals and aspirations appeared to be in decline, with much of the popular attention focussed on historicism and style, emblematic of corporate identity and patronage. But the fundamental themes of communal identity and accountability, and a tenacious concern for the particularities of place, remain very much at the heart of North American architecture.

The buildings discussed here are selected because of their strong identity, their uniqueness and for the paradigmatic role they have played in the development of North American architecture, however subtle or controversial these roles might be. They are diverse, reflecting the multi-faceted explorations of the period: technological, iconological, social, and cultural. Corporate headquarters share pages with subsidized housing. Projects reflecting the American fascination with spectacle and media—giant aquaria, baseball stadia, and a televangelist glass cathedral—appear next to projects that manifest the social concerns of this time and place in providing care for special groups: homes for the elderly, an intensive care unit for young cancer patients, and a library for the blind and handicapped.

Although it is sometimes difficult to draw the line between new projects and renovations, we have focussed here on new buildings, not because renovations are less important, but because they make up a class of buildings which deserve their own book. Similarly, the "America" of the title of this book refers less to a political entity than to an existing cultural interdependence and heritage shared between the U.S. and Canada. For this reason, the study of such cultural interdependencies shared between the U.S. and Mexico is the subject of another book. Although American architecture has benefited from the presence of projects designed by foreign architects, we have been concerned here with projects conceived by U.S. or Canadian architects, naturalized, or holding an American or Canadian license through which they obtained the job in question.

The projects are ordered chronologically, according to their date of completion. Taken together they make up a virtual city crossing the entire continent. The path through this collection starts with a modest wood frame art school perched above the Maine Coast and criss-crosses the continent several times, ending at a project just underway: a cultural center for a tribe of Native Americans, an ambitious project that combines the most advanced electronic technology with fundamental concerns for the landscape. What we find unique in this diverse juxtaposition of subjects and approaches is a sense of synthesis, as if these contrasts provide checks and balances out of which American architecture maintains its unique inventiveness, pragmatism, and vitality.

Any comprehensive project of this kind depends on the help of numerous groups and individuals. Many of the architects included in the book devoted time to discuss with us their work and the issues of American architecture today. Because we have included at the end of the book extensive documentation on each project, we have been particularly dependent on the time and generosity of the individual architectural firms which have provided us with this material. We would also like to express our appreciation for the creative contribution of the photographers whose work we include here. In particular, we would like to acknowledge the help of Norman McGrath, Gordon Schenk, and especially Erica Stoller.

We would like to express our deep appreciation to Mack Scogin, Chair of the Department of Architecture at the Harvard Graduate School of Design, who provided genial support for this undertaking. Many friends and colleagues there contributed greatly to our thinking on these issues. We are pleased to thank Jude LeBlanc, Mary McAullife, Mohsen Mostafavi, Spiro Pollalis, Linda Pollak, Edward Robbins, Dan Schodek, and Eduard Sekler for their valued conversation and friendship. We also acknowledge the generous help of several staff members at the Harvard Graduate School of Design: Hinda Sklar, Librarian, Mary Daniels, Special Collections, and Doug Cogger, Presentation Services.

Our thanks are extended to Stanford Anderson, who invited Liane Lefaivre and Alex Tzonis to spend a part of the Fall term of 1992 as guests of the Department of Architecture at the Massachusetts Institute of Technology. And many thanks to the members of the Design Knowledge Systems research group of the Delft University of Technology, in particular, Leo Oorschot, Yu Li, Caterina Burge, Catherine Visser, and John Linke Heinz. Our discussions with Joop Doorman were particularly fruitful.

We are deeply indebted to many friends—Anthony Alofsin, Spiros Amourgis, Richard Ingersoll, and Mary Otis Stevens, as well as Trevor Boddy, Christine Boyer, George Claflen, Emanuel Kelly, Micha Levin, Marvin Malecha, Bob Maltz, Tician Papachristou, Peter Papademetriou, David Plante, Donald Watson, and Stuart Wrede. The late Richard Pommer was most stimulating in his discussions with us about Critical Regionalism. We also benefited from conversations with Julian Beinhardt, Ed Eigen, Kenneth Frampton, Richard Hatch, Michael Sorkin, Tony Vidler, and Margo Wellington. Bob Berwick and Marilyn Matz, as usual, helped in more ways than they realized. We are grateful to Evangelos Rafalias for the working environment he provided. Special thanks also for their continuous support go to Sebastiano Brandolini, Luis Fernandez Galiano, and Toshio Nakamura.

Much research was carried out by our able student assistants from the GSD: Stephen Dietz, Christine Holland, Matt Hoyt, Victoria Meyers, Nancy Murdock, Christina M. O'Sullivan, Sandy Pei, and M. Wade Stevens. Thanks to you all.

Lastly, we would like to dedicate this book to our families for their love and support, to our students for the stimulation and contributions, and to Stathis Eustathiadis, for his magnanimity and irascible good cheer, without all of which this book would not have been possible.

Architecture in North America since 1960

CHAOS: A FORGOTTEN EPISODE IN AMERICAN ARCHITECTURE

At the beginning of 1961, *Progressive Architecture*, one of the leading American professional architectural journals, was having its annual meeting for its Design Award Program. As was customary, the jury used the opportunity to comment on the current state of architecture.

The architecture they were debating was the product of the second half of the 1950s. In an effort to break free from the orthogonal glass and steel box and the idea of the building as an undifferentiated "universal space," architects had developed a series of widely differing formal alternatives: volumes that were cylinders, hemi-

spheres, or prismatic rhomboids, with "plastic" columns and butterfly roofs, enclosed by sculptural surfaces and lacy screens. In their efforts to create a "monumental" and "humanist" architecture, the architects of the period were taking a great number of widely diverging paths, such as the historicist, the sensualist, the sculptural, and the ornamental.[1]

The "architecture of chaoticism," a free hand drawing by the magazine staff of *Progressive Architecture* for the series entitled "Sixties, the State of Architecture," by Thomas Creighton (1961)

Instead of criticizing this manifest lack of direction, Thomas H. Creighton, the editor of *Progressive Architecture*, concluded the meeting with a statement embracing the situation: "The profession of architecture, through its most articulate spokesmen, is perfectly willing to agree that a state of diverse design approach, which is readily acknowledged to be confusion and might well be termed *chaos* (our italic), exists today." Architecture in a state of chaos? The jury felt the question merited further attention. And so, following the meeting, Creighton decided to conduct a "sort of seminar by correspondence."

The response to his call was impressive, and the list of participants read like a *Who's Who* of the architectural world. Their comments mirrored the excitement and frustrations of the most prominent minds in American architecture at that time. On the basis of the written responses, Creighton organized a three-part series of the magazine, entitled "Sixties, the State of Architecture."[2] In the introduction to the first issue, Creighton put forth what he now called "chaoticism (a) major design approach which has to be recognized," and he explicitly called for "the acceptance and practice of the principles of chaos."

All participants were eager to take a position. For Walter Netch, who was, with Creighton, instrumental in shaping the discussion, the confusion arising from chaos was not necessarily a bad state to be in. The authority he cited was the great mathematician Norbert Wiener's *The Human Use of Human Beings, Cybernetics and Society* (1950).[3] By the end of the 1950s, this was a popular book, a major statement not only about the sciences and technology, but also about Western society's democratic aspirations. Wiener asserted that "confusion" was a fundamental characteristic of reality, and that "we are immersed in a life in which the world as a whole obeys the second law of thermodynamics: confusion increases and order decreases."

Pietro Belluschi, the dean of architecture at MIT, felt comfortable with chaoticism. "Confusion," he believed, "exists wherever there is life." He was echoed on the other side of the country by Berkeley's architectural dean, William Wurster, who found in chaos a potential for variety, as an enemy of standardization, which he "hated." John Johansen, the architect who tried to start a new "anti-stylistic" movement in architecture called "Kinetics," went further. The situation was, to him, "explosive." It resulted from new "rapid and effective communication," which opened new vistas and appetites for "remote cultures" and "historic monuments" following a period of "Bauhaus austerity." He also saw it as the outcome of "new functional requirements."

Of all the participants it was Philip Johnson who was the most content with chaos, or "foggy chaos," as he preferred to call it. "Why can't we just wander around aimlessly? The world is so full of a number of things ... Let us enjoy the multiplicity of it all. Let the students have a different hero every year," he wrote. He declared aphoristically, "the only principle that I can conceive of believing in is the Principle of Uncertainty."

Rafael Soriano, the Californian architect with a particular interest in advanced technology, was appalled, stating, "Our vision is befogged" (this had prompted Johnson's ironic comment on "foggy chaos"). Soriano accused "the monthly architectural press (which) blasts us with glamorous examples ..." He emphasized "the young who are playing with a variety of ideas a la mode" in an effort to be looked at as "different, even if they do not make sense to themselves or to anyone else."

Critics of the chaotic state of architecture included leading educators, such as Josep Lluis Sert, the dean of the Harvard Graduate School of Design, and Paul Schweikher and Serge Chermayeff, who were teaching at Yale. Prominent professionals, like Harry Weese from Chicago and Minoru Yamasaki, were also very negative about the situation. Mies was his caustic self: "Certainly, it is not necessary or possible to invent a new kind of architecture every Monday morning," he wrote, quoting his own favorite aphorism. Buckminster Fuller dismissed the whole issue. While many felt that confusion existed in architecture, he did not feel confused, he declared, unperturbed. "To those who have expected change," Fuller boasted, "little confusion exists."

Creighton, however, appeared to be orchestrating this event with higher ambitions in mind. It was crucial to him to formulate a way of coming to terms with chaos, and to find possible applications for it in design. He wished to cultivate what he saw as a fundamental state into something that had to be "admitted" and "defended" as a "design philosophy." Expecting it to become a lasting "condition," he argued that it should become a "movement." He even called for a chaoticist manifesto.

Chaoticism, however, did not catch on. Retrospectively, the incident of chaoticism in the context of the public debates of the beginning of the 1960s appears to be a minor, almost frivolous one. The superficiality of this architecture, overly concerned with the stylistic, formal, surface characteristics of architecture, was condemned by Lewis Mumford in an article that did in fact succeed in capturing the spirit of the time, "The Case Against Modern Architecture."[4] No one seemed interested in pursuing chaoticism and the initial excitement cooled quickly. Americans were preoccupied with different issues: changes in technology, the degradation of the environment, and problems in the cities.

These preoccupations were discussed by economist John Kenneth Galbraith in his critical work, *The Affluent Society* (1958).[5] His book challenged the complacency and routine thinking into which American society had sunk, hypnotized into perceiving itself as an affluent society. Galbraith pointed out that as a result of this mentality, Americans were unaware of the poverty in their midst. While affluent in terms of private goods, they were poor in terms of public essentials. In the end, they had been unobservant of the fact that the greater their wealth, the more trash they produced; and not only was no one willing to collect it, but there were fewer places to dispose of the discarded materials. Similarly, the unprecedented increase of automobiles created problems of both circulation and parking. "Magnificently efficient factories," Galbraith wrote, "a lavish supply of automobiles," and "vast consumption of handsomely pack-aged products" had led to "the agony of a city without usable air." He summed up the situation in a memorable phrase: "private opulence and public squalor."

Michael Harrington's book, *The Other America: Poverty in the United States* (1962),[6] was the result of a commissioned article in *Commentary* magazine at the end of the 1950s. It opened with a reference to *The Affluent Society*, a "brilliant book," Harrington commented, "widely misinterpreted." The effect of Galbraith's book on a large number of people had been that basic quantitative needs had been met, and the only economic problems remaining were "qualitative," to "live decently amid luxury," Harrington claimed. This discussion was taking place while there were estimates of 40 to 50 million poor people living in the United States. This poverty was "off the beaten track" for the middle-class Americans living in the suburbs. It was confined to the urban slums, and in contrast to the poor of previous generations, it was "immune to progress" and "impervious to hope."

In 1962, a third, equally explosive, publication was Rachel Carson's *Silent Spring*.[7] It opens with a dramatic description of an incident, of a town "in the heart of America where all life seemed to live in harmony with its surroundings ... prosperous, beautiful, even in the middle of the winter ... with countless birds (coming) to feed on the berries and on the seed heads of the dried weeds rising above the snow ... a strange blight crept over the area, and everything began to change." The description that follows competes with the most vivid accounts of Biblical catastrophes. But it was the reality of the natural environment assaulted, contaminated, and irrevocably polluted by the products of contemporary technology, observed and reported by a single scientist.

NEW FRONTIERS

Nothing could have been more different from the preoccupations of the *Progressive Architecture* symposium than the problems described in these three books. Indeed nothing could have been more remote from the issues raised in the symposium than those raised—at almost the same time—in John F. Kennedy's Inaugural Address (January 20, 1961), and further developed in his subsequent addresses: the State of The Union Message (January 30, 1961), the Program Outline for Economic Recovery and Growth (sent to Congress February 2, 1961), and the Special Message on Housing and Community Development (submitted to Congress March 9, 1961).[8]

The Kennedy texts offered a clear programmatic framework for cultural and societal change. They set up new policy priorities and institutional structures with a sense of urgency for renewal, change, and civility, and they redefined what it meant to be a citizen of America, and to be a citizen of the world. Among the major priorities that had a bearing on architecture were technology, the environment, and community.

In his Inaugural Address, Kennedy spelled out a commitment to "the wonders of science," although he also warned of its "terrors." Quoting Isaiah, he spoke of undoing "the heavy burdens" and letting "the oppressed go free." In the State of the Union Address, on the other hand, he drew attention to the state of the American economy, reporting that while the economy had recovered from the 1958 recession, the "most resourceful industrialized country on earth ranks among the last in the rate of economic growth." But he added: "We will do what must be done. For our national household is cluttered with unfinished and neglected tasks." Thus, he expressed the quest for "a decent home and a suitable environment for every American family," a promise not yet fulfilled, but for which he pledged a new Housing and Urban Affairs Department to be established in the Executive Branch. He also asked for classrooms "for two million more children who for the moment have no proper room to be taught."

The Economic Recovery and Growth Program Outline for Congress continues in the same animated spirit and in greater detail. The recommendations are prefaced by a statement of goals and problems declaring the American economy in a state of "economic decline and slack," whose actual production was "running behind the potential one." It called for a "new initiative and imagination" for "construction ... maintenance and improvement of ... housing ... community facilities ... more comprehensive and more practical planning for urban and metropolitan areas." It asks for "reduction of mortgage interest rates ... loans (for) many communities and public facility projects ... to quicken the pace of urban renewal works."

The President's Message on Housing and Community development focussed on community. It opened with the challenge that "our communities are what we make them." It included in addition to the provisions for housing for moderate income, and housing for rural veterans and the elderly, plans for revitalizing urban and metropolitan areas, citing the loss of population of central cities during the "fifties when our urban population as a whole grew rapidly." It also provided for land reserves and a "long-range program and policy for dealing with open space," to control "persistent patterns of haphazard suburban developments ... contributing to a tragic waste in the use of vital resources now being consumed at an alarming rate."

Community facilities and transportation in the cities were of major concern: "Nothing is more dramatically apparent than the inadequacy of transportation in our larger urban areas. The solution cannot be found only in the construction of additional urban highways ... other means of transportation which use less space and equipment must be improved and expanded." And the text concluded, urging that: "more important, planning for transportation and land use must go hand in hand as two inseparable aspects of the same process" as well as the need for experimentation. It asked for financing for tests and demonstrations of "new approaches to home design and construction."

One has to note here that the situation in Canada in the early 1960s appeared to be less dramatic than the one described by Galbraith, Harrington, and Carson, as well as by Kennedy. Not only had the Canadian environment suffered less from technology, but urban poverty was less of an issue, the phenomenon of public squalor being generally more confined and of a smaller scale. The public sector often acted as a partner with the private sector in maintaining and improving urban conditions.

As opposed to the Kennedy texts, and to the books of Galbraith, Harrington, and Carson, which all identified new problems, raised new questions, and urged rethinking, the debate in architectural circles about chaoticism, as well as the projects of the architects of the second half of the 1950s, seemed to be suffering from what Lewis Mumford had called "sclerosis." Buildings were seen only within the paradigm of the box, and the universal space as a constructive envelope, and although there were occasional variants, they were never seen as structures affecting the way people live and relate to each other as a community, or how they affect their environment.

With very few exceptions, the architecture of the 1960s was fundamentally different from anything built or proposed during the previous decade. Like the Kennedy texts and the books of Galbraith, Harrington, and Carson, the architecture of the new decade was an invitation to rethinking. It looked at buildings from the programmatic point of view and addressed issues of technology, the environment, and community.

The emergence of this new architecture coincided with the beginning of the new decade, marked by the entrance of a new generation into American culture and politics. Kennedy was simply its most charismatic spokesman, a man who, according to Richard Reeves, was "a surpassing cultural figure"—an artist, like Picasso, who changed the way people looked at things (*Time*, November 22, 1993). Indeed a major change was in the making: America was on the threshold of a Renaissance.

AN AMERICAN RENAISSANCE

The concept of Renaissance brings many things to mind: A moment in history of creative vitality, bursting out of a period of inactivity, dullness, and darkness; a group of people who take risks, break rules, make new ones; a dramatic opening of the horizon of inquiry; and a period that lasts for a brief moment in time.

In the history of American culture, such a period had been previously identified in the mid-19th century. F. O. Matthiessen, in his book of 1941, *American Renaissance*,[8] identifies the half-decade between 1850 and 1855 as a "concentrated moment of expression ... of imaginative vitality." It "saw the appearance of *Representative Man* (1850), *The Scarlet Letter* (1850), *The House of the Seven Gables* (1851), *Moby Dick* (1851), *Pierre* (1852), *Walden* (1854) and *Leaves of Grass* (1855)."

Similarly, during the first five years of the 1960s, there was a constellation of buildings emerging in the United States, buildings not only of exceptionally high quality and exceedingly innovative character, but also those of a germinal nature, whose impact would be felt in architectural thinking for years to come. The themes of the environment, technology, and community made up the framework within which these projects were conceived. Among them were Edward Larrabee Barnes's Haystack Mountain School of Arts and Crafts (1959–61, pp. 66–69), Louis Kahn's Alfred Newton Richards Medical Research Laboratory (1957–60, pp. 72–75), his Salk Institute (1959–65. pp. 94–97), Paul Rudolph's Yale School of Art and Architecture (1958–63, pp. 82–85), Venturi's Vanna Venturi House (with Short, 1961–63, pp. 86–89) and Guild House (with Rauch, 1961–65, pp. 98–99), and the Sea Ranch by Moore, Lyndon, Turnbull, and Whitaker (1963–65, pp. 90–93). These projects were followed closely in time (all three 1964–67) by Cambridge Seven and Buckminster Fuller's U.S. Pavilion at Expo 67 (pp. 110–113), Moshe Safdie's Habitat (pp. 116–19), and Ray Affleck and Associates' Place Bonaventure (pp. 120–23), as well as by Kevin Roche's Oakland Museum (1961–68, pp. 128–29) and Ford Foundation (1963–68, pp. 130–31). Buildings of a more restrictive character, focussing on specific issues, were Marquis & Stoller's housing project, St. Francis Square (1960–61, pp. 70–71), and the Kitt Peak observatory by SOM's Myron Goldsmith (1962, pp. 76–77).

This same framework of themes appeared in a number of books that revolutionized the thinking surrounding the built environment: Kevin Lynch's *The Image of the City*,[9] Lewis Mumford's *The City in History*,[10] Jane Jacobs's *The Death and Life of Great American Cities*,[11] Serge Chermayeff and Christopher Alexander's *Community and Privacy*,[12] Christopher Alexander's *Notes on the Synthesis of Form*,[13] Melvin Webber's *Explorations into Urban Structure*,[14] and Robert Venturi's *Complexity and Contradiction*. [15]

It is remarkable how Mumfordian this universe of concerns of the early 1960s was. Mumford's deepest intellectual ties were to the functionalist tradition. What distinguished his thinking, however, was the "multi-functionalism" of his approach, clear in the uniquely broad scope of his writings. For him, a well-functioning "humanist," "modern" architecture could not be dissociated from a well-functioning neighborhood, city, and region. Moreover, for him the definition of function had to be seen in terms of technology, environment, and community. This paradigm was a continuation of the American Functionalist tradition inititated by Horatio Greenough.[16] The materialization of Mumfordian "multi-functionalism" was never more faithfully displayed collectively than in the best projects of the American Renaissance during the early 1960s.

The reasons for Mumford's consistent preference for the regionalist expression of this paradigm are complex, and the dangers in using the term are obvious. His regionalism ran the risk of being confused with the backward-looking, sentimental regionalism employed in tourist or commercial projects since the second half of the 19th century. Even worse, it might have been taken as a support for the Nazi "Heimatsarchitektur" movement of the 1930s. It was known that Mumford, devoted to the ideals of community and democracy, was totally hostile to such a movement, however. He had made this point expressly in lectures in which he projected the figure of the 19th-century architect, H. H. Richardson as a prototype for this new kind of regionalism.[17] Yet the ambiguity of the term "regionalism" lingered, and still does, to a certain extent.

His critical and reflective notion of regionalism was associated with institutions for comprehensive regional planning and development in America and abroad, which were trying, before the Second World War, to establish a more balanced development— geographically, equitably, and ecologically—to their concerns about the disintegration of the natural environment and the community. It goes back to his 1920s and 1930s critique of the "internationalism" and "imperialism" of contemporary economy and culture, which he called "paleo-technic" regimes, that supported the exploitation of local resources by "outside holders of privileges," as opposed to his vision of a "neo-technic" order. For Mumford, the paleo-technic system, as prologued by bureaucracy and technophilia, had become not only exploitative morally, but also irrational economically and disruptive ecologically. Hence the emancipatory, restorative, and redeeming character of regionalism for Mumford, which he applied to the building, the city, and the larger geographical scale.

Mumford's most impassioned espousal of regionalism in architecture, as an alternative to the formalist architects of his day, is to be found in his October 1947 *New Yorker* article, entitled "What is Happening to Modern Architecture?" Mumford had written that modern architecture, which had begun as a long-term movement of emancipation and invention, was being reduced to a mere formal exercise, the "international style," as Henry Russell-Hitchcock and Philip Johnson had christened it at the exhibition they organized for the Museum of Modern Art in New York in 1932.

(Below) Charles Moore, section of Charles Moore House, Orinda, California (1962)

(Bottom) Charles Moore, axonometric of Charles Moore House, Orinda, California (1962)

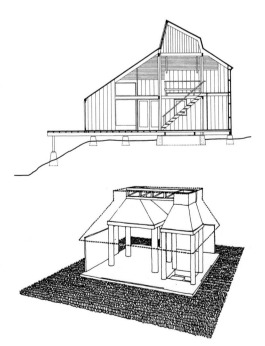

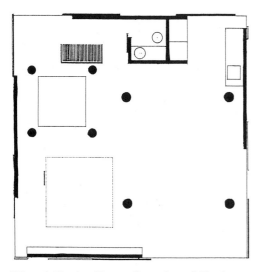

(Above) Charles Moore, floor plan of Charles Moore House, Orinda, California (1962)

(Below) Charles Moore, site plan of Charles Moore House, Orinda, California (1962)

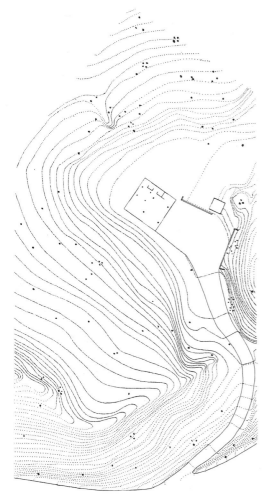

To this "assertively dogmatic," "sterile and abstract" stylistic turn, in the name of modern architecture, Mumford juxtaposed "that native and humane form of modernism one might call the (Californian) Bay Region Style ... far more truly a universal style than the so-called International Style ... since it permits ... adaptations and modifications." Mumford's regionalism was not against technology, nor did it support ethnic identity or local styles. It was an open system within which technology, the environment, and community would evolve openly in a complementary way.

CRITICAL REGIONALISM I

One of the most remarkable projects announcing the new architecture of the 1960s was the Haystack Mountain School of Arts and Crafts by Edward Larrabee Barnes (1959–61, pp. 66–69). In order to understand the immense appeal at the time of this modest project, one must realize how deeply it challenged the formalist architecture of the 1950s.

In a talk delivered by Barnes at Yale in March 1964,[18] he discussed the ideas behind the project. Like the forms of the building, Barnes's words appeared mild, calm, and ordinary. But the message was impassioned and polemical. He challenged architects to rethink basic issues of architecture, starting with the level of the program itself. Rather than presenting his ideas abstractly, Barnes decided to talk definitively about his experience of Mediterranean towns and the shock their design had produced on him. The key idea that had emerged from his exposure to this architecture was "continuity." Firstly, he described it as a continuity between individuals aggregating into a community, as opposed to the contemporary society "that is fragmented, fugitive, and often shallow"; secondly, continuity in time, where "each building is part of a process, not a world in itself," instead of the way architecture is practiced now— "in a highly competitive, building-by-building way." Finally, he discussed spatial continuity, between "adjoining buildings, their scale and color and mood, with respect for the spaces between buildings, realizing that this space may be important."

Barnes declared that architecture was at a watershed. "The day of putting architecture on a pedestal is over," he affirmed, "I am arguing for an architecture which is in harmony with its environment." He saw that the needed changes—for an enhanced sense of community, the importance of respecting building traditions, and the natural landscape—were radical, and would make it possible to leave behind the conformist paradigm of the previous decade. He called for a rethinking: "When we discuss the need for continuity, we must not overlook the vital need for change and even revolt."

The idea of continuity may have been influenced by Ernesto Rogers, the director of the Italian review, *Casabella-Continuità*, who had already applied the idea of continuity to architecture.[19] But Barnes was fundamentally drawing from the ideas of Lewis Mumford, in particular his broad theoretically and politically grounded definition of regionalism, in which the preoccupation with site constraints was linked for the first time with the concern for community, for the preservation of the natural environment, and for a critical alternative to a purely formalist or technocratic approach to architecture. Barnes, like many of his generation, had been greatly influenced by Mumford's writings about the environment while still an architectural student.[20] There was also a Mumfordian echo to Barnes's contemporary, Kennedy, who called for a reaction against the "blight and decay" and "tragic waste" of the "vital resource" of the "open land" destroyed by haphazard development. Barnes's project was regionalist in the Mumfordian sense, in the way it made the viewer reflect on the values of the environment, like the "old, bald, neutral tones, Yankee farmhouse which seems to belong to the ground whereon it stands, as the caterpillar to the leaf that feeds him" in the words of Greenough.[21] It was Mumfordian in the way it incorporated the idea of community, while belonging to the old American tradition of the progressive artists' schools, like Black Mountain, North Carolina, where the idea of community was central, and whose purpose, in the words of Percival and Paul Goodman, was to "irradiate society with people who have been profoundly touched with the excitement of community life."[22]

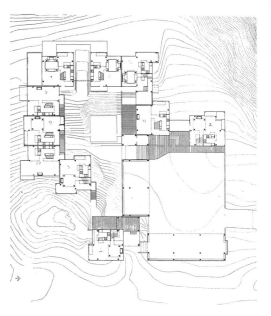

Charles Moore, site plan of Sea Ranch Swim Club 1, California (1963–65)

Like Barnes's project, the Sea Ranch by Moore Lyndon Turnbull Whitaker (1963–65, pp. 90–93) was conceived in a critical, Mumfordian regionalist framework. The environment was one of its central concerns. In the words of landscape architect, Lawrence Halprin, who participated in its design, Sea Ranch aspired to become an "organic community." And like the Haystack Mountain school, MLTW's project was conceived to be in a harmonious relation with the natural lay of the land, in order to disrupt the landscape as little as possible. Both projects, of course, were designed as unique communities. The inhabitants they nurtured were monocultural and elite. Haystack was a summer school for artists; Sea Ranch was conceived as a residential and recreational community, with facilities for hiking, fishing and abalone hunting, and sports grounds. They were not centers of work and production.

However, despite these limitations, both projects were designed with great concern for social interaction and for fitting into the environment in a way that was generally foreign to the architects of the 1950s. Both complexes were pioneering and encouraged a new awareness among the architectural profession. They opened the way to a kind of thinking that ultimately led to a series of projects which could have appeared completely different in their form and materials, but which were similarly devoted to the ideas concerning the relationship of buildings to the natural environment, such as Roche and Dinkeloo's Oakland Museum (1961–68, pp. 128–29), Arthur Erickson's Museum of Anthropology (1971–76, pp. 160–63), and Jersey Devil's Hill House (1977, pp. 178–79). In the 1980s and early 1990s we find this initial critical regionalism trying to come to terms with new technology, with projects such as Antoine Predock's Rio Grande Nature Center (1982, pp. 200–03), the Patkaus' Seabird Island School (1988–91, pp. 276–79), The Center for Maximum Potential Building Systems' Laredo Demonstration Blueprint Farm (1987, pp. 240–41), and James Stewart Polshek's Mashantucket Pequot Center (1993–, pp. 292–95).

This cluster of projects, diverse as they may seem, all share a symbiotic attitude towards nature, each having chosen a different way of expressing it: care for the selection of materials, response to the morphology of the site and landscape constraints, and concern about energy and the production of waste.

THE NEW RIGORISM

Louis Kahn was functionalist. The notion of a functionalist or "rigorist" architecture goes back to the 1760s, to Carlo Lodoli, a Venetian Franciscan friar. Lodoli was known as the Socrates of Architecture, not only for the purely oral nature of his pedagogy (he never published a word and his doctrine is known through the work of his followers, Francesco Algarotti and Francesco Milizia), but also for his attachment to the Socratic definition of beauty as being an expression of purpose, of use,[23] a tradition continuing in America through Horatio Greenough and extending, as we have seen, to Lewis Mumford.

There is something in Kahn of the moral stance of Lodoli and Greenough, not to mention Mumford, against the excesses of the architecture of their time. Kahn was a passionate critic of the architecture of the 1950s, which he found stalled in trivial and arbitrary conventions. "We're living in an era of new space demands, new things," he commented, "which are so fresh and unfamiliar that most minds are unable to identify a single image." In addition, the "wonderful resources" designers have at their command are going to waste because of the permissiveness of the times, leading to what he called the "mess of copying and re-copying," rather than innovative use.[24]

Kahn also had a clear sense of what had to be done. He was for re-examining "the nature of architecture" and its inherent constraints. In this, as is well known, he never lost his commitment to using architecture to strengthen community, to "strengthen our institutions," as he put it in a *Progressive Architecture* article of 1961. He preached for an architecture made up of essential elements responding to purpose, an architecture of pure functionality. He claimed that his influence in this was Socrates's functional definition of beauty, contained in the writings of Plato. He also claimed, more importantly, that he had been immersed since the 1930s in the tradition of American Functionalism, a tradition that drew from the Pragmatist movement and to its original ancestor, the sculptor and essayist, Horatio Greenough, who was responsible for coining the phrase, "form follows function."[25] Thus, Kahn's rethinking of architecture goes back to its essentials, to the "organic" principles of architecture, as Greenough had called them.

Certainly, an essential component of the functionalist tradition was the work of Mies van der Rohe and his followers of the 1950s. But the tradition had much deeper roots that stretched back to the 18th century. Function for Mies and his followers, as with most rigorists before, had been confined to what Greenough had called "the skeleton of our building." Kahn's rethinking permitted him, after diving into the fundamentals of functionalism and rigorism, to come up with a new aspect of function that had never received such prominence and analytic clarity, but also an aspect that was much more relevant to the contemporary reality: the function of mechanical services, circulation, and movement. Through this invention, Kahn liberated the architect from the prison-house of the universal space. With Kahn, the rigorist, functionalist vision of architecture was to be realized, not through the order, efficiency, and elegance of the construction, but through the effectiveness and robustness of the well-ordered mechanical and circulation systems of the building.

Kahn's new definition of functionalism, or service rigorism, also expressed an economic reality. Mechanical services were taking up more than 50 percent of the budget of buildings by the 1950s. In addition, it announced a technological reality. Mechanized movement in the built environment was becoming increasingly faster, more voluminous, and more complex. The socioeconomic reality also demanded that more attention be paid to the processes buildings contained, as the cost derived from the dysfunctionalities in the utilitarian buildings was mounting, and change was imperative.

Before applying his concept of "servant and served spaces" to the Richards laboratories, Kahn had already by 1953 exhibited in the Museum of Modern Art his plans for mid-town Philadelphia,[26] presenting a model of the city as process rather than three-dimensional urban organization. His model was poetic rather than analytical. Nevertheless, it was a breakthrough in his thinking and led the way to his subsequent masterpieces.

ACCENT ON ACTION

The idea of process related to the city was addressed in theoretical, analytical terms in books such as Leonard Riessman's *The Urban Process* (1964),[27] and in the influential *Explorations into Urban Structure,* edited by Melvin Webber (1964),[28] and in particular in the contribution to that volume by Donald L. Foley, "An Approach to Metropolitan Spatial Structure."[29] Foley stresses the urgent need to conceptualize *a-spatial* factors of the metropolis and relate them to its "spatial structure."

Apart from Kahn, the idea of process enters architecture gradually. The impatience with the closed, static buildings of the 1950s is spelled out in the article, "Jazz in Architecture" by Douglas Haskell.[30] He attacks "the square scene today," pointing to three examples: Mies's Seagram Building, Yamasaki's Wayne University, and The Lincoln Center by Philip Johnson, Wallace Harrison, and Max Abramovitch. The article points out to the possibility of the "jazz at Harvard" alternative by Josep Lluis Sert, whose syncopated Le Corbusier-inspired use of narrow vertical panels in the Holyoke Center and in the Peabody Terrace Housing (1963–65, pp. 100–01) appear to offer an alternative. The article goes on to praise Kahn's new "architectural order" for the Richards Medical Labs at the University of Pennsylvania.

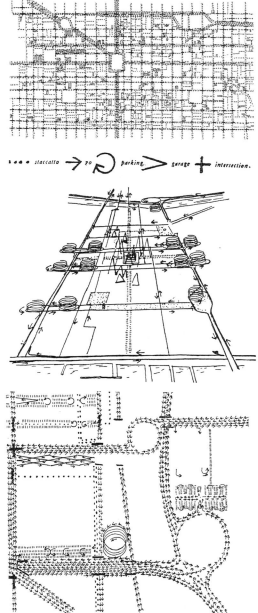

(From top to bottom) Louis Kahn, circulation pattern of Philadelphia Study (1953)

Gerhardt Kallmann's essay in the October 1959 issue of *Architectural Forum* makes the point much more forcefully—almost as a manifesto. Kallmann in fact coins the concept of "Action Architecture," as opposed to "abstract packages or indistinguishable boxes (of) space structure and envelope." He sees "pragmatic attitudes" replacing idealism and dogma. Kallmann refers to Kahn's Richards Laboratories (1957–60, pp. 72–75) as a call for an "esthetics of change, for flow patterns, for energy conservation in clusters (and as) images to reflect contemporary conditions of mobility and change."

A more daring idea of that time for conceiving the building as a process made out of mobile and immobile components was the Dulles Terminal of Eero Saarinen (1958–63, pp. 78–81). Here the space-consuming lounges and corridors typical of an airport are collapsed into mobile units, becoming bus-lounges. Through this device, Saarinen intended to reduce not only wasted space and effort, but to reduce the time travelers spent between arrival at the terminal and their boarding the aircraft. Saarinen's radical idea, however, had a rather limited follow-up, whereas Kahn's thinking, though relatively more conservative, had more far-reaching consequences.

Kahn realized that the more successful the machinery supporting processes contained in buildings became, the more disruptive it was to human comfort and communication. By the end of the 1950s, it had been universally recognized that the machine, whether in the form of the automobile or the air-conditioner, was an "enemy" of humans. Kahn's solution was not to destroy the mechanical enemy, but to master it. In this he was translating Lewis Mumford's "neo-technic" vision into architecture.

This is the message of Mumford's *Technics and Civilization* (1934).[31] It can be traced further back to the American philosophy of Pragmatism (especially in the Pragmatism of Dewey[32] and the Organicism of Frank Lloyd Wright). This mastering of the machine was the task that Louis Kahn set himself in his conception of a new topology of buildings, articulated into "servant," the space allocated to the machine, which had never before been given an architectural space treatment, and "served," the space for humans. The concept is inspired from many precedents, the closest one being the tower system for stairwells in Frank Lloyd Wright's Larkin Company Administration Building of 1904.

It was natural that this new functionalism would emerge from the design of not only a workplace, but of a new kind of workplace. By accommodating the machine, Kahn was also providing a means of giving unprecedented priority to community in the workplace at a moment when mechanization was taking command of it as never before. Confining the machine to its own "servant" realm would permit community to flourish in its "served" realm. The division between servant and served, machine and community, had, therefore, what one might call a political character. By allocating community a proper place in the building, Kahn was implementing what he believed to be the most important programmatic task of contemporary architecture—that is, to "strengthen our institutions." The idea of community in the workplace has always held a special attraction for Americans.[33] No one since the 1930s had espoused its ideals more fervently than Lewis Mumford. No one had given it an architectural counterpart, in America or in the rest of the world, before Lewis Kahn did in the early 1960s. This is the great contribution of the Richards Laboratories and the far-reaching, innovative Salk Institute (1959–65, pp. 94–97).

These two buildings by Kahn were more than unique feats expressed as single objects. Although they were single buildings, they implied a new building type—what Greenough had called a new "abstract type." After them, new buildings came to be conceived according to these new general principles of program-space organization. We see a direct impact of this type in I. M. Pei's Center for Atmospheric Research, near Boulder, Colorado, which achieved a harmonious relation between technology, community, and the environment. Rarely in history does a new type of building emerge permitting the fundamental rethinking of program—the Renaissance villa, the Chicago skyscraper, the 19th-century shopping galleria. This was the case with Kahn's two prototypes. It is interesting to add that at this moment in time, the context for such a breakthrough was the workplace. But this workplace was for a new kind of worker, different from the traditional blue-collar and white-collar worker, whom John Kenneth Galbraith saw as constituting a new class, and who would eventually come to be called the "symbolic analyst" by Robert Reich thirty years later.[34] This new group of people would emerge with their own demands of community, to which Kahn had tried to respond.

Kahn saw his work as leaving behind the structural exhibitionist calisthenics of the New Monumentality of the end of the 1950s, represented in the works of Minoru Yamasaki, Philip Johnson, and Edward Durrell Stone. In a separate way, so did Myron Goldsmith with his Solar Telescope (1962, pp. 76–77). For this observatory, the technology was neither destructive nor were the "symbolic analysts" in sufficient numbers to require their own realm of community, so that in turn neither the skeleton nor the "service" functions were given predominance. There is a distillation of the building to its essential organs, a composition consistent with a genuine, Organic architecture (as defined by Greenough) set off from its natural surroundings, but nevertheless in complete harmony with it. The building embodies the most naked kind of rigorism. This effect arises from the reduction of the structure to its essential, minimal elements, which barely disrupt nature, in comparison to the opposite effects of neo-monumental complexes. This unique project, which was as prototypical in its concept as Kahn's buildings, has remained—unfortunately, in our view—without progeny to this day.

THE RE-URBANIZATION OF THE BUILDING

Out of Kahn's prototype sprung many significant, and significantly different, buildings: Safdie's Habitat (1964–67, pp. 116–19), Kallmann McKinnell and Knowle's Boston City Hall (1962–68, pp. 124–27) and Paul Rudolph's Yale School of Art and

I. M. Pei's National Center for Atmospheric Research, near Boulder, Colorado (1967)

(Opposite page, from top to bottom)
Peter Millard, Central Fire Station (1961), New Haven; Paul Rudolph, bird's eye view of Married Student Housing, Yale University, New Haven (1960); Peter Millard, concept drawing of Central Fire Station, New Haven (1961); Peter Millard, Whitney Avenue Station, New Haven (1964)

© Carlin & Pozzi

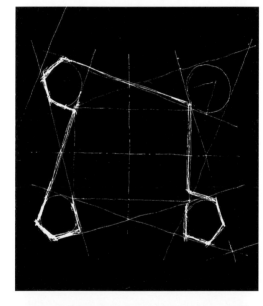

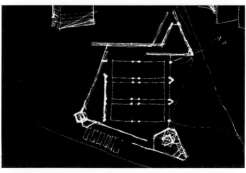

Architecture (1958–63, pp. 82–85). In all of them we find the articulation of servant realms attached to served ones as a means of sustaining community. In Rudolph's Art and Architecture Building, both the exhibition and the architecture studio areas emerge as the served realms. Rudolph's project draws from the Organic tradition as well: its served areas are not "universal," nor are they homogeneous. They are given their own individual height and light conditions, as their function requires, or to put it more accurately, as those requirements were interpreted by Rudolph for each location. Rudolph here combined Kahn's prototype with the Organic architecture of Frank Lloyd Wright—hence the service towers flanking a multitude of "served" levels, no less than 37, and the variety of lighting conditions.

But Rudolph's building was significant from another point of view. Characteristic of the American Renaissance we are discussing, was a new awareness of the significance of the urban fabric and the deteriorating quality of the cityscape. The disastrous impact of the urban renewal projects of the 1950s was becoming a focus of discussions beyond professional circles, simultaneously with debate over the destruction of the natural environment. This shift marked a return to another Mumfordian concern, which the architecture of the 1950s had ignored. The approach, however, that emerged at this moment was much more specialized, much closer to the disciplines of cognitive science, than Mumford had ever conceived. Visual organization and what Kevin Lynch, the MIT theoretician of urban design, would call the "imageability" of the city in his famous book, *The Image of the City* (1960),[35] became an object of systematic study.

The debate about the relation between the building and the city was centered at Yale, under the chairmanship of Paul Rudolph, and drew considerably from another source—less radical than Mumford's and less scientific than Lynch's and the other researchers at the Joint Center at MIT. Rudolph and the Yale circle appeared more traditionalist. Without rejecting the realities of new technology and the imperative of community, they were interested in drawing knowledge from the architecture of the City Beautiful, treating the external part of buildings as elements of a "city-scape," in a manner—to quote Trystan Edwards's *Good and Bad Manners in Architecture* (1924)—that expressed "sociable behavior" and "etiquette."[36]

The re-urbanization of buildings became the focus of Rudolph's teaching at Yale and of the program of the school he chaired in the early 1960s. In contrast to Lynch at MIT, who relied on scientific, empirical procedures, Rudolph used mostly intuition and historical precedent. But it fits, like Lynch's work, into a framework which one might call urban functionalism. This was a new, unprecedented way of thinking about architecture and the city.

One of the most significant features of the Art and Architecture Building was its servant Kahnian towers organized in a pinwheel scheme. In addition to internal needs, the scheme served also as an urbanistic device. There was a precedent for this, also, in Frank Lloyd Wright's Larkin building, but there were also other examples of buildings in Italian medieval towns playing the same role, in the "city-scape," as Rudolph interpreted them. The scheme made the building "turn the corner," but also fit into the overall New Haven cityscape, marking a point of termination at the long perspective of Chapel street, a view dominated by Yale University buildings.

The need to maintain a continuity of the urban fabric motivated the architecture of another New Haven architect, Peter Millard. Working as a chief designer in the office of Earl P. Carlin, mostly within the framework of Mayor Richard C. Lee's redevelopment program for New Haven, he developed a method for integrating buildings with their surroundings, best demonstrated in two fire stations for the city. Compared to Rudolph's Yale Art and Architecture Building, Millard's Central Fire Station is rigorist, stark, and prismatic in its form. But, like Rudolph's building, it serves as a component in an overall "city-scape" synthesis. And, like Rudolph, Millard used the pinwheel pattern in combination with Kahn's servant and served articulation. He applied them as a means to make the mass of the building respond to the irregularities of the site, but also to respond to the larger physical forms of the immediate urban context. He made the project play the role of a "gateway," its elements dominating grand vistas in the town's fabric, or, to use Kevin Lynch's terminology, a "definite (terminal), recogniz- able anchor which complete(s) and locate(s) the line." Millard's unique skill, as then Yale student Robert Stern has observed in his most cogent article on the firm,[37] was in bringing such urbanistic concerns down to detail and to the choice and manipulation of the materials. This concern is particularly true in another New Haven building—the Whitney Avenue Fire Station, in the neighborhood of colonial-revival houses. Stern conceived a formally rigorous treatment of the outer concrete wall "as a thin skin wrapped around a structural frame (a) clapboarded concrete surface." With its parsimonious formal means, it succeeded in capturing the deeper "imageability" of the urban structure, the identity of the "cognitive mapping" of New Haven, to use Kevin Lynch's terms.

A more ambitious, but far less successful, effort to re-urbanize architecture is Eero Saarinen's Stiles and Morse Colleges at Yale (1958–62). Designed to adapt to the scale, materials, and geometry of the neo-Gothic Yale surroundings, the neo-historicist result preempted 1970s postmodernism. But, in the early 1960s, the buildings created a scandal. In comparison to Rudolph and Millard, Saarinen's approach looked backwards. The complex related associatively with the previous Yale buildings, but failed to integrate itself into the cognitive map of the city.

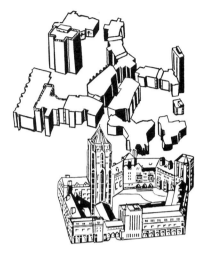

Ezra Stoller © Esto

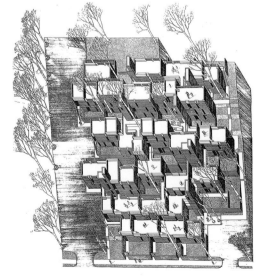

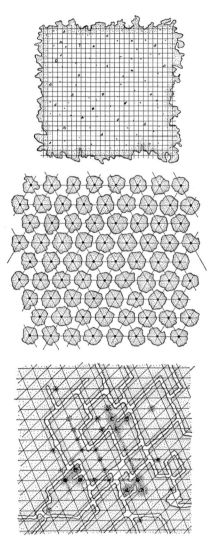

(Above) Kevin Lynch's illustrations from the Winter 1961 issue of *Daedalus*. (From top to bottom) "The Dispersed Sheet"; "The Galaxy"; "The Polycentered Net"

Opposite page
(Bottom left) Paul Rudolph, facade of Married Student Housing, Yale University, New Haven (1960)

(Top right) Eero Saarinen's sketch of the massing of Stiles and Morse Colleges, Yale University, New Haven (1958–62)

(Center right) Paul Rudolph, parking garage on Temple Street, New Haven (1959–63)

(Bottom right) Paul Rudolph, bird's eye view of Married Student Housing, Yale University, New Haven (1960)

Yale historian Carroll Meeks argues in his book, *The Railroad Station*,[38] that 19th-century cities had as one of their focal points buildings dedicated to movement. Rudolph responded to this challenge by trying to create a new building type: the urban, multi-story parking lot. The project was initially conceived to bridge a controversial highway that cut through the town and brought the automobile to the very heart of the city center. The idea of using a garage as an imposing element in the city was, in fact, Kahn's, and had been suggested almost a decade before. Rudolph's solution was not only different in shape—a linear volume rather than a silo—but it also dealt with the real problem of relating the scale of the parked automobile to that of a building for human use. Despite the highly sculptural quality of the work, the building ultimately failed to carry out the relation of the scale and facade of the building to the street. The fundamental failure was functional. In the end, Rudolph did not succeed in creating a satisfactory new building type. Bringing automobiles in large numbers into the heart of downtown was, by definition, leading to an intractable solution, as would be observed several years later, by Frank Gehry's parking structure for Santa Monica. Of course, the requirement for a downtown parking garage was a given in the program. Assuming this given, a possible solution would have been a multi-use building, which, among other functions, could provide housing for the cars. Clearly, the problem was not merely that of the cityscape, as, in the end, Rudolph had chosen to approach it.

THE RE-URBANIZATION OF ARCHITECTURE

The Yale circle's re-urbanization of architecture during the first half of the 1960s took place inside the framework of a general debate about the future of urban organization. The future form of the fabric of the man-made environment was discussed in a multi-disciplinary way. Architects and planners, sociologists and economists, ecologists and psychologists, political scientists and artists discussed, for the first time, issues on a common platform, and, also for the first time, computer models were brought in.

The Winter 1961 issue of *Daedalus*, dedicated to "The Future Metropolis," edited by Kevin Lynch and Lloyd Rodwin,[39] both from MIT and the Joint Center for Urban Studies, included as contributors prominent scholars of the country, such as Edward Banfield, Karl Deutsch, John Dyckman, Aaron Fleisher, Oscar Handlin, Gyorgy Kepes, Martin Meyerson, and Morton White, among others. Catherine Bauer Wurster, the former collaborator of Lewis Mumford in the 1930s, and Professor at the University of California at Berkeley, attended the conference, but was not part of the publication. The volume prefigured many of the urban functionalist themes of the decade. Most revolutionary was the essay by Karl Deutsch on social communication and the metropolis, where the latter was interpreted as "a huge engine of communication" whose objective should be the maximization of individual and social choice. Deutsch, an electrical engineer, as well as a political scientist specializing in systems thinking and conflict resolution, put forth a new model of the city as a switchboard, completely abstracting spatial or visual aspects. He saw in this model the potential of resolving conflicts in a global manner. Gyorgy Kepes, on the other hand, stressed the expression of imageability and communication in the cityscape through terms described in much greater detail by Lynch in his numerous subsequent publications.

John Dykman emphasized the importance of place as it relates to political participation, and urged designers to look not only beyond form but to look at economics as well. Kevin Lynch presented a distinct set of analyses of metropolitan form. Examining the impact of circulation and communication through modern technology, he saw three alternatives: the first, which he termed the "Dispersed Sheet," was a Los Angeles-like pattern; the second had more concentrated patterns, such as the "Core," the "Star," and the "Ring," and his third alternative was a combination of the first two, which he termed the "Polycentric Net."

During the 1960s, we see these issues reflected in the work of various researchers, but also in various architectural projects that express a unique urban consciousness. These were clustered in universities and they gravitated either towards Berkeley or towards MIT, Harvard, and Yale.

The West Coast thinkers, restating Karl Deutsch's model, held that older beliefs in the power of spatial configurations were mere superstitions. Designers were seen as unable to catch up with the actual changes in lifestyle and technologies unless they were able to free themselves from the obsession with placeness. Melvin Webber, the key proponent of this view, concluded that it was interaction and not place that formed the essence of the city and of city life.[40] These conclusions were the result of highly descriptive research documenting the real changes that were occurring in the American man-made environment as a result of new lifestyles and the new technologies of transportation and telecommunications, as well as forces of consumption. They encouraged the dispersal of the urban fabric and the liquidation of traditional city life. They recommended the encouragement of higher levels of non-spatial organization through total application of telecommunications in all areas of life, not only in the workplace, but also in education, culture, leisure, and entertainment. They saw in this fluid, multi-noded electronic world not only economic efficiency, but the fulfillment of a democratic ideal, the unconstrained maximization of the choice of the individual. No longer would there be a single community, but an endless number of overlapping communities.

The extreme opposite approach was adopted by the academic community of Harvard, MIT, and Yale. Its adherents clung to the imperative of community rather than accepting the inevitability of placelessness, which they saw their colleagues of the West Coast as espousing. In various degrees, most leading architects and theoreticians interpreted the physical organization of infrastructure (in particular public transit and the pedestrian networks) as a means of sustaining the sense, and the reality, of place—of "shaping community." This can be found in the architecture of, for example, Josep Lluis Sert, in Cambridge and Boston, as well as in the theoretical studies of Kevin Lynch and Serge Chermayeff.[41]

The most significant expression of these ideas in terms of real building complexes and urban infrastructure, emerge in the city of Montreal, coinciding with the world exhibition, Expo 67. With the participation of both public and private sectors, typical of Montreal, and typical of Canada, this was a clear effort to arrest the process of what John Kenneth Galbraith had called "private opulence and public squalor."

NEW BUILDING TYPES

A work that genuinely attempted to rethink fundamental aspects of architecture and offer a new building type was Place Bonaventure by Ray Affleck and his associates in Montreal (1964–67, pp. 120–23). The project was one of a series of attempts in Montreal to generate a mid-city complex which combined several facilities including transportation—cars, trains, as well as the metro. Bonaventure's success went beyond that of a built project. The project implied a powerful prototype, a true "Mega-Structure," as defined by Fumihiko Maki: "a large frame in which all the functions of a city or part of a city are housed, made possible by present day technology ... like the great hill on which Italians towns were built."[42] The project is truly a multi-functional city within the city, a gate to the city for train transportation, a subway stop, a three-floor bazaar complete with coffee shops and restaurants, a place to exhibit merchandise, an office space, places for assembly, a movie house, a conference center, and finally an artificial hill for a residential complex, a row house that can easily be seen as a row house type, clustered around playgrounds, swimming pools, and sculptural gardens.

Cambridge Seven and Buckminster Fuller's geodesic dome at Expo 67 (1964–67, pp. 110–13) was equally innovative, but in a different way. It explored the possibilities of a highly experimental technology supporting community in the context of new lifestyles. The building was not just a pavilion, it was a prototype of a new kind of built, urban environment. Departing from one of the city's metro stations, one would arrive to the Expo site. There one would transfer to the monorail which led the visitor directly into the dome, where he or she could immediately climb one of the escalators of the project. It was a demonstration of how a hierarchy of movement systems could bridge the whole metropolitan spectrum.

The architects conceived that, once inside the protecting shell of the dome, activities should be liberated, and that interactions between people should enjoy a high degree of freedom and flexibility. A mechanical circulation system moved the people effortlessly on different directions and levels. The dome projected an idea of an emancipated community, although attached more to leisure than to labor. The image of leisure, however, was that of active human contact and play, rather than spectacle and passive consumption.

Several of the designers of this period were interested in the issue of how to reconcile community and privacy. Moshe Safdie experimented with a new kind of urban lifestyle to be housed in his Habitat (1964–67, pp. 116–17), one that could combine advantages of suburban housing, openness and contact with nature, some degree of privacy, with city center densities that optimized shared resources. His experiment belongs to a number of other attempts to rethink the domestic environment. Serge Chermayeff, with Christopher Alexander, developed designs for high-density, low-rise housing. The accent was on providing internal courts to compete with suburban contact with nature, as well as to provide privacy and service distribution with an efficiency that was definitely un-suburban. Despite the title of the book, *Community and Privacy*, it dealt primarily with issues of privacy.[43]

At the other extreme, architects Mary Otis Stevens and Thomas McNulty attempted to counter Chermayeff's restrictive layout of the domestic unit, with their design for a house in Lexington, Massachusetts (1964), and rejected along with it the traditional patriarchal structure of the middle-class family, which they perceived as sustaining gender stereotypes and submitting children to a disciplinarian regime. They designed a house as an experiment in extreme openness, with a lack of individual privacy—a family house without any interior doors. Their design was conceived as a passageway encouraging continual movement and interaction, as a way of enabling collective, equal participation of every member of the family. In many respects, this search for openness was inspired by Buckminster Fuller's geodesic dome structures.

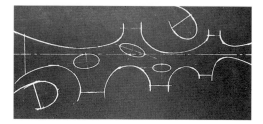

(Top) Otis Stevens and McNulty, aerial view of Lexington, Massachusetts (1964)

(Above) Otis Stevens and McNulty, concept drawing of Lexington, Massachusetts (1964)

(Below) Buckminster Fuller's drawing of the geodesic dome over Manhattan (1968)

Safdie wanted both privacy and community, and his Habitat 67 was a unique experiment of a very different scale and complexity. Its compact network of units and circulation to "support community" was an additional contribution to the ingenious pattern with which the units were assembled. Equally visionary was Safdie's technology developed in collaboration with Kahn's engineer, August Komendant, for producing the modules of prefabricated inhabitable units. The modules contained at the same time structure and mechanical services incorporated in their body, and were produced in a temporary, on-site factory. The modules were moved and placed by rail-riding derricks, while bathrooms and kitchens were prefabricated and dropped into place.

Both architects' projects were explicitly intended as prototypes, to be implemented later at a larger scale. Safdie dreamt of producing millions of units assembled along the same principles. As for Buckminster Fuller, he envisioned only one dome—but it covered half of Manhattan. In many respects, both projects were the equivalent in architecture of Kennedy's dream of a program for colonizing outer space.

Fuller's and Safdie's projects were still drawing from the spirit of rethinking and creativity of the beginning of the 1960s. They were not only overly optimistic, but also excessively deterministic, relying on technology as a means of achieving social ends. Although they were inaugurated four years after the assassination of Kennedy, with the news of the Vietnam War having already overwhelmed the nation, they were unaffected by the realities of urban crime and ecological destruction.

TOWARDS A SOCIAL ARCHITECTURE

Most of the projects we have referred to so far have rethought architecture in terms of the reconceptualization of spatial organization and the processes fitting within it. However, there was another path that challenged established ideas at that time, and that was in many respects more revolutionary, although its novelty was not expressed in spectacular morphological newness.

In his address to the Congress on housing and community development, Kennedy began: "Our communities are what we make them. We as a nation have before us the opportunity—and the responsibility—to remold our cities, to improve our patterns of community development, and to provide for the housing needs of all segments of our population." The 1949 congress, he commented, had a great vision announcing a national policy of "a decent home and a suitable living environment for every American family." There had been progress, he acknowledged. But this pledge had not touched "the 14 million American families who currently live in substandard or deteriorating homes, and has not succeeded yet in protect(ing) the other 39 million American families from the encroachment of blight and slums." His proposed policies were directed towards three fundamental national objectives: "First, to renew our cities, and assure sound growth ... Second, to provide decent housing for all ... Third, to encourage a prosperous and efficient construction industry."

Kahn had tried to design public housing in Philadelphia at this time. Despite his totally sympathetic attitude to the problem, he failed to understand the realities of life in such a project. Sert's efforts in Peabody Terrace (1963–65, pp. 100–01) to generate secure, community-sustaining housing, despite its success in enlivening the skyline along the Charles River, failed miserably on precisely these points.

With their non-profit, social housing project, St. Francis Square Cooperative Apartments (1960–61, pp. 70–71), Marquis and Stoller succeeded where many others had failed. It was sponsored and developed by a pension fund and was pioneering in expressing functionalist attitudes that were being discussed in academic circles found at Berkeley and elsewhere. The architects employed several design principles in the project which had been recognized by Jane Jacobs in her book, *The Death and Life of Great American Cities*[44] and in several other empirical studies about the behavior of people in housing. In particular, they looked at how open spaces were used in housing and how circulation and visibility patterns affected community and security. Clare Cooper, in her *AIA Journal* article of 1974, summarizing the results of an investigation which lasted more than half a decade, reported that in terms of a social environment, St. Francis Square was viewed by almost everyone living there as a friendly place. The creative significance of the project lay in the conception of the architectural program within which they considered the use of semi-private outdoor space, half way between completely private and completely public, with balconies and patios to make the apartments feel bigger and different from row-house public housing (where no fenced yards or patios separate the fronts of dwellings from public space), providing a total environment which was not only pleasing but functional. Another factor in its success was that the low-income residents were to be owners, not renters. This allowed the designers to concentrate more on the overall plan and landscaping than on the apartment interiors (which the residents would finish), creating an environment that was safe and interesting for children. The project managed to combine the convenience of an inner city location with suburban living qualities. This was the case with Safdie's project for Habitat, of course. But St. Francis Square did so with an extremely limited budget, and for a population that varied not only in race, but also in family size and composition. In addition, it included single adults and elderly couples. One proof of the success of the project was that few residents moved away; those who did move often did so within the complex, relocating in order to acquire larger or smaller accommodations according to their new needs. This kind of thinking was outside the realm of architectural orthodoxy in the previous decade, and was an exercise in democracy.

ARCHITECTURE ABOUT ARCHITECTURE, ARCHITECTURE ABOUT REALITY

Robert Venturi's small-scale projects, with their conventional functionality, low profile volumetric configuration, their literary allusions to history or to the context of surrounding buildings, seem to be set apart from any of the previous projects of the 1960s we have been discussing. There is, however, a deep affinity between them, in that Venturi's work, in line with other products of the American Renaissance, rethought fundamental tools of architecture. But he did so in a radically different way. He introduced the act of reflection of architecture upon itself.

The most significant project of this phase of Venturi's work is probably the house for Mrs. Venturi in Chestnut Hill, Pennsylvania (1961–63, pp. 86–89). On a purely utilitarian level, the building is impeccable, although not inventive in the sense of Kahn's Laboratory (1957–60, pp. 72–75) or Saarinen's Dulles Terminal (1958–63, pp. 78–91). But there is always something in the form which is unsettling. Why this clash of orthogonal and diagonal geometry? Why this contrast between front and back, and the two sides, why that particular roof structure? Why so much stressing of symmetry with a simultaneous abandoning of it?

These questions, surprising at first, initiate a critical look at its configuration in terms of possible intentions, alternatives, choices, and resolutions. In other words, what appears in the beginning to be slightly unconventional and artless, engages us in an internal contemplation concerning the meaning incorporated in the building, and beyond that, the meaning of architecture in our time. Slowly, we start reconsidering aspects of public and private, interior and exterior, solid and void, structure and separation. It is completely mistaken to see in all this an affirmation of the suburban house or a total rejection of it. On the contrary, it is an invitation to investigate ultimately epistemological aspects of architecture: How do we know things have to be the way they are? Or moral ones: Why should we accept that things should be done the way they are done? Venturi's architecture is very difficult, because to be engaged in this critical dialogue makes bare the devices of thought.

At first glance, Venturi may appear as a one-dimensional polemicist, juxtaposing his position with the 1950s—that is, the functional box. In *Complexity and Contradiction*, written at the end of the 1950s, he points to Philip Johnson's Glass House (1949), stating that "forced simplicity results in oversimplification." He compared it with Johnson's Wiley House, where an attempt was made to go beyond the simplicities of the elegant pavilion, by splitting and articulating private and public realms. But even here Venturi sees an oversimplification. The building reads like an "abstract theory of either/or." Venturi concludes that "less is a bore," reversing Mies's favorite dictum, "less is more." He is not asking simply for a return to complexity as a remedy to "blatant simplification" and "bland architecture." Without doubt, he stands for inclusiveness and richness, as opposed to what Yamasaki referred to as "serene" architecture. He welcomed contrast, but also conflict and even mess.

Venturi's buildings of that period are, to quote Harold Rosenberg's *The De-definition of Art* (1972),[45] engaging in visual debate with predecessors and contemporaries. And, to continue paraphrasing Rosenberg, are engaged with the problem of identifying an architectural identity—what it takes to be an architect and to make buildings.

Venturi's approach to architecture, an architecture about architecture, is expressed in a more complex building, the Guild House (1961–65, pp. 98–99). Here, however, an additional technique is introduced. The building overtly encompasses elements from its surroundings, it incorporates proportions, iconographic materials (such as the TV antenna), and other objects, as if it mirrors its environment. Later, this technique would be referred to as contextualism, meaning an effort to make the building dissolve into its surroundings to avoid cacophony. But that is not the case here at all. The realism of Venturi is not picturesque: it does not try to elevate aspects of place-ness, but on the contrary, it foregrounds placelessness. It is a "dirty" kind of realism, to use Bill Buford's term to name a movement very similar to Venturi's work.[46]

Venturi was initiating an architecture very much of our time. For the first time in North America, architecture was seen as a means of making a comment, as powerful as literature, painting, or film. It was about open questions—open wounds, one might say—with which the architect confronted us. The impact of these two innovative buildings will be one aspect of the 1960s that will be sensed for decades to come, even if the architecture itself of these future projects does not use the formal devices implemented by Venturi, or even his conception of a critical architecture. For the latter we will have to wait for Frank Gehry to start producing his extraordinary architecture, in particular his House (1978–79, pp. 180–83), the Santa Monica Garage, the Edgemar Mall in Santa Monica and the Weisman Art Museum (1992–94, pp. 290–91).

(Top) Frank Gehry, parking garage on Santa Monica Mall, California (1979–81)

(Above) Frank Gehry, close-up of parking garage on Santa Monica Mall, California (1979–81)

IN THE NAME OF THE PEOPLE: THE POPULIST MOVEMENT[47]

In the March 1968 issue of *Architectural Forum*, Robert Venturi and Denise Scott Brown published an article entitled "The Significance of A&P Parking Lots, or Learning from Las Vegas." In it they put forth an approach to public space which contrasted radically not only with their previous work, but also with the projects we have been discussing so far that have related to public space.

The article spells out for the first time the ideas that dominated the second half of the 1960s: the architectural and urban design role of the public itself, as the users and consumers of architecture. This was a bottom-up approach, rather than the top-down one that had characterized the first half of the decade, relying as it did on the architectural professional to carry out changes and improvements to society and culture, such as in the case of the Place Bonaventure (1964–67, pp. 120–23). The direction now was that of moving away from architecture as a solely professional institution, and in various degrees and ways, reverting the responsibility from the architect to "the people."

Where did this new development come from? By the time the Scott Brown and Venturi article was published, in 1968, major changes had occurred in America. The mood was radically different from that of the beginning of the decade. The excitement which the change of administration in the early 1960s had created was followed by agitation and even aggression. There was no end in sight to the Vietnam War. There had been two major riots in Watts, Los Angeles, resulting in 36 dead and over a thousand injured. On July 19, 1967, the Newark black ghetto rioted, with the material damage put at almost $200 million. An unprecedented power failure in Ontario Plant in 1965 blacked out parts of two provinces of south-east Canada and parts of eight north-eastern states. Urban renewal and federal aid for urban highways had by 1967 dislocated a total of 730,000 families. The two major political assassinations of Malcolm X and John F. Kennedy earlier in the decade had been followed, in 1968, by the assassinations of Martin Luther King and Robert F. Kennedy. To use Todd Gitlin's expression, the "years of hope" gave way to the "days of rage."[48]

All these events created a crisis of confidence. The establishment's authority was cast into doubt. There were other reasons, however, creating a "credibility gap" with the establishment, which paradoxically were sown by the establishment itself. In 1964, President Johnson declared his war on poverty in the framework of his populist program of The Great Society. In August, he signed the Economic Opportunity Act, appropriating $800 million. Yet it was clear by then that the problem of poverty and underdevelopment that Kennedy had spoken about was not only a question of economics. Traditional models of the Welfare State had failed to take into account the so-called "marginals," who became increasingly numerous as the ranks of the poor and the homeless grew. Poverty was seen as structural. The new poor were often unable to participate in the economy even when they were offered financial help.

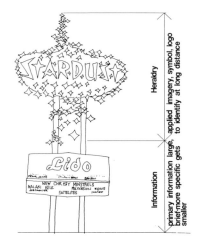

Venturi and Scott Brown's illustrations from *Learning from Las Vegas* (Cambridge: MIT Press, 1972)

God's Own Junkyard

The planned deterioration of America's landscape

PETER BLAKE

The cover of Peter Blake's *God's Own Junkyard* (1963)

The novel approach undertaken by the Johnson administration was to look into this problem from the point of view of the poor, rather than from the perspective of those in power. It was an unorthodox view, in a way diametrically opposed to the ideas of the Welfare State as developed ever since the time of the Enlightenment. The problem was thought to be in the thinking of the administrators, which was different from the way the poor perceived the world. Johnson put Kennedy's famous phrase in action, giving the poor "a real voice in their institutions." To administer this properly, the Economic Opportunity Act generated two organizations: Vista and the Community Action Program. It was up to them to find a way to implement the new programs. An approach emerged in this populist framework to turn the poor into participants in these organizations rather than passive recipients. The poor were labeled "sub-professionals," with the traditional roles reversed.[49] These sub-professionals were to teach the professionals about the needs of the poor and about ways to engage them in this new participatory framework. The idea was interpreted not only to encourage residents of poor neighborhoods to take part in administrative meetings, but to go one step further in encouraging them actively to take charge. Saul David Alinsky was one of the theoreticians of this approach, and his ideas often invited, if not incited, an adversarial attitude by the poor towards those in power.

Populism was visible both in the sphere of politics and in culture. The arts were marked by a break away from the Abstract Expressionist painting that had inspired the action architecture in the first part of the 1960s: the emergence of Pop art. Originally from Britain, this American-in-spirit movement emerged in the U.S. in the 1960s, sympathetic to the sensibilities of that period.

The idea of a pop architecture also originated not in America, but in Britain—although both movements could be said to be American in spirit. It occurred, more specifically, in the May 1949 issue of *Architectural Review*, by Gordon Cullen, a British writer fascinated by the vitality of American commercial culture. He usually wrote about the "townscape" and about picturesque squares of old cities, but this time his attention was devoted to "outdoor publicity." Cullen criticized contemporary architects for having overlooked street advertising as a source of inspiration simply because advertising was not produced by "professionals" and did not conform with the professional's view of "universal visual order." In a similar spirit, Peter and Alison Smithson, the British architects who were greatly responsible for preparing the ground for this movement in the United States during the 1950s, invoked such examples as Gropius's book on grain silos, Le Corbusier's fascination with airplanes and Charlotte Perriand's habit of bringing to the office every morning a new found object off the street. "Today," the Smithsons commented, "we collect ads."

The Smithsons were followed by Douglas Haskell, who published in *Architectural Forum* of August 1958 an article on architecture and popular taste in which he passionately defended the "common people" and "ordinary people" accused by "prestigious critics" of creating an environment that was "dreary, corrupt, scornful, infantile, and hopeless." For Haskell, these people—the common people—were attacked for no other reason than the "strangeness" and "novelty" of their designs. This split was no different from the one produced in the 19th century between the machine and architectural practice. Now, he concluded, the problem is "... the adaptation to an era of popular mass consumption (which would necessitate) new attitudes and new leaders." Haskell thought that this was only the inevitable triumph of the "democratic wilderness" and the "common people." He envisaged a new kind of architecture, "reduced to the barest suggestion of scaffolding to support the real show that goes on ... popular yet wonderfully abstract."

In 1965, Reyner Banham, writing for the British magazine, *The Listener* (August 5, 1965), would go further. Reviewing an exhibition at the Museum of Modern Art in New York, in an article entitled, "Modern Architecture, USA," he complained that motels, supermarkets, bowling alleys, filling stations, hamburger stands, and even private houses, were missing from the show. Banham demanded that "the people's recognition did not rest on abstractions, such as public taste." It rested on facts, on accepting the reality that 95 percent of all buildings put up in the United States were products of "frank and pleasurable emotional engineering," not answerable to a purely stylistic definition of quality, and whose quantity was so big that it could not be ignored anymore. Banham, an astute architectural historian, asked the question: Who knows what the creators of this new architecture look like, or if they exist?

One of the few American architects to respond to the Pop spirit was Charles Moore. In 1965, he published a long article, "You Have to Pay for the Public Life" in which he praises Disneyland as a public environment, a place which "allows play-acting, both to be watched and to be participated in a whole public world, full of sequential occurrences, of big and little drama, of hierarchy of importance and excitement ... rocketing bob-sleds." For Moore, these "fairy-tale fantasies, frontier adventure situations, jungles and the world of tomorrow" were experiences akin to looking at a Piranesi engraving or visiting Versailles.[50]

Denise Scott Brown's populism was of a broader and different scope than that of Cullen, the Smithsons, Haskell, and Banham, as her attachment to popular, consumer culture was not ironic. She was much closer in many respects to yet another Englishman fascinated with the reality of American street culture—Raymond Chandler—whose aim had been to turn the popular pulp fiction of his day into a serious genre. There was something more politically engaged about her view, and it came, as she has written herself, from the spirit of the Civil Rights Movement she encountered in the early 1960s as a foreign student, then a junior faculty member at the University of Pennsylvania. She saw *Learning from Las Vegas* (the book that followed the article) as springing from a sense of social commitment. She wrote: "Critics who ignore the social and cultural dimension in our thought see only historical sources in our symbolism. However, the ideas that led to the decorated shed were derived from a wider panoply of events than those that generated Radical Eclecticism." She saw her and Venturi's work as complementary to a broader reform—"Few architects and fewer historians heard the message of social planners. We did."[51]

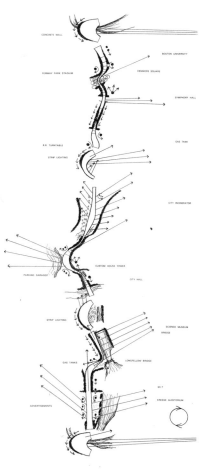

From Kevin Lynch and Donald Appleyard, *View from the Road* (Cambridge: MIT Press, 1972)

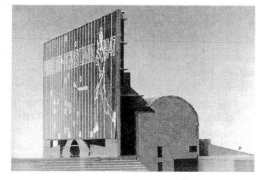

(Above) Venturi and Scott Brown's conceptual project for "A supermarket in California" (1979)

(Top) Venturi and Scott Brown's illustration from *Learning from Las Vegas* (Cambridge: MIT Press, 1972)

(Above) Venturi and Rauch, model of a design from the Football Hall of Fame, showing the facade's pop billboard imagery (1966–67)

In an article in *Architectural Forum*, she and Venturi reported findings from their teaching at that time at Yale. What they proposed as a design project for their students was a study of Las Vegas, in the same spirit as one used to study Rome. Las Vegas was documented and analyzed thoroughly with the intent to derive the new order from its apparently vulgar and degrading disorder.

Scott Brown's and Venturi's gesture both shocked and intrigued. Some important general conclusions were drawn, the first of which were the implications of automobile circulation to the perception of the environment and order, a topic, as we have seen, already investigated by Lynch's study, *View from the Road* (1964). Scott Brown's and Venturi's work went into greater depth and detail in analyzing design characteristics of the site, lighting, materials, and scale. They tried to develop maps capturing the quality of these spaces in Las Vegas Strip, equivalent to Nolli's map of Rome of 1748, and to identify "patterns." In this analysis they went back and forth between Las Vegas and Rome, the street and the Forum, and the triumphal arches and the billboards. As Scott Brown and Venturi said, our time and our environment are not "for heroic communication through pure architecture. Each medium has its day, and the rhetorical statements of our time will come from media which are more adaptable to the scale of our environment." And they concluded that instead of building monuments, architects should be building "decorated sheds" placed on the highway or on the strip, with big signs reading "I AM A MONUMENT."

Among the controversial ideas that emerged from the Las Vegas study was Scott Brown's and Venturi's split of architecture into two "Pop" categories: the "ducks" and the "decorated sheds." By "ducks," they meant the architecture of Rudolph, Millard, and the Yale school, whose forms tried to express their function. And by "decorated sheds," they meant the iconoclastic, anti-elitist solutions they clearly preferred.

Here, however, one realizes that, given the previous work of Venturi, neither the text nor the diagrams of buildings they proposed mean what they say. The objects that make up their projects were, to quote Harold Rosenberg again, "art-like equivalents of themselves."[52] Like Pop art, their architecture reached out not to real things, but to pictures of real things. Their esthetic consisted in seeing objects, like Pop artists did, as "pictures ... so that the Bowery or the suburban kitchen becomes ... an art exhibition ready for shipment"—in other words, "found art." There is, however, a second possible interpretation to Scott Brown and Venturi: that the design values of the Strip and the street were to be taken at face value.

One of the direct results of Scott Brown's and Venturi's manifesto was the emergence of super-graphics, meaning the adaptation of commercial signs to architecture. They were used in the interior of Grand's Restaurant (1962), but after *Learning from Las Vegas*, their use proliferated, most notably in MLTW's design for the changing rooms at the swimming pool and sauna in the Sea Ranch (1963–65, pp. 90–93), and in Charles Moore's own residence in New Haven (1966), as well as in the interior of the U.S. Pavilion at Expo 67 by Cambridge Seven (1964–67, pp. 110–13).

But populism in architecture had other facets. In 1963, a young planner, Chester Hartman, pointed to the great disparity between the needs of the poor and the norms that most architects were implementing in the design of their housing. "Physical factors alone have been stressed ... (they) are important, but they have no invariant 'objective' status, and can only be understood in the light of their meaning for other people's life, which in turn, is determined by social and cultural values." Hartman claimed that the architects' norms related to "middle class values" instead of the "working class orientation and life styles." The results were often meaningless and non-gratifying products for their users. Hartman belonged to the faculty of Harvard's Graduate School of Design where, already in the beginning of the 1950s, two young planners, John Dyckman and Martin Meyerson, were urging for the recognition of the "sovereignty" of the consumer and the need for the design professions and planners to be "responsive" to the consumer market in a democratic society. Hartman, however, viewed the problem as it related to the framework of the war against poverty in America of the 1960s, and the sovereignty of "the people" with respect to housing and the city.[53] His conclusions were very similar to those of John Zeisel and Brent Brolin. The former, a sociologist collaborating with Brolin, who was an architect, viewed their work as a combination of social research and design, replacing the official approach of architects to housing that had "a dehumanizing and degrading effect" (*Architectural Forum*, July–August 1968). Soon an army of behavioral and social scientists with or without the help of designers spread around the country, mostly documenting the failures of modern architecture in providing shelter or other facilities for the needy.

While Denise Scott Brown had tried to modify architectural morphology, without touching the central position of the architectural profession, behavioral and social scientists started demanding for themselves—in the name of the people—part of the architect's traditional responsibility in conceiving a project. An even greater extreme of populism called for the architect to disappear completely.

The radical positions of the social scientists gradually entered the mainstream during the early 1970s, with such projects as Levi's Plaza by Hellmuth Obata Kassabaum (1977–82, pp. 210–11), landscaped by Lawrence Halprin, where social scientists were involved at a very early stage of the design process, and who observed and interviewed the future users of the complex. As a result, the building contributed, in the words of Alan Temko, an architectural critic in San Francisco, to the anti-manhattanization of the town. Its relatively low massing offers a public space, not only through the geometry of the plan as it opens to a piazza, but also through the multi-functional organization of the building, which provides at the ground level services and activities that continue beyond the closing of the offices.[54]

Another change brought about by the populist movement, as it entered the mainstream, was to replace the pyramidal structure of the architecture profession—the design decisions being made at the top—with a matrix organization, where specialists and participants could carry out the design process together. This was the approach Moore Lyndon Turnbull Whitaker applied at Kresge College University of California at Santa Cruz (1970–73, pp. 152–53). From the very beginning, students and administrators were involved in the design. With enthusiastic participation, a course was offered at the university in the early 1970s under the title, "Creating Kresge College." Out of this interaction emerged creative results: a village-like street tied together the space of the complex, with a highly felicitous variety of accommodation to suit the needs of the students. Another project, though not populist in its visual expression, but deeply expressing the emancipatory aspirations for the freedom of populism as a social and political movement of the 1960s, was the Martin Luther King Center for Non-Violent Social Change, designed by Bond Ryder James (1976–81, pp. 196–99). With over a million visitors a year, the Center has become one of the most visited National Park Service sites in the United States.

Inscribed in the program of Johnson's Great Society was what came to be known as Advocacy Architecture, one of the more controversial results of populism. The person who coined the term, Paul Davidoff, was a law student and graduate from the planning department of the University of Pennsylvania in the late 1950s. In an article in the *Journal of the American Institute of Planners* (vol. 28, 1962. p. 108), he wrote: "It is not for the planners to make the final decision in transforming their values into policy commitments." The planner was to be involved in identifying how values were to be distributed among people, and how they were to be weighed against each other.

Advocacy Architecture drew mostly from the academic world rather than from the professional one. Many of these "storefront" projects, as these community-based architectural offices were often called, were headed by young design faculty members of the late 1960s, among them Kevin Lynch, Richard Plunz, Troy West, Melvin Charney, Richard Hatch, Max Bond, Karl Linn, Sim Van der Ryn, Christopher Alexander, Charles Moore, and Joseph Baker. Also out of the academic world came a final facet of populism that was more extreme than advocacy or participatory architecture. The seriousness with which this so-called counter-culture extreme was taken was demonstrated in a long article published in *Progressive Architecture* (August 1966), entitled "LSD, a Design Tool?" The answer is sympathetic to the drug and its consciousness-expanding architectural potential, reporting extensive experiments by designers using it and "the design uses to which they put their psychedelic experience." No real buildings came out of these aspiring utopian designers, to the best of our knowledge.

Support, both financial and ideological, for the different schools within the populist movement of the late 1960s, was short lived. There were many reasons for this. As we have already mentioned, the movement was financed primarily from The Great

Society programs. While the expansion of federal spending on the poor during the Johnson administration jumped from 12 billion to over 27 billion, funding for these programs did not increase. And increased social spending in the face of the increased military expenditure for the war in Vietnam proved elusive.

As The Great Society programs were being scaled back, the OPEC oil embargoes of the 1970s heightened public awareness of the vulnerability of energy resources. For the previous generation of designers, cheap energy made possible the air conditioning needed for people to inhabit the glass-skinned buildings of the 1950s, which were oblivious to orientation and local climatic conditions. While the "energy crisis" spawned a movement of designers such as Donald Watson and others who explored the implications of energy-conscious design,[55] both formally and technically, much of this activity was outside the professional mainstream. One exception was the twin office buildings, Enerplex, designed by SOM and Alan Chimacoff, in Princeton, New Jersey (1979–84), which were designed to showcase energy technologies. But as was noted in an evaluation of the project, the buildings were oriented more for energy than for people, and there were few spin-offs (*Progressive Architecture*, March 1989).

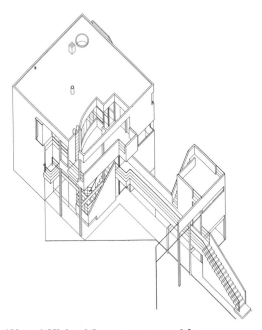

(Above) Michael Graves, axonometric of Benacerraf House (1967)

There was another significant factor, however: the mounting complaints of the wealthy that the administration was over-taxing them to support these social programs, which they said would create "a capital formation problem." This pressure would not be effective until 1978, when a new tax bill was passed, marking a turnabout of the whole enterprise of the Welfare State as it had developed since the 1930s. While the ultimate goal of the program had been to cement American society by eradicating inequality, the ideas of bottom-up activism had an extremely divisive impact. The end result was that populism, which had been aimed at lifting individuals from their oppressive poverty, led to the erecting of what the sociologist Richard Sennett called "barricades from within"—the endless splintering of participants into factions.[56] By the beginning of the 1970s, populism was abandoned both as a visual expression and as a procedural political framework in which to practice architecture.

Consistent with the unraveling of professional service institutions, a large part of the populist movement had challenged and undermined traditional design practice. This challenge created not only a major antagonism on the part of professionals and educators, but also fear. This was not merely the fear of the violation of vested interests and privileges based on the esoterics of a professional corporation: the architectural profession in the late 1960s faced with genuine dread the possibility that its fundamental position had been irretrievably lost.

(Above) Michael Graves, axonometric of Hanselman House (1967)

RETREAT INTO FORM

Not surprisingly, a reaction followed. By the end of the 1960s, a small group of architects appeared, who set out to return systematically to the formal architectural conventions that had developed in the 19th century. As a result, not only were populist

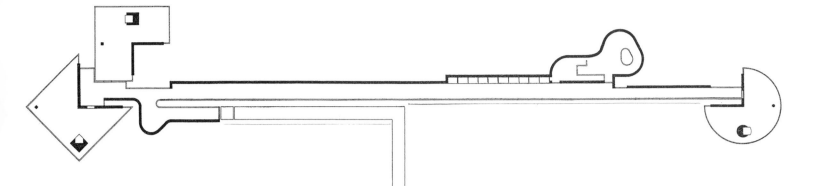

John Hejduk, floor plan of the ground level of House X (1980)

concerns abandoned, but there was a reaction against technology, the environment, and community.

Was this development a defensive posture against the threatened eclipse of professional knowledge, against the dissipation of professional power, as a result of the economic crisis? Was it what one might call a narcissistic reaction to losing control?[57] Or was it simply a failure of nerve, a response, perhaps, to the emergence of a new anti-Pop sensitivity in art which opted for the systemic, the hard-edged abstract, the structural, the primary, and the minimal? Or was it a sympathetic response to the emergence of the so-called neo-conservative politics as opposed to those of the New Frontiers and Great Society?[58]

One insight into this break with the concerns of the 1960s was expressed in a study published by the architect Mario Gandelsonas in collaboration with David Morton (*Progressive Architecture*, March 1972). "In recent years," Gandelsonas remarked, "there has been a re-examination of architecture," which he disparagingly referred to as the Functionalist tradition. As alternatives, he discussed two approaches that he saw as fundamentally opposed. One was science-related, using computer technology and mathematical models, which was engineering rather than architecture. The other approach was cultural. In Galdesonas's words, its aim was to find "cultural meaning" in architecture, to try to explain form and find rules of its use beyond those that relate to purely functional, practical, and physical needs.

The article presented for the first time in the United States the work of two young architects—Peter Eisenman and Michael Graves—who had at that time devoted most of their activities to teaching. His article argues that, in spite of their small scale, their work marked a new approach to architecture. Among his examples, he included Graves's Hanselman House (1967) and Eisenman's House II (1969–71, pp. 142–43).

Gandelsonas drew from the theories of semiotics of the 1960s for his analysis of these projects. He viewed the work of the architect as being the act of signification and the use of architecture as "reading." Only the drawing mattered, and design was seen as "the generation of form as a specific manipulation of meaning within a culture." (ibid.) What this "culture" referred to, however, was never specified.

A year later, the tendency Galdesonas had identified in the work of Graves and Eisenman was close to becoming a movement. In the May 1973 issue of *Forum*, Robert Stern, a professor of architecture at Columbia University, invited a team of critics to write about a group of architects called the New York Five—John Hejduk, Charles

Gwathmey, Michael Graves, Peter Eisenman, and Richard Meier—because he felt they "presented an opportunity (too rare these days) to discuss current architectural attitudes." The occasion was a book devoted to their work, limited mostly to a few private houses, published by the prestigious publisher, Wittenborn.[59]

To raise the level of excitement, Stern chose critics whose views were significantly different from those of the architects, such as Jacqueline Robertson (herself an architect) and the critic, Alan Greenberg. Especially critical were Charles Moore, who was part of the populist movement, as we have seen, and Romaldo Giurgola, the Chairman of the Architecture Department at Columbia, who, at that time, was preoccupied with social issues in relation to the workplace. The book, *Five Architects*, was introduced by Colin Rowe, an influential teacher at Cornell and "the intellectual guru," as Stern called him, of the new group. Rowe noted that the text was intended, implicitly, as "a response to Vincent Scully's introduction to *Complexity and Contradiction* and to Venturi's work." Whereas Scully had welcomed Venturi as the antipode of Le Corbusier, Rowe hailed the new group as Le Corbusier's heirs. In addition, Rowe's introduction was a vehement attack against the populist movement, as well as the whole decade of the 1960s, including the contribution of the architects of the American Renaissance. He declared that, rather than "constantly endorsing the revolutionary myth," it might be "more reasonable to recognize that, in the opening years of the century, great revolutions in thought occurred."

This call to Corbusian dogma contrasted with the hot turbulence of ideas and debates, not only of anarchic populism, but also of the polyarchic first half of the 1960s. In many respects, it marked a return to a 1950s spirit of "serenity" in architecture, as Yamasaki had called it, not so much in its forms or in its easy-going formalism, but in its abandonment of the idea of program and originality. In addition, this view of Le Corbusier was extremely reductive, as it concentrated mostly on the stylistic aspects of purism and very little on the rest of Le Corbusier's passionate investigations into the use of space, the functional typology of buildings, or even esthetics in a broader sense. Needless to say, Rowe's call to dogma was also an escape from the Mumfordian paradigm. Neither Rowe's introduction, nor most of the projects in the volume referred to the environment, to technology, or to community. And most of them paid only lip service to function.

Among the few exceptions was Richard Meier's architecture, more open to programmatic questions, eager to be seen as providing a social service in addition to performing a formal exercise. By then, Meier had designed a significant social housing project for the Bronx Development (1970–76, pp. 166–67), a point made by Romaldo Giurgola during the meeting. Gwathmey's house (1963–65, pp. 102–05), also included in the publication, paid attention to construction and to site, within an almost deliberate re-use of Corbusian elements.

Eisenman's projects appeared to be the most abstractly related to Corbuiser's Purism. The buildings looked like a formal analysis (for example, by Wolfflin, 1864–1945) of a Le Corbusier building rather than a building using Corbusian details.

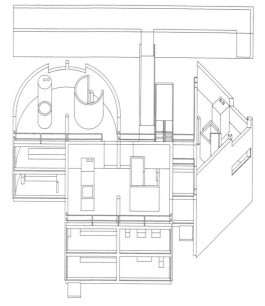

(Above) John Hejduk, axonometric of One-Half House (1966)

(Below) Charles Gwathmey, axonometric of Gwathmey Studio and Residence (1963–65)

In their abstraction, they appeared more like three-dimensional analyses of buildings than buildings that had come out of an analysis. As a result, they were labeled "cardboard" by critics, a characterization to which Eisenman, in the polemic formalist credo of the Five, did not object. It was the first time since the Second World War that such a thorough, virtuoso, formal analysis had been undertaken. Later, Eisenman would give a political meaning to this formalist position, "pre-empting the notion of the radical," as Diane Ghirardo, a professor of architecture and critic, would write in great frustration twenty years later.[60]

Hejduk's drawings were the most abstract objects presented in the book, but their abstraction was less analytical than intuitive. They appeared arbitrary and mysterious, because ultimately their logic was narrative rather than formal, an aspect that would become very explicit in his later publications. Graves's relation to Le Corbusier was the most curious: neither imitation nor analysis appeared to govern it. Fragments from Le Corbusier's buildings were elliptically transposed and assembled with no apparent stylistic or narrative reason, and with manifest delight in having none. Graves, in this sense, was probably the most original and the most radical exponent of what would come to be seen as a free-wheeling, narcissistic approach to architecture, as opposed to the "committed," disciplinarian one of the 1960s.

However, probably the most aggressive attack against the architecture of the 1960s at large and, to a great extent, against modern architecture, appeared in an article by Colin Rowe and Fred Koetter under the title "Collage City" (*Architectural Review,* August 1975). It opened with an attack against the Harvard Graduate School of Design, calling it a bastion of the American Renaissance mentality and one of the centers of the populist movement. It criticized the fact that the school had put out a brochure entitled "Crisis," to raise money for its program. But it was not the fundraising that drew the polemics of Rowe and Koetter: it was the title, typical of the "psychology of modern architecture"—apocalyptic, raising the threat of catastrophe and damnation, while promising the hope of salvation and an instant millennium. This "Savonarola syndrome," as Koetter and Rowe called it, universal in modern architecture, had to be suppressed.[61]

The article proceeds to trace this syndrome beyond architecture, in the history of culture, citing all utopias, from Le Comte de Saint Simon to Le Corbusier. According to Koetter and Rowe, utopias lead to one outcome only: disaster. Yamasaki's Pruitt-Igo, blown up in St. Louis on July 15, 1972, is referred to as a classic example of the results brought about by utopian thinking and design. Pruitt-Igo, in fact, became a general purpose myth serving the current reaction against the 1960s as well as the whole enterprise of Welfare State architecture. The tragic failure of this project was due more to economic and organizational reasons than to architectural design. The project was the first interracial public housing project in the U.S., and was named after the black war hero, Wendell Oliver Pruitt and the progressive writer, William J. Igo. Built under a public housing act of the 1950s, the project was plagued by funding shortages, and was never built and maintained in the manner originally envisaged by Yamasaki.

Koetter and Rowe's attack against the 1960s, and modern architecture in general, used long and complicated arguments which mostly repeated Karl Popper's and Isaiah Berlin's critiques of utopian thinking. Nor were their general conclusions a surprise: "It is better to think of an aggregation of small, and even contradictory, set pieces ... than to entertain fantasies about total, faultless solutions." This conclusion, however, coming from Koetter and Rowe, was inconsistent with their own previous work, as, for example, in a 1967 Museum of Modern Art show, when they had proposed a massive project very much in the radical utopian spirit of Le Corbusier.

Collage City was in fact little more than a manifesto for the architectural practitioners of the 1970s. Interestingly, its major references were historical. The cases presented were Versailles and the Villa Hadriana. Versailles was seen as a "radical criticism" of Paris designed by the "progressivist Louis XIV assisted by Colbert [sic] ... The rationalizations of a Colbert become handed down by Turgot to Saint-Simon and Comte and one begins to see something of Versailles' prophetic enormity." Koetter and Rowe argued that "the myth of the rationally ordered and 'scientific' society the accident free society rules by knowledge and information in which debate has become superfluous" has its origins in Versailles. Villa Hadriana, on the other hand, is a miniature Rome. It mirrors Rome's conflicts and chaos as "a conservative endorsement of Rome." Koetter and Rowe opted for the anti-utopian Villa Hadriana as a model.

Dressed in this analysis was a polemical argument—namely, that the incrementally accumulated built environment, despite its apparent disorder, had more chances of succeeding than one that had been conceived as a totality. This alternative was what Koetter and Rowe called "collage city," one that was put together as an "aggregation of small, and even contradictory set pieces."

In reality, using history more as a parable than a fact, the article was a repeat of the call for incremental planning that Jane Jacobs had already discussed in 1961, in *The Death and Life of Great American Cities*. But curiously, Koetter and Rowe's article condemned not only large-scale projects, as she had done, but also the utopian thinking of the political activists who had created so much havoc during the Johnson years, and who, in fact, had leveled the same criticisms against the biases of professional architecture, again as she had done. Koetter and Rowe argued for an incremental bottom-up intervention in the cities, rather than for "rational" planning. Equally curious was the attack focussed against Christopher Alexander, who had very little to do either with modernist urbanism or with socialist, centralized planning. "Collage City" in fact drew heavily from Alexander's "A City is Not a Tree," an intelligent critique of reductive planning ideas of the 1950s.[62] Finally, even more curious was the use of the idea of collage. Collage was a very appropriate metaphor for describing the emergence of artifacts from a slow evolution of the mutating and cross-breeding of existing products. It was in fact consistent with Christopher Alexander's idea of design methodology put forth in the above article. Koetter and Rowe correctly associated collage with the kind of thinking that Levi-Strauss had called *bricolage*. But now, suddenly, it was presented not as a creative method, but as a "method deriving its virtue from its irony."

How were the two sides of Colin Rowe's views reconciled? One appeared to support Purism and the pristine design of the New York Five, and the other a messy, ironic bricolage. The answer lies in that for Rowe, Purism was ultimately an opportunity for polemics, its target being the functional and contextual aspects of architecture, as well as scientific thinking and social values. The closest architectural interpretation of this idea was in the fastidious buildings of Michael Graves presented in the New York Five book, *Five Architects*. Here the seemingly arbitrary assemblage of Le Corbusier fragments was intentional. They were meant to be cartoons satirizing the aspirations and efforts of modern architecture, and more particularly, those of American architecture of the 1960s.

Irony worked, to quote Richard Rorty, as an antidote to the totalizing pictures of the world.[63] From this point of view, the idea of collage as irony was an antidote against the totalizing aspects of the technological, environmental, and social commitments of the architects of the 1960s. Since neither Purism nor Le Corbusier were essential to the "collagist" aims or methods, one should not be surprised that five years later Michael Graves would be designing buildings such as the Portland Building (1980–82, pp. 208–09) and the San Juan Capistrano Library (1981–83, pp. 220–21). They were characterized by a playful, free-wheeling collaging that exchanged Purism for an almost unrecognizable classicism. The reintroduction of classical architecture was one more step away from the 1960s and was not an arbitrary choice of Graves's alone, nor did it come only for the purposes of collage.

Similar historicist tendencies were emerging in Europe, expressing the same reaction against Action Architecture and echoing the negative response to the American Renaissance. They were also a result both of the post-May 1968 populist movement in Europe and of a major event which took place in New York in 1975, the same year of the publication of "Collage City."

The Museum of Modern Art put up a mammoth exhibition devoted to the Ecole des Beaux-Arts, with particular accent on the drawing and the historicist tendencies of its teaching. Arthur Drexler, the organizer of the exhibition, echoed Koetter and Rowe in his preface. Modern architecture was, in the "alarming phrase" of Walter Gropius, aspiring to be "total architecture ... Redemption through design ... was the mystic hope hidden within the humane re-ordering of earthly things. Today, in architecture as in everything else Messianic fervor seems naive when it is not actually destructive." Architecture, Drexler continues, has now to exploit the new situation created by the relaxation of dogma. Yet it should not take the path of Italian design, which "replaced moral imperatives with irony and humor." If there were no new beliefs, it would be impossible to reach any agreements. Offering as an alternative a non-dogmatic common conviction, Drexler suggested the Ecole des Beaux-Arts. And he concludes: "now that modern experience so often contradicts modern faith, we would be well advised to re-examine our architectural pieties."[64]

However, as much as this pristine and historicizing architecture of the early 1970s seemed opposed to populism, it was in many respects a continuation of the same beliefs. Ironically, both approaches shared one common enemy: the architecture of experimentation and the mass-scale reorganization of the environment typical of the American Renaissance. Both shared the same distrust of the Welfare State, the same admiration for anarchy, from a populist perspective in one case and a neo-aristocratic one in the other. Both singled out the same project of the Pruitt-Igo Housing in St. Louis by Yamasaki as a symbol of the devastating policies of the Welfare State.

THE FATE OF PUBLIC SPACE

While these formalist, mostly academic or small-scale studies thrived, at least a certain degree of experimentation and innovation survived in professional practice. The issues of technology, the environment, and community managed not to disappear completely, although they were now increasingly subjugated to private profit rather than supported by public funding. By the end of the 1960s, the kind of massive project which the Welfare State had supported directly and, more often indirectly, began to be replaced by another more massive type of project. Although these complexes were intended as private buildings, one of the main issues they addressed was "public space," a concept defined not by ownership, but by the kinds of activities that could occur in them, creating "a meeting place for the community."[65]

The emergence of the new kind of public space, accommodated within major private complexes, takes us back to 1968, the year that saw the completion of the Ford Foundation Headquarters in New York City (1963–68, pp. 130–31). A workplace for a private organization, although of a philanthropic character, the building provided exceptionally good individual spaces for its primarily white-collar workers. But it also offered as a unique amenity, a giant enclosed and landscaped court, with the explicit aim, according to the brief, "to offer a sense of the individual identifying with the aims of the group," as well as to act as a space between street and workplace; it also broke the routine lobby–elevator–corridor sequence, in an attempt to enhance a sense of community.

Gallerias and enclosed spaces have their origins in the 19th century, but never before had such an interior landscape court been designed in a workplace environment, and right in the midst of New York City. The technology and the spatial organization were also unprecedented. But did this make it a public place? The architectural critic, Kenneth Frampton, in *Architectural Design* (July 1968), criticized the building as being an "anti-agora," which, invaded by plants, excluded people in a prohibitive way. Yet the general perception of the space was different: it was seen as a prototype for a new kind of public space provided by a modern skyscraper, an alternative to the outdoor square in front of the Seagram Building, which had proved to be inhospitable, for climatic reasons, and costly to service as well.

Johnson/Burgee Architects and S. I. Norris Associates, ground plan of Penzoil Place, Houston, Texas (1976)

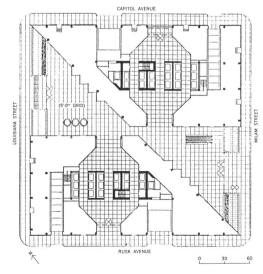

Kevin Roche's company applied the same idea of the internal court in his commission for the Deere & Company Headquarters West Office (1975–78, pp. 184–85), a workplace in an outlying suburban area. The need for such a space was felt to be even more important, given the remoteness of the complex from real, urban, public spaces. Here, the public space took the form of an enclosed central court, treated as an immense winter garden, measuring over 11,000 square feet. Unfortunately, because the building was located in greener surroundings, the court could not have the same refreshing effect as the Ford Foundation, situated in a mainly asphalt-covered environment. Not surprisingly, perhaps, in the Union Carbide Building (1976–82), Roche abandoned the idea of a single, central public space. Instead, to achieve a more collective identity, he proposed an egalitarian device, abandoning the traditional idea of the typical American corporation being organized according to the hierarchy of the company. "My argument against this was," he reflected during a meeting inaugurating the Temple Hoyne Buell Center for the study of American Architecture in 1983, "that the chairman of the board and the mail boy were essentially the same size. If they weren't then why didn't the chairman of the board wear an outsized suit and the mail-boy a very small sized suit? You wear a suit that is appropriate to your physical size, and since the physical size is more or less the same, offices should be more or less the same." The public space, therefore, is fragmented throughout the building.

Roche's suburban General Foods Corporation headquarters (1983) tries to recapture this idea of the central public space once more, but with variants of the "Beaux-Arts devices." The public space is approached through an axial road, which intersects with the center of the building and functions as a dining room. The historicist references combine with extremely inexpensive materials—"aluminum siding you can buy in a hardware store" (ibid.)—weaken the impact.

Of all Roche's projects, the Ford Foundation remains an unsurpassed prototype for a new paradigm for the work environment, and takes its place in this period with the other pioneering efforts to re-examine the workplace, such as Kahn's laboratory projects (Richards and Salk) and also the Levi Strauss headquarters by Hellmuth Obata Kassabaum (1977–82, pp. 210–11).

Another building, contemporary with the Ford Foundation, that introduced its own version of the enclosed mega-space, was John Portman's Hyatt Regency Hotel in Atlanta (1964–67, pp. 114–15). Portman acted as both designer and developer. This gave him special freedom to trade off innovation with efficiency. The complex grows around a court, a mega-atrium. Portman did not supply a real public space: there was no question of community, only of a simulation of collective identity, as had been the case with turn-of-the-century hotel lobbies. He did, however, provide an unprecedented kind of structure which, under different circumstances, like the Ford Foundation building, could act as an architectural precedent for a more genuine public space.

The opportunity to explore new models of public space came almost a decade later. It resulted very much from the fiscal crisis of the cities that occurred under the administration of Gerald Ford. In New York City, the announcement that President Ford had cut federal funds for the city was greeted in a *Daily News* headline as "FORD TO CITY: DROP DEAD."[66] But the crisis had deep repercussions for all the cities of the United States. It meant, among other things, that the preservation and creation of public spaces—one of the most costly aspects of cities—were to suffer. Within this context, it became clear that cities would have to resort to new tactics. One strategy was for private developers to provide public space in return for permits to build beyond the established regulations. The amenity envisaged was an enclosed mega-space, following in the pattern of Portman and Roche.

One of the most successful of such atria or "plazas," as they have also been called, was the IDS Center in Minneapolis Minnesota (1973), designed by Philip Johnson and John Burgee. In an article published in *Forum* (November 1973), under the title "A There There," Johnson described the context of the building in the most urbanistic, socially conscious terms. He referred to the location as a network rather than as a space used by "the people." His analysis of the environment, climate, and site was "a solution out of these constraints." Although he drew the solution from the precedent of the San Marco public square of Venice, the reference is neither one of nostalgia nor of ironic pastiche. It was instead an environment based on precedent, an urban place "splendid for girl watching and ice-cream buying ... both in air conditioned comfort." He went on to declare very explicitly that the plaza, in the conservative, historical heritage sense, was dead: "Long live the climate-controlled court." And he concluded by affirming the populist identity of the public place he had provided, merging the ideals of the 1960s with Gertrude Stein's acute observations about the placelessness of America, and declaring proudly: "there is a 'there there' now (for) the people."

The success of the IDS Center was based fundamentally on the movement of people, as well as their concentration within the building. By contrast, the shell of the building was neutral, if not drab, both inside and out. In the words of the *Forum* article (November 1973), in the end it was just another glass box. Conscious of the "boring and tiresome" characteristics of the building type, and in an attempt to keep their building from appearing monolithic and scaleless, Johnson and Burgee wrapped it in a skin made up of small panes of glass inserted into a grid pattern of sharply protruding mullions and muntins. As a result of the network of projecting lines on the glass box, the building resembled a birdcage (the architects' own expression), which was not much of an improvement over the conventional glass box. The cityscape had nothing much to gain from this kind of image.

The firm's Penzoil Place (1976) was the concept of IDS turned on its head. Although it was a glass box, it was far from drab. Located in the midst of Houston's skyscrapers, it had to compete for attention—notably against Johnson and Burgee's own RepublicBank Center (1983). Its power was in its "imageability," to use Kevin Lynch's term. It achieved this effect by eliminating the mullions and the muntins of the IDS building from the glass skin, which was now slick and dark, and opaque as crude oil. But where the Minneapolis building had used transparent glass to make its internal

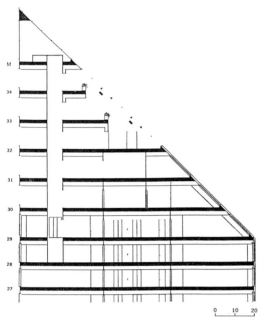

Johnson/Burgee Architects and S. I. Norris Associates, section of the roof of Penzoil Place, Houston, Texas (1976)

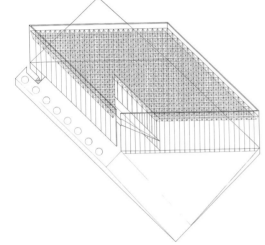

(Top) Gunnar Birkerts, Contemporary Arts Museum in Houston, Texas (1970–72)

(Above) Isometric study of the same building

public space both visible and beckoning to the passersby, Penzoil's glossy surface, which irresistibly attracted the eye of the beholder from afar, served only to keep out the gaze from close up. Undoubtedly, there was a "there there" once more, but it was way over there, on the highway, not here, on the street. But perhaps nothing was lost, as critic Richard Ingersoll pointed out, since in this "fifth largest city in the United States (which) will someday will be famous among urbanologists as the first modern city without streets," there are only "elevated freeways, parkways, feeder roads, six-lane boulevards" and endless "tunnels which connect over 50 downtown buildings … extending for a total of seven kilometers."[67]

Penzoil was a popular success, not so much among "the people," as among professionals and corporations. The critic, Peter Papademitriou, in an article, entitled "Is WOW Enough?" (*Progressive Architecture* August 1977) reported that two extra floors had been added to the project while it was under construction to satisfy the demand for new occupants, quoting a friend of Johnson's, who had ironically said that "it's a good thing Philip's not a nut about proportions."

Cesar Pelli's Pacific Design Center (Phase I, 1971–75; Phase II, 1984–88, pp. 156–59), was the first major building to employ the new mullionless glass sheathing technology. This strange architectural creature seems to float in a bustling sea of low-density, low-rise buildings in a predominantly industrial, though semi-residential, area in the trade center of Los Angeles. It soon came to be called the Blue Whale because of its mammoth size, its amorphous geometry, and the color of its skin. It was adventurous in forsaking the safe ground of the glass box of the 1950s, and of the more banal solutions typical of the 1960s for large shopping complexes and emporia. The Pacific Design Center was technologically highly innovative in the way it implemented a new glazing system which, confronted with the problem of scale, he chose to use in an effort to shrink the perceived bulk of the complex. His attempt to make the giant structure as unobtrusive as possible was received in a positive way by Californian critic Esther McCoy, among others.[68]

Pelli exploited new, highly sophisticated developments in sealing techniques to invent a new kind of rigorism in the tradition descending from Lodoli, Goethe, and Greenough, a rigorism of the skin of the building. This new rigorism, instead of being preoccupied with the skeleton, the organs, or intestines of the building, to complete the anatomical analogy, looked into the external essential part of its organism, which is its surface—its skin. This rigorism, applied to the "skin," quickly became mainstream, eventually degenerating into what critic Michael Sorkin has called "the equivalent in architecture of permanent press slacks."[69]

THE NEW GILDED AGE

By the beginning of the 1980s, there had been an upturn in the American economy, which had led to the massive enrichment of a minority and the decline of the middle and working class. Much has been written about this development, which occurred with the change of political administrations. Once again, there was an investment in building in Houston, Atlanta, Los Angeles, Boston, and in particular, New York City, which recovered from its mid-1970s fiscal crisis, at least partly, due to the active involvement of the city in the real estate business. Considering the intentions, the appearance, and the money poured into these projects—offices, hotels, and some luxury residential buildings—we can call this the New Gilded Age.

To illustrate the volatility of the times, the next building designed by Johnson and Burgee after Penzoil was the AT&T building (1978–83, pp. 212–13), a 647-foot sky-scraper for 1500 employees. Far from the glass box experiments, this new project was topped by a Chippendale-style pediment, covered in granite, and rested on piers and arches of a temple-like loggia of stone piers and archways. The project was celebrated by Paul Goldberger of the *New York Times* (September 18, 1983) as the "Harbinger of a New Era."

To understand why AT&T, even before its completion, was so admired by the media, why the project was featured on the cover of *Time* magazine, not under the name of the client, but under the name of the architect (Burgee, the co-designer, was left out, much to his frustration) and to see why it was celebrated in the pages of the American newspapers from Los Angeles to New York, one must understand it as a product of the "single minded greed" of the 1980s. This is how Anthony Lewis had referred to Johnson's International Place at Fort Hill Square in Boston. This appears to be the only rationale behind the triumphant march of the Towers of Excellence, Towers of Power, or simply the "block buster skyscrapers," as Herbert Muschamp (*New York Times*, August 6, 1992) would call the towers of the Times Square Development plan of New York by Philip Johnson.

Most of these projects appear to have found a legitimacy in the AT&T building's iconography, pseudo-classical collagist, civic-like appearance. Ironically, despite the AT&T's claims to elite culture, its style was populist. In fact, it seems that Philip Johnson acted obediently to the programmatic instructions he received, which requested an image for the building in the style of Norman Rockwell's paintings (*Progressive Architecture*, July 1994). What AT&T received, according to the same magazine, was a "pompous essay in pre-war corporate majesty." But what the city did not receive was a public space equivalent to the excess of volume that had been granted for the building. Not that there were not alternatives. Johnson simply acted too hastily to the new economic realities. Perhaps he was too eager to please. Under pressure and criticism by colleagues for this behavior, he admitted this, uttering his scandalous "I am a whore."[70] A more composed, reflective, and responsible design might have been more coldly received in the short term. But in the long term, it would have contributed more to New York's struggle for a public space and community.

A mere block away from the AT&T is such an alternative: Edward Larrabee Barnes's IBM Building (1973–83, pp. 214–17), built at almost the same time. It focussed on pragmatic, site, and technological constraints, empathizing with the needs and aspirations of the contemporary urban population. The building was less well received than the AT&T, yet in the long run it has succeeded in giving back to New York a genuine, although modest, public space. Certainly, such public spaces become by definition more public when they combine public services, such as links between pedestrians and transit, places for eating and meeting informally, together with a symbolic representation of community. Two other examples, Hugh Stubbins's Citicorp (1970–77, pp. 172–73) and Helmut Jahn's State of Illinois Building in Chicago (1979–85, pp. 236–37), are both more successful from this point of view.

Adjacent to the IBM and AT&T towers, perhaps the best example of the excess of the 1980s, is the Trump Tower by Der Scutt (1979–83, pp. 218–19). For the people of New York City, the effect of such buildings might be equated with those drugs that offer temporary relief and euphoria only to be followed by negative, if not disastrous, effects. The point here is not about traditional notions of the split between poor and rich and the violent reactions the poor might have to the conspicuous exhibition of wealth by a minority. Nor are we referring to the contrast between public space identified exclusively with opulent emporia, as opposed to the forgotten, mean streets. We are in fact referring to the identification of public space with a celebration of conspicuous consumption in the framework of American developments in the 1970s and 1980s. During this time, the average American indulged in a 47 percent increase in personal spending while his income increased by only 38 percent. He saved less than the inhabitant of any European Community country, with the exception of Greece; any Middle Eastern country, with the exception of Egypt and Jordan; and any East Asian and Pacific Rim country, with the exception of Papua New Guinea. As Edward Luttwak points out, this led quickly to a curious "capitalism without capital" and to an end of the American Dream.[71] From this point of view, the monumentalization of consumption has been at odds with public interest, which, after all, has been embodied by successful public spaces for centuries.

Unlike the engineering feats of the previous century, such efforts today, whatever their conceptual inventiveness and quality of execution, are not enough to encapsulate as images the idea of collective effort or community. Neither SOM's John Hancock Center (1965–70, pp. 144–45) nor Gunnar Birkerts' Federal Reserve Bank of Minneapolis (1967–72, pp. 146–47), technological masterpieces though they are, achieved through their success as structural rigorist essays a recognition in the minds of the public at large, as public symbols standing for public places. Not that technology or functional rigorism are unimportant in defining community. Other types of rigorist work, as Cesar Pelli has demonstrated in the Pacific Design Center or Jahn in his United Airlines Terminal Complex (1987, pp. 240–41), are more successful in achieving this.

Neither does the combination of huge masses of high-density, mono-culture workplaces, as a uniform corporate identity, and equally giant public lobbies create sufficient conditions to generate public space, as in the case of Pelli's World Financial Center Towers and Winter Garden (1980–88, pp. 248–51). Ironically, this concentration of buildings can act as a prohibitive factor for the participation of the plurality that makes up the real public—something which, to return once more to the 1930s, Rockefeller Center could achieve.

A decade later, in the 1990s, the situation became radically different economically, politically, and psychologically. On August 6, 1992, the new architecture critic of the *New York Times*, Herbert Muschamp, published an article on the front page of the arts section with the title, "For Times Square, A Reprieve and Hope Of a Livelier Day, Gone are the Glowing Towers. Think Gaudy!" On November 1 of the same year, announcing the suspension of the Johnson project for Times Square, he would declare: "Time to Reset the Clock in Times Square." The magic was gone. Social, technological, urbanistic issues were reemerging. To the monumental, funereal-pecuniary style Johnson Towers, Muschamp would juxtapose a Times Square which had to be recognized as "more than a place ... a social contract written in form, color, light, rhythm." Accordingly, Robert Stern, head of the new design team, stressed the importance of the street rather than the building as such, and promised "an urban pageant."

The news about AT&T's maturity was no better. The tower was not well received by the public, as opposed to the architectural critics who saluted it almost unanimously (one exception was Ada Louise Huxtable, whom Paul Goldberger had replaced as the architectural critic at the *New York Times*). By the end of the 1980s, as the magic was dying, it became clear that the building had failed functionally, socially, and culturally. The populist "cultural" associations, which glowed on the printed page and on the television screen, were dysfunctional from the urban point of view. It was a failure typical of narcissistic expectations destroyed by everyday reality. Thus, under the title "Remaking Public Spaces that Didn't Quite Make It, A New Philosophy at the AT&T Building," the *New York Times* announced the changes to the ground floor tower "in the belief that the result would be an amenity that is far more engaging and welcoming than the existing arcade and covered pedestrian space." (September 27, 1992.) Interestingly, Barnes's IBM Tower proved to have succeeded where the AT&T tower failed, in all aspects, although initially, being a plain urbanistically, technologically, and socially conscious building, it was criticized for not adding to either "the dignity or life (of) the cityscape" (*New York Times*, March 28, 1983).

It is important to note that the client who commissioned the revision of part of the the Johnson scheme, very ably reshaped by Gwathmey, Siegel and Edwin Schlossberg, was not a "welfare state" bureaucracy or "socially conscious" institution, but the immensely successful contemporary corporation, Sony. As the new owner of the building, Sony decided to carry out many modifications to undo the original monumentality of the work. It also decided to house its own avant-garde products in the redesigned ground floor of the tower. By happy coincidence, the products displayed are dedicated to interactive information technology. These exhibits, designed especially for children, include robotic equipment that is accessible for experimentation in creating infinite virtual and hyper-active realities. The redesign of the Johnson tower did not provide a place for contemplation, not even for a tranquil sandwich. But a place it will be, something which the original design failed or refused to give to the needy public of the city.

Despite its success, the new space, revamped by Sony, as *Progressive Architecture* observed, was a failed attempt at preserving public space in Manhattan: "The Bill of Rights doesn't accompany the flaneur, and certainly not the homeless coming inside the commercial space" (July, 1994). "Sony is about communication, dealing with people—music, movies, video," Mr. Gwathmey said, adding, "They wanted to dispel the elitist image and engage the building with the ground and make it participatory" (*New York Times*, September 27, 1992).

THE NEW CRITICAL REGIONALISM

As the gilded age began to de-urbanize New York and other American cities, that is in the early 1980s, another tendency began to appear in architecture. It included projects that were smaller both in number and scale, and dispersed over the continent. In a conscious rejection of the gilded tendency, its two main concerns were the quality of the environment and the community.

The notion of community these projects presents is more than simply aggregating and moving large crowds through built emporia, as was the case with the large-scale urban developments. The idea of community was linked with environmental quality and implemented through carefully relating building and site, including existing older structures and paths of communication. In most of these projects, ecological factors, energy considerations, and choice of materials were integral to the framework of each region.

It was such concerns that brought together a number of practitioners and theoreticians at a four-day seminar on Critical Regionalism at the College of Environmental Design held at the California Polytechnic Institute at Pomona in 1989.[72] At this seminar, the developments of the past decade were identified as a disruption of historical continuities and, in particular, of a long line of socially and environmentally conscious efforts in American architecture. Spiros Amourgis, the organizer of the conference, pointed out that, during the decade between the mid-1970s and mid-1980s, a historicist "dogmatism" had prevailed, resulting in grave misconceptions about the modern legacy and the loss of valuable knowledge of precedent, including technological achievements and technology being seen as a means of supporting new ideas of the region. The architect Marvin Malecha pointed out that values concerning the ecosystem and social quality, advocated at the turn of the century in America, had also been put to the side during this decade. In his contribution, Douglas Kelbaugh noted how, by "alluring motifs and forgotten styles," recent practice violated rather than integrated with local history.

Despite the views at the Pomona seminar, the participants did not aim to define themselves as a group with a dogma. The notion of Critical Regionalism to which they subscribed simply brought together a rather diverse number of designers with varying kinds of practices and individual creative ways of looking at architecture: they were united by a common commitment to the issues that Mumford had put forth first before the Second World War, and that were burning with an even greater urgency.

One finds these issues addressed, for example, in Esherick Homsey Dodge and Davis's lyrical aquarium structure which extends out into Monterey Bay (1978–84, pp. 224–27) and brings together old buildings with new facilities, exploiting the "found" resources rather than importing and imposing alien ones. This project captures a whole world of what Edward Barnes called "continuities" in the American mind—shared experiences and memories about the immigrant and the sea—as powerfully as the best pages of American literature. Steven Holl's Berkowitz Odgis House (1984, pp. 230–33), overlooking the Atlantic Ocean as it meets Vineyard Sound on Martha's Vineyard, makes an equal impact, although it employs fundamentally different means and is in a very different idiom. While Esherick presupposes no knowledge of literature, only fragments of collective images of piers, canneries, weedy lots, wood, chipped pavements, tin, and iron—one does not need to read Steinbeck to have such memories—Stephen Holl's ship-like structure may perhaps be alluding to Herman Melville. The delight in this house lies in unpacking its poetic metaphors.

Both the aquarium at Cannery Row and the house on Vineyard Sound are uniquely American buildings, offering two extremes of immigrants' experience of the Ocean: the Atlantic and the Pacific. They are also at two different ends of the experience of a social spectrum, the first to be enjoyed collectively, the second individually.

In contrast, Andres Duany and Elizabeth Plater-Zyberk's Seaside Plan (1980–, pp. 194–95) and Arquitectonica's Atlantis (1978–82, pp. 204–07) employ regional attributes profusely. They also appear to have an image of collective form, the first reflecting the village and the second the Unité d'Habitation (Le Corbusier's housing project in Marseillles). They are, however, very different from Esherick's and Holl's projects. Their virtuoso application of regional elements and collective form images do not appear to be critical. They are more scenographic, even illusionistic, settings. Without doubt, they have both been great commercial achievements, but in a broader cultural sense, they fall short of contributing to the development of a new consciousness for the public. Both appear to a superficial observer to

© Michael Moran

(Top) Judith Chafee, Jacobson House, Arizona, 1982. The indigenous trellis—ramada—covers the structure of the house.

(Above center) Tod Williams and Billie Tsien, study sketch of the entry stairs of New College, University of Virginia, Charlottesville (1992); (above) aerial view; (below) cross section

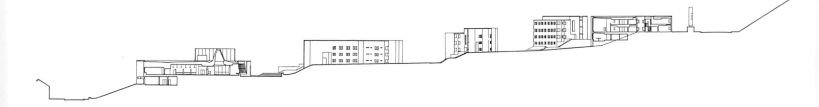

Carlos Jiménez, concept sketches of Houston Museum of Fine Arts Administration and Junior High School Building, Houston, Texas (1991–94)

employ, in a virtuoso manner, the attributes, color, shape, and textures of their region, but they do so in a flashy, mock-regionalist way, numbing all sense of affectivity and care.

Antoine Predock's Las Vegas Library and Museum (1987–90, pp. 268–71), on the other hand, and Ricardo Legorreta's Solana IBM Center just outside Dallas, Texas (1988–90, pp. 264–67), employ regional elements with remarkable creativity, as they serve environmental and social ends while carefully avoiding easy associative simulacra of locality.

Douglas Cardinal's Museum of Civilization (1982–89, pp. 252–55), as critic Trevor Boddy has observed, draws its forms from the natural land formation rather than from the quotations of neo-Gothic historicism of most monumental buildings in Ottawa.[73] Nestled in a bend of the Ottawa River on the border between Ontario and Quebec, it, like Gatje, Papachristou and Smith's Richard B. Russell Power House (1978–85, pp. 228–29), located on the Savannah River at the border between South Carolina and Georgia, combines and elevates a mundane collective experience of a tour into an experience of community and communion with nature. Both projects teach their visitors about "regional" values as they move through the building along a sequence of objects—machines, artifacts, landscape settings—that places both buildings on yet another border: between architecture and landscape design.

On a much smaller scale, Fay Jones's Thorncrown Chapel (1979–80, pp. 190–91), on a wooded hillside in Arkansas, and Judith Chafee's Jacobson House in the Arizona desert (1982)—two other extremes of the American environment—employ traditional elements of the region. Both employ these basic means in an unprecedented way, demonstrating how regional values can be brought down to aspects of detail and detailing. Jones uses the simple, local light-wood construction techniques in order to keep the disruption of the surrounding fauna to a minimum. Chafee tranforms the ancient, indigenous ramada trellis structure into a covering for the house below, providing shade. Its orientation allows diurnal breezes that flow up and down nearby mountain slopes to pass through, adding to the coolness created by the house's traditional, heavy masonry construction. There is community implicit in both projects in the care and discipline with which they are related to the ecological system, in ways that reach beyond the values of individual gratification.

A concern with ecological aspects, explicitly interwoven with technological experimentation and the imperative for sustainability of community, is evident in the Laredo Demonstration Blueprint Farm by the Center for Maximum Potential Building Systems (1987–, pp. 240–41). The Roosevelt Solar Village for the elderly (1981–83, pp. 222–23) by Kelbaugh + Lee, funded by the Farmers' Home Administration, grew as a continuation of the existing neighborhood with a sophisticated passive solar heating system. In Antoine Predock's Rio Grande Nature Center in Albuquerque, New Mexico (1982, pp. 200–03), and Jersey Devil's Hill House (1977–79, pp. 178–79), the experiment is with the section of the landscape, how to insert the building into the natural profile of the land formation.

Taking an entirely different path, Tod Williams and Billie Tsien's New College at the University of Virginia in Charlottesville (1992) and their Neurosciences Institute at the Scripp's Research Institute in La Jolla, California, recall, through their remarkable siting, to some extent, the craftsmanship of Aalto's complexes, where the irregular relationships between the pieces of the composition are highly contrasted with the prismatic order of its components. The contrast makes us aware of the unique character of the landscape, conforming to the irregular shapes of the terrain. Other fine examples of integration into the landscape are Clark and Menefee's Middleton Inn near Charleston, South Carolina (1978–85, pp. 234–35) and Fernau and Hartman's University of California at Santa Cruz Student Center (1989).

Carlos Jiménez's rigorist, minimalist projects in Houston—such as the Houston Fine Arts Press (1985–87, pp. 242–45), and his new Houston Museum of Fine Arts Administration and Junior High School Building (1991–94), show how the exploitation of something that everyone else takes for granted—in this case, the uniqueness of the local Texan light, which in his highly individual and expert way Jiménez plies like a building tool—can be used to create a poetic version of the kind of "solar and bio-climatic" design as defined by Jeffrey Cook.[74] The buildings are not merely formal exercises in the poetics of order and light, however. They are highly functional. They have the clarity and rationality of organization found in a Chermayeff urban prototype. The hierarchical functional zones relate to the access from the street, even if the surrounding urbanity is only a ghost. The same can be said about the way the building meets the street in the front and in the back. From this point of view, the buildings respect the values of the site to come rather than the actual situation.

Equally elegant and straightforward in its means is the Seabird Island School by Patricia and John Patkau (1988–91, pp. 276–79), designed for a Native Canadian Salish Band, north of Vancouver. In addition to the immensely poetic way in which the countless planes of the complex roof configuration harmoniously echoes the natural jagged geomorphological formations of the mountains nearby, the project is a new architectural hybrid, a fusion of cultural traditions—European and Native Canadian— that seem to have only just come into a meaningful and mutually fulfilling dialogue. Aside from its extraordinary high level of formal excellence, however, the building is remarkable for another reason. The explicit mandate of their sponsor, the Government of British Columbia, was to use the project as a means of reinforcing a sense of community among the Band. Using the same kind of participation techniques that Charles Moore and his associates employed in Kresge College (1970–73, pp. 152–53)—not surprisingly, as Patricia Patkau was a student of Moore's at Yale— the architects spent months discussing the project with the Band before submitting the final project. The Band members themselves undertook the construction of the building, using detailed models made by the architects as guides. A measure of the project's success as an exercise in participatory democracy is the masterly construction of this highly complex structure.

Opposite page
(Top) Eric Own Moss, Gary Group, part of the four-building complex of Paramount Laundry and Lindblade Tower in Culver City, California (1988)

(Center) Side wall of the Gary Group, stabbed with C-shaped re-bars and slung with chains

(Bottom) The top of the front wall, its tilted, intentionally rough appearance giving the impression of destruction and abandonment

Eric Owen Moss, Lindblade, Culver City, California (1989)

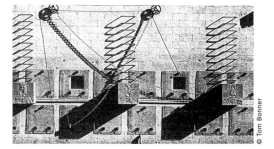

© Tom Bonner

DIRTY REALISM

What if, however, there is no positive context to which a project can respond, what if the surrounding region is one of devastation, of anomic and atopic graveyards of urbanity? What if the ruptures created by the bombing out of inner cities and the razing of neighborhoods in between are the forgotten carcasses of a paleo-technic no-man's land, which Lewis Mumford called the "anti-city," caused by post-war attack on cities in the name of urban renewal?[75]

There are, let us argue for now, two different ways of reacting to such "dirty real" sites. One is to ignore them, to carve out a small enclave within them, and build a new world within the old. The other is more confrontational: it engages the context in its own terms, incorporates the chain link fences, the industrial grade materials, the rust, and the disorder.

The second movement parallels a tendency in American literature which the former editor of *Granta* magazine, Bill Buford, called the Dirty Realist School of writing. He referred to a generation of writers disenchanted with their seniors' postmodern flight from reality into fabulism. The writers he referred to, by contrast, set out to chart the dirty realities of what Buford called the "dark underbelly" of everyday life in the late twentieth century and to take a hard adversarial look at everyday life in a world cluttered irrevocably by the "oppressive details of modern consumerism."[76]

The first "dirty realist" building was Robert Venturi's Guild House (1961–65, pp. 98–99). It was in this retirement home, placed between parking lots and highways, that a chain link fence first appeared. Images of physical decay, decomposition, and destruction dealt with from a critical, moral outlook—a technique as old at least as mannerism in architecture—are also employed in a most inventive way by SITE, a group of New York sculptors, poets, sociologists, and architects. The group, which has been called the "enfants provocateurs promoting a theory of de-architecture, mocking consumer culture" developed a large number of projects concentrating on the representation of time and change as it related to the process of undoing the building. Besides Surrealism, Duchamp, and other, more recent, avant-garde art, their roots can be found in the counter-culture of the 1960s. Their most celebrated projects are a series of department stores for the Best Products Showrooms, built mostly during the 1970s. The facades of these stores are shown going through various stages or modes of unmaking, tilting, dissolving. In one of their latest works, the Forest Building (1978–80, pp. 192–93), the structure is being broken apart by plants and trees. The ecological connotations are obvious: although their intentions were moralistic, their "living iconography" tended to be easy and playful.

Dirty Realism assumed a more complex expression with the architecture of Frank Gehry, starting with his own house (1978–79, pp. 180–83), but extending over a large number of projects throughout the 1980s. According to Mike Davis's *City of Quartz*, Gehry appears to have drawn inspiration from his experience as a defensible designer in Los Angeles, employing "vandalproof," "high-profile," "low tech" security devices, later to become basic motifs in his work.[77] Davis added in an exaggerated way that Gehry's work was nothing but a scenographic set in a hellish picture of Los Angeles. Gehry, in fact, had perfected a new technique of drama, where to quote Shelley's *Defense of Poetry*, "the connection of poetry and social good is more observable."[78]

The design of his house therefore is more than plain Dirty Realist. Using Duchampean and Surrealist techniques, mixing past and present, memory and projection, and everyday routines with extraordinary accidents, he returns once more to Shelley's poetics of the sublime, "familiar objects be as if they were not familiar." More recently, after the Vitra Museum (1987–89), Gehry has moved into a frenzied mode which is close to generating movement simulating forms which he claims are inspired by the multi-membered goddess Shiva. Despite this choreographic turn, his work appears to remain still faithful to holding up the mirror with particular interest in the subtle violence and deadening effects of architectural monotony.

Among the younger generation that carried this critical tendency to a higher pitch is Eric Owen Moss, an architect working in Culver City, an industrial wasteland of Los Angeles. There is something rap-like in the way, one after the other, his buildings react to their hostile surroundings, countering them with a mirror-like reflection of their own image. Paramount Laundry Office (1987–89, pp. 256–59) is a remodeling of an old warehouse. With its columns askew, and the strange shrapnel-like metallic structure on the roof, it looks like the architectural victim of a collision, an attack, or a war. Even more warlike is his Lindblade Building, where the wood roof beams covered with galvanized steel, and the untreated steel reinforcing rods are held in place with bolts over steel-sash windows, suggesting a fortified bunker, armored against the assaults of a hostile world. His complex known as the Gary Group is equally brutal, with its concrete walls stabbed with C-shaped steel re-bars, wrapped in sadistic chains and wheels. Urban hell never had a better portraitist, and rarely such a committed assailant, in architecture.

What was the meaning of picturing a cruel reality through architectural means? Was it to express an attraction to the sadistic qualities of hardness, harshness, and brutality found in the man-made environment of today? Was it, to quote Kant's famous passage from *Observations on the Feeling of the Beautiful and the Sublime* (1764), the fact that this "portrayal of the infernal kingdom arouses, along with horror, enjoyment"?[79] Was it an attempt to unseat uncomfortably complacent, conformist beliefs about gang violence, brutality, and crack cocaine?[80] Was it a representation of the impossible conditions in a worsening urban environment for meaningful contact and community? Or was it a poetic expression of a moral indignity at the widening gap between the two extreme strata of American society and the widening indifference of part of the population towards it?[81] It was probably a mixture of all these.

There were other efforts, though less extreme, to develop a critical architecture at that time. Michael Sorkin's writings and imaginary dystopian projects are doubts about the possibility of a humane architecture and urbanism in our time.[82] Turning to the San Francisco firm of Holt Hinshaw Pfau Jones, there is something hyperbolic

© Holt Hinshaw Pfau Jones

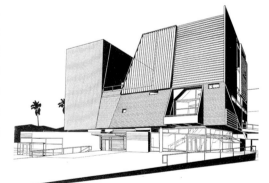

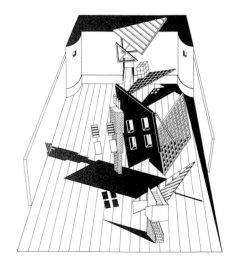

Opposite page
(Top) Holt Hinshaw Pfau Jones, Central
Chiller Plant at UCLA (1990–94)

(Center) Holt Hinshaw Pfau Jones, San Jose
Repertory Theater, San Jose, California
(1994–95)

(Bottom) Lars Lerup's rendering of
Love/House (1984)

about the way in which they incorporate the technological vocabulary of industrial facil-ities into their designs, along with something precarious. The tilted planes, connected to the main structure through an ominously over-complicated and truss-like network of metallic rails, ducts, and wires seem frozen on the brink of an explosion or collapse. The architects mean to point out the destructive potential, even violence, inherent in the all too inhumane paleo-technic mentality that has ravaged so much of the contem-porary surroundings. This intent is expressed in a moving and monumental way in their Astronauts' Memorial at Cape Canaveral (1988–90). But it is equally at work in their more workaday Paramount Pictures Film and Tape Archives (1989–91, pp. 272–73), and their Central Chiller Plant at UCLA (1990–94), where the mechanical plant seems to be bursting forth out of the brick walls, which are tilted towards the outside.

Also confrontational, although on a much smaller scale, is the work of Lars Lerup, at the time based in San Francisco. His erupted, fragmented houses also seem on the brink of destruction. They are intended as "assaults," in the words of the architect, on the hypocritical values of the middle-class suburban family house (1984).[83]

As we have seen, Dirty Realism appeared almost at the same time as Critical Regionalism, in the early 1960s. Of all the tendencies that evolved from the end of the 1970s to the present, these were, and continue to be, the two major critical schools of thought. But, departing from the same state of dissatisfaction, the same adversarial attitude, they seem to have arrived at extremely different conclusions. Critical Regionalism—as embodied in the community conscious projects of Marquis and Stoller's St. Francis Square or Hellmuth Obata Kassabaum's Levi's Plaza—is restora-tive, healing, and reformist of the *status quo*. It recognized the belief that there are still possibilities for solutions. Dirty Realists, on the other hand, do not believe in solutions. We wrote at the beginning of this section that there are arguably two approaches to cases of urban devastation. In fact there are more. Among these are both the approach taken by the urban functionalists of the early 1960s, and that taken by the populists of the late 1960s. Both these groups of professionals believed, in the face of strong odds, in the possibility of community and, moreover, developed techniques for enhancing it. The Dirty Realists are not engaged in this functional type of thinking—at least so far. They are, for the moment, simply expressing a deeply felt anger at the scale with which urban decay has been allowed to happen, creating an architecture, while up against the wall and desperate in the face of chaos.

CONCLUSION

Chaos. By the beginning of the 1990s, chaos seems to be, once again, the center of architectural debates. It seems we are back where we started, at the beginning of the 1960s, when architecture was declared to be in a state of chaos. Is this to say the circle is complete? That things have not evolved over the years?

This is obviously not the case. As we have shown, the development of North American architecture during the past thirty years has been tremendous. There were breakthroughs in the morphology and typology of buildings: Kahn's new functional topology of "servant" and "served," Buckminster Fuller's conception of a total, well-tempered environmental system, Affleck's design of a multi-layered, multi-functional public urban complex that linked transit, commercial, leisure, work and residential uses, and Safdie's artificial hill town. In spite of their often brutalist appearance and mostly naive determinism, these are marvelous inventions, contributing new ways of controling and organizing buildings internally and relating them to an urban fabric, by exploiting new technologies, expressing new programs, and experimenting with new lifestyles. Equally unique were the design explorations of Paul Rudolph and Peter Millard in New Haven, in the role buildings play in shaping the image of the city, generating an urban cognitive map.

New ways were sought for harmonizing buildings and the landscape, both natural and man-made, exemplified in such buildings as Edward Larrabee Barnes's Haystack Mountain School of Arts and Crafts, Moore Lyndon Turnbull Whitaker's Sea Ranch Condominium 1, Louis Kahn's Salk Institute of Biological Studies, Kevin Roche's Oakland Museum, and Arthur Erickson's Museum of Anthropology in British Columbia, as well as more recently, in the rigorist structures of Carlos Jiménez and the complex configurations of John and Patricia Patkau at the Seabird Island School.

Complementing these functional and environmental contributions were projects promoting public space, again in novel ways, such as Levi's Plaza by Hellmuth Obata Kassabaum, which emerged from a dialogue with a community of users and the surrounding urban landscape; Oriole Fields at Camden Yards (1988–92, pp. 282–85), a unique home for the American fascination with spectacle and sport, born on the land of one of the most depressed areas of paleo-technic obsolescence; and Marquis and Stoller's St. Francis Square and Moore's Kresge College. Their strengths, as Simeon Bruner has observed about social-urban excellence, are not always visible and cannot be easily drawn or photographed because these buildings are about the quality of human interaction, the quality of the process through which these projects came about, and the organizational concurrence between public and private institutions.[84]

Another facet of the development of U.S. and Canadian architecture since the 1960s has been the pioneering design experiments, generating new kinds of facilities to help the disabled and ill. Stanley Tigerman's Illinois Regional Library for the Blind and Physically Handicapped (1975–78, pp. 168–71) and Morphosis's Cedars-Sinai

Comprehensive Cancer Center for Children (1991, pp. 274–75) are unprecedented architectural offerings in an effort to alleviate human suffering.

Rich and diverse as this architectural production was, it had major limitations. Many of these projects never addressed satisfactorily the issue of race. The issue of gender and the hidden injuries of the dispossessed has been ignored by almost all. None succeeded in demonstrating that they were legitimate social products beyond closed dogma and arbitrary authority and power. These failures are a major obstacle to recognizing that the architecture of the past three decades has succeeded in expressing our contemporary ideal of human dignity, which a democratic society needs.

To many, it appeared that this failure was due to the lack of theory, of a higher level of abstraction capable of giving a better grasp of the role of architecture and a better sense of direction. The emergence of critical architecture in North America emerged as a response to this lack. Never before had architects commented on their surrounding reality while at the same time baring their own professional devices in such a penetrating, analytical way. Never before had the parts of a building been loaded with so much signification, so entangled in multiple webs of cultural references. And never had it been so skillfully taken apart with the surgical knife of semantic analysis as in the works of Robert Venturi, Denise Scott Brown and, later, Peter Eisenman, Frank Gehry, Steven Holl, Eric Owen Moss, and Holt Hinshaw Pfau Jones. From this point of view, Venturi's Vanna Venturi House and Guild House mark the beginning of one of the most significant tendencies of our time. They transformed our perception of architecture: that it was capable of commenting about the world as well as being present in it. Architecture has never been the same since.

Yet despite the force and acumen, the sophistication and brilliance of this massive critical activity, there is a sense of void in U.S. and Canadian architecture. Questions about morality and responsibility, with very few exceptions—one of which is James Freed's moving Holocaust Memorial Museum (1986–93, pp. 286–89)—are either not posed or they are obscured in abstract and abstruse formalist complexes. With the rare exception of projects such as James Polshek's Mashantucket Pequot Museum and Research Center (1993–, pp. 292–95), interweaving archaic culture with avant-garde communication technology, building, and landscape, the conflict between identity and otherness, community and globalism, the natural and the mechanical— a conflict that is one of the major preoccupations of the end of century—is also glossed over.

In the last analysis, architecture as a *techne* is about making people happy, while as an *episteme*, it is about finding an answer to the basic question of how one should live. One has a feeling that architecture's current preoccupation with its own means, its own intellectual tools, has disoriented the best minds in the profession away from the core of architecture towards the periphery. Architects have lost sight not only of facts but also of values that are important to the public at large.

Identifying the multiplicity of subjective points of view, which critical architecture has been busying itself with, while a good thing in itself, is not enough. To be critical, although necessary, is not sufficient for architecture to perform well, especially at moments of crisis. Routine and dogma may be obstacles to change, but there is no virtue in open-ended possibilities as such, unless they are accompanied by a framework of commitment and values. A democratic society is, after all, a tool, a mechanism, and, one might say, a technology, following the Pragmatist philosopher, John Dewey. It is a technology for doing things, and doing them satisfactorily, and not simply an expression of an adversarial state of mind. Concern for values, being reminded of the question of how one should live, of the definition of happiness, together with the preoccupation with the quality of technology, the environment, and community were at the center of the American Functionalist paradigm that emerged in the writings of Horatio Greenough, Ralph Waldo Emerson, Henry David Thoreau, and Lewis Mumford.

As we move to the end of this century, we believe the Mumfordian "multi-functionalist" paradigm continues to be as pertinent as ever. How it can be put into action remains an open question. We can only agree with John Dewey that the best practice is one that permits a continuous learning process, which is by definition always a creative one.[85] In other words, creativity is not the making of something out of nothing. It generated new things through an elaborate process of re-using past experience and design knowledge in unknown future contexts. The more variant and numerous the experiences, the greater the potential for creative design, and for better and novel responses.

From this point of view, we see in the variety and difference of the projects of the last thirty-five years that we have been discussing in this book, neither chaos, nor masterpieces in the attic, nor skeletons in the closet, but precious precedents born in the midst of acute social, technological, and environmental crises—from which an unprecedented architecture is to be born.

Notes

1. See, for example, Nicholas Pevsner, "Modern Architecture and the Historian, or the Return of Historicism," *The Royal Institute of British Architects Journal* 68 (April 1961). See also the issue entitled, "The New Sensualism," *Progressive Architecture* 40 (October 1959).

2. Thomas H. Creighton, "Sixties, the State of Architecture," *Progressive Architecture* (March–May 1961).

3. Norbert Wiener, *The Human Use of Human Beings, Cybernetics and Society* (Boston: Houghton Mifflin, 1950).

4. Lewis Mumford, "The Case Against Modern Architecture," *Architectural Record* (April 1962).

5. John Kenneth Galbraith, *The Affluent Society* (Boston: Houghton Mifflin, 1958).

6. Michael Harrington, *The Other America: Poverty in the United States* (New York: Macmillan, 1962).

7. Rachel Carson, *Silent Spring* (Cambridge, MA: Riverside Press, 1962).

8. F. O. Matthiessen, *American Renaissance: Art and Expression in the Age of Emerson and Whitman* (London: Oxford University Press, 1941).

9. Kevin Lynch, *The Image of the City* (Cambridge: MIT Press, 1960).

10. Lewis Mumford, *The City in History* (New York: Harcourt, Brace & World, 1961).

11. Jane Jacobs, *The Death and Life of Great American Cities* (New York: Random House, 1961).

12. Serge Chermayeff and Christopher Alexander, *Community and Privacy* (Garden City, New York: Doubleday, 1963).

13. Christopher Alexander, *Notes on the Synthesis of Form* (Cambridge: Harvard University Press, 1964).

14. Melvin Webber, *Explorations into Urban Structure* (Philadelphia: University of Pennsylvania Press, 1964).

15. Robert Venturi, *Complexity and Contradiction in Architecture* (New York: Museum of Modern Art, 1966).

16. Mumford's vision of "multi-functionalism" is put forth polemically in his "Case against Modern Architecture" (see note 4 above). His position is stated clearly for the first time in "Monumentalism, Symbolism and Style" (*Architectural Review*, April 1948), where he writes: "There is not a single function to be satisfied but a whole interrelated series ... as modern architecture matures it must become multi-functional" (p. 44). His definition of "multi-functionalism" included "a humanistic canon ... (which) provides accordingly for all the dimensions of the human personality"—mechanical, but also symbolic and social.

17. See Tzonis and Lefaivre, "Lewis Mumford's Regionalism," in *Design Book Review* 19 (1991): pp. 20–25 and Lewis Mumford, *The South in Architecture* (New York: Harcourt, Brace & Company, 1941).

18. Edward Larrabee Barnes, *Perspecta* 9 (1965).

19. The concept of *continuità* was central to Ernesto Roger's concerns as an architect and as a writer in the post-war period. Roger's definition was highly original: it was an

early synthesis of the modern and the traditional, and the architectural and the social. He changed the title of *Casabella* to *Casabella-Continuità* when he became its editor following World War II, a period when the magazine became the most important forum for the critical debate about architectural and urban issues.

20. Private conversation with the authors. New York, winter 1979.

21. Horatio Greenough, "American Architecture," *Form and Function: Remarks on Art, Design, and Architecture* (Berkeley: University of California Press, 1969).

22. Percival and Paul Goodman, *Communitas* (Chicago: The University of Chicago Press, 1947).

23. Xenophon, *Memorabilia* III, VIII, 5, 6.

24. This statement is Louis I. Kahn's contribution to the debate organized by Thomas Creighton (see note 2).

25. See note 21 above.

26. *Perspecta* 2, 1954.

27. Leonard Riessman, *The Urban Process: Cities in Industrial Societies* (New York: Free Press of Glencoe, 1964).

28. Melvin Webber (ed.), *Explorations into Urban Structure* (Philadelphia: University of Pennsylvania Press, 1964).

29. Donald L. Foley, "An Approach to Metropolitan Spatial Structure," in Melvin Webber (ed.), *Explorations into Urban Structure* (see note 28 above).

30. Douglas Haskell, "Jazz in Architecture," *Architectural Forum* (September 1960).

31. Lewis Mumford, *Technics and Civilization* (New York: Harcourt, Brace & Company, 1934).

32. For further reading, see Larry A. Hickman, *John Dewey's Pragmatic Technology* (Bloomington: Indiana University Press, 1990).

33. Robert Reich, *The Work of Nations: Preparing Ourselves for 21st-Century Capitalism* (New York: A. A. Knopf, 1991).

34. See note 33 above.

35. Kevin Lynch, *The Image of the City* (Cambridge: MIT Press, 1960).

36. Trystan Edwards, *Good and Bad Manners in Architecture* (London: P. Allan & Co., 1924).

37. Robert Stern, *Perspecta* 9–10 (New Haven: Yale University Press, 1965).

38. Carroll Meeks, *The Railroad Station* (New Haven: Yale University Press, 1956).

39. Kevin Lynch and Lloyd Rodwin (eds.), "The Future Metropolis," *Daedalus* (Winter 1961).

40. See note 28 above.

41. Particularly committed to the idea of community was Serge Chermayeff and Alexander Tzonis, *Towards an Urban Model* (Yale, 1967), with contributions from Jerzy Soltan, Jacqueline Tyrwitt, Roger Montgomery, Melvin Webber, and Karl Deutsch, among others. See also Serge Chermayeff and Alexander Tzonis, *The Shape of Community* (Harmondsworth: Penguin, 1972).

42. Fumihiko Maki, *Investigations in Collective Form* (Washington University School of Architecture [special publication] 2, 1964).

43. See note 12 above.

44. See note 11 above.

45. Harold Rosenberg, *The De-definition of Art* (New York: Collier Books, 1972).

46. See Bill Buford's introduction to "Dirty Realism," (ed., Bill Buford) *Granta* 8 (Cambridge, England, 1983).

47. For a fuller treatment of this phenomenon, see Alexander Tzonis and Liane Lefaivre, "In the Name of the People," *Forum* ([Dutch] October 1976).

48. Todd Gitlin, *The Sixties: Years of Hope, Days of Rage* (New York: Bantam, 1987 and 1993).

49. Allen J. Matusow, *The Unraveling of America* (New York: Harper and Row, 1984).

50. Charles Moore, "You Have to Pay for the Public Life," *Perspecta* 9–10, 1965.

51. "Denise Scott Brown," in Ann Lee Morgan and Colin Naylor (eds.), *Contemporary Architects* (Chicago: St. James Press, 1987 [second edition]).

52. See note 45 above.

53. See A. Tzonis and L. Lefaivre, "In the Name of the People" (note 47 above) for more extensive bibliographical sources, in particular, Chester Hartman, "Social Values and Housing Orientations," *Journal of Social Issues* vol. XIX, 2 (April 1963).

54. Alan Temko, "Levi's Choice—The Be Good or Be Great," *No Way to Build a Ballpark and other Irreverent Essays on Architecture* (San Francisco: Chronicle Books, 1993).

55. Donald Watson and Kenneth Labs, *Climatic Design* (New York: McGraw Hill, 1983).

56. Richard Sennett, *The Fall of Public Man* (New York: Knopf, 1976).

57. Alexander Tzonis and Liane Lefaivre, "The Narcissistic Phase of Architecture," *Harvard Architecture Review* 1 (Spring 1980).

58. Peter Steinfels, *The Neoconservatives* (New York: Simon and Schuster, 1979).

59. Robert Stern, *Five Architects* (New York: Wittenborn, 1973).

60. Diane Ghirardo, "Peter Eisenman's Bogus Avant Garde," *Progressive Architecture* (November 1994).

61. Colin Rowe and Fred Koetter, "Collage City," *Architectural Review* (August 1975): pp. 66–91.

62. Christopher Alexander, "A City is Not a Tree," *Design* 206 (February 1966).

63. Richard Rorty, *Times Literary Supplement* (June 24, 1994).

64. Arthur Drexler (ed.), *The Architecture of the Ecole des Beaux-Arts* (New York: The Museum of Modern Art, 1977).

65. Bernard J. Frieden and Lynne B. Sagalyn, *Downtown, Inc.* (Cambridge: MIT Press, 1989).

66. *Daily News* (October 30, 1975).

67. Richard Ingersoll, "Tunnels of Love," *Archithèse* (January 1990).

68. Esther McCoy, "The Blue Bombshell," *Progressive Architecture* (October 1976).

69. Michael Sorkin, *Variations on a Theme Park* (New York: Noonday, 1992).

70. Philip Johnson in *The Charlottesville Tapes* (New York: Rizzoli, 1985): p. 19.

71. Edward Luttwak, *The Endangered American Dream* (New York: Simon and Schuster, 1993).

72. See Spiros Amourgis (ed.), *Critical Regionalism, The Pomona Meeting Proceedings* (College of Environmental Design, California State Polytechnic University, Pomona, 1991).

73. Trevor Boddy, *The Architecture of Douglas Cardinal* (Winnipeg: NeWest, 1988).

74. Jeffrey Cook, "A Post-Industrial Culture of Regionalism," in Spiros Amourgis, *Critical Regionalism. The Pomona Meeting Proceedings* (see note 72 above): pp. 164–80.

75. Lewis Mumford, "Megapolis as Anti-city," *The Urban Prospect* (New York: Harcourt Brace Jovanovich, 1968).

76. See note 46 above.

77. Mike Davis, *City of Quartz* (New York: Verso, 1990).

78. Percy Bysshe Shelley, *Defense of Poetry*, 1822.

79. Immanuel Kant, *Observations on the Feeling of the Beautiful and the Sublime*, 1764.

80. American Social History Project, *Who Built America?* (vol. II, New York, 1992, p. 660).

81. Edward Luttwak's phrase for the phenomenon is the "Third-Worldization of America." See note 71 above.

82. See note 69 above.

83. Lars Lerup, *Planned Assaults* (Cambridge: MIT Press, 1987).

84. Simeon Bruner in Philip Langdon, *Urban Excellence* (New York: Van Nostrand Reinhold, 1990).

85. This is a general theme of John Dewey's writings, in particular of *Democracy and Education* (New York: MacMillan, 1916). For a fuller treatment, see Larry A. Hickman, *John Dewey's Pragmatic Technology* (Bloomington: Indiana University Press, 1990).

Detail of Venturi and Rauch's Guild House,
Philadelphia, Pennsylvania (1961–65)

© William Watkins

Edward Larrabee Barnes
HAYSTACK MOUNTAIN SCHOOL OF ARTS AND CRAFTS
Deer Isle, Maine
1959–61

(Above) Site plan

(Opposite above) Diagonal elevation
of the view from the sea

(Opposite below) View from the hillside

The Haystack Mountain School of Arts and Crafts is a summer community of eighty students and faculty who work and live on a south-facing lichen-covered granite slope overlooking the sea. The site was not a mountain as the name suggests, but came from the previous location of the school on a farm near Haystack Mountain. A main flight of steps runs down to the shore, and branching walkways and decks link the workshops and cabins together. Big studio windows point up to the trees, while ribbon windows look out to the sea. The wood construction is balloon frame. The walls and steep tilted roofs are shingled and, over time, the wood has turned silver, looking in Barnes's words, "like a Maine fishing village."

The approach from the road is over a slight rise to a crest of rock above the sea. Straight ahead is the main stair down. The first deck serves as a "Town Square," a place to gather and to eat outside the dining hall. Each of the four workshops—for pottery, carpentry, weaving, and graphics—have generous teaching decks. The wash house steps downhill under a continuous roof. The site is a steep, rocky, 90-foot slope down to the sea, with few usable shelves on which to place living and working quarters for the summer community—a simple place to work, to meet, a place in harmony with nature. Because the school is attended only in the summer, there is no insulation or central heating. The cost of construction in 1961 was about $5 per square foot.

In discussing his design at the time, Barnes said: "There is nothing esoteric about architectural ideas. They can be drawn on the backs of envelopes. A flight of steps to the sea. A banked garden ... The important thing is to express the idea clearly and see all the implications ... There is no better way to do architecture than to have a strong architectural idea and be true to it."

To grasp why such a modest project and such mild-mannered words struck a deep chord among architects and the general public of the time, one must understand the context. The late 1950s was the ebb of post-war conformist, neo-monumentalism that Lewis Mumford had criticized for having deserted the ideals of modern architecture:

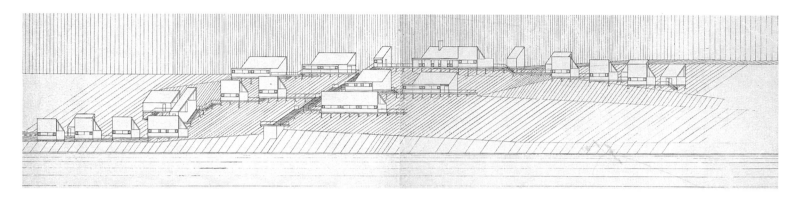

that is, rational employment of resources, respect for the environment, concern for the social quality of space, and emancipation from the arbitrary, despotic ideologies of the past. In other words, the modernism that the new generation wanted to dispense with. Barnes's project, despite the fact that the prototype of its unit goes back to the beginning of the 1950s (it was designed by Barnes for Robert Osborn in 1951) appeared to respond to the specific needs of the new decade. On one hand, it criticized the dominant tendencies of modern architecture; on the other, it offered a clear alternative, one which concretely manifested, through its structure and architectural representation—despite the small scale of the complex—a commitment to a number of values. These were a harmonious relation with nature, community, and a new sense of freedom and experimentation. As opposed to most of the projects of the 1950s, at least the ones that were recognized during the decade as important, the complex demonstrated a

© Edward Larrabee Barnes

(Above) Section

(Left) Pathway linking the units

(Opposite) Communal space

© Joseph Molitor

careful orientation and siting. Similarly, not only did it not ruin the landscape, as many contemporary projects, even of that scale, did, but it took great care to ensure that any such disturbance was minor. Ignoring contemporary discussions about plasticity of structure and the sculptural quality of construction, it chose a pitch of roof and a stark geometry for the units, borrowing from the local New England shelters, as they were the best adapted to the climatic conditions of the region. A whole generation of architects, both from the East Coast and West—for example, MLTW's Sea Ranch (1963–65, pp.

90–93)—uses it as a point of departure. Finally, oblivious to calls of monumentality, it broke the complex into units that were meaningful from the point of view of needs of privacy, as much as from the aspirations of collective thinking and exchange of ideas.

Thirty years later, while very little had changed in the weathered project, Barnes recollected in his understated manner: "I felt that it was a very necessary statement to make ... I've always been drawn to making things as simple as possible if you can do that without making them inhuman or dull or oppressive."

As the critic Robert Campbell has remarked (*Architecture*, February 1989), the Haystack Mountain School of Arts and Crafts "is a building that, in its day, helped point an important new direction for American Architecture." Today, "it has ... the status of a New England classic." And one might also add that, although so interwoven with the American Renaissance of the early 1960s, its message about nature and community is as current today as it ever was.

© Joseph Molitor

Marquis & Stoller
ST. FRANCIS SQUARE COOPERATIVE APARTMENTS
San Francisco, California
1960–61

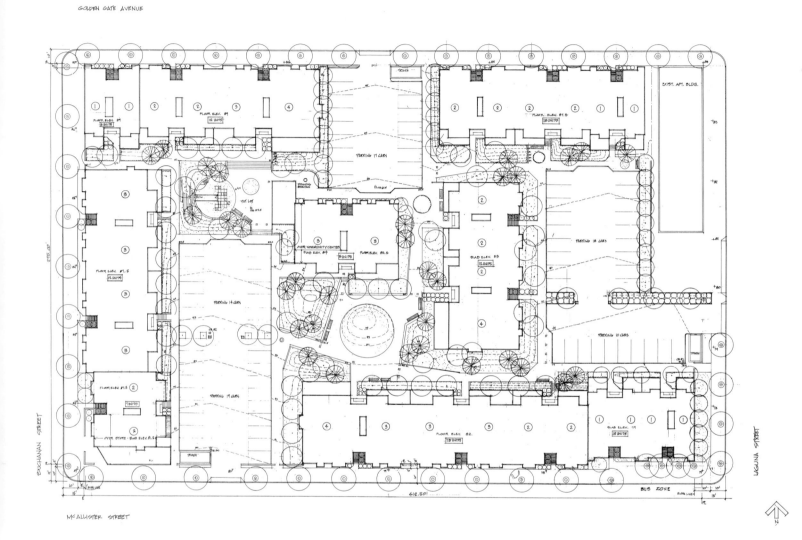

Site plan

St. Francis Square, located in the Western Addition urban renewal area of San Francisco, is one of the most successful efforts to date in providing moderate-cost urban housing. The 299 garden apartments were designed in 1960 by the local firm of Marquis & Stoller, in conjunction with landscape architect, Lawrence Halprin.

The non-profit project was sponsored and developed by the Pension Fund jointly administered by the International Longshoremen's and Warehousemen's Union and the Pacific Maritime Association. They established a non-profit corporation to provide moderate-cost housing, financed under the FHA 221d3 and FNMA National Housing act, U.S. Federal housing finance programs, that provided low interest-rate mortgaging.

A deliberate decision was made early on to invest large portions of the effort

and available resources in the total physical environment of the project, rather than in the individual dwelling units or buildings. This is significant in that from the onset, the undertaking was constrained by an extremely limited budget, and every decision had to be weighed on a scale of benefits. Carefully designed, simple, and efficient apartments were planned, but individual "architectural" features were de-emphasized.

Considerations of building massing, spacing between units, and the movement of the inhabitants through the landscaped communal areas all became of paramount importance.

The dwelling units are flats without split levels or complex arrangements, and are stacked three stories high in groups of six, around stairwells (three units on each side) to form each building. They are linked and arranged as blocks of sub-communities,

© Stoller Partners

© Stoller Partners

© Karl Riek

Public spaces inside the project

comprising approximately 100 units surrounding and facing on to open spaces in the center of each block. Plans for pitched roofs and complicated fenestration were abandoned in favor of simple geometry. Resources went instead into decks, terraces, landscaping, walks, fencing, and graphics such as signage providing directions and information.

A major decision was reached to ask the city to vacate the two streets cutting through the site, and when it acquiesced, it became possible to combine four blocks into one superblock: three blocks of housing adjoining a city school on the fourth block. In an unusual move for a housing scheme in the U.S., parking spaces were relegated to the periphery of the project, and while residents might be forced to walk some distance to their houses, the elimination of all vehicular traffic on the site provides major advantages, one being that children can play and ride their bicycles without ever crossing the street.

Walks, sitting areas, gardens, and other spatial arrangements are linked together in such a way as to knit the grouping of the buildings into one community. To further emphasize the long-term commitment to community, the apartments were sold as cooperatives to qualified buyers with income limitations set by the FHA. The apartments were sold out before construction was finished, and today St. Francis Square continues to be much sought after as affordable housing, over thirty years after its completion.

Louis I. Kahn
ALFRED NEWTON RICHARDS MEDICAL RESEARCH
LABORATORY, UNIVERSITY OF PENNSYLVANIA
Philadelphia, Pennsylvania
1957–60

Aerial perspective

This building caused tremendous excitement, among not only architects, but the general public. The design was exhibited at the Museum of Modern Art in New York, and there was an almost record number of visitors (August Komendant, *18 Years with Architect Louis I. Kahn*, Chapter 1). The reaction of the users—the doctors working in the laboratory—was not so favorable, however. The glare of sunlight disturbed their work, and equipment installation was inflexible. They complained that Kahn had designed a monument to himself and not a functional building. Nevertheless, the building is usually accepted as one of the most significant buildings of the post-war period.

The Richards Building was commissioned in 1957, in a decade that saw widespread expansion of medical schools. The building's program was complex: it included the departments of physiology, microbiology, research surgery, and public health, along with the administrative offices of the Johnson Foundation. Its 8 stories contain about 75,000 square feet of floor space and separate facilities for animals. Interior space was divided into open bays, with utilities running through vertical service towers and spaces in the ceiling.

Of the cluster of the four 8-story towers of the original project, three were "served" towers, containing studios, offices and labs, and one was a "servant" tower, containing animal quarters and utilities. Each of the

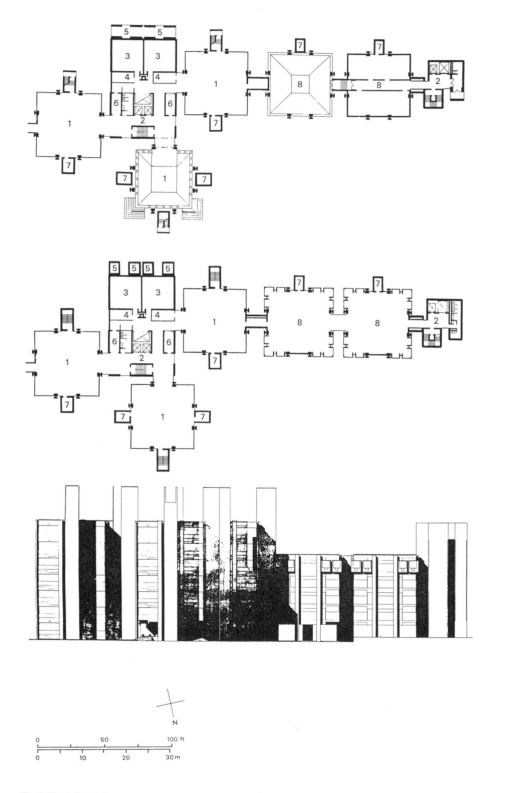

(Top) First floor plan

(Center) Typical laboratory floor plan

(Bottom) North elevation

towers connects at every level with the others. The scheme was very much the result of the crowded conditions of the University of Pennsylvania campus.

The memorable form of the towers, however, was defined by Louis Kahn's radically new interpretation of the program and by his highly original vision of what architecture ought to be. Revolutionary as this way of understanding a program might have seemed, critical of contemporary mainstream professional practice, and signaling a return to monumental prototypes of the past—the towers of San Gimignano and Bologna have been frequently cited as precedents—Kahn's project was deeply attached to the idea of modern architecture, particularly in its commitment both to technology and community. More specifically, this meant the breaking up of the traditional horizontal academic laboratory, restructuring it into four large towers, articulated as servant and served spaces. The plan fascinated because it moved away from the "standard corridor type layout," seen as "unsatisfactory because of its linear nature-yielding spaces which were inhospitable, anonymous, inflexible." (James Marston Fitch, *Architectural Forum*, July 1960.) The scheme took the idea of the modernist "box"—the universal Miesian "space"—and replaced it with a new notion of architectural "place," an environment structured to enhance the sense of "community." Kahn referred to the MIT corridors with names on them, pointing out that this was exactly the wrong environment for the contemporary scientist (Jurgen Joedicke, *Documents of Modern Architecture*, p. 212).

Kahn's scheme is based on an idea of architecture that goes back to the 18th-century "rigorist" principle that the form of a building should be the explicit representation of its function. But while rigorists (for example, the Venetian theoretician of architecture, Francesco Lodoli) reduced function essentially into construction, and the way forces (that is, structural loads) travel through the structure of a building, Kahn saw in function the circulation of people, goods, and air. In short, everything that the mechanical utilities

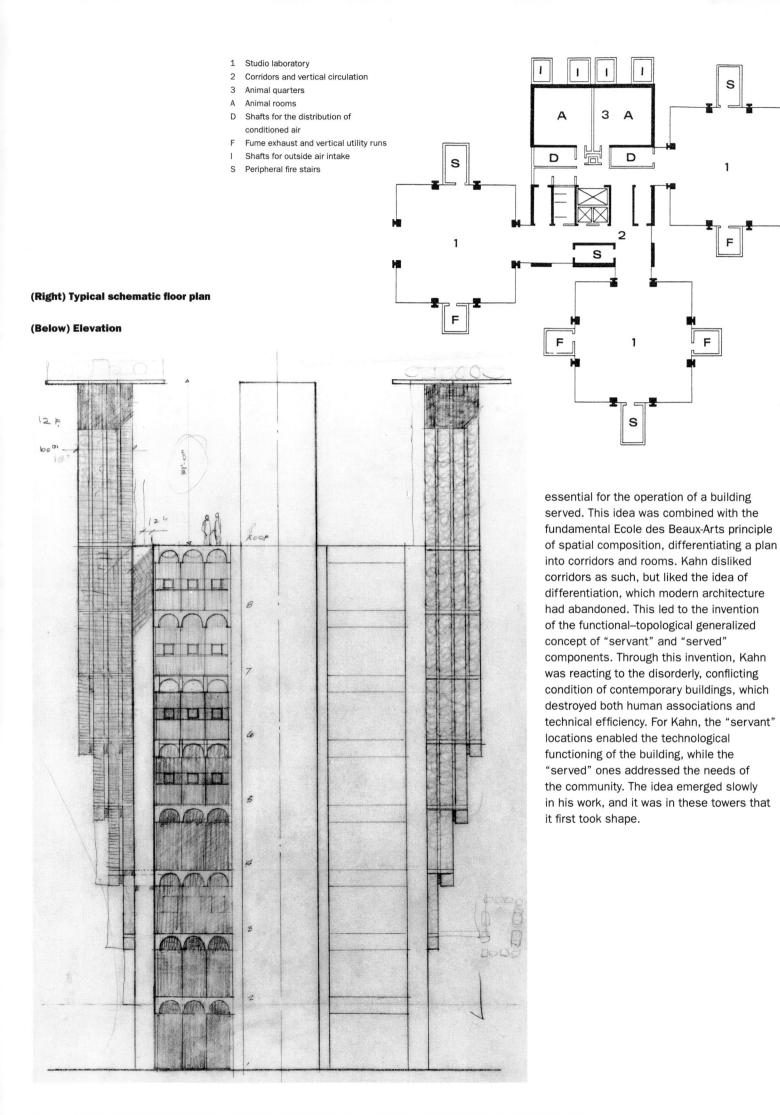

1   Studio laboratory
2   Corridors and vertical circulation
3   Animal quarters
A   Animal rooms
D   Shafts for the distribution of
    conditioned air
F   Fume exhaust and vertical utility runs
I   Shafts for outside air intake
S   Peripheral fire stairs

(Right) Typical schematic floor plan

(Below) Elevation

essential for the operation of a building served. This idea was combined with the fundamental Ecole des Beaux-Arts principle of spatial composition, differentiating a plan into corridors and rooms. Kahn disliked corridors as such, but liked the idea of differentiation, which modern architecture had abandoned. This led to the invention of the functional–topological generalized concept of "servant" and "served" components. Through this invention, Kahn was reacting to the disorderly, conflicting condition of contemporary buildings, which destroyed both human associations and technical efficiency. For Kahn, the "servant" locations enabled the technological functioning of the building, while the "served" ones addressed the needs of the community. The idea emerged slowly in his work, and it was in these towers that it first took shape.

(Above) Facade

(Right) Assembly diagram of the skeletal framing for the towers

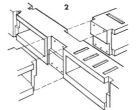

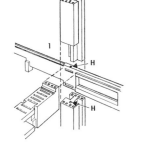

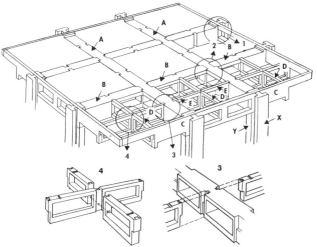

Skidmore Owings and Merrill
ROBERT R. MCMATH SOLAR TELESCOPE
Kitt Peak, Pima County, Arizona
1962

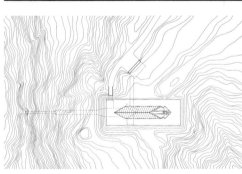

(Top) View of the structure on its
sublime setting

(Top right) Detail

(Above) Site plan

(Above right) Section of the structure

The Association of Universities for Research in Astronomy need not have commissioned an architect to design the structure destined to house the world's biggest solar telescope: a team of astronomers and structural and mechanical engineers could have carried it out with great competence. But the committee responsible for the project, including Dr. Robert McMath, the astronomer after whom the complex was named, decided that in addition to being both functional and economical, the structure "must be beautiful." It is interesting to note that Dr. McMath's opinion about the observatory was diametrically opposed to that of the 17th-century astronomer, Cassini, who clashed with the architect of the first modern observatory, Claude Perrault, believing that the building was only an instrument, to the exclusion of any esthetic considerations.

The committee was fortunate in their choice of Myron Goldsmith of SOM, an architect who trained under Mies van der

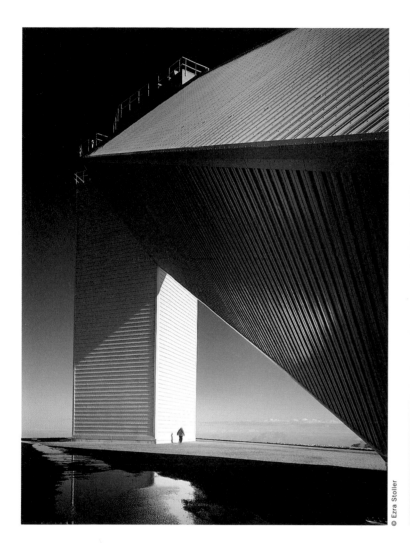

Rohe at the Illinois Institute of Technology. No doubt the beauty of the remote site itself was to a great extent responsible for Goldsmith's decision to work with the team. Located 45 miles south-west of Tucson, Arizona, at the southern end of the Rocky Mountains, Kitt Peak not only presented excellent sky conditions for a solar telescope, but the 85-acre summit area of gently rolling grasslands, interspersed with groves of native trees and outcroppings of rock, offered one of the earth's most beautiful landscapes.

The design program was three-fold: (1) a structure to support the number one mirror on a concrete tubular cylinder 26 feet in diameter, 100 feet above the mountaintop, with the lateral movement of this tower caused by wind or thermal forces allowed to be a maximum of one-thousandth of an inch—less than the thickness of a human hair; (2) a skin to surround the supporting structure made up of a steel frame covered with copper sheets that would be cooled by tubes circulating a solution of water and glycol; and (3) the inclined tube, which was to be partially buried in the mountain and partially formed by the superstructure, as well as being cooled by a similar system to ensure lower temperatures at the bottom than at the top during the constant daily and annual temperature fluctuations. This was to prevent an inversion of the air column with its attendant turbulence—any such changes would distort the mirror and impair the optical quality of the telescope.

The result was an object of dramatic purity and starkness. Perhaps never before has the dictum "form follows function," expounded by the 19th-century American sculptor, Horatio Greenough, had a more astounding architectural embodiment. Goldsmith's design is not merely an exercise in the machine esthetic: it is a machine. The design was truly guided by, to quote Greenough once more, "the love of the concrete." The sole determinant of form was the task of housing the machinery that would gather light from the sun, 93 million miles away. And yet there is something not just beautiful, but sublime in the Kantian sense, in the way this building brings together the earth and sky, and architecture and science, turning one of the most demanding technological programs into a structure from which to observe the nature of our universe.

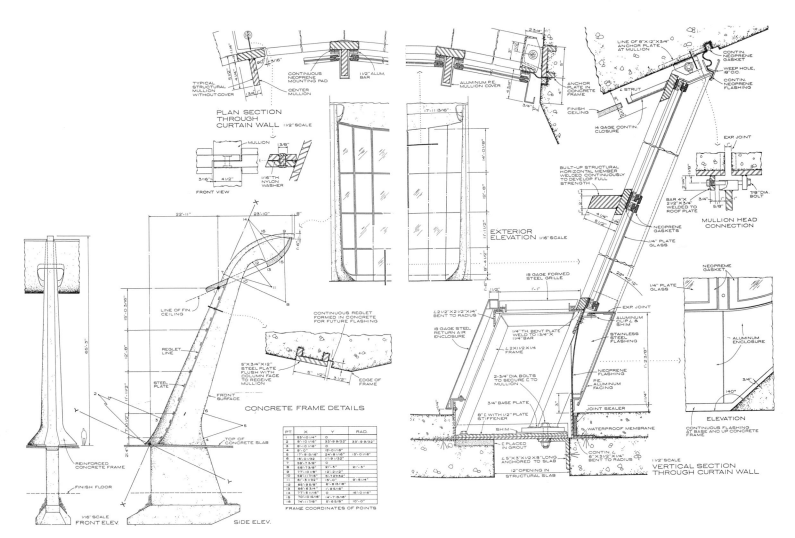

Construction details

Eero Saarinen's approach to the design of the new airport for the Washington D.C. area was a radical departure from common practice, and started with a fundamental analysis of the whole problem of the large terminal for jet airplanes. Saarinen's solution was—instead of bringing the planes to the terminal—to develop a system of mobile lounges that would serve as the waiting area until the departure time, and that would then be rolled away to the aircraft parking area near the runways. The passengers' long walk to the boarding gate is eliminated, and the noise and fumes of the planes kept away from the terminal.

No less daring was Saarinen's conception of the terminal building itself. Freed by the mobile lounges from the finger structures and adjustable loading ramps of traditional terminal buildings, it is viewed as a gateway through which the arriving visitor passes en route to the nation's capital. The concept is derived from an early sketch by Erich Mendelsohn. The walls of this gateway appear dematerialized and one is left with the illusion that the roof is hovering suspended in space. The structure has been likened to a flipped-up scroll and a hammock hanging between trees. Daylight pours in all around through clear, untinted glass, shaded by the catenary curve of the overhanging roof.

Despite the elegance of form and the insistence of structural clarity, there are in fact several games being played between structural expression and structural fact, the most conspicuous being that the roof and its supports are entirely separate elements, but the break between roof and support is not where it is expressed. The original plan calls for future extensions to the terminal at either end, and this has been anticipated in the

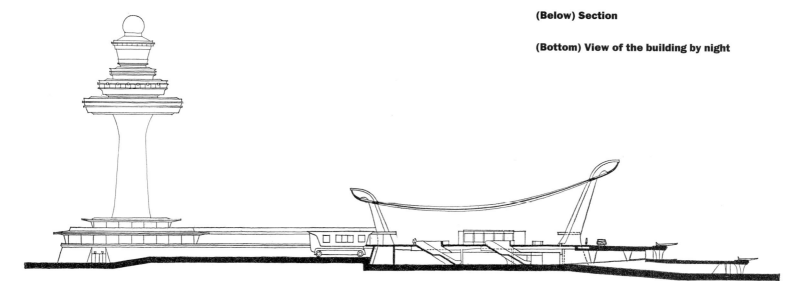

(Below) Section

(Bottom) View of the building by night

Ezra Stoller © Esto

(Below & below right) Ground plans

(Bottom left & bottom right) Views from the outside

(Opposite left) Soaring form of the roof

(Opposite right) Interior

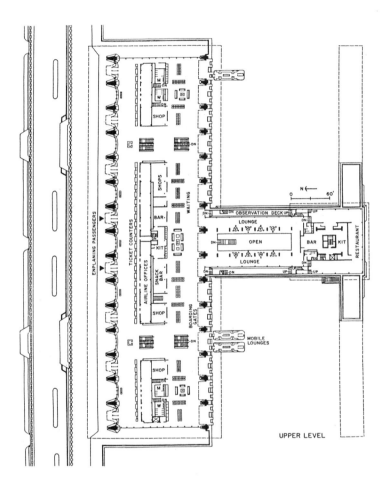

UPPER LEVEL

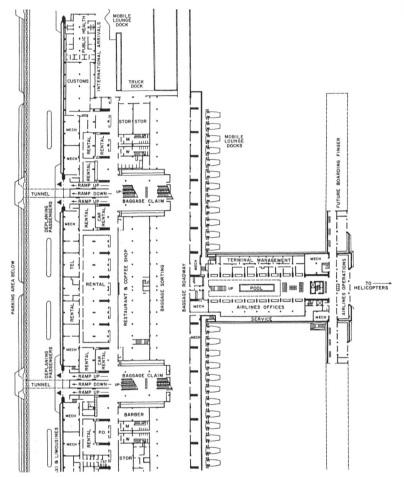

design of the end walls and their relationship to the other glazing.

Ironically, despite the rational basis of the concept, the transport of passengers by the mobile lounges has been the least successful aspect of the terminal and not as widely imitated as the designers and critics of the day had envisioned. What has proved more successful are the access routes, and pedestrian and vehicular movement designed for the master plan, which Saarinen drew up for the airport in conjunction with landscape architect, Dan Kiley. The gracefulness of the terminal is reflected in the easy flow of the traffic approaches and exits from the terminal building.

Edgar Kaufmann, Jr., in his August 1963 article in *Progressive Architecture*, wrote about how Dulles was the first full-sized statement of a new attitude, long awaited, in which the resources of modern life are treated as servants, and humanity triumphs over the miracles of applied science. One of the lessons from Dulles, however, is that no matter how liberating the technology of applied science may seem, we still have little ability to control or predict its outcome.

Paul Rudolph Architect
YALE SCHOOL OF ART AND ARCHITECTURE
New Haven, Connecticut
1958–63

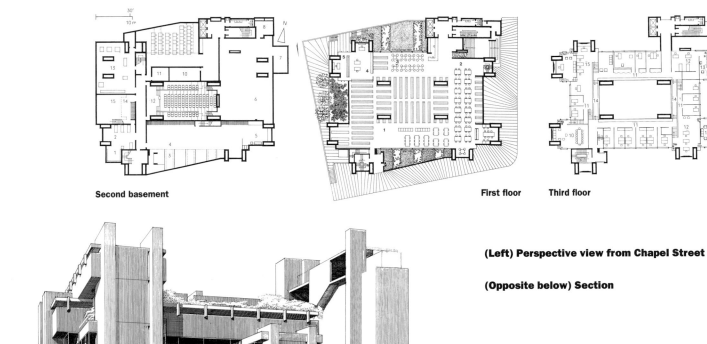

Second basement   First floor   Third floor

(Left) Perspective view from Chapel Street

(Opposite below) Section

This building is perhaps the most daring effort of the early 1960s to revolt against the tyranny of the Miesian "universal space" glass box and to offer a clear alternative to it. Rudolph was given the chance to conceive and build this 7-story composition, consisting of no less than 37 levels of fugue-like, overlapping, and interpenetrating platforms. He was at the time Chairman of the Department of Architecture, thus serving as the main representative of the client (Yale University), as well as being the architect. This unusual dual role was both a rare opportunity and a mixed blessing, as Nikolaus Pevsner indicated in the building's dedication speech, because the architect was deprived of the creative potential of constraints posed by a perceptive client.

The Art and Architecture Building was one of Rudolph's last major projects

commissioned in New Haven, where he had designed the City Garage, or for Yale University, for which he had designed the Forestry Laboratory and the Married Student Housing; in fact, it was one of an astoundingly large constellation of 26 works commissioned by the President of Yale University, A. Whitney Griswold. Griswold was obsessed with architecture. When he assumed the presidency of the university, the campus was dominated by Gothic historicist buildings, designed to make, in the words of *Time* magazine, "scholarship look more scholarly." (November 15, 1963.) Most of these buildings were built during the 1930s, sustaining single-handedly the economy of New Haven. Griswold was committed to complement this eclectic architecture with "buildings in the idiom of (our) time" (*Architectural Record*, April 1962).

He saw himself more as a "patron" than as a "client." He raised the money, selected the architects and during his 13-year tenure, "produced Yale's architectural Renaissance." (ibid.) Among his architects were Louis Kahn, Eero Saarinen, Gordon Bunshaft, and Philip Johnson. "Their stunning results," *Time* magazine declared, "made Yale more of a laboratory than a museum." Griswold's attitude to architecture was shared during this time by the leaders of the New Haven community, which acted in concordance with the university. It was in this inspiring euphoric context that the Art and Architecture Building emerged.

On the lower stories, the building houses the sculpture and basic design studio, along with a lecture auditorium. The library occupies the ground floor where one finds a small entrance. On the next floor there is

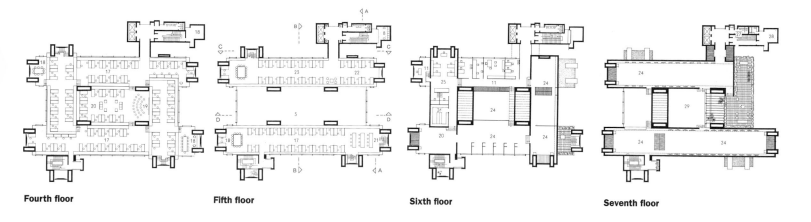

Fourth floor   **Fifth floor**   **Sixth floor**   **Seventh floor**

a large space for exhibitions as well as for social events. The space is surrounded by discussion alcoves, and adjacent to it there is an architectural jury pit. At this level is the main entrance to the building, reached by a grandiose stair. Vincent Scully referred to it as the "most dramatic entrance in the United States of America, bar none." ("Art and Architecture Building, Yale University," *Architecture Review*.) The large space is surrounded by open mezzanines serving the administration offices; from these mezzanines one can look down all the way to the library space. A similar multi-story arrangement is occupied by the architectural studios and, on one of the mezzanines, by the City Planning Department. A channel-shaped concrete bridge crosses the space and a 14-foot statue of Minerva overlooks it. At the time of the opening, the architectural drafting room was considered the most successful space of the building. The last 2 floors contain the painting and graphic art studios. They are basically long open galleries illuminated by clerestories or skylights. A cafeteria and a guest apartment were located on a penthouse level at the top.

The basic concept of the building was the "pinwheel scheme," locations clustered off a central major space, a rectangular enclosed court overlooked by long, rectangular mezzanines. "Once having adopted the pinwheel scheme," Rudolph wrote in *Architectural Record* (April 1962), "the architectural problem became one of articulating it in three dimensions. A structure was adopted which allowed each leg of the pinwheel to be at a different

height, giving a kind of overlapping and interpenetrating series of platforms." The basic frame was then "manipulated to vary the spaces in an intricate way which grows out of the use of the building." Originally, the idea was to arrange the whole structure around one court, but this was rejected by the fire department. Rudolph had to compromise by cutting the volume into two: the 2-story exhibition hall, serving as the meeting-heart of the institution, and the design hall as the major workshop area.

There are many precedents of the scheme. Rudolph himself repeatedly cited Frank Lloyd Wright's Larkin Building, and, without doubt, the concept was enriched by Kahn's idea of

servant towers surrounding a service community space, originating in the Richards Laboratories at the University of Pennsylvania (1957–60, pp. 72–75). The hollow corner towers at the perimeter of the building contain the primary vertical air passages of the heating and air-conditioning system. The general contractor, George B. H. Macomber Company, and the structural engineer, Henry A. Pfisterer, worked hard to enable the scheme to come about without any alterations to Rudolph's design. The total vertical continuity sought by Rudolph, however, was unacceptable to the local fire department, and despite much criticism from the architectural community, the plan

(Below) Skyline of New Haven

(Bottom left) Corner detail

(Bottom right) Rendering by the architect

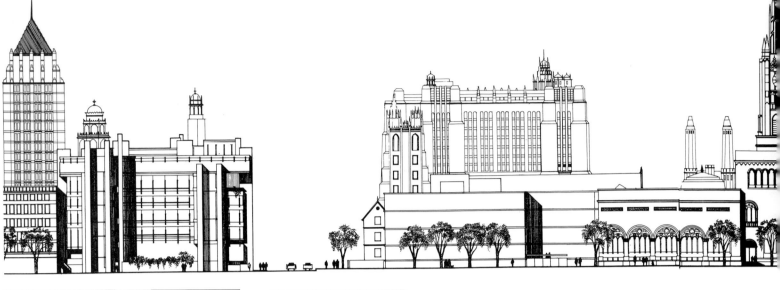

Ezra Stoller © Esto

was compromised to ensure compliance with the fire code. In 1969, six years after Griswold's premature death, the building stood almost in ruins, devastated by a fire that would have burned it to the ground had it not been for these changes in the design.

The "pinwheel scheme," while chosen strategically to house the service functions, turned out to be problematic, voluminous, and cumbersome in an institutional building the size of the Art and Architecture Building. Equally important was Rudolph's desire for the configuration to express the idea of community and concourse, for the building to fit into the urban context, specifically at the corner of Chapel Street. Reacting against Mies's propensity to design *ex nihilo*, as well as Gropius's approach to design "from within," Rudolph tried to rethink architecture

in terms of an "urbanistic continuity," a tradition he saw deserted by modernist architects. The pinwheel scheme was therefore adopted because, "since the building is on a corner its role in the cityscape is to turn that corner." It was also considered appropriate because with its vertical tower elements, it was almost like a form of punctuation terminating the composition of the long street of Yale buildings, creating an urban sculpture.

Inside, the building further revealed Rudolph's ideas. His treatment, much imitated around the world, of the concrete walls, with their deep vertical striations and rugged texture, aroused, in Pevsner's unhappy phrase, the "tweed" feeling, or, even worse, the "collegiate Shetland

sweater." And next to this roughness was the elegance of the bisected nautilus shell in the exposed concrete (*béton brut*), and the heavy cargo netting juxtaposed with the orange velveteen on the floors. There is an aura of Piranesi in the interior of the building, in the light torrents, in the stair gorges, and in the effects of space swirling around and soaring up. It is of interest that at the time the building was being conceived and constructed, the art historian, Carol Meeks, a few yards across from Rudolph's office and the site of the building, had been lecturing on Piranesian space, based on his famous engravings of the *Carcere* and on the significance of an architecture of "mood," which he tried to trace in history and project on to the future.

(Below left) Articulation of the corner

(Bottom left) Lounge

(Below right) Studio

Ezra Stoller © Esto

Ezra Stoller © Esto

Ezra Stoller © Esto

Venturi and Short
VANNA VENTURI HOUSE
Chestnut Hill, Pennsylvania
1961–63

© George Pohl

Here is an almost minimal suburban house. It stands on a flat, open site in Chestnut Hill, a suburb of Philadelphia. Designed by Robert Venturi for his mother, the house includes an extra bedroom for the architect, on the ground floor, and a relatively large room above used as his studio.

Few buildings of such small size have had such a big impact and received such passionate criticism in the history of contemporary architecture. The firm's brief calls the house "a seminal work." Indeed, the project shaped to a great extent the path the company took, and contributed to a new way of looking at architecture. But the *Architectural Review* (February 1966), in its first reference to the house, simply labeled it "mannerist," and identified it with a *laissez-faire* approach to life, comparing it, on the same page, with a completely nondescript suburban house which the *Review* called "mainstream." Little did the *Review* know what awaited the project. And while the building has frequently been called artless, ugly, and preoccupied with trivia, it has also been recognized as a major work that opened a new era in architecture.

One of Venturi's very early works, it has—like many early works in the career of any artist—an autobiographical and programmatic character. The building confesses, so to speak, the first experiences of the author with canonical buildings of the past, and the excitement and conflicts they aroused in him. It also projects, paradigmatically, a new set of design norms concerning the relations between building and site, form and function, and building as object and statement about building. Above all, the building stands as an exemplar of how to reach a global, final architectural synthesis from a multitude of conflicting needs and values, all demanding simultaneous satisfaction from the new product—not by brutal reduction, but by crafty compromise.

The architect has always described the house in terms of conflict and paradox. The current brief calls it "complex and simple," "open and closed," "big and little." These concepts, in their contradictory, paired juxtapositions, represent architectural strategies of composition rather than qualities physically present in the work.

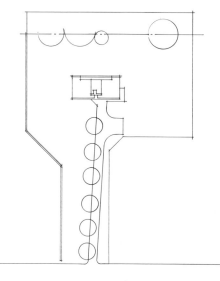

(Top) Back of the building

(Above) Site plan

(Below) Section

(Right) Side entrance

(Bottom right) Entrance

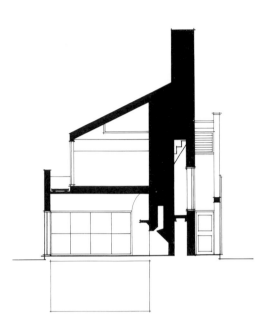

Although they are strongly reminiscent of the design principles of Aldo van Eyck, who had also asked (a decade earlier) for an architecture of enrichment and inclusion, rather than reduction and elimination, the spatial tactics in Venturi's work are different.

In an earlier description of the work, in the Yale architectural magazine, *Perspecta*, of 1965, Venturi describes the following characteristics of the composition: "It contains things within things in plan. An interior multiplicity distorted to fit its rigid bounds and forced to accommodate its exterior symmetry. It contains things behind things in elevation: an interior multiplicity appropriate for a house protruding beyond the parapets of its two parallel walls, and manifesting itself in the irregular positions of its windows."

It continues by referring to the differences between back and front, the juxtaposition between the continuous roof shape in the back, and the "violent" roof complex in the front elevation. It contrasts the basic rectangularity of the interior partitions with the segmenting diagonals of the entry and circulation, describing "the segmental wood trim pediment" as "an ornament" whose purpose is to contrast with the diagonal shapes of the roof in order to magnify the scale of the entrance and to stress the planarity of the stucco wall.

© Rollin R. La France

(Left) Facade

(Below & bottom) Elevations

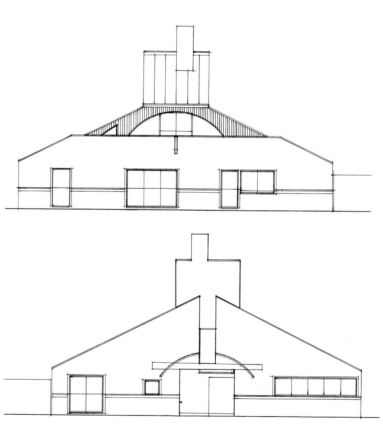

The inspiration of the spatial tactics in Venturi's work is without doubt drawn from Italian mannerist architecture. It also draws on Aalto's and Kahn's method of achieving a product of richness through a step-by-step appropriation of a large list of formal and functional requirements, gradually inserting new parameters in the composition, increasingly deforming in each subsequent stage the spatial configuration. The result of this "inclusiveness" is the manifest "complexity," as well as the "contradiction" in the final design.

For example, there is no coherence between the internal organization of the house and its outside envelope. This discontinuity is demonstrated in the two most significant outside elements—the front and the back walls, which appear appliqué-like, rather than leading to, or opening from, the inside. While they are plain and planar, the two sides are busy and fragmented. The overall outline of the building, with its overstressed gable roof, is symmetrical, but the openings that puncture it are distributed in a non-symmetrical manner. The interior is complex, compact, almost crowded. The fireplace is "too big," and the mantle "too high" for the size of the room. In front, the entrance loggia is wide, high, and central; its over-size scale is emphasized by the contrast with the other doors and with its shallowness, and with the size and expedient position of the inner entrance behind it. The applied wood molding over the door increases its scale, too. A similar technique is followed with the dado. It increases the scale of the building by being higher than would normally be expected.

"Complexity" and "contradiction," however, are not ends in themselves; they are the by-products of the overriding goal to achieve a richer, closer-to-reality artifact. The work is paradigmatic not only in terms of the goals it defines for architecture but also for the methodological design means it suggests. The author starts with a formal, elementary tripartite plan within which the

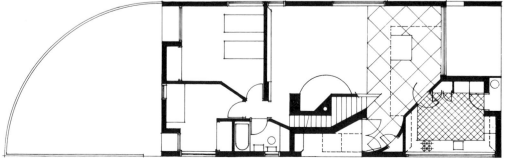

basic home activities are located. Then follows a sequence of design operations. New objects are introduced or those previously placed are moved, pushed, cut or squeezed, as more functional considerations enter into the problem. Is this casting the process of making architecture a problem-solver? Yes and no. Yes, because the outcome of the process is extremely habitable; and no, because it leads to a puzzle, to a product that compels examination of its very process.

This is clearly a difficult architecture, highly charged cognitively. An extremely practical artifact, where space lost to circulation is minimal, and the location and configuration of the individual rooms is most commodious, it is at the same time an architecture that addresses general and fundamental issues that go beyond architecture proper, at least as traditionally defined. It is architecture about architecture. What makes the house for Mrs. Venturi so significant historically is that it was the first building to be explicitly intended as such. It initiated a world-wide movement that has increasingly dominated architecture to the present day.

MLTW (Moore Lyndon Turnbull Whitaker)
SEA RANCH CONDOMINIUM 1
Sea Ranch, California
1963–65

Floor plan for all 10 units

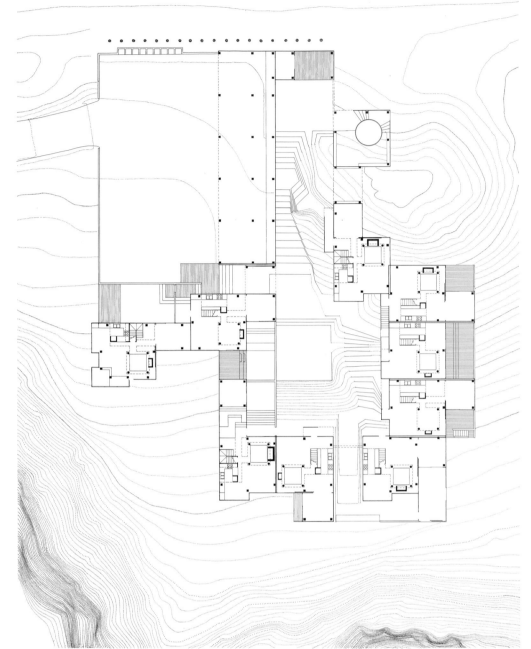

The site is a great open space, a 5000-acre coastal meadow, once occupied by a sheep ranch, and just 100 miles from San Francisco. This rugged, windswept, green expanse, originally dotted with rough-sided barns and sheds, sprawls over a distance of 10 miles, hemmed in only by a forest of great fir and redwood trees to the east, and craggy, sandstone, surf-pounded cliffs of the Pacific Coast to the west.

The harmonious way in which the Sea Ranch Condominium 1 settles into this almost mythopoeic site is remarkable. With its inclined silhouette of sloped roofs following the natural slope of the hills towards the sea, with its towers bracketing the outline of existing rock forms to mark their distinct location, with its unadorned, unpainted, natural redwood sheathing, it is an immensely lyrical response to the land.

Sea Ranch began in a visionary spirit. Albert Boeke, the developer, put together

the team of architects with landscape designer, Lawrence Halprin. It was planned as an experimental community for two thousand families, an idea that grew out of optimistic aspirations typical of the 1960s— to develop an alternative to the conformity and oppression of the man-made environment, and to revive a sense of community and place.

In the years when ecology was still a new term, the architects called their project "an organic approach to planning that is not only aesthetically involved with the landscape but ecologically involved as well." The intention was to preserve the coastline, the beaches, the Gualala River, the great stands of timber, the trail hiking, the fishing, and the abalone hunting. "The notion of entering this wild and accessible area," wrote Halprin, "and making a community seemed a great challenge ... I was convinced that the Sea Ranch could become a place where wild nature and

human habitation could interact in a kind of intense symbiosis." (*Progressive Architecture*, February 1993.)

Every level of the original design bears the mark of the "native character" of the site. Halprin's landscape design included the linking of houses by fences and wind-protected garden courts rising gently from the meadow to meet with hedgerows and serve as windbreaks, a common practice in the region. A further means of integrating the project was to give the buildings forms taken from the local vernacular of barns and sheep sheds. Conscious of the incongruous effect of their decision, the designers asserted that: "We rejoice if we can find a product intended for one use and reuse it in another memorable fashion. Ours is the pragmatism of simple indigenous construction, common sense, plus the poetry of traditional materials used in familiar ways to make very special, albeit unfamiliar places."

(Left) Vernacular farm building

(Below) View from the road

(Bottom) Site plan

There is a long Californian tradition of building residences in the unadorned, unpainted local redwood, which Sea Ranch follows. The Condominium buildings are constructed as a giant cage of stepped and lapped Douglas Fir girts bolted outboard to groups of rough-sawn fir columns. The exterior of the cage is enclosed by rough fir boards vertically nailed with tongue and groove joints. Asphalt-impregnated building paper was placed outside the rough sheathing and this water barrier was in turn covered with redwood boards.

There is a unique coupling of formal rigor and sensuousness experienced in the surface textures and impressions: smooth, uninterrupted lines, natural hues, as the shafts of sunlight and shadow play upon them, and the scent of so much exposed timber near the ocean and the quality of the joints and copper flashing of the complex. "The details are our fingerprints," Turnbull wrote. "Our detailing could be described as non-detailing ... the joinery is so simple and logical that it appears to be only common sense and not eye-catching elaborations." (*Global Architecture Detail*, 3, 1976.)

Within the walls of Condominium 1, perhaps the most memorable place is the bedroom in the form of a four-poster bed, of the type one imagines the first pioneers in California could have slept on, but whose posters are 2 stories high, which, for reasons of privacy, canvas curtains can enclose like tents. The resulting spatial experience— which can be traced back to Charles Moore's own house in Orinda, California (1960–62)— of being in one sheltering "aedicular" structure embedded inside another, is a strange and pleasurable experience, perhaps enhanced by, and enhancing, the sense of

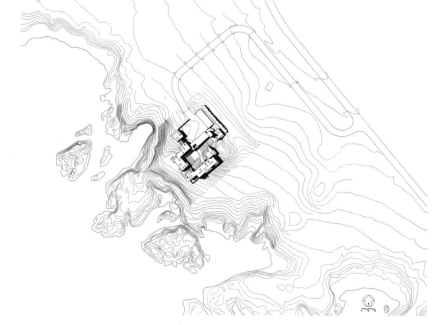

© Morley Baer

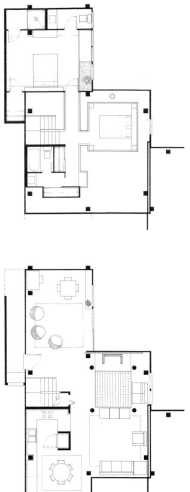

(Above) View from the hillside

**(Above right) Floor plans, indicating
the location of the bedroom structure**

**(Below) Bedroom structure, embedded
inside the bigger structure of the dwelling**

**(Opposite) View from the ocean of
the ten units comprising the original
condominium**

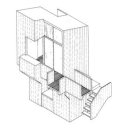

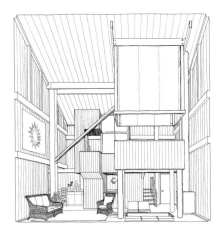

dwelling in an environment approaching natural wilderness.

According to architectural critic Donald Canty, writing on the occasion of the prestigious Twenty-Five Year Award bestowed on the project by the American Institute of Architects in 1991, Sea Ranch remains surprisingly close to the spirit of the original designers. This spirit is perhaps best summed up by Donlyn Lyndon: "We believed our task was to make places for people. Beyond the pragmatic, they must be appropriate and engage the mind and be delightful to the spirit." (*Progressive Architecture*, February 1993.)

Sea Ranch, like Barnes's Haystack Mountain project (1959–61, pp. 66–69), was very much a project reacting to the architecture of New Monumentality and debased modernism. This generation tried to rethink architecture and reorient it towards the original goals of the modern movement, which they saw by then as deserted and betrayed. As Lewis Mumford had already suggested in the 1940s, with a premonition of the coming crisis, the goals included the idea of the region in a deeper sense—that is, respect for the natural environment, a judicious use of natural resources, a commitment to community, and an open, reflective mind to design. Today, although so much has changed in the world of architecture and in the world at large, these questions still remain unanswered, with Sea Ranch an inspiring prototype.

Louis I. Kahn
SALK INSTITUTE OF BIOLOGICAL STUDIES
La Jolla, California
1959–65

**Section through laboratory showing
sunken courts and studies**

Dr. Jonas Salk, having invented a polio vaccine, used the proceeds from his discovery to establish an institute devoted to medical research. When the idea for an Institute for Biology Research first occurred to him, the image of a monastery at Assisi, which he had visited in 1954, sprang immediately to mind. Its arcades, columns, and courtyard provided him with the spatial concept he sought for the new social and intellectual organization he envisioned.

The Institute was to have three major elements: laboratories, a meeting-house, and community for married students, resident scientists, and their assistants. There was also to be a library with reading rooms and meeting-places, where everybody could come together to pass free time and exchange ideas. This was a totally new concept. The atmosphere was to be not just scientific, but humanistic as well, so he planned a swimming pool and a 500-seat lecture hall that could also be used for concerts and theatrical performances.

At the time Salk was looking for an architect to create his vision, the Richards Medical Research Building (1957–60, pp. 72–75) was much in the news, and he decided to commission its architect, Louis Kahn.

The location chosen by Salk was in La Jolla, north of San Diego on the Torrey Pines Mesa. Kahn had been to the breathtaking site, a high ground overlooking the great

expanse of the Pacific Ocean, with a deep canyon through the property from east to west, scattered with shrubs, cactuses, and lemon trees (August Komendant, *18 years with Architect Louis I. Kahn*, pp. 41–2).

Back in Philadelphia, Kahn decided that the laboratory would be parallel to the ocean at the east end of the canyon, the meeting-house to the north, on a small hill close to the high cliff of the shore, and the community to the south. All would be within walking distance from the labs, and all would command extraordinary vistas.

The planning of the scientists' facilities was difficult because it was unprecedented in its conception. Salk wanted more than just the traditional, functional work place; he wanted something as innovative as the Richards Laboratory. Consequently, Kahn consulted the scientists about their habits, but there were almost as many opinions as there were people consulted. For instance, one scientist, asked what size the library should be, estimated room for about 45,000 volumes, while another said, "15,000 will be more than plenty." (ibid., p. 44.)

The design process was notoriously complicated and has been documented many times. The end result implemented and further developed the idea of servant and served spaces, first employed by Kahn in a vertical manifestation in the Richards Center, and now interpreted on the horizontal

(Left) Perspective of housing

(Below) Site plan and doodles of housing

(Bottom) Perspective of laboratories and courtyard

plane. There were ten towers, five on each side of the court, housing 36 studies. Each tower was comprised of 4 offices, except the easternmost, which had only 2. Two 45-degree diagonal walls in each tower created bays with views to the ocean, one for each study.

The characteristic of this work most commented on is the sculptural quality of the bare surfaces and the unprecedented combinations of materials—the juxtaposition of travertine and concrete. Several types of concrete were blended with pozzolan and other mixtures to produce a warmer color. Plywood forms were coated with polyurethane to ensure the consistency of the finish on the concrete walls.

In spite of the pristine appearance of the finished buildings, there is nothing simple about its structural system. There was no question of pre-casting for the project, as opposed to the Richards Laboratory, because the first floors were below grade and there was no space available for a huge crane to operate. All the buildings had to be poured

(Above) View from the sea

(Left) Internal court

(Opposite) View towards the sea

Ezra Stoller © Esto

in place. The structural problem was that in a seismic terrain it was thought that only a steel structure could have adequate ductility. The local authorities, on hearing that the building was going to be a rigid-frame concrete structure, said "no way." However, as August Komendant would not take no for an answer, the problem was solved by introducing lead–zinc-covered steel-plate interfaces between the Vierendeel trusses and the supporting columns, and by providing adequate length for column tendons in order to create elastic joints for the framing (ibid.).

As Komendant explains, the pre-stressed Vierendeel trusses were devoted to supporting the floors at the top and bottom chords, thus providing space for mechanicals between the floors—the servant components of the complex. This servant space provided very rigid horizontal support for the overall structural system. The proof of the structural

soundness of the Vierendeel system was not late in coming. Soon after the laboratories were finished, the area was shaken by an earthquake, and while other buildings in the area had cracks, the Salk buildings had none (ibid.).

What happened to the garden that was meant to be enclosed by the two wings of the Institute? Kahn had been to Mexico, and the work of Luis Barragan had impressed him so deeply that he invited him to help choose the plants and trees for the space. When he entered the space, Barragan approached the concrete walls, touched them, and said not a single tree or blade of grass should interrupt it: "By doing so you will have a facade—a facade to the sky!" (ibid., p. 72.)

As Dr. Richard Rietz, a scientist turned design consultant, observed, "The Salk is a watershed laboratory of our time … It introduced open laboratories, modular lab

planning, ease of communication between scientists, reconfigurable utilities and services." And he contrasted it to the 19th-century laboratories of long corridors with poor support spaces (*Progressive Architecture*, October 1993).

Francis Crick, who has been at the Salk for 17 years, has said that most scientists are so absorbed by their research that they are ready to work even in "cubby holes and little corners." One Salk technician, however, reported that every year at sunset on the vernal equinox, the staff would sit around the linear fountain in the central plaza and look to the west. As the sun set into the ocean, it would transform the fountain into a pool of fire, an experience one observer likened to being at the center of the universe.

Venturi and Rauch
GUILD HOUSE
Philadelphia, Pennsylvania
1961–65

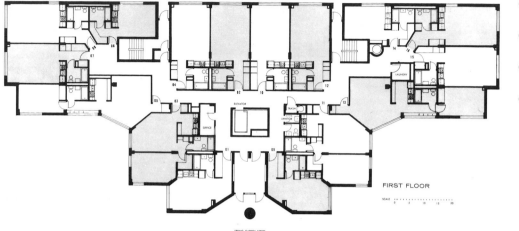

(Left) Ground plan

(Below) Setting on the city edge

(Opposite above) Facade

(Opposite below) Back of the building

FIRST FLOOR

© Venturi, Scott Brown and Associates

Like the house for Mrs. Venturi in Chestnut Hill, Pennsylvania (1961–63, pp. 86–89), the Guild House is a relatively modest building for its type. Yet it was just as epoch-making, because, like the Chestnut Hill project, not only was it a utilitarian artifact, but it also had a reflective function. Whereas Venturi's mother's house was architecture about architecture, this was architecture about reality—the reality of the city, old age, and how contemporary society deals with these issues.

It also coupled the practical with the theoretical in a most uncompromising, pragmatist manner. The architectural program called for 91 apartments for elderly tenants, with 2-bedroom, 1-bedroom, and studio units. The site was small, urban, and within view of downtown. It was located next to the East Poplar, an area of urban renewal, where the Friends' Neighborhood Guild—the same client as the Guild House—sponsored the first American self-help cooperative, as well as an interracial redevelopment project in 1952.

Like the Chestnut Hill house, the plan was from the point of view of room dimensions, circulation, lobby, materials, and detailing, stripped to a minimum, while all the basic needs of the elderly concerning comfort and safety were satisfied in complete accordance with the standards of that time. However, as with the Venturi house, the work maximized other aspects. The objective of community was enhanced by an unusually large space placed at the top floor, in contrast to the routine practice of relegating this kind of

room to the basement. The architect worked closely with the Executive Director of the Friends' Neighborhood, Francis Bosworth, who, both understanding and ambitious, tried to "resist flattening out the building into a crackerbox" (*Progressive Architecture*, May 1967). The configuration of the plan touched the street at the center, at the entrance, respecting the street line, while stepping back at the rest of the facade "in a series of Victorian jogs," to offer the elderly tenants the opportunity of having more varied views of street activities.

The formal architectural quality of the work is exceptionally high, especially within the narrow budget limits. The most simple, basic esthetic means were chosen in order to have the least interference with the functional requirements, while achieving

simultaneously a significant esthetic impact. As with the Chestnut Hill house, scale plays a very important role. The scale of the windows or of the brick is altered according to their distance from the street to imply the presence of a civic order, despite the fact that the building is a humble facility for the elderly.

The same contrast is to be found between the low programmatic prose of the institution and the high poetics of the tripartition of the composition—of the oxymoron embedded in superimposing the arched window at the top with the central column at the bottom, or making references to eminent precedents, such as Philibert de l'Orme's Château d'Anet, and most paradoxical of all, the gold anodized TV antenna.

© William Watkins

© Venturi, Scott Brown and Associates

What was the intention behind these contradictions? Stylistic gymnastics? Irony? Critical comment? What was the effect upon the users? What this building, as with the earlier Venturi house, provides, is a work of art, part of the art movement of the 1960s, multivalent and cryptic, but also inviting an open number of interpretations, as with the work of Jasper Johns, Andy Warhol, and Robert Rauschenberg.

The work provides an exemplar of an inclusive, rather than reductive, artifact— of an "accommodating" and "compromising" design, rather than one of simplification and rejection. More importantly, after a long period of an architecture of built "solutions," this was an architecture that appeared more effective in problem-stating, by posing new questions about the utilitarian and the contemplative, the poetic and the ordinary, the institutional and the practical. It used architecture in a completely novel way, neither to incorporate passively existing constraints, nor to try to ignore them in a utopian manner, but to frame a contemporary reflection of reality.

Sert Jackson and Gourley
FRANCIS GREENWOOD PEABODY TERRACE
Cambridge, Massachusetts
1963–65

(Below left) Concept sketch

(Below right) Site plan

(Opposite above) View from the river

(Opposite below) Views of the court

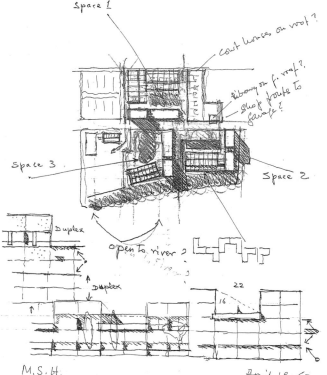

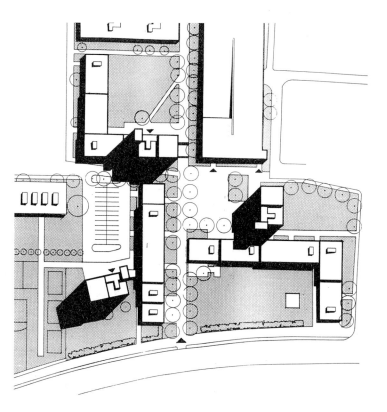

Peabody Terrace aimed at satisfying the growing needs of Harvard University for housing its graduate students as well as for providing a community for young families. The project supplied a dense, 85-unit-per acre pattern for 500 minimal apartments, ranging from efficiencies to 3-bedroom units. It also included a central square, a drugstore, a cleaner's and dryer's shop, washing and drying facilities on the ground level, a place for sunbathing on the top, and meeting and seminar rooms. The paved plaza was intended for outdoor gatherings, while additional courtyards were introduced to offer social amenities, such as a children's playground and a spray pond.

The project consists of three 22-story towers linked by bridges to the lower buildings, terraced apartment buildings of 3, 5, and 7 stories. The first 3 stories are walk-ups. Starting with the fourth floor, the rest of the apartments are served by elevators that stop at every third floor. The intervening levels are reached by stairs from the stop levels. This scheme was efficient from the point of view of elevator installation and usage, and permitted the use of relatively slim towers. The project was, however, criticized for its excessive circulation areas.

Special effort was made, unique at this time, to integrate the building complex with its environment. The elegant silhouette of the towers was chosen so that they would not dominate the surrounding smaller wooden houses. The lower apartment type was designed to relate the high-rise towers to the scale of these smaller buildings. A brick-paved walkway was laid out through the complex to join it with the neighborhood to the north, and with Memorial Drive and the river bank to the south. The quadrangle pattern adopted for the previous Harvard Houses (undergraduate student dormitories) along the Charles River was used by the new housing.

The work reacted against the radically monumentalist, anti-historicist excesses of modernist architecture, as well as the overwhelmingly institutional mood of the area. The mixed massing of Sert's project, borrowed from the new urban design principles applied in Holland after the war, and the gridded facade pattern—both, in fact, having very little to do with the immediate context of the complex—helped to scale down the size of the housing and make it appear less formal. They also recalled, romantically, Mediterranean residential structures, giving to Harvard a more city-like atmosphere and a patina different to the kind lent by its neo-Georgian designs.

Without doubt, the introduction of Peabody Terrace revolutionized what Kevin Lynch called the "imagibility" of Harvard and of the Cambridge bank of the Charles River. In addition, through its informal domestic character, the project gave a more urbane, less institutional character to the area. The feature on the project, in the October issue of *Progressive Architecture* in 1964, praised it for its "fluent continuity … from old to new," and the June 1994 issue of the same magazine asserted that "Peabody Terrace foretold an emerging respect for history and context."

As Jane Holtz Kay pointed out, the Peabody Terrace was an attempt to move beyond aloof megaliths (*The Christian Science Monitor*, April 8, 1983). "An urban campus," Sert is quoted as saying, "is a

© Phokion Karas

© Phokion Karas

© Phokion Karas

cultural center within a city, and should set an example of good planning and good design for the city. It is, in a way, a micro-city and its urbanity is the expression of a better, more civilized way of life." Yet the work did not succeed in escaping the pitfalls of the modernist beliefs that kept architecture from coming into contact with everyday reality. As *Progressive Architecture* (June 1994) remarked, citing Tod Aufiero, a Harvard Graduate School of Design alumnus, "all needs of the original program could have been accommodated in four-story structures". In this manner, many problems brought about by the choice of the tall towers could have been avoided from the beginning. There were similar choices made, causing major problems to the present inhabitants of Peabody Terrace, dictated not by "necessities, but by Modernist preferences." (ibid.)

Today, the firm of Bruner/Cott, experts in revitalization, is in charge of renovating the thirty-year old buildings, giving new life to a work which, without doubt, contributed significantly to the understanding of the much-neglected subject of urban housing, showing how it can be a unique means of enriching the cultural wealth of our cities.

Charles Gwathmey
GWATHMEY RESIDENCE AND STUDIO
Amagansett, New York
1963–65

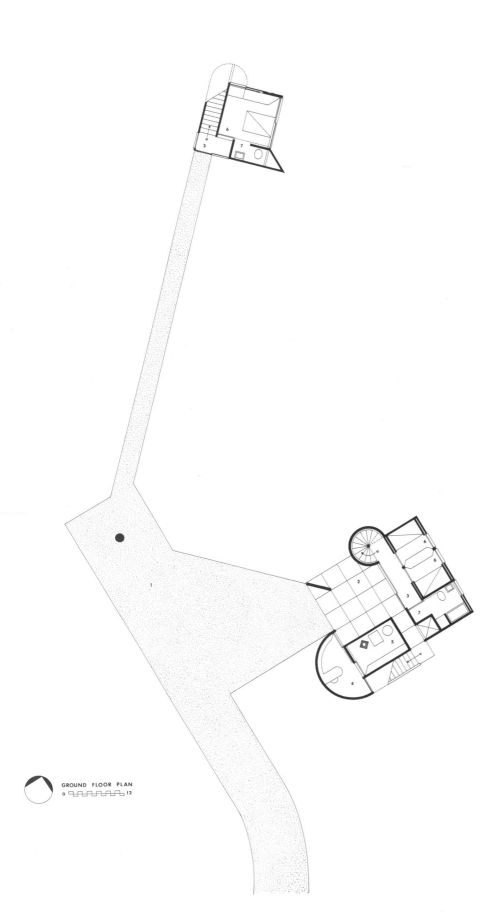

Ground floor plan

GROUND FLOOR PLAN
0 ⌐⌐⌐⌐⌐⌐ 12

At the time the project was first conceived, the site was a one-acre flat field with the adjacent areas still undeveloped. Anticipating future development in the region, a program was conceived to allow for phased construction at the site that would not be destroyed by the inevitable additions to the area beyond the site. This careful staging of the work was characteristic not only of budgetary constraints, but of the total choreography and control by the young architect, Charles Gwathmey, in designing his first project—a house and studio for his parents.

The main house is a small 1200 square feet in plan, but 30,000 cubic feet in volume, a distinction clarified by the designer as a composition of volumetric, rather than planar, assemblages. By organizing the building vertically, the programmatic and site constraints were satisfied through the manipulation of section as well as plan. The ground floor contained the guest rooms, workroom, and covered terrace. The public living spaces—living room, dining room, and kitchen—occupied the next level up, a double-height space, and the master bedroom and bathroom on the top. By raising the public spaces a level above grade, the designer was able to capitalize on the extensive views as well as breaking with the more common connection between principle living spaces and the ground.

A year after the house was completed, a second structure was added, accommodating a guest room and a full studio. The section of the second structure was derived from the main house, but by siting it 45 degrees to the initial structure, creating, in the words of the architect, "a perceptual form dynamic

© Gwathmey Associates

(Left) Porch of the main structure

(Below) Axonometric view of smaller unit

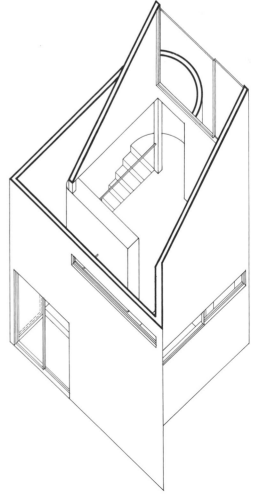

between the two volumes." Another relationship was established with the second building. While the first is clearly anchored to the ground, the second appears precarious, and seems almost to move.

The buildings are wood frame, with cedar siding on both the exterior and interior. Their volumes are primitive and minimal, and their geometric forms are manipulated in response to site, orientation, program, and structure. According to Gwathmey, they appear to be carved from a solid, rather than resulting in an additive assemblage. Light cast on these simple but photogenic volumes plays an important role in underlining the dynamics of form of the composition.

(Left) View of west facade

(Below) Axonometric view of bigger unit, ground floor

(Below left) Axonometric view of bigger unit, top floor

© Gwathmey Associates

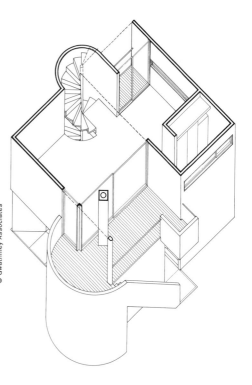

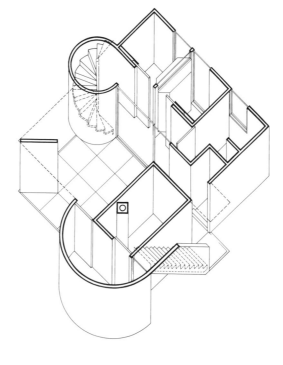

(Opposite) View of ceiling from the top of the stair

© Gwathmey Associates

Marcel Breuer and Associates
WHITNEY MUSEUM OF AMERICAN ART
New York, New York
1963–66

(Right) Section

(Far right) Basement plan

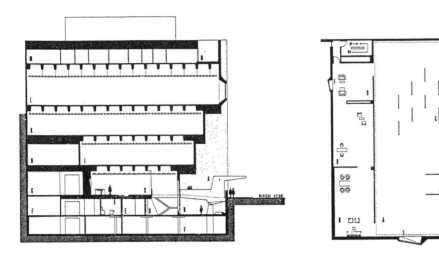

From its origin as a single studio space in Greenwich Village, to an undistinguished but large building on West 54th Street, the Whitney Museum finally found a home commensurate with its importance as a cultural institution in East Manhattan, at the corner of 75th Street and Madison Avenue, the heart of the "uptown" galleries district. The designer of the new building was Marcel Breuer, one of the pioneers of the modern movement, a collaborator of Gropius, a Bauhaus master, and, later, a teacher at Harvard.

By the beginning of the 1960s, Breuer, with major commissions around the world, was one of the leading architects to react against the idea of an architecture as a modernist "box" dictated by the representation of functionality, and to enter into a very personal area of exploration—one of expressive qualities, of the sensual texture of building materials and of abstract, "plastic," spatial relations of built form. According to Breuer (*Sun and Shadow, the philosophy of an architect*, 1954), architecture was not just a matter of utilitarian concerns. It was, in his words, about:

> The void you touch with your elbows
> The taste of space with your tongue
> The fragrance of dimensions
> The juice of stone.

Although Breuer conceived architecture as "sculpture" (*Progressive Architecture*, October 1966), he did not renounce the imperative of functionalism. On the contrary, for him a building was "a sculpture with rather serious functional requirements" (ibid.). That was why, he argued, even when a building "follows free lines, it should always be clear that these lines are built, that they did not just grow" (*Sun and Shadow*, 1954).

Breuer's Whitney Museum was to influence Gordon Bunshaft's Hirshhorn Museum in Washington, D.C. and I. M. Pei's Everson Museum in Syracuse, but it has no formal historical precedents in architecture. This is what made it uniquely daring. Its forms originated in the sculpture of the 1950s. Sculptural manipulation is obvious in the interior of the building. A rich interplay of varied materials and textures characterizes the interior walls, in their flame-marked warm gray granite and sand-colored concrete. The surfaces of the materials are contrasted. The granite is sometimes rough, sometimes smooth, sometimes polished to a high gloss. The concrete is in certain places bush-hammered, and in others marked by the carefully chosen planks of the wood forms. Patterned granite carved with niches is employed to line the trustees' room. The search for sculptural effects extends even to the building's details: the bronze hardware, the solid teak doors, transoms, railings, and the floors—variously bluestone and parquet—the teak paneling, the bleached canvas wrapping around the gallery walls, not to mention the granite benches, display panels, and light fixtures designed by Breuer for the lobby. Space itself is

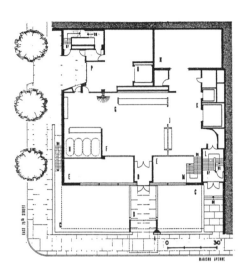

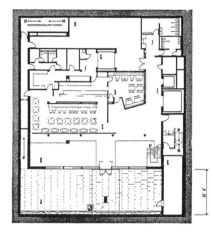

(Far left) Ground plan

(Left) Upper story plan

conceived as sculpted, best exemplified by the stairwell.

Functionally, the organization of the building achieves an optimal allocation of activities within a relatively tight envelope. The top floor is taken by offices, above which is a large mechanical penthouse, while storage, public restrooms, and a cafeteria with a view of the sculpture garden, are located at the lowest level. The moat between the street and the building is very successful in accommodating a high-quality space for a sculpture garden, and in providing a pleasant café in contact with the outside, even though it is below ground level.

An important factor contributing to the functionality of the work is that, despite sculptural concerns, the overriding principle of the composition is the idea of universal space: (1) the building is divided into plain rectangular parallelepiped volumes; (2) their plain volumetric definition is not violated by structural elements even when they are given the freedom to be "plastic"; (3) the particular needs for space division are satisfied by using display panels subordinated to larger space envelopes; and (4) spaces do not leak or interpenetrate.

Despite its unprecedented form, the building fits felicitously into the corner of Madison Avenue. At that location, the character of the neighborhood is rather varied and highly three-dimensional, with two Gothic revival churches, the Parke-Bernet Building, the flamboyant Rhinelander Mansion, as well as many apartment buildings and brownstones, as Hamilton

Smith, the associate designer of the Museum, pointed out (*New York Times*, July 20, 1985). While potentially a massive building, its scale is reduced significantly by the slope on the top of the Madison Avenue facade, which conceals the two top office floors.

The seven large, irregularly shaped, enigmatic windows, which offer the Museum-visitor contact with natural light, a view, and street life, as well as a sense of orientation, are also devices through which the building, from the outside, assumes a scale, enhancing its relationship to its surroundings, although in highly unorthodox ways. One might say that its expressionism is, in many respects, in affinity with its Gothic neighbors.

As one discovers, strolling up or down Madison Avenue with the crowds that pass through the museum daily, the unique sculptural identity of the Whitney—its ingenious set-back profile, the unexpected moat, the playful bridge, and ceremonial gate—succeeds in offering a public place to the city.

Ezra Stoller © Esto

(Above) Exterior, with sculpted windows

(Opposite) Close-up of sculpted windows

Ezra Stoller © Esto

Cambridge Seven Associates, Inc. with Buckminster Fuller
UNITED STATES PAVILION EXPO 67
Montreal, Quebec
1964–67

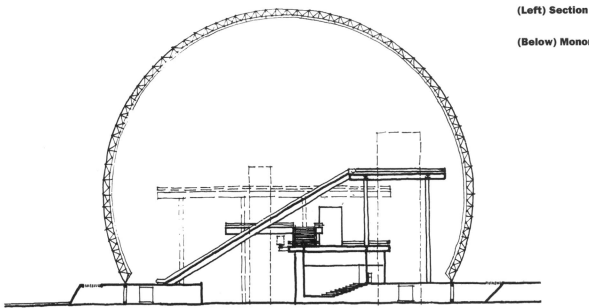

(Left) Section

(Below) Monorail

During the first discussions on the concept of the United States Pavilion for Expo 67, the sponsor and designers decided to downplay both the Great Society (President Johnson's ambitious program to improve the welfare of Americans) and the Vietnam War—very obvious facts of life at the time—and to use a theme that would educate and entertain in a soft-spoken way. The exhibits illustrated the American creative spirit in cinema, painting, sculpture, folk art, and space exploration. The shimmering dome and the movement within created one of the most dramatic images at the exposition.

The site is in the middle of the St. Laurence, on the Ile Ste. Hélène, immediately across from the new metro station built for the fair. One of the confounding challenges of a geodesic dome is in determining how it meets the ground. In this case, the skillful integration with the landscape, through the use of the retaining walls and forecourt, brings the sphere down to earth in as graceful a manner as possible.

The decision was made to use a simple, three-quarter sphere, a modified geodesic dome. The dome rises as high as a 20-story building and is animated by people moving through it, both by day and night. The transparent acrylic panels—effectively the skin of the dome—had a green bronze tint that reduced the light transmission from 93 percent at the bottom to 45 percent at the top.

Inside the dome, concourses, platforms, and balconies connected by long escalators formed the architectural skeleton of the pavilion. Visitors were taken to the topmost exhibition platform on one of the longest escalators in the world (145 feet) to descend by shorter escalators, from exhibit to exhibit. The continuous pedestrian circulation system allowed large crowds to pass through the exhibits without congestion and excess signage. The Expo monorail passed through the dome, giving passengers a preview of the excitement within.

The framework of the geodesic dome was made of tube steel infilled with clear acrylic panels. As the brief called for a pavilion life of only six months—the time that the Exposition was to be opened—the instructions were to spend nothing on the longevity or easy dismantling and reassembling elsewhere after the fair. This stringent budget requirement also applied to the interior structures: the platforms, stair towers, and escalator supports were of very straightforward structural steel framing, with gypsum wall-board ceilings, walls, and edges, none of which were designed for a long life. It is ironic that the basic dome structure and framework of the interior platforms are still there over twenty years later.

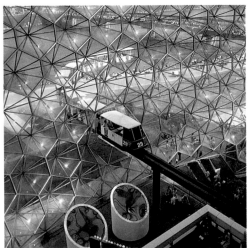

© Cambridge Seven

The brief called for the building to be air-conditioned—a difficult task for a large-volume, transparent sphere during the six months of summer. This requirement meant the provision of very large air-handling equipment and large volumes of supply and return conditioned air. All of this was housed adjacent to the main floor level, using the ground form and theater mass to lessen the impact of its scale. The sun load was diminished by the innovative use of computerized blinds that opened and closed, and that were designed to track the sun in its path from morning to evening.

(Right) Ground plan

(Below) View from outside

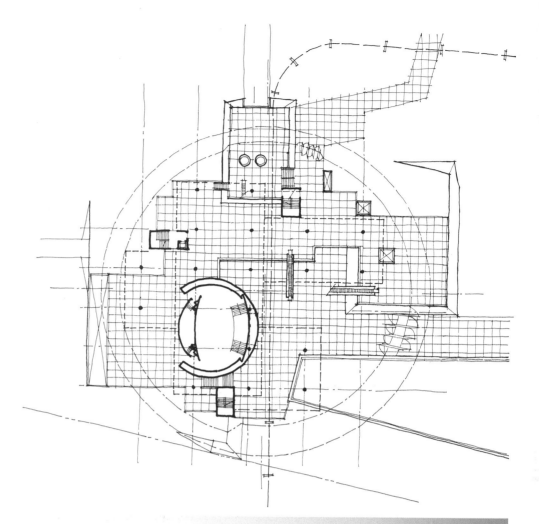

(Right) Circulation pattern

(Below) Night view

(Opposite) Interior with Pop super graphics

© Cambridge Seven

© Cambridge Seven

The pavilion created some controversy. Governor George Romney of Michigan said that it was "pretty on the outside," but "full of trivia on the inside" (*Time*, June 2, 1967). Also critical were the then Soviets, who considered it "just a tiny bubble." But for the majority of the visitors, it was the biggest success of the show. It was likened to London's Crystal Palace Exhibition of 1851 and was instantly assured a place in history. Unfortunately, in 1977 the acrylic cladding of the dome burned. Since then the pavilion has been an empty—though well-preserved—ruin. The City of Montreal is turning the center into an environmental awareness center, with an emphasis on water. Two Montreal firms, Blouin Faucher Aubertin Brodeur Gauthier Architects and Desnoyers, Mercure & Associates won the competition for the project.

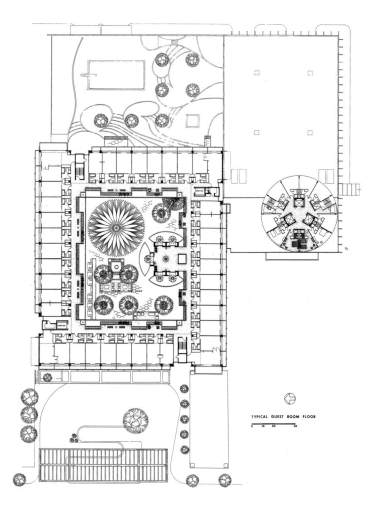

TYPICAL GUEST ROOM FLOOR

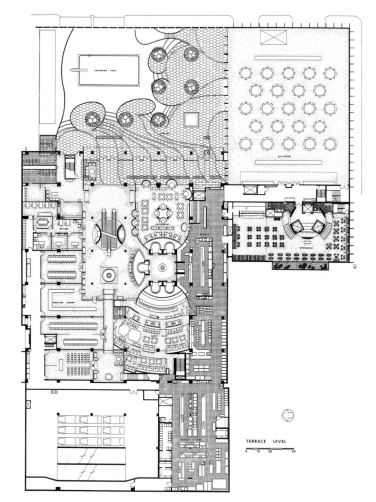

TERRACE LEVEL

When it opened in May 1967, the Hyatt Regency revolutionized luxury hotel design. The huge building houses 800 guestrooms, rising 20 stories above the atrium, with 40 rooms per floor. Interior glass elevators overlook a garden-like lobby with a sidewalk café, coffee shop, and lounges, and terminates above the skylighted roof at a revolving restaurant beneath a blue dome. Below the lobby are a fine restaurant, a night club, ballroom, convention and exhibition facilities, and a pool deck and underground parking for 500.

The hotel was so successful that more buildings were added. Now the 1352-room Hyatt Regency is a major force in the Peachtree Center complex—a major commerical development—and serves as an anchor to the downtown convention center which boasts over 6000 hotel rooms.

John Portman's hotel also revolutionized ideas of urban planning. At about the time

when James O'Connor wrote *The Fiscal Crisis of the State* (New York: St. Martin's Press, 1973) and federal support for urban renewal began to dwindle, Portman—one of the country's most successful architect-developers—took matters into his own hands as a self-styled urban visionary. His 1976 manifesto, written with New York City Architectural League President, Jonathan Barnett, entitled "The Architect as Developer," deals with the failures of the city planning of the 1950s and 1960s, which razed whole areas of cities and put nothing in their place. Here Portman envisaged a new persona for the architect as much as for the developer, one that went back to the 18th-century entrepreneur-builders, against the current tendency for over-specialization and autonomy of architecture. Portman's vision demanded a more spatially and technically expert entrepreneur. It was a powerful image that had a tremendous

impact on the practice of the profession during the 1980s.

The idea behind the hotel was, in his words, "to open the dense, congested city center, adding public space while providing an environment to evoke and enhance positive human reactions. The building was 'exploded,' freeing the core of the building and evolving a huge atrium space. This space allowed natural light, trees, water and the feeling of an outdoor piazza into the interior." As in the case of Portman's ideas about the architectural professional, which reach back to the 19th century, this glorification of the centralized atrium space goes back to both commercial and hotel buildings of Victorian times, the Second Empire and the American Gilded Age. Portman's re-invention, however, was based on the most up-to-date technology and an understanding of the most current lifestyle dreams and aspirations of a certain section

(Left) Interior view

(Below) Exterior view

(Bottom) Longitudinal section

© Portman

© Portman

of the urban population of the great North American cities.

A measure of the success of Portman's vision, the Peachtree Center has grown around the initial core of the Hyatt Hotel over a thirty-year period into a 13-block complex which includes three of his hotels: the Hyatt Regency, the Westin Peachtree Plaza (1976), and the Marriott Marquis (1985). The complex also includes 8 office towers, including One Peachtree Center Tower (1992), a retail Mall, and the Atlanta Market Center.

Without doubt, Portman has been not only a visionary practitioner, but also a form-giver. He was an inventor of a new building type, as well as of a new way of living, and has been widely imitated over the last twenty-five years. These buildings have been very successful. And the paradox of their success is that they responded to a deep need against which they ultimately turned. The irresistible attraction of the atrium space was that in the midst of a hostile, anomic city, it offered the alternative of a protected concourse. Given its fundamental programmatic definition, however, it fell short of providing a place for a genuine community. As much as Portman's buildings have been successful on their own, they still stand as evidence of the tendency of our time to produce a highly polarized environment nurturing corrosive contrast.

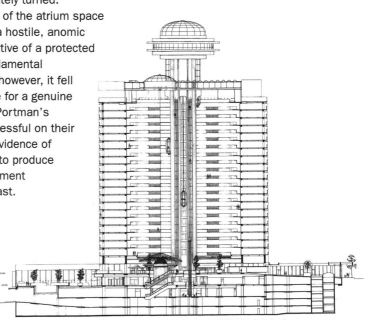

LONGITUDINAL SECTION

Moshe Safdie and Associates
HABITAT
Montreal, Quebec
1964–67

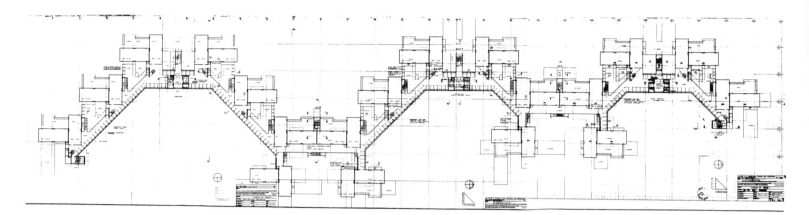

(Above) Site plan

(Right) Section

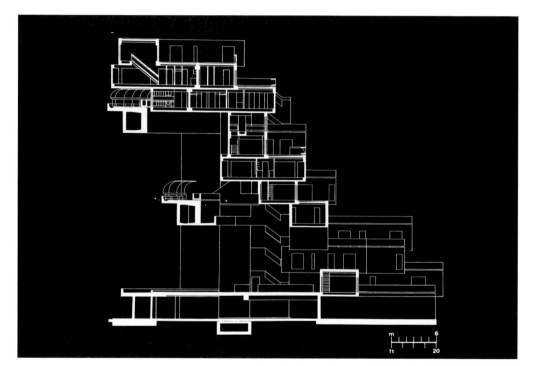

Habitat was a key theme of Montreal's 1967 Exposition, a pressing issue for many national and international organizations around the globe. Habitat, the modular 158-unit apartment building complex designed by Moshe Safdie, was the prototypical housing showcased at the 1967 Exposition. The original idea was conceived by Safdie as his thesis project. Reyner Banham (*Architectural Forum*, July–August 1971) referred to it as "the final year thesis that got built." It was intended as a response to the needs, aspirations, and potentials for solving the world's settlement problem. If a monument in our time, in the sense that the tower of Eiffel is a monument, is a structure that succeeds in incorporating in a memorable

image the said fundamental needs, aspirations, and perceived potentials of a people at a given place and moment, then the three-dimensional space structure of the Habitat deserves that title. It captured the zeitgeist of the mid-1960s, a time still shaken by the Kennedy assassination and the destruction of the Vietnam war, but dominated by an affluent middle-class culture, still free of major crime, still unconcerned about ecological issues, still growing economically, and still believing in the ability of technology to solve social problems.

Three governments financed Habitat. The federal government contributed 50 percent, with the rest provided by the Province of

Quebec and the City of Montreal. The scheme is an experimental system proposing new ways of structuring, constructing, and servicing habitable space, applying mass-scale prefabrication to housing, by aggregating apartment units into a collective whole, and shaping this aggregate into the form of a sustainable community. Habitat challenged "the system at the level of industry, the practice of labor, the by-laws, and the state of the building art of the time." (Safdie, *Beyond Habitat*, p. 102.)

The architect expected that assembly-line techniques would provide savings to pay for more amenities for the inhabitants. He was even more optimistic that this approach would contribute to solving shelter shortages

© Graetz

View of the harbour from Habitat

around the globe. To explore such possibilities, Safdie, after designing Habitat, traveled to the Soviet Union (*Progressive Architecture*, October 1966) to examine industrialized techniques for housing.

Being only a prototype, the building of the Habitat far exceeded the cost of a mass-produced artifact exploiting economies of scale. The cost of what was built for the Expo—which was only a portion of the initially planned 1000 apartment units, the number chosen to guarantee a minimum viable housing cluster—was estimated at Canadian $42,000,000. The general contractor signed for the built part, which contains much of the essence of the original concept, but it was scaled down to only 158 units, a $10,500,000 (US $7,000,000) contract. The final cost was US $22,000,000. It is interesting to note (see the *New York Times*, June 3, 1986) that the project was sold, almost twenty years after its completion, to a limited partnership formed by the tenants for Canadian $11,400,000 (US $8,100,000). The price was much lower than the initial cost, but the Canadian

Government was happy to escape from what it perceived to be a financial albatross, "a combination of rent controls and government-wide anti-inflation measures (which) had the effect of allowing rents to slip as much as 50 percent below market." (ibid.) However, the project has not been a bad investment for society: beyond its cultural value, as an experiment for a problem that still remains unsolved, it has supplied important knowledge.

Each unit of the 10-story project—a mechanical plant and vehicular access form an additional sub-level—is comprised of one, two, and three prefabricated modules, measuring 17½ feet by 10½ feet. Each inhabitable unit was at the same time a structural unit. A sub-floor for each unit contains most mechanical services. The module was mass-produced in a temporary on-site factory. It took two days to produce one load-bearing unit including floor and walls. The pre-cast modules were lifted and placed by rail-riding derricks. Prefabricated bathrooms and kitchens were dropped into place.

The units are clustered around independent elevator and stair shafts. There are three such clusters, each with their own garden entrance. They are connected by horizontal shafts and interior streets. The streets are covered by sheets of curved acrylic. For each unit, including the smallest at 600 square feet, there is a private terrace provided by part of the roof of the unit below. The drainage for the roofs is internal to the unit. In a post-Kahnian way, the main distribution trunks for the various mechanical systems, elevator shafts, and pedestrian walkways are integrated with large horizontal and vertical structural components. For this intriguing structural organization, the engineer was August Komendant, the technological colleague of Louis Kahn.

Habitat was intended as "an alternative to suburban housing" (Safdie, *Beyond Habitat*, p. 118), as well as a reaction to the oppressive conditions of the existing urban housing in the advanced industrial countries. Like Le Corbusier's proposals, it was a radical, technology-based alternative which, at the same time, was created out of Mediterranean precedents, one reminiscent of "Aegean hill villages and the Arab towns." These precedents are intriguing, not as historicist, formalist nostalgia, but as "generic" "building systems" (ibid.). Their structure of repetitive components was designed to offer high-density arrangements with efficiency benefits, combined with the possibilities of a sophisticated urban life. But, more significantly, inherent in the system of the compact network of units "grouped along alleys and streets," was its ability to support the community.

(Left) View of the facade

(Below left) Construction axonometric and details

(Below) View of the back of the building

(Bottom) Terrace

© Safdie

© Timothy Hursley

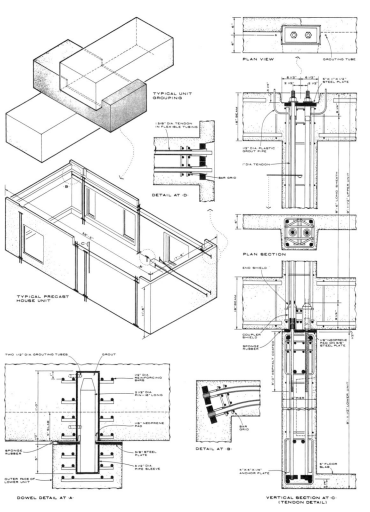

TYPICAL UNIT GROUPING

DETAIL AT ·D·

TYPICAL PRECAST HOUSE UNIT

PLAN VIEW

PLAN SECTION

DOWEL DETAIL AT ·A·

DETAIL AT ·B·

VERTICAL SECTION AT ·C· (TENDON DETAIL)

(Top) Aerial view

(Left) View from the Saint Lawrence River

(Above) Close-up

Affleck, Desbarats, Dimakopoulos, Lebensold, Sise
PLACE BONAVENTURE
Montreal, Quebec
1964–67

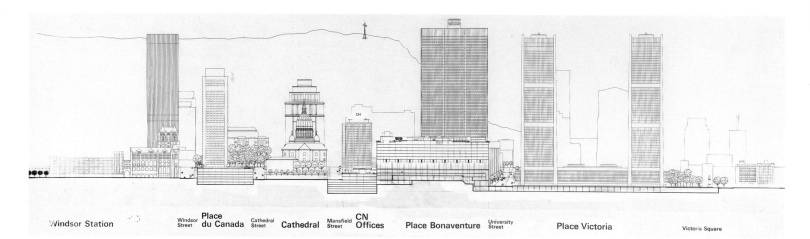

Windsor Station — Windsor Street — Place du Canada — Cathedral Street — Cathedral — Mansfield Street — CN Offices — Place Bonaventure — University Street — Place Victoria — Victoria Square

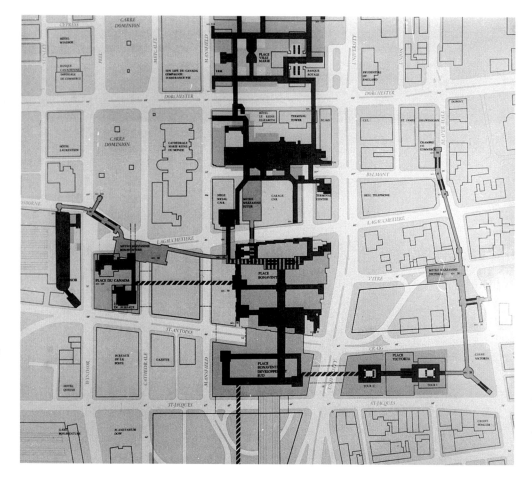

**(Top) Project shown against the
Montreal skyline**

**(Above) Downtown Montreal
underground linkages**

Place Bonaventure was designed to cover a 6-acre site located along the railroad tracks on the edge of downtown Montreal. To the west of the building was an abandoned lot not far from the printing press of a local newspaper. To its front was the back of the Queen Elizabeth Hotel, an ungainly bulk harkening back to the early 1950s. To the east was a 6-lane offshoot of the Trans-Canada autoroute. And, to the south, was a lower lying zone, scattered with abandoned, early 20th-century industrial sheds built to accommodate the neighboring, once bustling, harbor area of Old Montreal. Just beyond this area on the Saint-Lawrence River, rose a series of immense grain silos of the Five Roses Flour Mills.

At a time when most downtown buildings in North America were designed for a single use, Place Bonaventure broke new ground by combining a shopping concourse with convention and exhibition facilities, a merchandise mart, offices, a hotel, and a winter garden. In addition, this multipurpose urban complex combined one million square feet of a wholesale merchandising market; approximately 400,000 square feet of retail shopping; an exhibition/convention hall of approximately 6 acres; 100,000 square feet of office space; and underground parking for 1100 cars.

Among the most vaunted of the building's amenities was the rooftop hotel and garden, accommodating 400 rooms and a 5-acre landscaped garden, reached via express elevator. Hotel rooms look inward over the gardens designed by Sasaki, Dawson, and

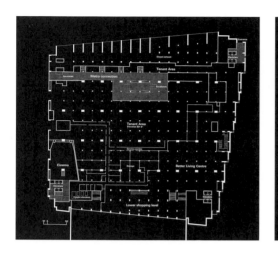

(Above) Underground level: shopping,
cinema, connection to the metro

(Above center) Top floor, hotel level

(Above right) Shopping concourse level

(Right) View looking north

De May, conceived as a Canadian setting with moving water, lakes, streams, and waterfalls, with deciduous and coniferous trees, shrubs, and rock formations. These spaces have an outdoor swimming pool, heated in the winter, where guests can swim even during the frequent snow falls in below-zero temperatures that beset the city. Certainly, this is a utopian extravaganza realized for the very lucky few. Pursuing, however, this utopian vision, one might project through it a new mixed-use building type whose very top would be devoted to housing, and whose characteristics would display not the traditional stellar isolation of

the skyscraper, but a much more down-to-earth urban quality like the one achieved by the Bonaventure Hotel complex.

The building is different from most multi-use buildings in that it forms an integral part of the city life in the surrounding highly public realm of downtown Montreal. The reasons for this success are the numerous connections to transportation networks—public and private, vehicular and pedestrian. The building sits on top of a major transportation network, including the extensive underground walkways linking Place Ville Marie, Queen Elizabeth Hotel, Canadian National Headquarters, and Central Station for rail

transportation and the subway system. Thousands of people pass through the building every day, by foot, rail, road, and metro.

The building has been criticized for its roughly hewn, elephantine, exposed-concrete megastructure image, its dwarfing scale, and its aggressive attitude towards the city. True, the surroundings, although so close to downtown Montreal, were more of an edge condition rather than a city center. True, Montreal, because of the severity of its climate, is less conducive to street life than to inward, galleria activities. But without doubt, the building made no effort to appear

(Right) Section

(Below) Roof garden

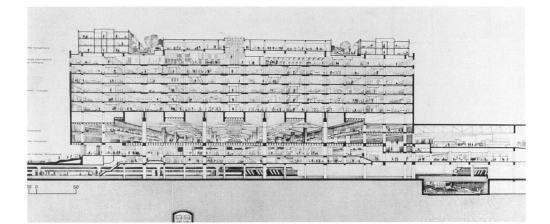

© Michael Drummond

anything more than a large warehouse. Contextually, on the other hand, it is not in conflict with other structures across the river (left behind by the old harbor), which are being conserved as part of the city's heritage. From this point of view, the complex emerges as a bridge between these paleo-technic memories and the much more civic life of the present.

Place Bonaventure has been one of the most successful urban projects of the past thirty years, characteristic of the dynamism and urbanistic aspirations of Montreal and of North America in the 1960s. More than this, it remains an urbane building type fit for the complexities of our time. Affleck and his associates were lucky to have the support of their clients to realize their vision. Affleck said: "I have always been particularly interested in the social aspects of architecture, which, in my opinion, revolve around the sharing of space between a variety of people who are, in effect, in touch with each other through sharing the same space. This is one space shared daily by thousands of people who come here to work, shop, meet, visit, or merely pass through."

(Left) Roof garden

(Below) Facade detail

© Drummond

© Michel Proulx

Kallmann McKinnell & Knowles
BOSTON CITY HALL
Boston, Massachusetts
1962–68

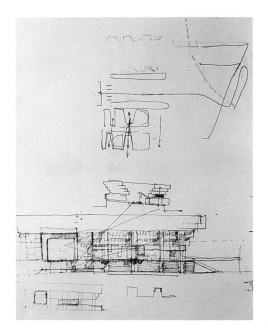

(Above) Concept sketch

(Right) Section

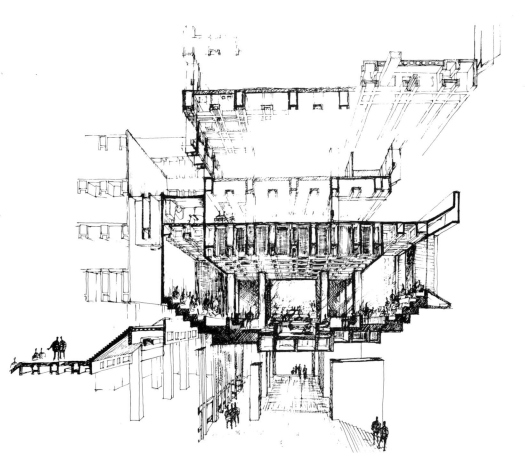

The Boston City Hall is a rare case in America of a major public building resulting from a national competition. The site is in the heart of historical Boston. At the time of the competition, it was part of the Government Center urban renewal area, planned for the Boston Redevelopment Authority by I. M. Pei & Associates. The aim of the plan was to reorganize existing financial, administrative, and residential activities, as well as to rejuvenate the declining commercial neighborhoods of Scollay and Dock Squares.

Following the ideas of the period, the decay of the area was seen as having been caused by the antiquated fabric of the city; thus, renewal was conceived mainly as opening up new ground for new buildings to come. The plan drew extreme criticism for ignoring the pre-existing fabric and, as a result, destroying the social associations on which it depended. It was a key target in Jane Jacobs's first book, *The Death and Life of Great American Cities* (New York: Random House, 1961). Yet the existence of such a

master plan, especially in the North American context, was not altogether negative. Due to the plan, which was rare at such a large scale in the U.S. at that time, the new City Hall could find a well-structured spatial context in which to fit.

The scheme provided, according to the brief, for a plaza, for "the active participation and involvement of Bostonians in the function of the city ... dignified and serious ... in a democracy vital and involving everybody." Recreation activities were to take a secondary place. In its clear geometrical pattern of radiating brick-paved planes divided by strips of granite, the Plaza has the character of an outdoor room "of noble and civic proportions" strongly reminiscent of Italian public places.

However, due to the lack of a genuine historical background and collective memories and tradition of rituals, the space is perceived as too distant by the average citizen, in comparison to the Italian precedents it resembles. A stronger

integration with cultural and commercial activities, at the programmatic level, could, perhaps, have helped make a more familiar, friendlier public place, without placing the goal to create a "civic and monumental" outdoor room for Boston at risk. The same, multi-functional integration program for the building would have enabled it to "serve" better as a genuine "concourse for the city."

In addition, the square was treated more as a symbolic and visual object than as a place to be used for civic meeting and discussion. Finally, introducing design elements that enhanced the environmental quality of the area, as James Marston Fitch remarked (*Architectural Review*, 1970), would not necessarily have excluded poetic and monumental aspects. But all this would have required a different approach to the plan of the urban condition as well as a different building program.

Within the confines of the program, Kallmann decided to apply his principles of "Action Architecture" as a means of providing

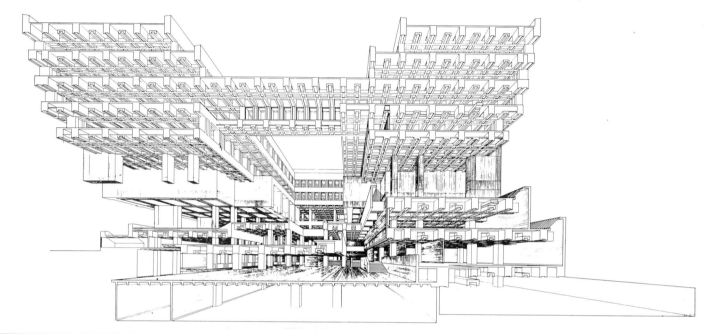

© Vanderwarker

(Left) Interior

(Below) Site plan

a public building beyond the confines of the New Monumentality approach of the previous decade (*Architectural Forum*, October 1959). In this article, Kallmann argued for an architecture emerging out of process and improvisation, very much along the lines of John Johansen's kinetic architecture. Contrary to the Mummers Theater (1964–70, pp. 138–41), however, Boston City Hall's spatial *ad hoc* happenings are subjugated within a strict compositional frame, an overall classical taxis. Despite many irregular or serial spatial patterns occurring within the building, its tripartite division of base, middle body, and cornice-capital, is dominant. So is the accentuated termination of the composition at the corners and at the top, and, certainly, the consistency of the superimposed rhythmic patterns.

This syncretist approach between classical and anti-classical systems was achieved with some help from recent precedents—in particular, Le Corbusier's La Tourette, as was noted at the time. But the scheme has an

original esthetic as well as a functional solution.

The building houses suites for the mayor and the city council and 30 municipal departments. It is divided into three zones: a lower level which contains offices that serve the public frequently; a middle level with the formal public spaces; and the less frequently visited departments located in the rectangular crown of offices above. The sequence of interior spaces conforms more to a drama of scale and light, rather than to practical constraints of accessibility. Special theatrical effects are also reflected in the choice of materials: polished metal, bronze paneling, African mahogany, concrete, and brick.

A year after its completion, the AIA granted the project an Honor Award, which stressed the fact that it achieved "its civic purpose not by size nor by height, but by its rich, expressive form." Yet the vision of civic purpose and expressive form was to a great extent nostalgic and literal, rather than actual

Back of the building

© Kallman, McKinnell & Knowles

and real. Sibyl Moholy-Nagy wrote that "the eclecticism of the project was characterised by an austerity not to be found in the orgiastic citationism of many architects since then. Still a building aspiring to communicate the actuality of democracy in our time finds a pathetic servant in mobilizing nostalgia." (*Forum*, January–February 1969.)

At the moment of its completion, the City Hall stood not only as a unique example of excellence in a public building in North America, but also as a voice of protest against what Ada Louise Huxtable called, in her review of the project in the *New York Times* (February 8, 1968), the "values of cheapness over quality as a form of public virtue."

After more than twenty-five years, the building's image as the center of Boston's municipal government plays a key role in making the cognitive map of the city more legible and more memorable, surviving the assault of urban renewal that preceded it. The Boston Society of Architects nominated it for the AIA's Twenty-Five Year Award, citing its presence as "a continually instructive symbol of a community and one of this country's most successful architectural expressions of the democratic ideal."

Kevin Roche John Dinkeloo and Associates
OAKLAND MUSEUM
Oakland, California
1961–68

(Below) Site plan

(Bottom) Section of the entire project

The competition brief for the City of Oakland's new civic museum complex was for three separate buildings: an art museum, a natural history museum, and a cultural museum. The winning scheme, designed by Kevin Roche, was of a unified structure that combined architecture and urban landscape in an important civic park space.

The project was also viewed by the city leaders as part of a revitalization of the downtown. The new Oakland Museum was to be not just a museum of the history, culture, and environment of California, but a civic meeting place and cultural center for the residents of the city. Consequently, it was to be designed for the comfort, convenience, and psychological needs of the museum-goer.

The building, which is mostly underground, occupies four blocks, and is conceived as a walled garden with large welcoming entrances. The galleries are arranged so that the roof of one space becomes the terrace of another. A pedestrian street connects the different levels and the other functions—namely, auditorium, classroom, galleries for temporary exhibits, a restaurant, offices, and a parking garage. Each area opens directly on to lawns, terraces, trellised passages, and broad flights of stairs. The entire museum is built of a light-colored concrete with a sand-blasted finish.

Integral to the design of the museum is the extensive landscaping by Dan Kiley. The intention behind it was to introduce plants of varying textures and growing habits throughout the garden, where they would complement and soften the rigid geometry of the structure. The 38,000 trees, shrubs, and vines include native and exotic species, and a special artificial soil and irrigation system that was developed to reduce the weight of the planter boxes on the roof terraces. Since the building was completed, the landscaping has grown over the entire building, gradually submerging its form and creating a lush, colorful garden.

The building is widely used by visitors and by locals as an escape from downtown activity. Classrooms and special programs for children ensure that the site is constantly animated, and the wide walls that surround the planting are just the right height for them to sit on. This is a bold re-interpretation of the idea of the museum. It offers not only a place in which to contemplate nature, history, and art, but provides a rich social experience for its community.

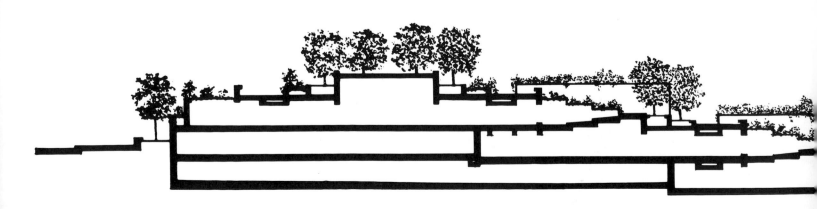

View of the complex

© Roche Dinkeloo

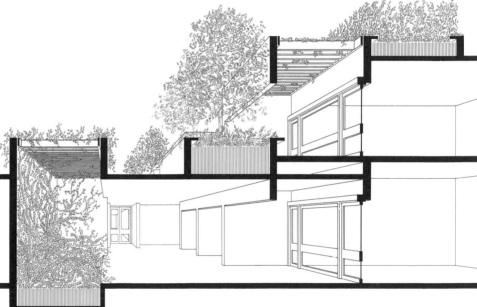

(Right) Section

(Below) Aerial view

Kevin Roche John Dinkeloo and Associates
FORD FOUNDATION
New York City, New York
1963–68

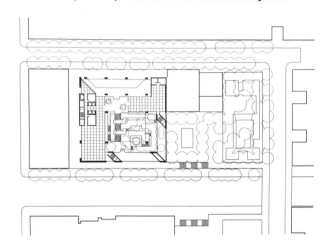

(Below left) Ground floor

(Below) Site plan

(Bottom) Park inside the urban workplace

© Roche Dinkeloo

Unlike conventional New York office buildings, which isolate the occupants and store them in cubicles, depriving them of a sense of their working community, and limiting their physical environment to views of other similarly stored inhabitants, the Ford Foundation creates a unique environment for its occupants—a space that allows members of the Foundation staff to be aware of each other, to share common aims and purposes, and that assists them in fostering a sense of a working family.

To achieve this environment, the architects deliberately avoided a high-rise tower. The building is as low as possible and conscientiously observes the lines and planes created by other buildings on the surrounding streets. The scale of the project shifts on 42nd Street, where it terminates the thrust of that street, the volume appearing large, while on the more residential 43rd Street, the scale is more modest. Roche considered the building as a dividing line between its commercial and residential neighbors, and given the special nature of the work carried out by the operation of the Ford Foundation, decided that this should not be an office building, but a new type of work environment, one that connects workers not only to the larger organization, but to the city as well.

The plan is *C*-shaped, which serves both to shelter and provide a view out to the parks and river beyond. By enclosing the roof and the open portion of the *C* with glass, a large garden court was created—a park intended for staff and public alike—with trees and shrubs and flowering plants, a place to enjoy greenery, even in winter. Each office has a sliding door opening into this park, which further enhances the atmosphere of the offices, and creates a sense of wellbeing. And unlike its contemporary, the inward-looking atrium lobbies of John Portman's hotels (see, for example, the Hyatt Regency Atlanta, 1964–67, pp. 114–15), the Ford Foundation looks out through the greenery across the city.

One innovation in this building is the use of the 6-foot modular grid. The standard module in American offices before this had been a 4-foot grid, or half the dimension of what was considered to be the minimum

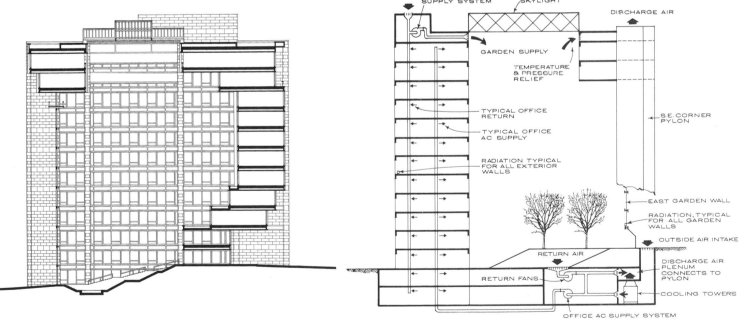

office space for one person. But in this uniquely structured work environment, where people of unusually high academic caliber and their staff direct the 14 national and international programs of the Foundation, the increased modular grid translates into larger windows and column breadth.

Given the economic realities in New York City, it is unlikely that any corporation would contribute such an architectural gift to the city today. Only a non-profit organization such as the Ford Foundation could conceive of a totally new concept for the work environment, and create a building 12 stories high with nearly a third of an acre as park.

The Ford Foundation was an extremely innovative building type, influencing the development of "atrium" projects in Manhattan and all over the world.

(Top) Street view

(Above left) Section of the offices

(Above) Section of the garden atrium

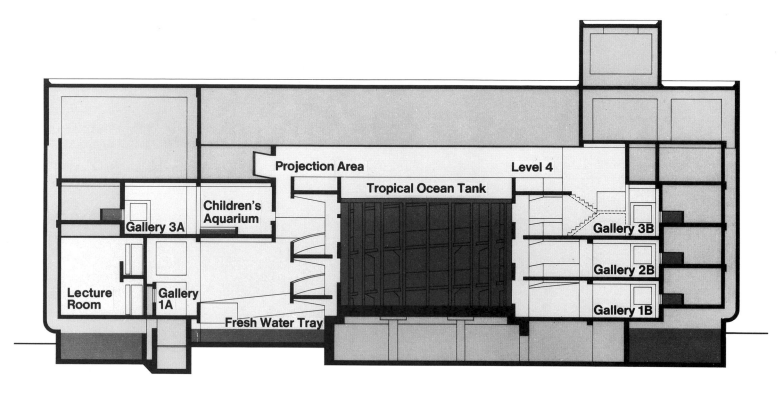

Section

Cambridge Seven Associates is that rare phenomenon in American architecture: a true collaboration. When the seven partners founded the firm in 1962, they were determined not to limit themselves just to the design of buildings. From this early collaboration of architects, graphic designers, film makers, and exhibition designers, grew a company that became best associated with two building types: aquariums and subway stations. In both of these they exceled in the design of the movement of people through spaces with a maximum of visual stimulation and interest. Their first project, the New England Aquarium, established their virtuosity in not only building and graphic design, but also in using architecture as an instrument of urban revitalization. This pattern was followed in their design for the National Aquarium in Baltimore, and a large sequence of international projects.

When the program for a new Boston aquarium was first proposed, the executive director, Donald M. DeHart, wanted to exhibit in addition to fish, "the world of water ... as it relates to our communities in the areas of health, recreation, aquaculture, industry, and commerce, since man's proper utilization of

water is crucial to his survival on this planet." (*Progressive Architecture*, December 1969.) The ingenious solution of the architects was to design a 5-level Giant Ocean Tank which was a free-standing cylinder in the center of the building, 40 feet in diameter and 4 stories high. Its 200,000 gallons of salt water teemed with sharks, sea turtles, stingrays, and other marine animals. Surrounding the base of this tank was a rectangular basin of water, the so-called Fresh Water Tray. It contained 150,000 gallons of fresh water and housed live toads and frogs, wading birds, and lizards, along with many species of fish.

The circulation depended on two sets of ramps, one for people moving upwards, following the perimeter of the museum's walls, and one for the descending flow of visitors, spiraling down the central Giant Ocean Tank. In the terms of one of the architects (Peter Chermayeff), the idea arose by merging a Le Corbusier scheme with Frank Lloyd Wright's Guggenheim, then "filling the center space of the Guggenheim with water." (*Progressive Architecture*, December 1969.) These ramps, according to the architects, minimized the distance of the viewer from the exhibits, and the double circulation route

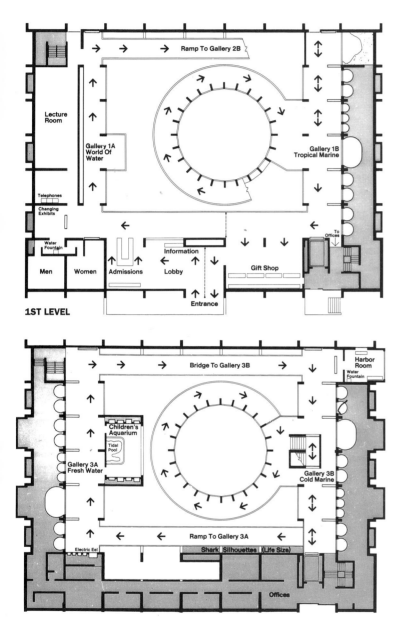

1ST LEVEL

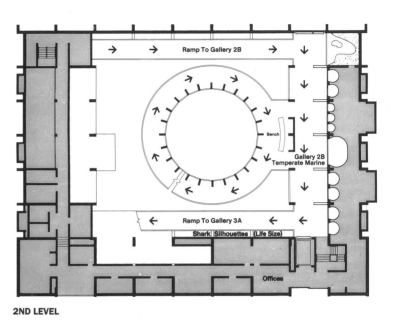

2ND LEVEL

3RD LEVEL

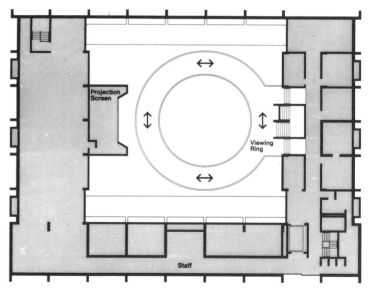

4TH LEVEL

provided for constantly changing views, allowing the visitor an experience of the undersea world from both near and far, and from above and below.

Another major innovation in the aquarium was the use of multimedia graphics, a strategy further developed in the design for the U.S. Pavilion at Expo 67 in Montreal (1964–67, pp. 110–13). Throughout the aquarium, large-scale graphics, including a mural, 20 x 45 feet, of black silhouetted sharks on a blue ground, illuminated by

blacklight, are as much a part of the show as the inhabitants of the tanks themselves. Among the elements exhibited across the circulation path, is a yellow submarine floating in space. Projected over a blue neon wave outline against a cork wall, it is a direct allusion to the ecologically conscious spirit of The Beatles song.

The aquarium interior is a total underwater environment, with no natural daylight, but a combination of undulating neon and blacklight that provides the ambience

of a deep-sea world. The architects have compared this to being in some ways analogous to European churches, where the structure, space, lighting, and works of art all combine to create a special atmosphere or mood. With crowds of over 6000 visitors per day, many of whom are school children, it is less an atmosphere of religious introspection, than of great exuberance and enjoyment, a destination for busloads of young pilgrims, celebrating the natural environment of their New England heritage.

(Left) Spiral ramp

(Below) Section

(Opposite) Inside view

© Cambridge Seven

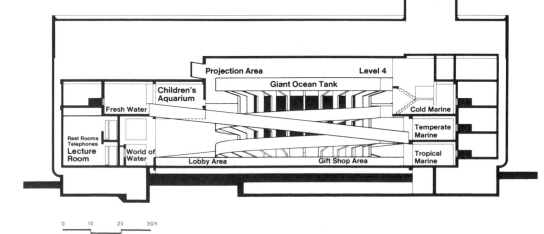

Projection Area   Level 4

Giant Ocean Tank

Children's
Aquarium

Fresh Water   Cold Marine

Temperate
Marine

Rest Rooms
Telephones
Lecture
Room   World of
Water   Lobby Area   Gift Shop Area   Tropical
Marine

0   10   20   30 ft

© Cambridge Seven

Paolo Soleri
ARCOSANTI
Cordes Junction, Arizona
1970–

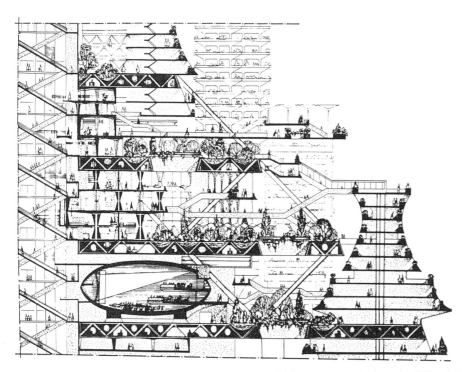

© Arcosanti

(Above) Section

(Above right) View from the top of the building

Rising against the basalt cliffs of the north Arizona desert, a prototype community emerged in the 1970s that was to combine compact urban structure with large-scale solar greenhouses on 15 acres of a 4000-acre preserve. The project is the lifetime work of Paolo Soleri, an Italian-born architect who had worked with Frank Lloyd Wright at Taliesin West in the 1940s.

Following his work with Wright, Soleri returned to Italy in 1950, where he was commissioned to build a large ceramics factory, Ceramica Artistica Solimene. The processes with which he became familiar in the ceramics industry led to his award-winning designs of ceramic and bronze windbells and for over 30 years, the proceeds from these windbells have provided the funds which allowed him to test his theories of architecture and urban design work.

Arcosanti is Soleri's prototype town for 5000 inhabitants. Phase 1 (representing only 3 percent of the projected town) is the habitat developed in the first twenty years of work on the site. Located at Cordes Junction, in central Arizona, the project is based on Soleri's concept of "Arcology," which he defines as architecture coherent with ecology. Arcology advocates cities designed to maximize the accessibility associated with the urban environment; minimize the use of energy, raw materials, and land, reducing waste and environmental pollution; and allow interaction with the surrounding natural environment.

The site is the side of a mesa in the high desert. The buildings command a view of the canyon to the south and mountain ranges far to the west. The irony of designing a dense urban structure in the middle of the desert is not lost on Soleri, who feels that it is only in the isolation from the profit pressures of land developers that he has the space and freedom to try out his concepts. A similar rationale is articulated by Pliny Fisk in developing his Laredo Farm in south Texas (1987–, pp. 240–41).

The completed structures of Phase 1 include two enormous vaults incorporating residences; two large apses housing a bronze art foundry, a ceramics facility, studios and residences, a multi-use structure which includes a gallery, bakery, cafe, and residential units, administrative offices; conference and lecture rooms; design studios and workshops; an amphitheater, music studios, and performance space; a swimming pool and guest rooms. Soleri's grand vision is for this desert oasis to become ultimately a mixed-use, 24-hour city.

© Arcosanti

As Sibyl Moholy-Nagy writes in her early critique of Soleri's work (*Forum*, May 1970), none of this is very original in the context of the utopian megacity that started after World War II. The Archigram Group, Plug-In City, or the much more detailed propositions of the Urbanisme Volumetrique of architects R. Anger and M. Heymann, also proposed high-density, technological environments. But as she notes, several principles separate Soleri's work from these predecessors, and none more strongly in his insistence that his arcologies be completely separated from the old urban centers. This emphasis is on esthetics, not technology, and the basis for his community is not economic, but philosophical—a biological humanism reminiscent of Wright's Broadacre City.

Ultimately, Soleri's ideas may be more influential not as a model for how to build cities, but as a reminder for us of the need to confront the consequences of low-density, high impact cities, which are the norm across the southwestern United States, from Houston to Los Angeles. The broad following of Soleri disciples in the 1970s—when Arcosanti was a popular destination for those pursuing alternative lifestyles—were often searching for alternatives to the perceived and real failures of the urban renewal projects of the 1960s. Ironically, Soleri is better known today for his wind chimes and bells, which hang from redwood decks and balconies throughout the West, than for his pioneering ideas that architecture and ecology are inseparably linked.

View from the ground

Johansen and Bhavnani
MUMMERS THEATER
Oklahoma City, Oklahoma
1964–70

Architect's drawing

No other building of the 1960s expressed more demonstrably the idea of action and movement as the Mummers Theater by John Johansen. The components of the building resemble construction cranes with mega-gadget parts, arrested momentarily mid-course in a complicated operation of transporting or erecting a futuristic structure.

The Mummers Theater represented a total break with the traditional, conservative architecture of Oklahoma City, or the more recent efforts of the early 1960s in that city to revitalize the downtown area by imposing what Peter Blake, in *Architectural Forum* (March 1971), called a "neo-Yamasaki," "New Monumentality" complex of buildings, whose "smashing vistas to nowhere" emerged alien to and alienated from the authentic life of the city. As an alternative, Johansen wanted to bring a new vitality drawn from "humble or crude and vulgar utilitarian" artifacts.

In order to express this vitality in architectural terms, Johansen proceeded to identify the parts of the building involving circulation, then to assemble them in the same informal manner in which machines are put together, without any rules of composition. Johansen called the new esthetics "Kinetics." Responding to a deep "fascination with movement," it was meant to replace not only any classical

compositional frame confining the building to a hierarchical structure, but also the very basic idea of spatial well-formedness as a design principle. Like the avant-garde theater productions the complex housed, prominence was given to action and improvisation rather than to space and order: "Kinetics is here to perform greater service, and to delight in."

A sense of virtual movement was achieved by conceiving the building in terms of its "individual parts," "enclosures, generalized or specific, to accommodate function," and then "connecting," "supporting," and "placing" all the parts without the guidance of any regulatory geometry. As one can see from the theater complex, the apparently chaotic result of assembled "containers," "supports," and "connectors" implies tension and movement. Johansen would have been even more content if the parts had really been moving, like cable cars and exposed elevator cars, and not "by illusion, as in the baroque period."

Johansen's "Kinetics" was a set of simple rules to avoid the straitjacket of spatial order, which—as with Picturesque garden design rules that generate infinite variety—lead, paradoxically, to a coherent whole, that of topology rather than shape and size. It was also a system that could easily accommodate functional needs, as one can see from the project itself. The building

© Balthazar Korab

(Above) Aerial view

(Right) Concept drawing

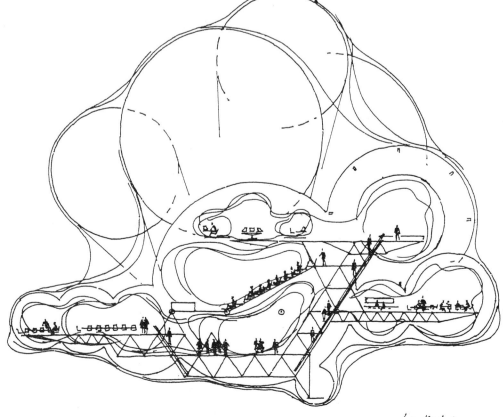

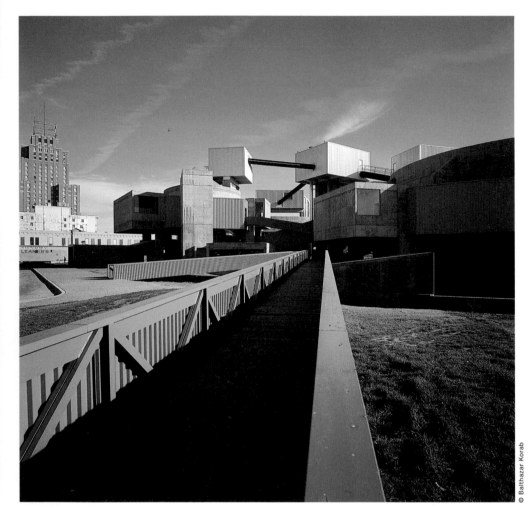

contained a thrust-stage theater, an arena theater, and a rehearsal hall, all located on the same level. At the level below was the entrance and the lobby. All mechanical equipment was on a level above the theaters and outside the building enclosure. Johansen believed that this was an efficient and direct way to keep their noise out. The administrative services, the offices, the storage, some mechanical systems, and the dressing areas were placed in the basement, and were lit by skylights.

Kinetics, however, had very little to contribute in helping the building integrate into an existing fabric. The action the building represented recalled the heroic, lone, frontier settler, rather than the disciplined, institutionalized, urbanized citizen.

The chaos out of architecture Johansen created in the Mummers Theater is an optimistic celebration of the joy of action and the freedom technology can offer in transcending bureaucratic, institutionalized bounds—the same studied improvisation as in the jazz and Action-Painting of the time. This optimism is what makes the building, despite superficial similarities, have very little in common with the more recent deconstructive chaotism.

© Balthazar Korab

(Above) Approach to the "facade" of the complex

(Right) Ground plan

(Opposite) Detail

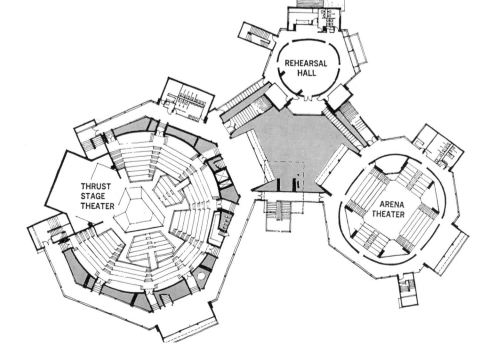

© Balthazar Korab

Eisenman Architects
HOUSE II
Hardwick, Vermont
1969–71

© Norman McGrath

(Left) Facade

(Below left) Axonometric study

(Below) Axonometric study

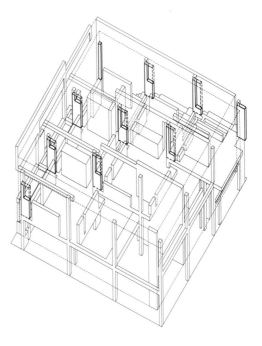

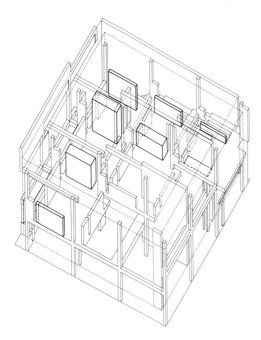

House II, a second house for an academic couple, was designed and built at the ebb of a number of radical tendencies that shook established ideas and practices of architecture, not only in America, but also in Europe and Japan. These were, on the one hand, movements that were highly politicized, and, on the other, sharply science-oriented, particularly towards the behavioral sciences. In both approaches, traditional questions about formal, spatial aspects of architecture were disregarded.

Eisenman's work, together with that of the other members of the so-called New York Five group, provided a polemic alternative to fill in the gap as these radical fronts receded. Central to this group, as Mario Gandelsonas remarked (*Progressive Architecture*, March 1972), was the idea that buildings are objects to "read" rather than to use. The accent was on form and space as generators of "discourse," whose rules were purely formal or "autonomous." House II demonstrates this new direction in a most extreme and forceful manner.

The architect describes the project brief as "an attempt to simulate the presence of trees and hedges which were non-existent on the barren hilltop, through the use of a sequence of columns and walls," and the "transition from the extroverted summer life to the introverted security of the winter fireplace." This description of contextual elements is curious, in that a close examination of the design—or any of the architect's numerous writings from this period— shows very little related to either context or program.

The house appears to be an intricate spatial configuration resulting from a number of formal operations on geometrical elements, devoid of any external reference, to function or to cite. The idea is reminiscent of the grammatical syntactic operations of Chomskean linguistics, which take place independently of a pragmatic context. This analogy, and it is only an analogy, was used profusely by Eisenman, only to be later abandoned.

(Below) Axonometric study

(Right) Back of the building

(Below right) Axonometric study

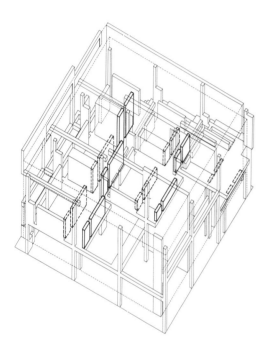

© Norman McGrath

In House II, the "spatial system," he remarked, "provide(s) for a continuing and countermanding dialectic." The elements used are the column and the wall, but they constitute basic shape-objects to relate to space-constraining systems, such as grids and planes, to be organized by elementary design operations, such as "shifting square volumes along a diagonal given line," while ignoring function, construction technology, symbolism, and iconographic value.

Clearly the results are so abstract that one has the impression that the house has nothing to do with a real building. "Cardboard architecture," said Eisenman, "is not a pejorative term but a rather precise metaphor describing ... my work." With that he meant the exclusion of meaning in determining the shape of an artifact and the high precision and control needed for formal manipulation of architectural space.

Eisenman has argued, to justify his disregard for function and meaning in House II, that "the program of the house is known ... an infinite set of combinations for its solution in physical terms ... its importance to me is that it allows the concern for function to be reduced ... there is little polemic or new meaning available in the particular arrangement of its functions." There is a passionate, and utopian, spirit in this purposely meaningless building that seeks to identify a pure core of architecture, one insubordinate to any scientific or social norm. But there is also a failure of imagination in this contempt for program and function, a failure not of an imagination of forms, but a failure of that most humane of all human activities—what John Stuart Mill called "social imagination."

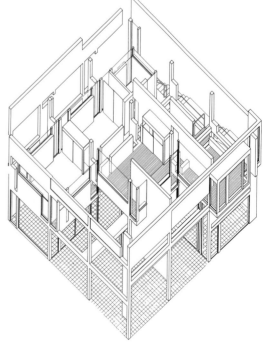

Ezra Stoller © Esto

(Far left) Facade

(Left) Elevations

Known as "Big John" to Chicago's population, the John Hancock Center is a multi-use complex, with 711 apartment units, ranging from efficiencies to 4-bedroom luxury residences, office space, and central area commercial entrance lobbies. Additional facilities include amenities such as restaurants, health clubs, swimming pool, and ice skating rink, and a transmitter for the city's major television stations. Initially two high-rises were planned for the site, a 70-story apartment and a 45-story office tower. But because the two towers would have occupied most of the site and would have impaired each other's privacy and lighting conditions, it was decided to construct a single tower where the offices would be on the lower floor and the apartments on the higher floors.

The building is a Miesian glass and steel skyscraper stretched to about double its normal height, rising 1107 feet above its plaza. In order for such a tall structure to be able to withstand the Chicago winds, it was tapered from bottom to top, then tightly braced by a reinforcing diagonal truss tube structural system. The result is a highly

articulated structural tower that provides a vertical city of work and residential environments—yet another innovative experiment in a city that is the birthplace of the high rise and the locus of so much of its evolution.

Engineered by Fazlur Khan, the structure of the John Hancock Tower consists of regularly spaced exterior columns interconnected with diagonal members. Its uniqueness and simplicity are due to the minimum number of diagonals added in the plane of the exterior columns, creating a rigid box effect. The diagonals, columns, and spandrel beams (which also act as ties) intersecting at their center line virtually eliminated moments caused by stress due to asymmetry. Also, by providing a heavy tie beam at levels where the diagonals intersect at the corner columns, the diagonal members were made to participate in accruing gravity loads and could therefore become inclined columns.

A large number of initial studies were made to select the optimum relationship between the diagonals, columns, and horizontal spandrel beams. Furthermore, in order to retain the structural integrity of the

rigid tube system, while keeping in mind the need for simple fabrication and erection, a linear slope of all the four exterior faces of the building was decided upon. The resulting solution is a 100-story building with base plan dimensions of 165 x 265 feet, narrowing to roof plan dimensions of 100 x 160 feet.

According to the designers, an optimum structural system made it structurally feasible to build a 100-story building for the equivalent cost of a normal 40-story framed structure. The successful use of this structural system was possible only because an equivalent architectural solution could be developed. Thus the project is an example of one of the most significant recent integrated efforts by architects and engineers.

In this new structural system developed for economic efficiency and optimal engineering, even the distribution of the multi-use occupants of the building was submitted to calculation. It was necessary to find not only the proper shape of the building, but also the exact number of stories to satisfy fully the original gross space requirements of this mixed-use skyscraper. Because an apartment floor plan should not have a depth of more than about 130 feet for efficient planning, and because office floor plans can have considerably larger depth, it was a logical solution to put the apartments over the office space. The end result was a building that combined structural efficiency with an urban efficiency of stacking a residential tower above an office tower. A model of efficient design in a high-density urban context, it succeeds also as a memorable image of rationality.

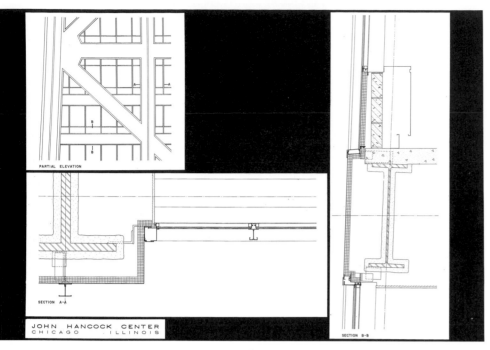

PARTIAL ELEVATION

SECTION A-A

JOHN HANCOCK CENTER
CHICAGO · ILLINOIS

SECTION B-B

(Left) Construction detail

(Below left) Section

(Below) Construction detail

(Bottom) Structural system

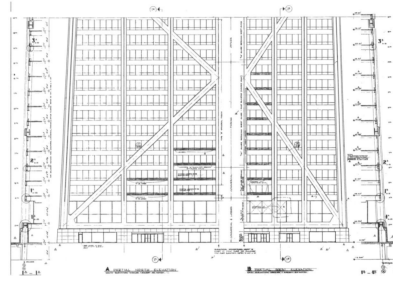

A PARTIAL NORTH ELEVATION

B PARTIAL WEST ELEVATION

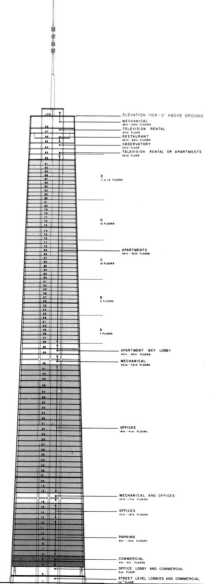

ELEVATION 1106'-5" ABOVE GROUND
MECHANICAL
98th-100th FLOORS
TELEVISION RENTAL
97th FLOOR
RESTAURANT
95th-96th FLOORS
OBSERVATORY
94th FLOOR
TELEVISION RENTAL OR APARTMENTS
93rd FLOOR

E
11 or 12 FLOORS

D
10 FLOORS

APARTMENTS
46th-92nd FLOORS

C
10 FLOORS

B
9 FLOORS

A
7 FLOORS

APARTMENT SKY LOBBY
44th-45th FLOORS
MECHANICAL
42nd-43rd FLOORS

OFFICES
18th-41st FLOORS

MECHANICAL AND OFFICES
18th-17th FLOORS
OFFICES
13th-16th FLOORS

PARKING
6th-12th FLOORS

COMMERCIAL
4th-5th FLOORS
OFFICE LOBBY AND COMMERCIAL
3rd FLOOR
STREET LEVEL LOBBIES AND COMMERCIAL
1st FLOOR

COMMERCIAL AND SERVICES
CONCOURSE FLOOR

CONCOURSE

© Ezra Stoller Esto

Gunnar Birkerts and Associates
FEDERAL RESERVE BANK OF MINNEAPOLIS
Minneapolis, Minnesota
1967–72

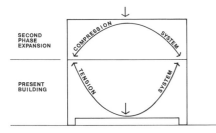

(Above) Catenary members

(Right) Plaza

The 108,000-foot-square site of the Federal Reserve Bank occupies a full city block at the end of Nicolet Mall, which was developed as a pedestrian and shuttle bus spine in the downtown core of Minneapolis. The building is conceived as two buildings in one. The first is underground and contains the bank's secure areas, vaults, and service functions.

The second houses clerical and administrative operations in a glass office block that spans the gap between two great concrete towers. This glass building is supported, like a suspension bridge, by two "catenary" members, so called because it follows the natural curve of a chain—*catena*—when hung freely between two fixed points. The curve is also echoed in the curtain wall of the facades; below the curve, the glass tips forward, and above it, tips slightly backward. The extraordinary idea of combining a bridge structure and a high-rise recalls Buckminster Fuller's Skyscraper Suspension Bridge of 1928–29.

In concept, the structure is simplicity itself. The two catenaries, one on either side of the building and 60 feet apart, support the two major facades; the top part of each facade rests on the catenary, and the bottom part hangs from it. The facades are in turn rigid frames that support the 11 floors that span between them. The tendency

of the supporting towers at either end of the building to topple inward is checked by two 28-foot trusses at the top, and the space in between them contains the mechanical equipment.

There was no precedent for the bank's structural system. No occupied floors had ever spanned 275 feet before. In order to get the necessary stiffness (much greater than that of a roof or a highway bridge), the engineers had to use the full 10-story height of the two side walls for rigid structural frames.

Several types of truss were considered, but the system that turned out to be the lightest and most economical ($47.00 per square foot) was a braced suspension system. The primary supporting members are catenaries composed of cable and welded steel plate. All floors are transferred to these catenaries, which are braced against asymmetrical loads by an 850-foot-deep truss at the roof.

This is not a structurally exhibitionist scheme whereby techniques are displayed for the sake of engineering gymnastics and muscle flexing at the expense of livability and functionality. A virtue of this unique structural system is that it allowed a potential 50 percent expansion of the office portion of the building, by adding 6 more floors to the top of the initial structure.

One result of this design was that the building has eminently flexible and pleasant work spaces, with views of the outside unhindered by interior supporting walls or cores. Unfortunately, the potential of the suspension structure to have a passage under the building is not exploited. A second result is the highly memorable shape on the urban horizon, an inverse arch. "Ask anybody in Minneapolis about the Federal Reserve Building," Charles Moore wrote. "If they draw a blank, then describe a catenary curve with your hand, and they will know what you mean." (Charles Moore and Gerald Allen, *Dimensions*, p. 61.) The suspended form, however, does not indicate in any way where the entrance to the building is, a significant point for such a major urban structure, with disorienting effects, for both the user of the building and the city at large.

Also unsuccessful was the creation of an immense, 2½-acre public plaza equipped with a fountain, seats, planting, sculpture, electrical and television outlets, and provisions for a temporary stage—the wrong scale for an amenity to be able to sustain community needs. In addition, there is a lack of intensive articulation through urban furniture and landscaping that would have provided a more hospitable context. The problem of access only adds to the

© Balthazar Korab

© Balthazar Korab

(Above) Plaza

(Above right) Structural skeleton

(Right) Section perspective

(Below) Facade

© Balthazar Korab

shortcomings of the project. Since the plaza slopes up to a point high above the street on one side, it does not invite—or indeed even allow—a flow of pedestrian traffic across it. Because the entrance to the bank is not from the plaza, but from the street below, not even the people who go into it cross the plaza. As a result, the bank's present to the city of a public space is to a great extent wasted, despite the immense investment in the idea.

The building demonstrates that even the most ingenious architectural solution will fall short as an urban solution unless it is accompanied by a sound strategy concerning the pedestrian and vehicular circulation patterns of the city. But the Federal Reserve Bank also shows how an unprecedented architectural invention, totally devoid of historical connotations, and technological in its rationale, can become a memorable civic object, offering a sense of identity and imageability to a whole city.

Louis I. Kahn
KIMBELL ART MUSEUM
Fort Worth, Texas
1966–72

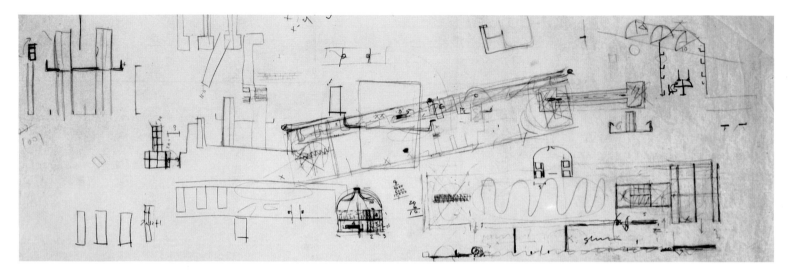

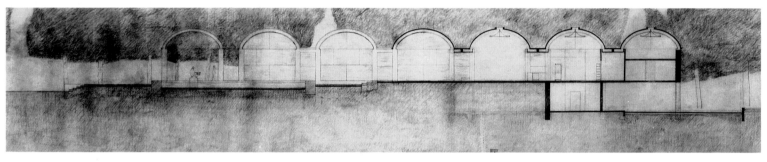

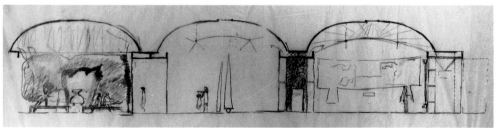

(Top) Various plan studies, sections, axonometrics, and details

(Above) Site section

(Left) Sketch section

The generative cell for the complex is a post-tensioned reinforced concrete cycloid vault, 100 x 22 feet, supported by four columns at each corner, from which emerged the plan of the Kimbell Museum. The megaron-like cell, as in many Mediterranean settlements, is repeated over a slope forming a harmonious 3 x 5 composition matrix, out of whose tripartite side the central unit is removed, creating an outdoor court. Passing through the court, one enters the building, penetrating the megaron from the side. Two open portico units stand at the right and left of the court, flanking the entrance. The composition is one of the most minimal and most grammatical demonstrations of classical taxis.

The vaults are split down the middle. Light descends through this split, washing the curve of the vault. The resulting configuration can be seen as a synthesis between the long, linear megaron, lit through the sides, and the pantheon-type dome lit from above. It marks a significant addition to the Santorini cumulative vault prototype, so cherished by Le Corbusier, out of which grew the Kimbell system. According to August Komendant, a consultant to the project, the Kimbell's use of the cycloid shells, the special post-tensioning of shells, and the post-tensioned two-skin, long-span floor system and walls, are all genuine innovations (August Komendant, *18 Years with Architect Louis I. Kahn*, p. 126).

In addition to the galleries, the museum houses an auditorium, a library, a bookshop, and a kitchen. In accordance with Kahn's "servant" and "served" analysis, the areas under the vaults—the focus of the exhibition area—form the served space, while the in-between spaces, along the vaults, form the servant space. Thus, servant and served are structured in zones rather than in discontinuous towers, as in the Richards Laboratories (1957–60, pp. 72–75), and in discontinuous horizontal bands, as in the Salk (1959–65, pp. 94–97); in the case of the Kimbell, they offer a more flexible solution.

Of course, this flexibility has its limits. The vaulted structures of Santorini that Kahn

© Ezra Stoller

based his design on are traditionally never more than one story high. This restriction turned to a disadvantage, forcing him to place many of the museum's functions underground, in the basement. The staircase leading down to it—though universally acknowledged as a masterpiece of detailing—does little to allay the fact that access to natural light is eliminated.

The fact still remains, however, that, up on the ground level, to move across and along the cellular grid of the Kimbell, under the

gentle light reverberating off the soft low curve of its valuts, is one of the unique spatial experiences in world architecture—credit for which also goes to the lighting expert, Richard Kelly, who collaborated with Kahn on the project. Perhaps nowhere is this spatial experience more dramatic than when one leaves the brilliant glare of the Texas sky behind, passes under the first outdoor vault into the gallery, and crosses the threshold into the hushed, serene, transcendent luminosity of Louis Kahn's masterpiece.

Interior

Modular repetition of the vaulted megaron

© Ezra Stoller

Cycloid vault covering the side passageway

KIMBELL ART MUSEUM • 151

MLTW (Moore Lyndon Turnbull Whitaker)
KRESGE COLLEGE, UNIVERSITY OF CALIFORNIA AT SANTA CRUZ
Santa Cruz, California
1970–73

© Mark Darley/Esto

(Below left) Court

(Below) Site plan

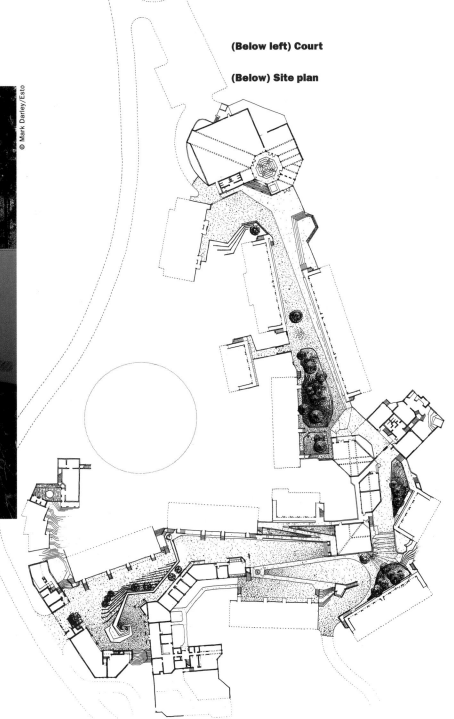

The site of Kresge College is a heavily wooded knoll overlooking Monterey Bay. Two sides of the site are precipitous, while the other slopes gently to the south. The program called for a residential college to accommodate 325 resident students and an equal number of off-campus commuters. Program requirements included student rooms, a library, classrooms, faculty offices, as well as dining, recreation, and common areas. Students and faculty requested a "non-institutional" alternative to typical university classroom and residences, which needed to be accomplished within a very tight budget. From the very beginning, students and university administrative staff were involved in the design. A course was offered at the university in 1970, called "Creating Kresge College," which drew enthusiastic student participation.

The answer to the challenging requirements generated from this process resulted in small, two-story buildings grouped along a pedestrian pathway of a picturesque configuration, sited to respect the trees and terrain. This pathway creates a unique public space and a center for the college where people can meet. The idea of the street is to enrich college life in much the same manner that a street does for village life.

The residential accommodations reflect the architects' interests in offering students choices about how to live. Instead of the typical double-loaded corridor, they designed four-person apartments, each with a living room, two bedrooms, bath, and kitchen. Other, more adventurous students were given a "do-it-yourself" situation in eight-person groups. Walls, roofs, basic plumbing and cooking facilities were provided, but the students built intermediate floors and walls of their own design. All rooms are furnished with a modular cube system that allows for unlimited arrangements.

The structures that house special functions are strategically placed markers

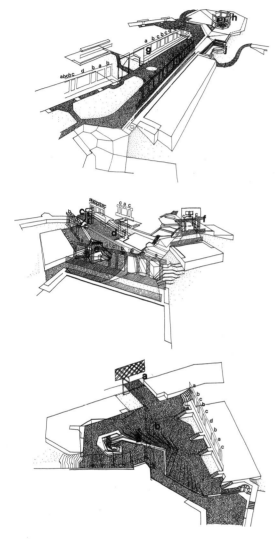

(Above) Sections

(Right) Entrance

© Mark Darley/Esto

along the street. The octagonal court at the upper end provides an entry to the town hall space and restaurant. The library is denoted by a two-story gateway. Other public facilities, such as the telephone booths, are enlarged to become street markers commenting on the importance of communications in student and faculty life. The college is designed as a mixture of the serious and the playful, a place where educational processes can occur in both traditional and untraditional ways.

APARTMENT PLAN

DORMITORY PLAN

10'/3m

Craig Zeidler Strong
MCMASTER UNIVERSITY HEALTH SCIENCES CENTRE
Hamilton, Ontario
1967–72

(Right) Ground plan

(Below) Facade

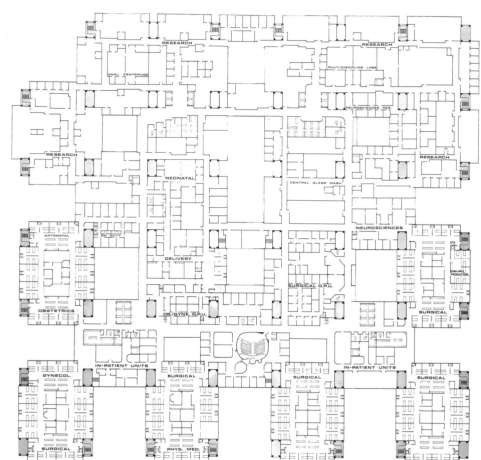

ONE HALF MINUTE WALK

© Balthazar Korab

The McMaster University Health Sciences Centre's sheer size may at first seem to threaten its basic purpose—to provide healthcare for the individual. There were two main reasons given by partner-in-charge of design, Eberhard Zeidler, for why the Centre was planned as one vast structure rather than as several small ones: firstly, the economics of providing comprehensive healthcare for the region, and secondly, the importance of bringing together and training personnel in several health professions (not just the medical profession), and to educate the healthcare team together.

The Centre was planned to integrate physically all aspects of health education, but not in isolation from other medical and educational services in the region. The Centre was to serve its immediate neighborhood, exposing the students to this level of care. According to Zeidler's brief, "A teaching hospital cannot exist on its own, independent of society. Its teaching program, its size, its facilities,

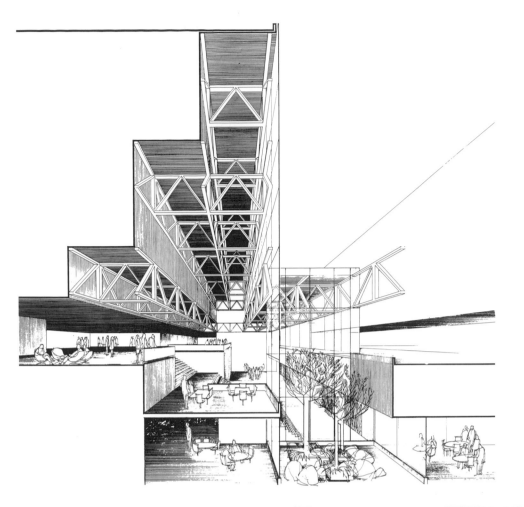

in room relationships without structural interference.

Called "obsolescence-proof" by the World Hospital Congress in 1969, the four-level complex was the first integrated patient-care, educational, and research complex to incorporate interstitial space with an incremental mechanical system, a significant advance from Louis Kahn's Salk Institute (1959–65, pp. 94–97). A servo-system concept, integrating structural and mechanical systems, separates changeable and permanent building elements for ease and economy of inevitable future change and growth.

(Above) Section

(Right) Night view

and its goals must reflect the needs of society and respond to those needs."

The original site was 13 acres on the McMaster University campus, which were to increase to 27 acres by the final stage. The health functions of the complex face towards the neighboring community, while the research and educational functions face the university campus; this division serves not just as a symbolic function, but as an expression of the basic fabric of the institution.

The 1,761,500-foot-square building includes a 418-bed teaching hospital, 403,000 square feet of research facilities, teaching facilities for approximately 900 students, and an underground parking garage for nearly 1000 cars. The basic structural module size of over 8000 square feet can accommodate any future use anticipated in a health sciences center. The module size was determined not so much by large room sizes as by the need to achieve maximum flexibility

Cesar Pelli & Gruen Associates, Inc.
PACIFIC DESIGN CENTER
Los Angeles, California
Phase I 1971–75
Phase II 1984–88

Cylindrical circulation element

© Joe C. Aker

The Pacific Design Center is 4½ acres of blue spandrel glass covering 750,000 square feet of merchandise mart for home furnishings. Rising on a 16-acre site in a Los Angeles neighborhood, this behemoth is located in an area dominated by small-scale, low-rise, mostly commercial buildings, and shops interspersed with a few homes. The major problem the architect had to address was scale—how to insert a huge building in the center of a low-rise context.

According to the eminent West Coast critic, Esther McCoy, Pelli used a glass skin to minimize the bulk of the building, and used as low relief mullions as possible to enhance its smooth uninterrupted surface. In addition, he chose to avoid the traditional orthogonal box associated with glass and steel buildings. Instead the building's glass skin was pulled as tautly as possible over its

structure. The structure itself was no bigger than its functional requirements demanded, with all superfluous volume eliminated. Its sculptural shape was an expression of functional demands.

The most distinctive formal feature of the building—the rounded element extending the length of the roof—simply follows the outline of the barrel-vaulted galleria on the top level. The obtuse-angled volume that flanks the rounded element is the mechanical services zone tucked into the structure next to the galleria. The cylinder on the south side of the building was an efficient solution for vertical circulation.

Inside, the building is laid out as "village streets," a pattern typical of merchandising marts. But beyond the strict interpretation of the building code, Pelli added other amenities. A large terrace on the third floor

offers a good vantage point for admiring the surrounding city, and spacious viewing platforms are supplied at each landing for viewing the unique cityscape of Los Angeles.

The use of such a fragile material as glass may seem an odd choice in an earthquake-prone site. In fact, it was engineered to withstand earthquakes of up to 8.2 on the Richter Scale, thanks to its rigid high-strength steel-welded frame resting on a continuous 30-inch concrete mat. In Pelli's words, the structural system is effective because "the glass just hangs there and shakes within its neoprene gaskets and has hardly any effect on the structure." (Barbaralee Diamonstein, *American Architecture Now*, p. 179.) Glass was also an economical solution. Comparing the Pacific Design Center to Beaubourg (Centre Georges Pompidou, Paris)—two buildings about the same size, built

© Balthazar Korab

around the same time—Pelli noted that his design cost somewhere in the region of a quarter as much as its French counterpart (ibid.).

Phase II, the Green Building expansion, includes a showroom area, parking for 1900 cars, a conference center with an auditorium that accommodates 450 seats and a public plaza. An outdoor amphitheater seating 300 people was incorporated on the plaza, along with a 5000-foot-square gallery for architectural and design exhibitions. Phase II is connected to the original structure at the terrace and first floor levels. Phase III includes an additional 400,000 square feet of showroom space and parking for 640 cars.

The project became a highly influential prototype, from the programmatic, organizational point of view, as well as the technological one. The Pacific Design Center

is probably the building that launched the idea of Skin Rigorism. Structural Rigorism relied on the compositional and sculptural effects of the skeleton, the proportion and rhythm marked by the structural elements. And Functional Rigorism depended on the expressiveness of the shape of the inhabited volumes. The rigorism of the skin, however, as exemplified in the present building, exploited its own mirroring capacities, translucency, and transparency, and its seamlessness, its precise detailing, its flexibility, as well as the very mystery of covering and concealing.

In this glass idiom, Pelli became a pioneering poet. Many buildings were to come, not only in California and Texas, but all over the United States and the rest of the world, trying to exploit the potential of the new idiom he manifested in the "Blue

© Atlantic Filmworks

(Top) View of the Blue Whale

(Above) Stairwell

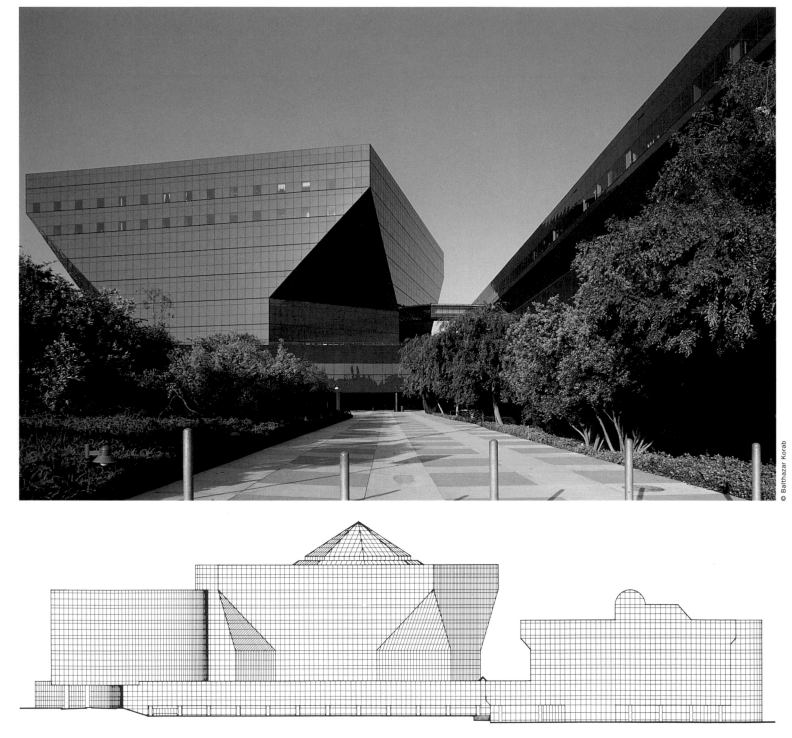

Whale," as the building became known, although it dramatically, and almost magically, turns from bright blue in the daytime to flaming red at dusk as it reflects the setting sun.

The "Blue Whale" is an illustration of how a building devoid of any historical references and whose configuration is dictated by a radical rethinking of construction rationality, technological control, and innovative, efficient industrial materials, can become, in its own non-monumental way, an urban landmark.

(Top) Phase II

(Above) West elevation, Phases I, II, & III

© Balthazar Korab

© Joe C. Aker

Arthur Erickson Architects
MUSEUM OF ANTHROPOLOGY, UNIVERSITY OF BRITISH COLUMBIA
Vancouver, British Columbia
1971–76

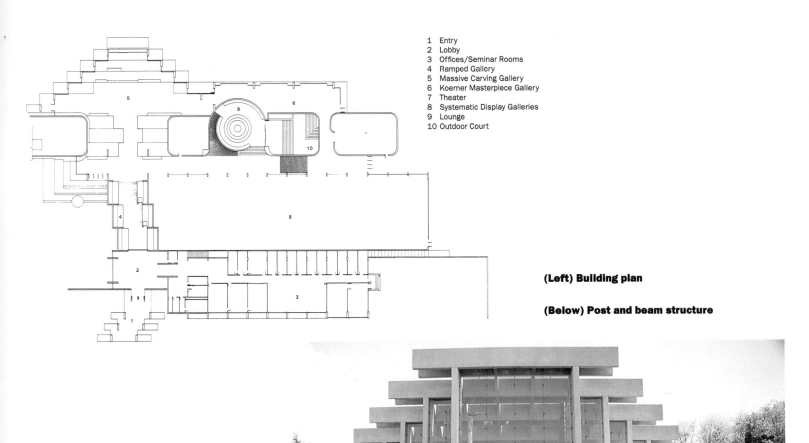

1 Entry
2 Lobby
3 Offices/Seminar Rooms
4 Ramped Gallery
5 Massive Carving Gallery
6 Koerner Masterpiece Gallery
7 Theater
8 Systematic Display Galleries
9 Lounge
10 Outdoor Court

(Left) Building plan

(Below) Post and beam structure

© Erickson

The Museum of Anthropology was funded by the Federal and Provincial governments to house the 1200-piece collection of North Pacific Coast cultures from the collection of the University of British Columbia. The site selected for the new museum was a wooded slope on the edge of the Point Grey cliffs, overlooking the Pacific Ocean, and framed by the Straits of Georgia and the North Shore Mountains. The design of the building started from a belief, articulated by the architect, Arthur Erickson, that: "Architects foremost should be listeners, since architecture is the art of relating a building to its environment, and this requires listening to what the environmentalists say—listening to total context. For architects, this is as much a process of creation as it is of discovery, and building is not so much designed as it is decreed by the context."

As in the case of traditional villages, the museum building stretches parallel to the shore. Carved totem poles are placed near the building in the same relationship with their surroundings as they would have had in their original settings. This conception, also incorporating an artificial lake, was taken, according to Erickson, from a Haida village on Anthony Island, on the tip of the Queen Charlottes. Kenneth Morris designed the landscaping to evoke the character of a traditional Northwest Coast native Canadian village (*Arts Canada*, October–November, 1976). The monumental wooden doors are carved in low relief by Ksan craftsmen in Hazelton, British Columbia.

© Erickson

Erickson modeled his remarkable structure on the Kwakiutl longhouse frames. Whereas the posts, cross beam, and ridgepole of the native Canadian structure are carved from cedars sewn together through slanted awl holes, in the museum, pre-cast posts and pre-cast, post-tensioned beams are tied together by invisible bolts.

Although Erickson's building bears not the slightest formal resemblance to Frank Lloyd Wright's architecture, clearly he is influenced by his writings on "organic" architecture, in particular where Wright advocated making the spaces in a building all come together with the natural setting of the building, so that "light, air and vista permeate the whole with a sense of unity." (Frank Lloyd Wright, "Prairie Architecture," 1931.) One might even add that Erickson's work is experimenting to an unprecedented degree with certain initial findings of Richard Neutra.

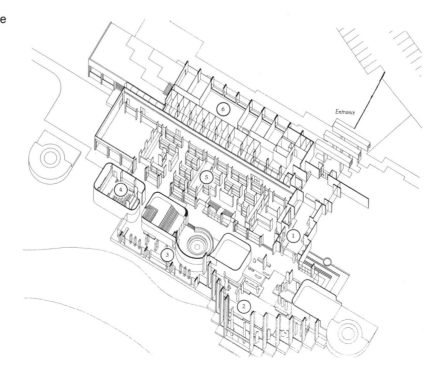

MUSEUM OF ANTHROPOLOGY, UNIVERSITY OF BRITISH COLUMBIA • 161

© Erickson

View from outside

Accordingly, in the Museum of Anthropology, the sequence from the entry to the lobby, to the ramped gallery, and into the Great Hall, then to the small object gallery, is a sequence of spaces that does not begin or end abruptly. Conceived as a pathway, the floor follows the gentle slope of the land. From the entrance, one descends an easy ramp through three small exhibition halls representing the three major cultures—the Nootka of the south coast, the Kwakiutl of the middle coast and the Haida of the northern region. These rooms are intended to resemble clearings in the woods, and are skylit only. The ramp leads down to a longhouse frame that becomes the gate to the Great Hall, where carvings range from 8 to 45 feet in height.

In order to maximize contact with the surrounding landscape, the Great Hall is as transparent as the structure permits. This is where the building excels. Its panels of floor-to-ceiling glazing build up dramatically to the large west wall and the views beyond, thanks to the technologically advanced Pilkington-suspended, tempered-glass system. Erickson has written: "I have been anxious to find, wherever I build, the right response to light. The Northwest Coast is a particularly difficult area with its watery lights, which are capable of soft and subtle moods. The Coast demands transparency in buildings, or skylights bathing walls with a gentle introspective light." (*Architectural Record*, May 1977.) The transparency is intended to recreate the atmosphere of a British Columbian Forest, the natural setting for the pieces it contains, with views of the mountains, sea, and forests. The play of light and shadow shift constantly, washing the masterpieces in the soft, mist-filled light of the region, and one has the feeling of walking on a fern-covered forest floor (*Arts Canada*, October–November, 1976).

© Christopher Erickson

(Above) The Great Hall

(Left) Smaller gallery

© Erickson

Site plan

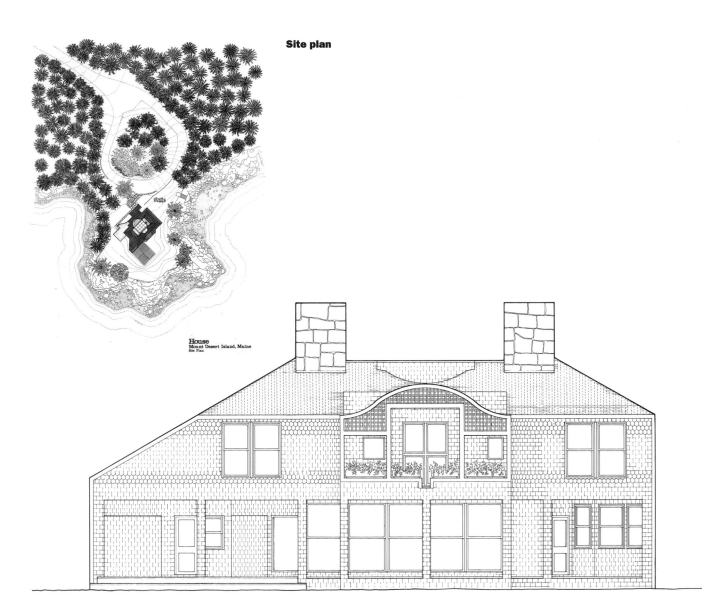

House
Mount Desert Island, Maine
Site Plan

Elevation

"Stompin' at the Savoy" is the title of an article written by Robert Stern in the May 1973 issue of *Architectural Forum*. The article criticized projects of his contemporaries, the so-called New York Five, for what Stern called their compulsive "modernist" tendencies. Implicit in this criticism lie Stern's own ideas about architecture. Here is a partial list of these principles as they emerged in the text:

1. Architectural experience should not be divorced from culture. Neither should architecture stop contributing "to man's understanding of his place in relationship to the natural world and other man-made objects."

2. The complexity of a project should not lead to perceptual confusion. Buildings should be habitational "on a strictly pragmatic basis."

3. The exterior expression of buildings should not be at odds with the materials used, neither should it produce cramped, dysfunctional spaces. An architecture that ignores orientation and environmental issues—that is, "insistently new, abstract and divorced from the place in which it is built: from its landscape and from its architectural traditions which are after all, the record of experience over a long period of time"—is in trouble.

(Above) Facade

(Right) Main floor plan

(Far right) Second floor plan

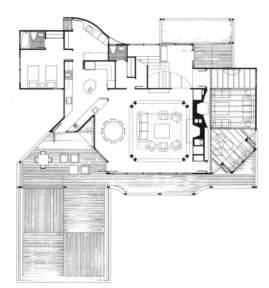

No project of Robert Stern applies these principles so well as his modest year-round vacation house, called "Points of View." Located in Mount Desert Island, Maine, the shingle-style cottage was "intended to capture the spirit of holiday pleasure that one usually associates with the rambling shingled cottages that are so characteristic of the island community on which it is built."

The configuration of the house, its double-chimney pattern, the low, simple prismatic volume and roof outline, all enhance the character of the landscape. By pointing to its individual cues, they make its image more understandable and memorable. The play between order and informality of the plan layout reflects the easy routine and relaxed improvisational style of a leisurely lifestyle. The comfort and intimacy of the different types of introverted niches is as important in the design as the "points of view" from which to look at the landscape. Both needs are satisfied by evoking traditional precedents: the covered entry porch, the stair "for sitting on as well as walking," the decks, and the verandahs.

This traditionalist house, neither nostalgic nor pastiche, is a prototype of how a prototype, still applicable, can be creatively re-instantiated with devotion and technical excellence, and in this way kept alive.

Richard Meier & Associates
BRONX DEVELOPMENT CENTER
The Bronx, New York
1970–76

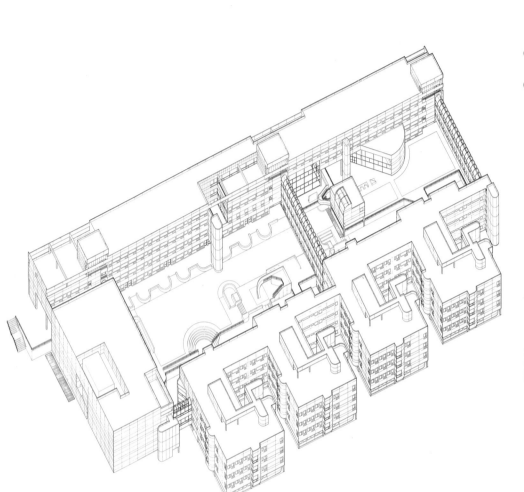

Bright, precise, and white silver, the Bronx Development Center sits in the midst of a dirty, desolate, grim triangular traffic island bounded by railway trucks to the west and the Hutchinson River Parkway to the east, neighboring a large dilapidated warehouse. Unexpectedly, it is a hospital, a highly equipped treatment center for the mentally retarded.

The Bronx Development Center was originally planned as a total-care residential facility for 750 physically disabled and mentally handicapped children. It now houses 380 residents and serves also as an out-patient facility. While the program's complex technical requirements demanded particular attention, Meier writes that the design is, above all, an attempt to create a sense of place that responds to the special feelings and needs of the residents.

Given the conditions of the neighborhood, Meier's strategy was to create a layout that opens inward to a realm where the resident is protected from the external setting. The two major programmatic elements divide around the lateral axis of the composition: the public and support services wing in the rectangular block on the west, and the residential units and services in the east block. A gymnasium with an indoor pool and a physical therapy building are on the south, and the two courtyards, each with a glazed corridor at its northern edge, complete the composition.

Not only are the highly controled configuration of the building and materials in total contrast to the conditions of abandonment and harshness of the surroundings, but the very nature of Meier's architectural language—the orderly combinatorics of the composition, with its elementarist, geometrical volumes, the gentle exactitude of the meticulously finished fine aluminium skin, punched out by exquisitely detailed, round-cornered windows—emerges as emblems of a special community, dedicated to the care of these special children.

© Ezra Stoller Esto

(Above) Internal court

(Left) Entrance

© Ezra Stoller Esto

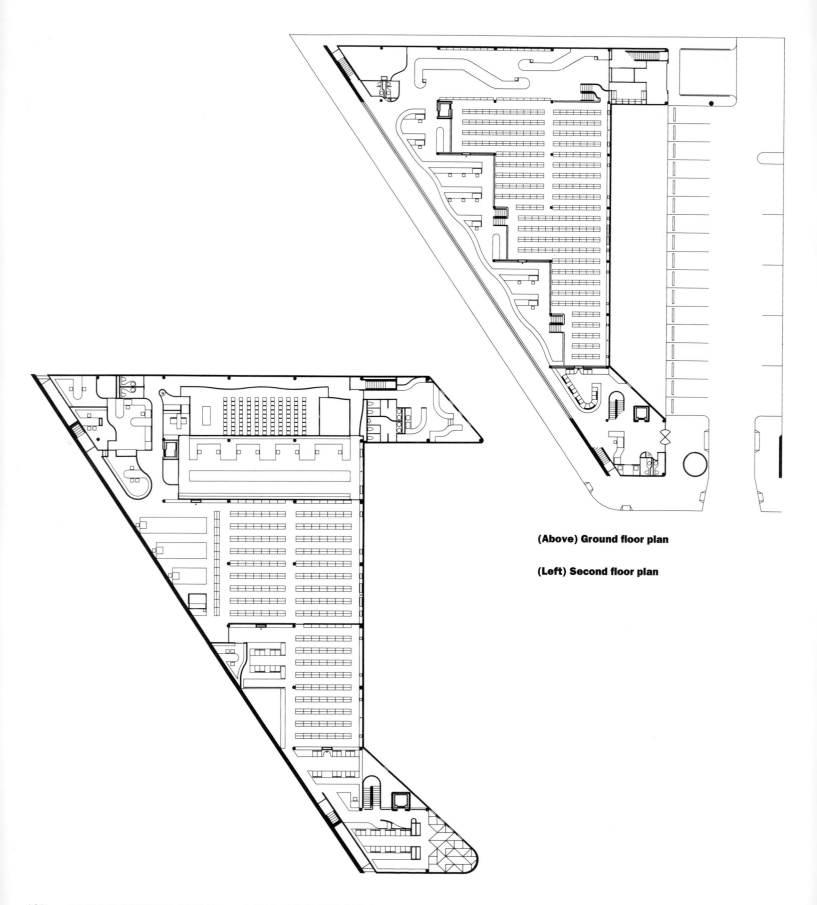

(Above) Ground floor plan

(Left) Second floor plan

Stanley Tigerman wrote in December 1977 that most of the buildings he had designed had come into being very slowly—in some cases, very painfully—and he confessed that some of them show that torture. Not so, he said of the Illinois Regional Library for the Blind and Physically Handicapped, the basic scheme for which he designed in a matter of a few days. The reasons he cited for this were his "sympathetic response at the earliest meetings with the client group and that the difficult site, in combination with rigorous building and parking requirements, left very little room for willfulness."

The site is an isosceles triangle, located on the south-west corner of the University of Illinois at Chicago campus. The facade of the building is dominated by the use of metal panels. They are finished in red baked enamel. Color is also used for structural members, which are bright yellow. The exposed mechanical and electrical elements are blue. The long elevation is concrete, and the undulating shape of the 165-foot-long window set into it reflects in elevation the circulation plan located inside. Through this device, the building conveys how it is used. Curving interior walls, built-in elements, and a linear plan also convey the functional organization of the building. Most importantly, color and spatial pattern are used to achieve a cognitive map of the facility to assist the blind visitor to use the library with the greatest ease. If memorized, it can assist the blind visitor in moving through the library with a minimum of difficulty.

Tigerman has written extensively about the project and he has devoted particular attention to explaining the apparently paradoxical use of color here. The entire idea that a "library for the blind" is furnished in very bright colors is apparently curious. Explains Tigerman, there are certainly many

Entrance

"rational" reasons for the bright colors: (1) the "legal" definition of blindness does not necessarily mean "total" blindness—the last thing a person sees before becoming totally blind is very bright color bathed in light; (2) blind people have sighted relatives and friends, who will convey the building's highly colorated state; (3) the building is located directly across the street from a bland brown brick University in an economically deprived neighborhood in a colorless city; and (4) it suggests an informality and humor challenging the serious condition of the user.

All of this adds up to Tigerman's general intention to strike out at the overly serious way in which libraries have always conveyed the humorless intentions of learning as a particularly American dream not to be tampered with. The library for the blind was intended to be a building that conveyed wit and humor.

Tigerman views the building iconographically as a mixed metaphor. He reveals the sources himself: they are derived from the "modern movement" in architecture, specifically Le Corbusier and Hejduk (Barbar House). These are often neutralized by system-referencing elements, such as the red walls, gray concrete, and the yellow structure. Tigerman views "metaphorical illusions ... implicit in the program" as "loaded with poignancy (blindness) rather than the current modish thinking that superimposes metaphors on unsuspecting programs."

Tigerman takes particular delight in anthropomorphic ideas. He points to the circulatory system "printed" on the building face. Part of the strategy of his poetics is the use of "inversions and reversals" which are "everywhere and nowhere." As a result, for example, "the apparently lightweight steel

© Tigerman

Borrowing facilities

panels are made opaque while the apparently heavy concrete wall is made transparent through the device of the horizontal, undulating cut." These latter "transmutations represent ... the irrationality connected with blindness, the schizophrenia between the program and the general state-of-the-art," and what the architect calls his own "inconclusive struggle with both."

This is without doubt a functional project, which is at the same time original in its functionality, but it is also a project that has a reflective value demonstrating the fruits of cognition, as well as being a reflection on cognition and its limits. This is one of the most uniquely creative projects of the author and his generation, demonstrating how constraints derived from scientific, empirical

study, far from frustrating invention, can be the very catalyst of ingeniousness. Furthermore, the overpowering devotion of the architect to serving the needs of a traditionally deprived part of society makes the building a symbol of sharing and responsibility.

Hugh Stubbins & Associates, Inc.
CITICORP
New York City, New York
1970–77

Profile

© Norman McGrath

A dramatic urban presence in New York City, Citicorp is a unique condominium development, combining on one site an office tower for Citibank, a church for St. Peter's Lutheran congregation, low-rise shops and offices surrounding a public atrium, a pedestrian plaza, and a connection to the subway. The challenge implicit in designing this building was significant in two respects: one dealt with the question of public and private needs, the other involved solving the problem of an orientation towards people in a project of such size and complexity.

The tower, rising 914 feet from the street, is physically and visually one of the most distinctive buildings in midtown Manhattan. It is unique both in how it meets the ground and in how it meets the sky. Best known for its unusual sloping crown, the building is perhaps more successful in the animated plaza at its base. Early sketches show several variants of the diagonal top—terraced garden apartments, as well as solar collectors were explored—but were either not cost-effective or did not meet the city's zoning ordinances.

Bright aluminum and reflective glass enclose the 46 floors of the tower. In order to provide air, light, and space at the street level, the building is elevated on four 114-foot-high columns that support the volume at the midpoint of each facade, leaving the corners cantilevered into space. Several factors strongly influenced this particular design: zoning, the politics of real estate assemblage, economics, and esthetics. Developing the site in this way enabled the pedestrian functions of plaza, church, retail areas, building lobbies, subway entry, and galleria to nestle around the base of the tower. The development of a major public space at the plaza was considered a risky move. Previous attempts to copy the quasi-public spaces of Rockefeller Center had not been successful, but the well-received shopping mall, The Market at Citicorp, where 20,000 people a day promenade, eat, and spend money led to the proliferation of such plazas elsewhere in the city, but nowhere with the success of the original (*Progressive Architecture*, December 1978).

Technological innovation was significant within the complex and allowed construction

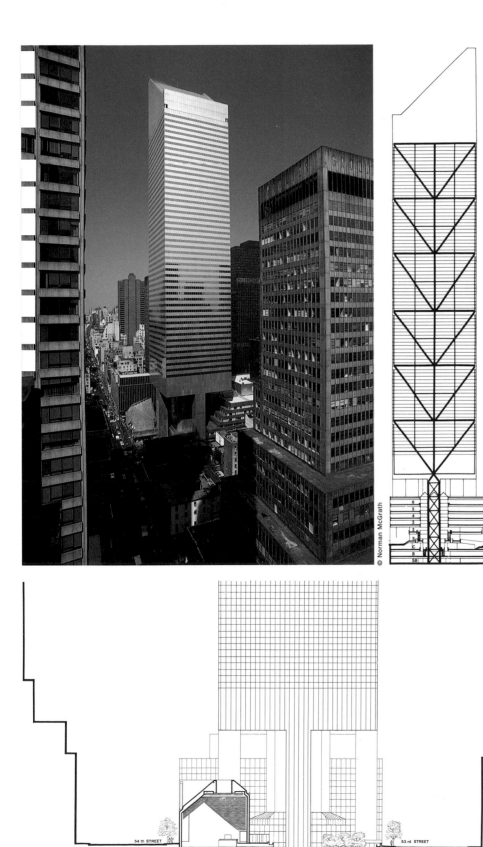

© Norman McGrath

(Far left) Facade

(Left) Elevation

(Below left) Section

to be achieved within a modest budget. Diagonal bracing, clear-span floors, and the first use of a tuned-mass damper to moderate tall building motion are all part of the unique structural design. Other technological advancements motivated by the recent oil embargoes and resulting attention on energy conservation, included a heat-reclamation system, custom-designed, low-brightness lighting, a computer-based building management system, and double-deck elevators as important elements of energy conservation within the complex.

Stubbins writes about his belief that structure is of great importance, and how it should be forthright, logical, and honest. But in fact, the big columns are not an honest expression of structure, for as his collaborator, structural engineer William Le Messurier, points out, they could have been designed to appear much thinner. The choices for the size of the columns—like the angle for the distinctive top—are less about technology than about esthetics, and in both cases the architecture reflects the design sketches of the architect, and not the calculations of the engineer.

I. M. Pei & Partners
NATIONAL GALLERY OF ART EAST BUILDING
Washington, D.C.
1968–78

What is striking about the East Wing of the National Gallery of Art is the highly geometrical configuration of its volumes, with the extending planes implicitly dividing both the inside of the complex and the outside landscape. This is no surprise to a city whose layout is dominated by axes and radiating patterns. But while the plan of L'Enfant was controled by well-known principles of 19th-century Beaux-Arts sculpture and painting composition, I. M. Pei's project emerges very much as an object belonging to the hard-edge minimal sculpture of the 1960s. Situated on a 9-acre trapezoidal site inscribed in the original L'Enfant plan of Washington, the 604,000-foot-square East Wing of the National Gallery of Art extends across the east–west axis of the original building (now named the West Wing), and relates to it in scale, materials, and location.

Pei's building complies with a diagonal division of the site by forming two complementary triangles interconnected by a triangular central courtyard. Similarly, it complies with the materials. Clad in the same pink-hued Tennessee marble as the original gallery, the color of the exterior walls of the East Wing changes from deeper shades at the base, becoming lighter towards the top.

The marble of the facade and of the paving of the entrance plaza extend into the central triangle of the garden court, the major focal and circulation area of the complex, integrating further the inner heart of the building with its surroundings. Balconies and bridges with the same concrete and pink marble dust aggregate as the exterior long-span exterior beams cross through and overlook this great central space. The court is dominated by a skylight of insulating glass with an aluminum sunscreen, supported by a welded steel space frame made up of 25 tetrahedrons spanning 16,000 square feet and rising 80 feet at its highest point.

A secondary skylight is located above the café in the underground corridor that connects the two wings. This pyramidal skylight sits in a landscaped plaza paved with cobblestones—the focal point of a fountain that cascades down the skylight, visible to the visitors below. As an idea, it was the

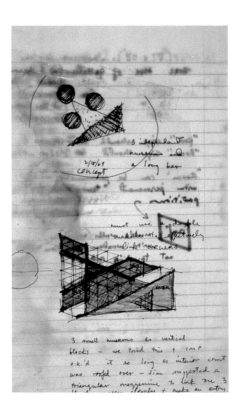

(Above) Conceptual sketch

(Above) Aerial view

(Below) Floor plans

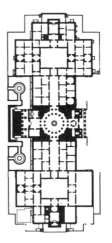

prelude for the pyramid that would appear three years later in Pei's grand entrance for the Louvre. The pyramids of the East Wing, however, seem almost lost in the open plaza, and it is only from inside that the daylight and water cascade can be experienced.

The gallery spaces are diamond-shaped pods, reshaped into hexagonal rooms for more effective exhibition space. Each pod has its own skylight, stairway, and elevator, and the three pods are linked by long-span gallery bridges. The gallery spaces, while carefully crafted, seem dwarfed by the impact of the great atrium court, dominated by the Calder sculpture suspended from the skylight. There is a problem here of scale and transition that Pei's composition does not appear to take into account.

A five-story reading room and six levels of library stacks are accommodated in a triangular study center adjacent to the museum proper. Related to that are seven floors of offices for curators, administrators, and academics, with a penthouse overlooking the roof-garden for a boardroom, executive offices, and staff repertory.

The building has been generated out of strong formal determinants. It has been, even more, the result of the overwhelming constraints of L'Enfant's 18th-century city plan of Washington, for which Pei develops a tight logic of relentless rational geometry. In the Illinois Library for the Blind (1975–78, pp. 168–71), Stanley Tigerman appears to use the triangular site as a foil against which the building reacts. Pei's building, however, seems to have an inner coherence, a spirit reminiscent of Louis Kahn's buildings in Bangladesh, from which the angular geometry flows out to the surrounding landscape.

In the end, the building is less about context than about geometric abstraction, a masterly response to the abstraction that is a key preoccupation of most of the works it houses.

© Ezra Stoller/Esto

© Ezra Stoller/Esto

© Ezra Stoller/Esto

(Top) Main entrance hall

(Above) Staircase

(Right) External view

Richard Meier & Partners
THE ATHENEUM
New Harmony, Indiana
1975–79

(Below left) Site plan

(Below) Upper level ramps

(Bottom) Side of the building

New Harmony was one of the most significant American utopian communities. Founded by a German Lutheran group in 1814, the town was sold in 1825 to Robert Owen, the Welsh industrialist known for his socially experimental New Lanark mills in Scotland, and his writings on utopian communities, which embodied his belief about how education and the environment could improve man and society. The Owen family still lives in New Harmony and is active in preserving the memory of the movement. In 1973, Historic New Harmony, Inc. was founded to acquire properties in the town for the restoration of the community. In addition to the preservation of the buildings, one of the activities of the group was to develop tours of the site that would allow the modern visitor to experience the relationship between a utopian social vision and the resulting community.

The program of the Atheneum asked for a 180-seat auditorium, four exhibition galleries for permanent and changing exhibits, observation terraces, visitor facilities, and ticketing. While Meier's project satisfies the program, the work stands in great contrast to the log cabins and brick buildings of the historic settlement. Not only does the steel-framed, white porcelain-paneled building levitate in its context, but the very organizing principles of the edifice

stand out from those of the other New Harmony structures.

Meier intended the project to serve as a place of arrival, as a threshold and starting point for those arriving for a tour of the historic town. The idea of an architectural promenade and historic journey was central for the architect in the conception of the scheme. The site is at the north-west border of the town, where the building is placed on an 8-acre grassy mound near

the banks of the Wabash River. For the visitor who arrives by boat, a path leads through the field directly to the entrance of the building, which is oriented to the riverbank. A three-story plane, set at a 40-degree angle to the podium, which anchors the basic reference grid of the complex, is intended by the architect to acknowledge the point of arrival. (Other visitors approach the building from the parking lot to the south.)

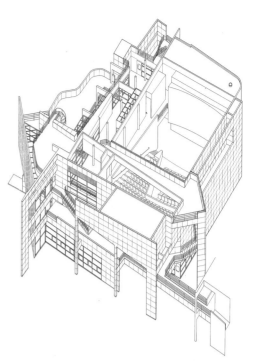

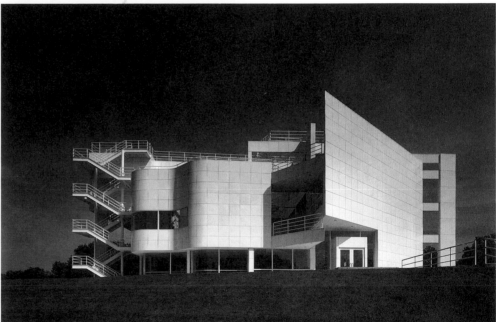

(Above) Outside view

(Above right) Axonometric

(Right) Facade

Once inside, the visitor faces an internal circulation ramp, which leads through the most important parts of the building. Its role, from the brief of the architect, is as a "chief mediator and armature," and is fundamental to the whole scheme. "As the ramp winds upward from the orthogonal grid," continues the brief, "it regains the five-degree orientation of the path from the river (and) the entire building is set in motion." There is the "orthogonal grid" on which "another grid cranked on a five degree diagonal" is "overlaid" to "induce a compression of spaces." This 5-degree shift is to "inflect one circulation path towards another" and to "force a visual perception of spaces narrowing, then opening." (*Progressive Architecture*, February 1980.)

The brief uses many empathetic metaphorical terms—"compression," "tension," "resonance," to describe and justify a complex, and at the same time

highly geometrically controled, space arrangement of the interior. But Meier does not belong to the tradition of expressionist architects interested in empathy and feeling. His is an architecture obsessed with "pure visibility effects," looking at, aligning, and framing objects in space. No wonder, museums would play an increasingly important role in his development. The Atheneum is conceived very much as a device, a most sophisticated instrument, one is tempted to say, despite the total absence of any contraptions, for controling the experience of observing a collection of objects which happen to be, in the case of New Harmony, a set of historical buildings on a historical site.

The organization of the Atheneum as a pure optical phenomenon based on regulatory lines and geometrical, spatial coordination systems recalls Doxiadis's study from the 1920s of the Propylea as a

visual gate to the Acropolis (republished by MIT Press, 1972). There is a 19th-century mentality about his highly abstract, formalistic analyses of place, which lack any reference to meaning and use, nor is there any reference to ritual and community, which was so integral to the classical site. Similarly, there is something detached about the way the Atheneum relates to one of the most intriguing social experiments on the North American continent. This approach might have a rationale from an objectivist point of view, as an effort not to prejudice the visitor about the history of New Harmony. The Atheneum is not, after all, a memorial to the utopian town. Meier lets, therefore, the log cabins, the brick structures, and certainly the guides themselves speak for the historical significance of the community. But in doing so, he may have relegated the role of the architect to that of a mechanical curator rather than that of a reflective designer.

Jersey Devil
HILL HOUSE
La Honda, California
1977–79

(Right) Aerial view

(Below) Site plan

© Bob Moore

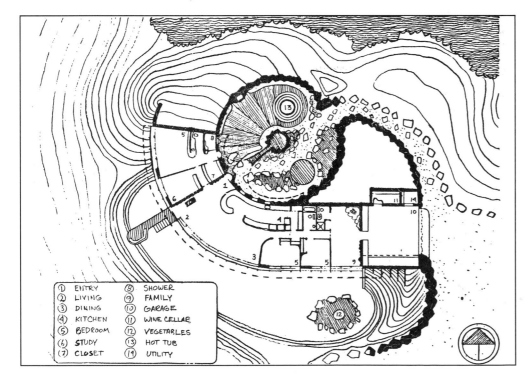

① ENTRY	⑧ SHOWER
② LIVING	⑨ FAMILY
③ DINING	⑩ GARAGE
④ KITCHEN	⑪ WINE CELLAR
⑤ BEDROOM	⑫ VEGETABLES
⑥ STUDY	⑬ HOT TUB
⑦ CLOSET	⑭ UTILITY

After receiving his Masters degree in architecture from Princeton in 1971, Steven Badanes joined up with John Ringel to form one of the more unusual design partnerships, Jersey Devil. Since then, the group has produced more than a dozen houses and small projects, known as much by their fine craftsmanship as by the fact that the designers live on the site during construction. As Badanes explains, this allows them the freedom to adapt the design throughout the entire building process to whatever exigencies arise. In this mode of working, the three-dimensional reality provides inspiration and solutions to problems that are elusive on a sheet of paper.

The aptly named Hill House is sited on a spectacular ridge top, 10 miles from the Pacific Ocean and 50 miles south of San Francisco. The house sits in a south-facing bowl, opening to the generous sunlight. Winds of more than 100 miles per hour buffet the site, so the designers chose to bury the house into the hillside to present a low profile to the coastal storms. To further complement its integration with the landscape, the house uses earth berms, stone from the site, and a turf-covered roof. The thermal mass of the concrete and stone stabilizes the temperature, and with its

(Right) Front yard from the roof

(Below) Front yard from the ground

(Below right) Section

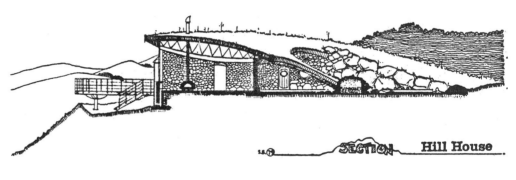

passive solar features makes the house a low-energy user. Because the house is only a few miles from the San Andreas Fault, it required over 15 tons of reinforcing steel as a precaution against earthquakes.

The sod roof is supported on prefabricated lenticular roof trusses, sheathed with plywood and covered with insulation, a continuous waterproof membrane, drainage gravel, and topsoil. As all interior walls are non-bearing, the designers were free to build them in whatever shape seemed best to suit their place and purpose. Some are straight, some are bowed; others are warped or undulating, and all stop one foot short of the bottom chord of the trusses—with plexiglass glazing between the wall and ceiling for acoustic separation—to emphasize that the partitions are non-structural.

Most striking on the interior are the finishes and details, particularly the light fixtures, designed by a Jersey Devil member, Jim Adamson. Ducts emit light instead of air, and overturned flowerpots set amid the trusses cast a warm glow on the tile floor below. Other materials used in unconventional ways are the Almaden wine bottles, used as clerestories, and Perrier water bottles, used as glazing in the garage wall culverts.

With parallels to Frank Lloyd Wright's houses in its siting and reminiscences of Goff in the use of materials, the Hill House best exemplifies the tradition of design builders pursuing their craft with lively wit, great skill, imagination, and a strong affinity for place.

Frank O. Gehry & Associates
FRANK GEHRY HOUSE
Santa Monica, California
1978–79

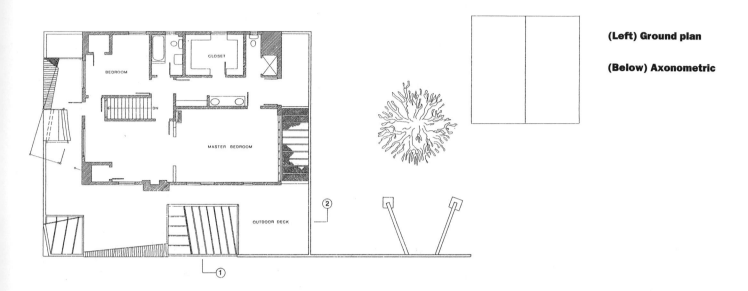

(Left) Ground plan

(Below) Axonometric

The original structure was a 2-story, gambrel-roof, "Dutch colonial" house in the nondescript suburban context of Santa Monica. As a reaction to what he called this "dumb little house," Gehry peeled away the pink asbestos shingles over white clapboard and revealed the original structure underneath. The back of the house was also torn away and the studs exposed. Some places inside were stripped down to the bare core. The ceiling was peeled away and the original lath turned out to be redwood. Around the building he built a 1½-story-high wall of corrugated metal with chain-link screens in the rear loggia, turning the old house into a core and the new house into a wrapper for it. The original structure was made into one big room behind the wall of the new structure. The corrugated metal shell added about 800 square feet to the old house. On the asphalt pad of the driveway he placed the dining room.

Gehry was enthusiastic about his design: "I got fascinated that you could look through the new house, and see the old house as though it was now packaged in this new skin. The new skin and windows in the new house would be of a totally different aesthetic than the windows in the old house." (Barbaralee Diamonstein, *American Architecture Now*, 1980.) But the reaction of the neighbors to the corrugated metal, chain-link mesh, trapezoidal forms and tilting masses was different. They were startled and angered, and one tried to sue him (ibid.).

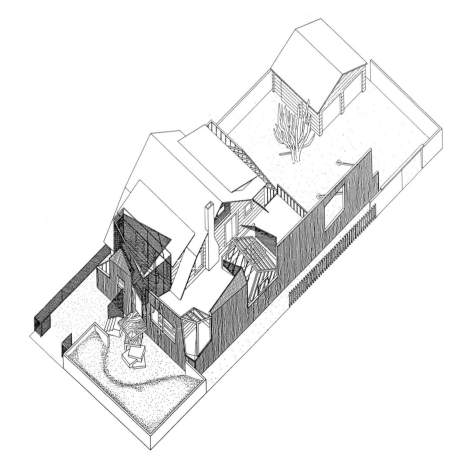

When Gehry was interviewed in 1980 by Barbaralee Diamonstein about why he had identified so strongly with "cheapskate architecture," he replied, with feigned *naïveté*, that "I had a lot of poor clients." (ibid. p. 35.) But there is nothing naive

about this building. The unfinished quality of his work is inspired by paintings by Pollock, De Kooning, and Cézanne that "look like the paint was just applied." (ibid.) It is easy to see that the source for the industrial roughness of his surfaces is the sculpture of his friend and sometimes collaborator, Richard Serra. But the strongest influence in this design is Marcel Duchamp's surrealist work, *Nude Descending a Staircase*. "I am interested in surrealism," he declared, qualifying the house as "very surreal" (quoted by John Pastier in his criticism of the building in *American Architecture of the 1980s*).

The house is conceived as a series of *tableaux*, whose purpose is to subvert domesticity. The window in the kitchen and its chain link "shadow structure" above it were meant "to read as a cube falling out of a box—as if it were trying to escape from the enclosure that was put around the old house." The windows of the old house are glazed over and turned into mirrors. One of the window panes at the front of the house is made up of two non-perpendicular panes of glass, creating a surprising illusionistic effect at night. The slight angle of one of the panes allows it to be perpendicular to a street light that is across the road. In the evening one looks out of that window and sees all the interior lights in the house are reflected on one pane overlaid on the streetlight, which is in turn reflected in the other, blurring the separation between the two. The surreal effect is heightened by the use of chain-link fencing as flooring for a small, almost inaccessible walkway leading nowhere.

Like much of Gehry's work, this building is about the fear of boredom and the flight from stultifying conformity. If ever the anxiety of growing staid and loosing one's sense of rebelliousness had an architectural expression, this is it. But his design devices are more than mere applications in architecture of accomplishments in avant-garde sculpture and painting. Gehry, as this project demonstrates, is obsessed with architecture and its unique means of expression. The building is an object to think with, like any work of art. But it is specifically constrained by the use of space and the specifics of the site on which it is anchored. Being obliged to work with these constraints, the building reacts to and reflects upon the reality of its use and of its surroundings.

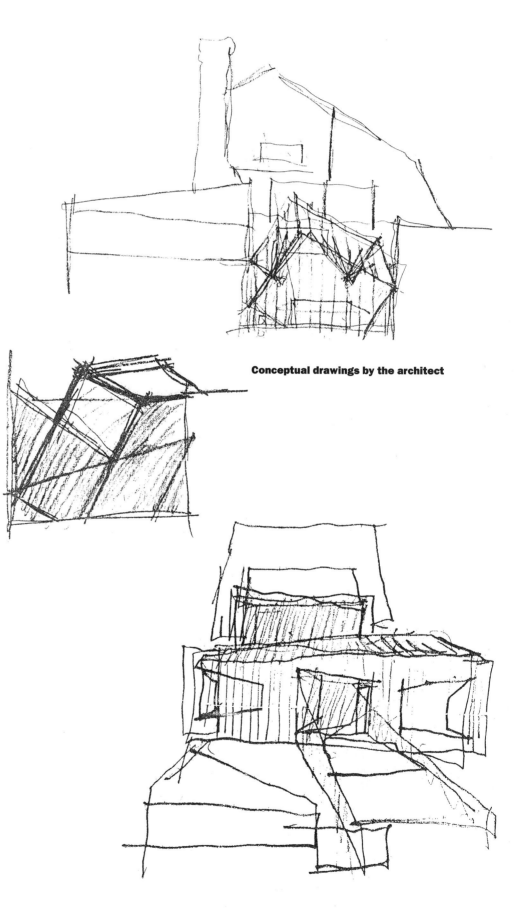

Conceptual drawings by the architect

© Tim Street-Porter/Esto

© Tim Street-Porter/Esto

Kevin Roche John Dinkeloo and Associates
DEERE & COMPANY HEADQUARTERS WEST OFFICE

Moline, Illinois
1975–78

(Below left) Site plan

(Below) Facade

(Bottom) Section

The Deere & Company administrative center was designed by Eero Saarinen and completed in 1964, after his death, by Kevin Roche and John Dinkeloo. The new West Office Building is an expansion of the headquarters, and nearly doubles the usable area of the original structure. Located on a knoll west of the administration building, it balances the composition of the auditorium of the original project, and is similarly connected by means of a bridge to the administration facility. The exterior of the building is based on the original curtain wall, modified to meet current energy conservation requirements.

To avoid the psychological problem of people working in an annex, the architects determined that the addition needed to have an identity of its own; and that identity became a center—an enclosed, covered, planted court, around which the open workstation office space is arranged. The resulting perennial garden, which is

60 feet wide, slopes down one level from the main entry to connect to the cafeteria at the lower level, and serves as a relief space for the transition between work and meal. The rocks that form the surface of the garden came from the Iron Mountains in Michigan, and their presence seems singularly appropriate to the environment created by the exposed, weathered steel building. The barn-like, skylighted roof of the central courtyard helps to give the illusion of greater height and more space.

The construction is organized on three levels and the plan presents a slight shifting of the two main volumes, underlined by the diagonal course of the interior circulation. Both the cafeteria and the offices are completely open to the central garden. This connection acts as an absorber of extraneous ambient noise so that the working environment is remarkably quiet.

The frame of the building is in untreated steel and the walls are in reflecting glass.

The overhangs of the horizontal structure support a *brise-soleil*, also in steel, which runs around every floor. The ceilings are polished aluminum slats that, reflecting the greenery of both the outside and inside court, pick up the dappling light in a kind of diffused glitter and help to extend the natural landscape into the workplace.

The Deere & Company Center is one of a series in the investigation that Saarinen, and later Roche, undertook in their systematic rethinking of the workplace appropriate for the new kind of worker— that is, the information processor—the new technologies of communication, and the transformation of transportation patterns in the urban fabric. As opposed to the Ford Foundation (1963–68, pp. 130–31) atrium building type, this is a villa in the park. As Kevin Roche has remarked (*Architectural Record*, September 1984), the project has "a classical ante-bellum composition." Its significance lies, however, not so much

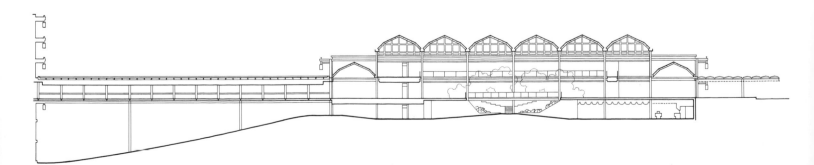

(Left) Ground plan

(Below & below left) Inside views of the court

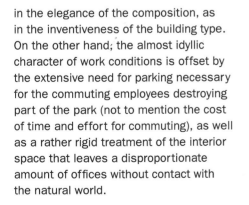

in the elegance of the composition, as in the inventiveness of the building type. On the other hand; the almost idyllic character of work conditions is offset by the extensive need for parking necessary for the commuting employees destroying part of the park (not to mention the cost of time and effort for commuting), as well as a rather rigid treatment of the interior space that leaves a disproportionate amount of offices without contact with the natural world.

© Roche Dinkeloo

Arthur Erickson Architects
ROBSON SQUARE AND PROVINCIAL LAW COURTS
Vancouver, British Columbia
1973–79

© Wayne Thom

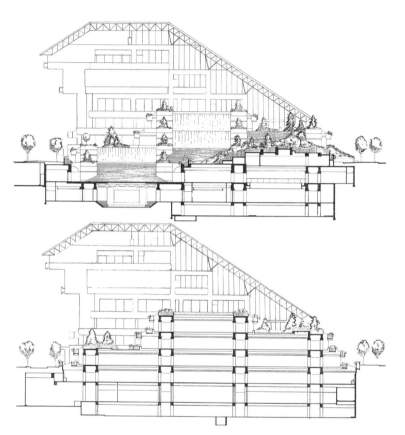

(Left) Entrance to the complex

(Below) Sections

Arthur Erickson could have proposed a soaring, vertical "monumental" solution for this gigantic project. Instead he chose Frank Lloyd Wright's Fallingwater as a model. This is why the Robson Square and Provincial Law Courts, occupying three city blocks of downtown Vancouver, is a low-lying structure, broken down into stepped horizontal planes, and why it incorporates pools, streams, and waterfalls along with luxuriant vegetation (over 50,000 plants) and rock formations, all expertly landscaped by Cornelia Hahn Oberlander.

Owned by British Columbia's Provincial Government, this civic center comprises three distinct sections: the 35,000-foot-square Law Courts building, the 350,000-foot-square Robson Square government office building with outdoor plazas, and a turn-of-the-century neo-classical courthouse and annex, renovated for the 45,000-foot-

square Vancouver Art Gallery. The program also includes a media center, winter ice skating, cafés, underground rapid transit station to connect the pedestrian retail malls beneath the neighboring shopping centers, and numerous open space and pedestrian amenities. None of the buildings reaches beyond a height of 7 stories, the height of the old courthouse which was preserved and adapted for new purposes.

The Law Courts occupy the top block. The building has a glass roof, and strong exposed post-and-beam structural elements. The Law Courts concourse soars to an 86-foot height from which it offers vistas of the old courthouse. Stairs on the east side of the lobby grandly transport the visitor up to smaller tiers of semi-public galleries leading to the courtrooms. The common gathering area in the immense atrium-like concourse is offered as a novel way of opening up the

workings of justice to the public. It apportions public spaces to the glass-enclosed western half, and the judges' chambers and jury rooms to the more enclosed eastern part, with the courtrooms situated at the center of each level.

The middle block accommodates a city square, as well as the public service grouping of Provincial Government offices. It is designed as a low-rise terraced structure, whose entire roof area has usable landscaped open space. Building service spaces, mechanical plants, and parking are provided on two levels below the office space. An underground truck tunnel system along one street handles deliveries and other services to and from the complex. The tunnel minimizes the presence of vehicles in the pedestrian areas of the complex. A prominent feature of this block is what Erickson dubs the "stramps": the

(Above left) Stramps

(Below left) Entrance

(Top) Law Courts building

(Above center & above) Landscaping

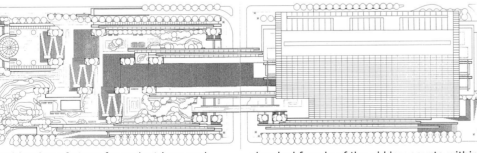

combination of steps for pedestrians and ramps for handicapped access that take their lead from the cascading levels of government offices down to the open plazas below.

The last parcel contained an old courthouse and annex that had previously been turned into a museum. As opposed to many projects of urban renewal, the Erickson scheme retained the beloved neo-classical building. The complexities of this part of the program involved how to integrate the neo-classical facade of the old law courts within the modern complex, and how to provide easy access to the sculpture terrace at the second level without distracting from the main gallery entrance colonnade. Erickson achieved this integration without any recourse to nostalgia or difficult analytical formal devices. As a result, he offers to the public an approachable experience of how old and new, tradition and innovation, might be complementary rather than in conflict.

The project was conceived, in the architect's own words, as a "a meadow sanctuary of civic and communal values, government offices wrapped in nature's nurturing guise." As Erickson himself points out, its civic amenities are becoming increasingly clear as the property values around it rise and tall buildings begin to fill in the surrounding cityscape. The project appears as a manifestation of the reverse of the nightmare phenomena of what John Kenneth Galbraith called "private affluence and public squalor," and a hope for public architecture as one of the prerequisites for a sustainable democracy.

Johnson Burgee Architects
GARDEN GROVE COMMUNITY CHURCH
Garden Grove, California
1976–80

(Below) Facade

(Bottom) Plan

© Gordon Schenk

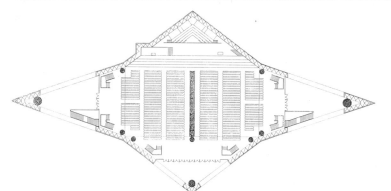

"It is higher, wider and longer than Notre Dame in Paris." So boasts architect Philip Johnson of his creation, the Crystal Cathedral, in May 1980, after its completion. The dimensions of the glass temple are indeed impressive: the length of the building is 400 feet (122 meters), the width is 200 feet (61 meters), and the height is 120 feet (36·5 meters). In fact, the comparison is a clever deceit: because of its unusual star-shaped configuration, the floor area is only half as large as Notre Dame.

The original church, commissioned by the Reverend Robert H. Schuller, was designed by Richard Neutra in 1959, with a bell tower added in 1967 by the senior Neutra and his son, Dion. When the congregation outgrew the old church, Schuller decided to build a new structure. The brief called for a new church that could seat 4000 people, be flooded with light, and respect the older Neutra structures. Schuller's credo was that God should be enjoyed in the presence of the sky and the surrounding world, not in a forbidding stone environment: "The ideal church would be a park where people could sit in communion with nature." In reality, the building is set in an asphalt park, a 300-car parking lot, not unlike a suburban mall. As a drive-in cathedral, the congregation can stay in their cars and listen to the broadcast of the sermon. Schuller urged Johnson to redesign the early proposal with complete transparent cladding, stating that "the view

of traffic and surrounding life is all part of God's world."

Johnson has achieved tremendous controversy regarding the project by associating it with other famous exemplars. In addition to Notre Dame, he has referred to both the Norman Foster Sainsbury Centre for the Visual Arts in Norwich, England (same triodetic steel frame to support the roof and walls, and reflective glazing and natural cooling) and Mies's Friedrichstrasse proposal for Berlin, with its triangular glass office tower as precedents for the church. These are, however, unconvincing examples because of the fundamental dissimilarities between projects. Sainsbury, for example, has the end walls free for the view, and a far more restrained geometry. These dissimilarities have been pointed out by several critics, only to enhance the project's visibility.

There is a strong Hollywood quality about the design, combining feats of technological achievement with an almost childish approach to culture and symbol. Similarly, the building is a curious hybrid of technical complexity and simple-mindedness, operatic luxury, and Calvinistic austerity. The main

space has no heating or cooling system at all. Solar gain is sufficient in the mild winters to maintain comfortable temperatures for the congregation, and the reflective glass and natural ventilation from the operable windows and opened wall sections keep the space from overheating in the summer. But to open the pivotal doors, the building uses the same high-tech space technology as at Cape Canaveral. The transparent skin is a highly reflective glass allowing only 8 percent of the heat and light to penetrate, an effect quite noticeable when the walls are opened and the congregation gets a direct view outdoors.

The building has been critiqued for its poor acoustics, awkward layout, poor sight lines, and bad detailing of the glass cladding, but even by this functionalist yardstick, the great central space outweighs its shortcomings. The use of light and space is unlike any other cathedral, but in some ways it is more like a sports arena. And while the central space is uplifting for the congregation, it serves primarily as a backdrop for the television ministry numbering in the millions. From this point of view, it is a most successful building functionally.

Puzzlingly, the post-Marxist architectural critic and historian, Manfredo Tafuri, linked the all-crystal appearance of the building to the *glas architektur* of the European utopian avant-garde. (*Domus*, July 1980.) He sees, however, that the perfection of its geometry—"the facets of the prisms, the inviolability of the inside in particular, due to the glass system nullify all attempts to read symbolic value into those references"—make the design more like a Lichtenstein painting using quotations. Despite its excessive acoustic environment, he sees in it the noise of the world being banned from it.

For most of the congregation, the religious experience has changed from being a community in an enclosed space to the isolation of individuals watching a video screen in the privacy of their own home. For this reason, the dematerialized shell of the cathedral seems a particularly apt metaphor for the absence of any physical identity which characterizes this particular religious community in an age of electronic technology.

Fay Jones & Maurice Jennings, Architects
THORNCROWN CHAPEL
Eureka Springs, Arkansas
1979–80

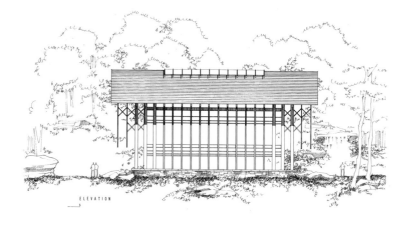

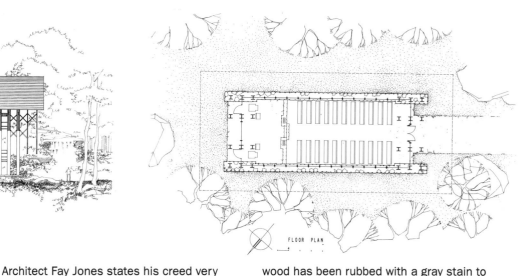

(Above) Side elevation

(Above right) Ground plan

Conceptual sketch

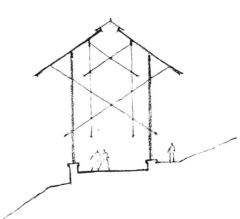

Architect Fay Jones states his creed very succinctly: "I am very concerned," he writes, "with the tenets of organic architecture. In trying to apply Frank Lloyd Wright's basic principles, I see the site as a determining factor in what a building becomes. It is in the realm of interchange between nature and man-made things that each can benefit from the other."

The site, located in the Ozark Mountains of Arkansas, is a level area on a hillside thick with oaks, maple, and dogwood, with a stone bluff on one side and sloping woods on the other. The idea of a chapel on this site came to the owner when he realized that travelers always stopped at the same place to admire the view. In order to do justice to the inspirational quality of the place, the landowner decided to build a chapel to welcome wayfarers. His brief to Fay Jones was to create something that would not damage the land and that would enhance "the spirituality of the place" (Colin Amery, *Financial Times*, February 19, 1990).

Because the setting was so fragile and access to it so difficult, no mechanical equipment could be used without destroying the foliage and rock formations. Instead, the chapel had to be built only from pieces—two-by-fours and two-by-sixes—that could be easily carried by two men up a narrow footpath.

The chapel is small, being 60 feet long, 24 feet wide and 48 feet tall. The material is mostly local Arkansas wood and stone—southern yellow pine, rising from a fieldstone floor and two low fieldstone walls. All of the

wood has been rubbed with a gray stain to blend with the bark of the surrounding trees. Like Wright, Jones often designs all aspects of the building in order to create an "organic" whole, and every aspect of the Thorncrown Chapel has been detailed meticulously, including benches, lecterns, and light fixtures.

As in many of his projects, Jones has sought to combine Wrightean organic architecture with a historical archetype, which is Gothic in this case. Then, in a process he calls "operative opposite," he exploits the opposite characteristic of the archetype. At Thorncrown, he reverses the Gothic characteristic of a heavy compressive structure of stone and makes its inverse as a light tensile structure of wood. This means that the building is not pushed together from the meeting of great weights, but tied together from the inside through the connection of slat-like members overhead. An extraordinary construction detail is that the centers of the steel truss connectors above the central aisle of the church, have been left hollow, creating a series of empty lozenges sparkling with light.

The result is, in the words of Colin Amery, "a primal sense of place," which instead of disturbing the surroundings, "elevate(s) them by the gentle imposition of a geometry inspired by nature." (ibid.) In this, Jones remains true to the Transcendentalist tradition that characterized the thinking of an architect not only like Frank Lloyd Wright, but poets and philosophers like Emerson, Whitman, and Thoreau.

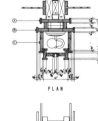

PLAN

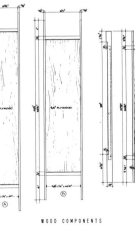

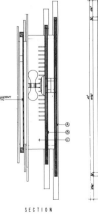

SIDE　　FRONT　　SECTION　　WOOD COMPONENTS

(Above left) Front

(Above) Interior

(Left) Details of construction

SITE Projects, Inc.
BEST FOREST BUILDING
Richmond, Virginia
1978–80

Architects' concept drawings

© Esto

(Left) Facade

(Below) Model

SITE began in the heady atmosphere of the New York art scene in the 1960s, when a sculptor, poet, sociologist, and architect came together to exhibit their images and profess their theory of "de-architecture." This, they claimed, was a new method or perspective for examining the built environment and expanding its meaning. By shifting the concerns of architecture from traditional formalism to information and commentary, SITE intended to heighten a public level of communication.

In 1972, the Best Products Company, Inc., the largest catalogue showroom merchandiser in the U.S., commissioned SITE to develop a series of special showrooms—each a unique work of art related to its environment—in various locations throughout the country. While each subsequent Best showroom has its own particular message, several themes run through much of their work. Perhaps their best-known image is that of the unfinished or ruined building look. This theme has become less important as two often recurring themes have become increasingly visible—responsiveness to energy and nature.

While not their best-known project, the Forest Building is an example of the group's evolved thinking over the past twenty years about the relationship between building and nature. Located in a densely wooded suburban site, the building is sited and constructed so as not to destroy existing vegetation. The forest is allowed to penetrate and envelop the showroom. This phenomenon is exaggerated by the surrounding asphalt, giving the appearance of architecture invaded and consumed by nature. A 35-foot gap between the facade and the actual front wall of the store, and an irregular cleft at either end of the building, imply that Best's regular brick box has been rent asunder by giant oak trees.

In a recent article (*Amicus Journal*, Summer 1993), SITE co-founder James Wines writes: "In the post-industrial world, any architecture whose work continues to draw inspiration from the machine age is hopelessly out of touch with reality. Such movements as 'high-tech, neo-constructivism, and neo-modernism' have become our contemporary equivalents to the Beaux-Arts; meaning a dated and nostalgic catalogue of style motifs that have nothing to do with the Age of Information and Ecology. Architecture now is about rediscovering humanity's debt to the earth and converting this awareness into a new iconography."

Continuing in this vein, whose antecedents lie in Picturesque, Romantic, anti-mechanistic American thinking of the 19th century, he calls for an "architecture desperately in need of a spiritual, theoretical, and philosophical reunion with nature (where) architects should see their structures as narrative fusions of ideas that connect shelter to the earth." With its imagery of ruin and vegetation run wild, the Best Forest building is perhaps more a reminder of the consequences of ignoring the potency of nature than a model for how best to take it into account.

Andres Duany, Elizabeth Plater-Zyberk, Architects Inc.
SEASIDE PLAN
Seaside, Florida
1980–

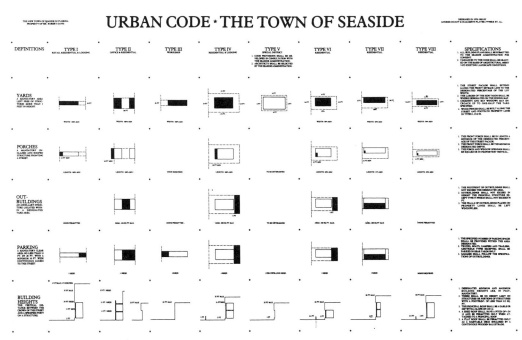

URBAN CODE · THE TOWN OF SEASIDE

© Duany/Plater-Zyberk

(Below) Site plan

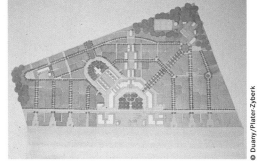

Seaside is an 80-acre beachfront site on the Florida Panhandle along the Gulf of Mexico. The program was for a resort town, conceived to approximate the size and components of a small town. The aim of Duany and Plater-Zyberk was to "turn away from the methods of contemporary real estate development toward those of traditional American urbanism." To this end, the retail center was conceived as a downtown commercial district, the conference facility doubled as town hall, and a portion of the recreation budget was dispersed to create small civic amenities throughout the town. What the architects referred to as the civic character of the town was further reinforced by reserving sites for public buildings such as a chapel, a primary schoolhouse, a fire station, and a post office, to be shared by adjacent communities. The program has expanded to include a service station and a workshop district, and the town is still evolving.

In Duany and Plater-Zyberk's plan one factor was key: The Code. All the houses were built to fit in with a strict building code concerning architecture, urban design, and landscape. The architects devised a simple one-page document that allowed the purchasers of the individual plots to commission architects, who then had to follow the prescribed code. They devised

a plan for development with zoning laws that create comprehensible streets and squares, strong focus on the town hall and clear distinctions between private and public buildings. There are eight building types, covering aspects of lot frontage, porches, fences, footpaths, location of parking lots, heights of roofs, proportional relation of public spaces and heights of roofs, towers, and boundaries between zoning types. Materials are also tightly controled. Houses are mostly timber with tin roofs, giving the place the air of a 19th-century southern town.

A study of towns carried out by DPZ throughout the American South indicated that a community of genuine variety and authentic character could not be generated by a single architect. The firm therefore designed only a small part of Seaside, and many buildings were given over to other designers, among them Steven Holl, Deborah Berke, Silvetti and Machado, and Leon Krier.

The code was intended to generate an "urban environment similar to that of a small southern town prior to 1940," where the emphasis was on creating human environments that favored pedestrians over automobiles and where zoning and building codes brought cohesion to developments through architectural

diversity. Plater-Zyberk supports the idea that "a strong neighborhood identity in a city is a good structure as long as there is a public realm. Sociologically, everybody wants a strong neighborhood identity in compensation for the universalization of culture in the 20th century." (Beth Dunlop, *Architectural Review*, July 1989.)

Despite its nostalgic historicism, the project, influenced very much by the ideas of Leon and Robert Krier, and to a great extent by Robert Stern, is much closer to pre-war beliefs about architecture and its potential. In many respects, it can be likened to the developments in Israel, especially Tel Aviv. The strong utopian environmental determinism is, however, counterbalanced by a sense of economic realism. The urban principles translated into a sound investment for the developer Robert Davis, who, having built modernist townhouse complexes in Coconut Grove, decided that something else was needed to attract "all those doctors and lawyers who sought a delightful summer community and a shrewd real-estate investment." (ibid.)

As an indication of Seaside's overwhelming success, the firm has been involved in 40 projects since it was started, from Orlando to Vero Beach, Cape Cod, California, Washington, and Alabama. On the other hand, Seaside is an affluent

(Left) View from the sea

(Below left) Pedestrian path

(Below) View from the land

neighborhood and its success has occurred under optimum sociological conditions.

Some big claims have been made about DPZ's work, most notably by Vincent Scully (*New York Times*, January 27, 1991), who sees it as "the revival of the vernacular and classical traditions and their re-integration into the mainstream of modern architecture in its fundamental aspect: the structure of communities, the building of towns."

Seaside has also been the target of criticism. Commenting on its strongly historicist preoccupation, its escapist esthetics, but also its programmatic identity, Herbert Muschamp bemoans "the old-fashioned fantasy" it thrives on as the embodiment of the "rage for simulation which has loomed large on the American landscape in recent years."

(*New York Times*, April 11, 1993.)

Duany and Plater-Zyberk have proposed a clear set of urbanistic tools, an excellent manifestation of how they can be implemented to the smallest detail. Yet, no matter how rational or based on empirical testing, these tools are unreal in the context of the largest reality of contemporary North America. Not only is the model based on purely architectural criteria, excluding technical and environmental complexities,

the very basis of their project—socially, economically, and culturally—is rooted in the principle of separation and exclusion. Hardly the image of contemporary, multicultural, dynamic America. The idea of the project is applicable only as a segregated appendix to the intestines and organs of the larger urban corpus within which business will continue as usual, unless other fundamental systemic alternatives are provided.

Bond Ryder James & Associates
MARTIN LUTHER KING, JR. CENTER FOR NON-VIOLENT SOCIAL CHANGE
Atlanta, Georgia
1976–81

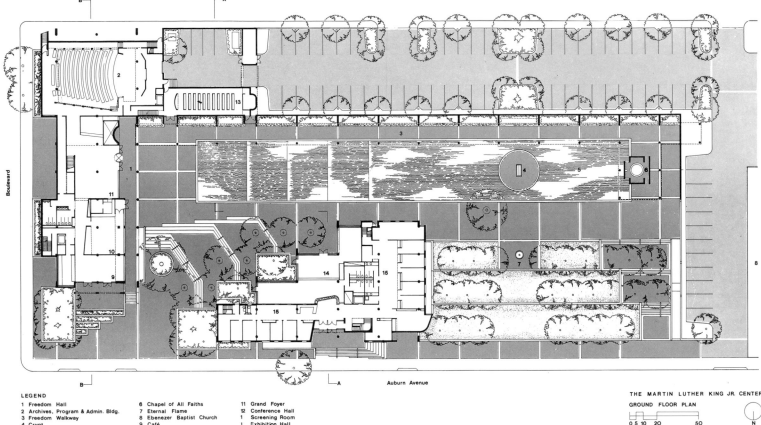

THE MARTIN LUTHER KING JR. CENTER
GROUND FLOOR PLAN

0 5 10   20   50

N

LEGEND
1 Freedom Hall
2 Archives, Program & Admin. Bldg.
3 Freedom Walkway
4 Crypt
5 Reflecting Pool
6 Chapel of All Faiths
7 Eternal Flame
8 Ebenezer Baptist Church
9 Café
10 Bookstore
11 Grand Foyer
12 Conference Hall
1 Screening Room
1 Exhibition Hall
1 Programs

Site plan

The Martin Luther King Center for Non-Violent Social Change is located next to the Ebenezer Baptist Church on Auburn Avenue, the traditional main street of Atlanta's black community. The church marks the street's transition from a commercial to a residential area, and the King family residence—Martin Luther King Jr.'s birthplace—is on the next block to the east.

This is one of the earliest major projects of the firm, and remains its masterpiece. The architectural concept emerges out of a number of important constraints related to the meaning of the project, its historical and physical context. The firm describes these constraints as follows. Immediately following his assassination, Dr. King's crypt was placed on the vacant site next to Ebenezer, beneath a tree in which he had played in his youth. This open land was later designated as the site for the Center because of its association with the church, the family, and the activist black community around Auburn Avenue.

The building program grew out of the initial work by Richard Dober and was developed by the architects through discussions with the King family and associates. The architects were asked by the clients to read the writings of Martin Luther King and to discuss his campaigns with his associates. The clients stressed the need for a program that would be both spatial and symbolic. They wanted the Center to represent Dr. King's ideas, philosophy, political heritage, and the mission of the civil rights movement.

The Center includes archival, administrative, public, educational, and informational spaces. The small open-air chapel, Freedom Walk, the construction materials, and the reflecting pool are used to symbolize some of Dr. King's views and relationship to other liberation movements. The crypt, set in a pool of moving water to suggest the continuation of the civil rights movement, refers specifically to the historic march on Washington, D.C. in 1963.

(Right) Grounds

(Below) Buildings of the center

© Bond

© Gordon Schenk

MARTIN LUTHER KING, JR. CENTER FOR NON-VIOLENT SOCIAL CHANGE • 197

(Opposite) View of the center from the pool

© Schenk

(Above) Covered passageway

(Right) Aerial view

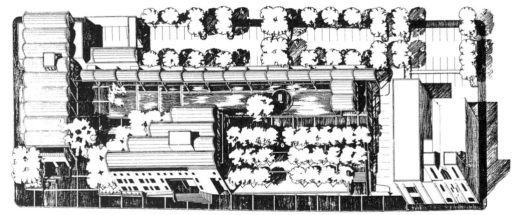

The site is organized so that the visitor can enter from the Ebenezer Church to the west or from the birthplace to the east. The two major buildings relate both to the adjacent streets and to the center of the compound. The southern entrance to the site is marked by steps and a ramp to emphasize gently the transition from street to site. A grove of trees also marks this transition, while allowing views of the crypt from Auburn Avenue.

The King family asked that the Center be built of humble materials and ones that would express his heritage. The architects selected local brick, pre-cast and poured-in-place concrete, West African Sapele wood, and Southern U.S. pine and white oak. A special construction technique was used for the brick vaults. Each vault is one brick thick, and was assembled as a curved wall on the ground. The vaults were then carefully lifted and placed on to pre-cast concrete beams. Following vernacular construction that is often additive by nature, the buildings of the Center suggest repetitive compositions through the expression of the vaults and the division of the program into several elements. Divisions in the brick paving reflect the column spacing of the arcade, which are of concrete, separating the brick and glass of the walls.

The architects felt it was important that the Center should not appear overpowering, given the associations that monumental public buildings have for many black southerners, and so they sought to develop a civic scale that was neither domestic nor monumental. In this effort, they conceived of an architecture which is truly universal, beyond the confines of the mainstream architectural textbook tradition, deeply moving in the intentional poverty of its architectural means.

Although not originally built as a tourist site, the Center has become one of the ten most visited U.S. Park Service sites in America. With nearly a million visitors each year, the Martin Luther King Center plays out its role in fulfiling the dream of a just society.

© Schenk

Antoine Predock Architect
RIO GRANDE NATURE CENTER
Albuquerque, New Mexico
1982

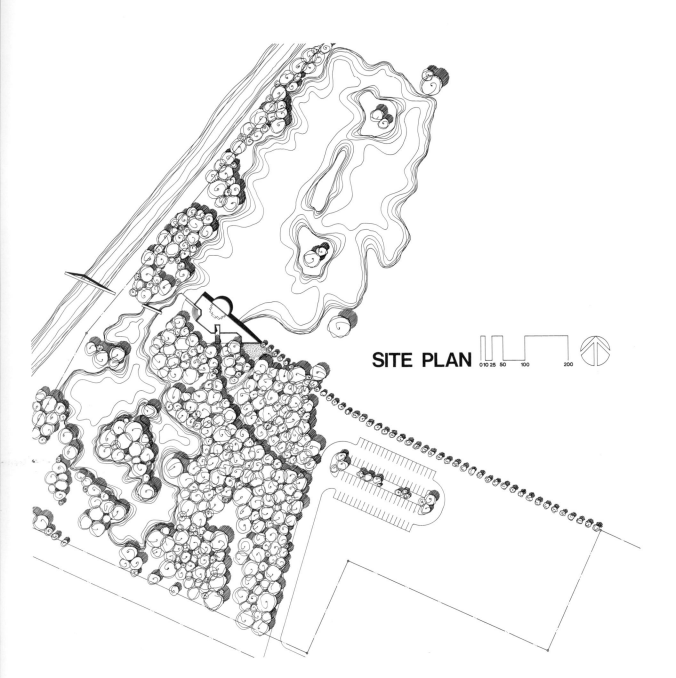

SITE PLAN 010 25 50   100   200

The New Mexico ecosystem, rich in flora and fauna, is rapidly disappearing and being destroyed by expanding urbanization and agriculture. The Rio Grande Nature Center and Preserve is an attempt to raise the awareness of the ecological significance of the region, its moving beauty, and its threatened future.

The Rio Grande flows 1900 miles (3000 kms.) from the mountains of Colorado to the Gulf of Mexico. It is possible to see, as it passes through the city of Albuquerque, how it has been overwhelmed by the growth of the city. The remaining open fields are vestiges of a beautiful pastoral setting which once stretched the length of the city. The natural wetlands ecosystem still harbors a diverse set of processes that contrast sharply with those of the semi-arid mesas. Acquisition of the site by the state of New Mexico offered the potential of maintaining important connections between the city and the river, its symbiotic agricultural development, and a prime wildfowl preserve located in a migratory flyway.

Antoine Predock developed a master plan for the Rio Grande Nature Center and Preserve, incorporating environmental, legal, historic, and recreational concerns for the 170-acre site, responding to the resources of the site and the problems posed by development. Functionally, the Nature Center itself is an unobtrusive bird "blind," where visitors have panoramic views of the wildfowl areas with a minimal disturbance of the environmental system. The materials are cast-in-place concrete walls, colored concrete floors, and galvanized steel doors and

(Above) Interior

(Right) Ground plan

© Timothy Hursley

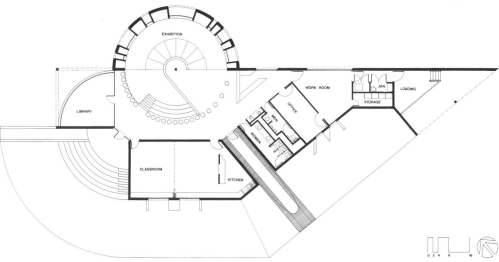

windows. From the main approach, the berms and bunker-like perimeter structure blend into the wooded environment.

Located at the edge of a cottonwood grove on the shore of the pond, the building uses elements of "river-bottom vernacular" for basic building materials, such as the 8-foot diameter corrugated drainage culvert that forms the tunnel entry into the Center. The architect wanted the visitors to become aware from the first moment of the salient feature of the building and site: water. He saw this experience to be enhanced through the use of "vertical, eight-foot high, water-filled tubes (that would) encircle a sunken ramped exhibit and viewing area." In addition, "light shimmers through these tubes from skylights to create an underwater effect." In an intricate combination of the traditional picturesque strategy, combined with modern technology, Predock's composition incorporates a ramp descending "physically and symbolically to allow strategically framed views of vast forage areas, the marshlands, and a reverse-periscope underwater image of the aquatic world."

The Center is designed as an educational facility, with children in mind. As a gesture to the frequent school-age visitors, window sills are low and the culvert entrance has a special appeal: "I remember as a kid running through metal culverts, clicking sticks along the side," Predock says, "and the kids really respond to it." (*Progressive Architecture*, December 1984.)

Peter Papademetriou, the American critic long associated with the architecture of the Southwest, sees the Rio Grande Center as marking a transition in Predock's work away from the "puebloid modern" of his earlier projects to a search for other vernacular forms, and that his use of a Corps of Engineers esthetic presents perhaps a "tougher realism than the coziness of adobe forms," and offers an alternative definition of "regionalism for the emerging Southwest."

Just as importantly, perhaps, Predock uses his talents of composition and narration in a deeper critical regionalist sense, inspired by Mumford's call for a more intelligent symbiotic relation between humans and their surroundings.

© Timothy Hursley

(Opposite) South facade

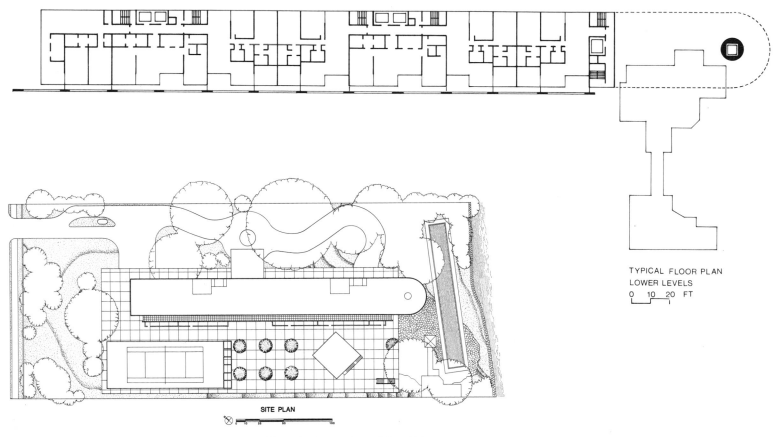

TYPICAL FLOOR PLAN
LOWER LEVELS
0   10   20   FT

SITE PLAN

(Top) Typical floor plan

(Above) Site plan

The television show, *Miami Vice*, placed Arquitectonica's name in the credits, along with the names of the stars of the show, to acknowledge the opening shots which showed the firm's Atlantis Building. *Money* magazine used another of their buildings as the setting for a full page advertisement of itself. No other firm, perhaps, better represents the architectural ideals of the 1980s, which emphasized private luxury and glamour.

A 20-story luxury condominium, Atlantis was Arquitectonica's first big commission. Designed to be seen from a speeding car, the north facade of the building is covered in reflective glass, surmounted by a 23½-foot high bright red triangle, and emblazoned with four bright yellow triangles. In the middle of the building an immense 37-foot square piece has been pushed out, and through the resulting gap, the bright green head of a palm tree bobs and sways. The south elevation was hardly less delirious—a colossal, bright royal blue stucco facade framing a grid-like series of balconies, at the base of which rests the 37-foot-square cube

(containing a health club), which had been pushed out of the building's center, lying just where it landed.

The exuberantly youthful building made a big splash in Miami, despite complaints about the claustrophobic boxiness of the apartments they housed (Ellen Posner, *Wall Street Journal*, July 17, 1984). These functional drawbacks were more than outweighed by the luxurious amenities of the building, in particular the hole in its center, which was termed a "sky court" by the architects. With its curved yellow walls and looped red staircase, the sky court provided for the residents of the four adjacent apartments an exotic outdoor environment, complete with hot tub and whirlpool bath, and breathtaking views overlooking Key Biscayne.

After the success of Atlantis, so many commissions followed in Miami imitating it, that the city's image is now practically trademarked by Arquitectonica. The firm's highly recognizable style, consisting of purist, prismatic, oversized geometric shapes in flashy colors, is the work of Laurinda Spear,

© Norman McGrath

© Norman McGrath

(Left) View of the missing center

(Below) Section of the block and sky court

(Opposite) Sky court

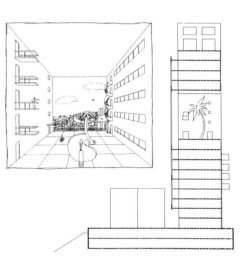

one of its five founding partners. One of the most prolific women practicing architecture in America since Julie Morgan—she has designed over 70 buildings to date—she shared at 25 years of age a prestigious *Progressive Architecture* award (*Progressive Architecture*, January 1975) with Rem Koolhaas for the design of a housing project in Miami, which introduced the oversized stark geometrical forms in striking colors. So novel did it appear to Paul Rudolph, that he termed it "surrealistic," and Peter Chermayeff likened it to the work of a "mad poet." Arquitectonica, however, with an extreme sense of realism and rationality, succeeded in turning this novel vision into a built project, one that has met with the clients' enthusiastic approval.

© Norman McGrath

Michael Graves Architect
PORTLAND BUILDING
Portland, Oregon
1980–82

Studies by the architect

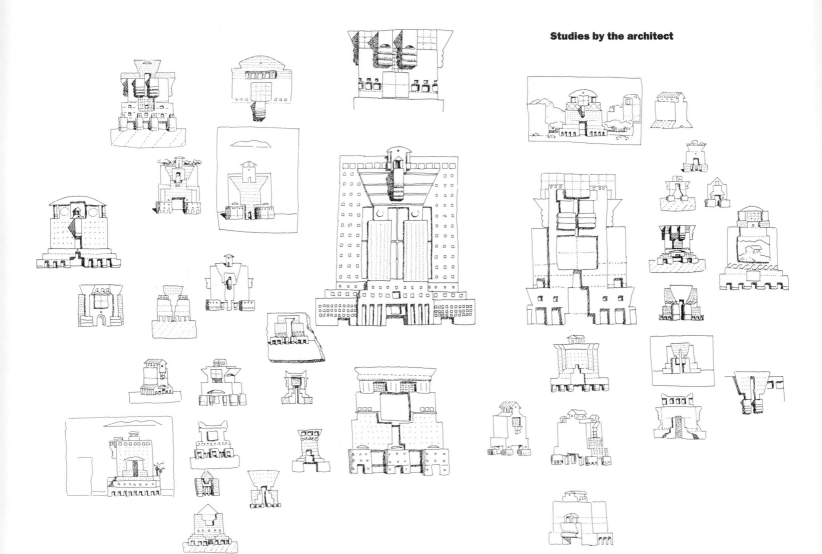

Studies by the architect

"There is an emerging tendency that views the system of architecture as a system of cultural meaning," wrote Mario Gandelsonas, in a *Progressive Architecture* article of March 1972. According to this approach, a building is "read" rather than used. Gandelsonas identified Michael Graves as one of the most important architects within this tendency, part of a general re-examination of the functionalist tradition. The Portland Building was his first big commission and, if not his most important, his most talked about and ambitious project in this direction.

The site is located in downtown Portland, Oregon, next to the City Hall, the County Courthouse, the public transit mall and across from the city park, on a 200-foot perfectly square block. The 362,000-foot-square building resulted from a design competition sponsored by the city and advised by Philip Johnson. The finalists were, in addition to Michael Graves, Arthur Erickson and Mitchell/Giurgola.

The building houses the city's municipal offices. Its 15-story block also includes, on its first two floors, an auditorium, two meeting rooms, a visual arts gallery, and a restaurant. The city services are located behind a large window of reflective glass.

The scheme expresses the negative attitude of the 1970s and 1980s towards modernist architecture. But it also manifests what Susan Doubilet, the *Progressive Architecture* critic, called the divided intentions of the client "on one hand ... want(ing) to make a statement ... on the other hand ... restrict(ing) the

architect with a rather low $51 per square foot budget." (*Progressive Architecture*, February 1983.)

Thus, the ambitions of the client to become visible on an international scale allowed the architect a major opportunity to display magnificently his playful nostalgic form and colour polemics. The client's aspirations were fulfilled. The project ultimately came to be known internationally, due to the intricacy of Graves's images. The stringent budget, however, shows through. It is evident in the location of the circulation of the building in the core—the most efficient, conventional solution—as well as in the choice of the squat shape of the building, which was the least costly or rather the most "pragmatic," as the architect saw it.

(Below left) Facade

(Below) Side

This preference for efficiency, however, came into conflict with the functional requirements of an office building. In addition, the "Plain Jane arrangement," to quote the architect, led to an over-confining, two-dimensional treatment of the facades. This restriction precluded a plastic architectural articulation. It did not exclude, however, a "painterly" facade made up of materials more than paint. It is probably the architect's preoccupation with "reading" the building, however, that led to a reductive, scenographic mock-up. In addition to its controversial esthetics, the Portland Building's paint-dependent facade, as well as its other materials, for example the enameled metal, poses formidable problems of maintenance for a public building, as pointed out by Thomas Fisher (*Progressive Architecture*, February 1983).

Linked with the facade is a fundamental esthetic problem which emerges not so much out of its two-dimensionality, as from the way Graves had applied the idea of "reading" to the building. The facades are blown up straight from a small size model without evident consideration for scale. It is like enlarging the type of a text without altering its content. A model, however, is like a summary of a text which cannot be turned into a short story or a long novel without fundamental structural changes. Here, not only is the giant column of the facade out of scale, but the whole colour scheme also suffers. Unfortunately, the question of scale and the relationship between thumb-nail sketches and large-scale realization when it concerns color is better handled today by stage designers, rather than by architects who use color. This craftmanship is clearly lacking in the

Portland Building. The most important question, however, is why color, and why this particular color palette, was chosen for this location and this particular program. Both the urban, contextual, and the programmatic aspects of the question remain unanswered. Perhaps all one is meant to read in the building is a question mark. Certainly we have to recognize that the sheer fact that Graves tried to re-introduce color into the architecture of large complexes and especially public architecture, and that he raised these questions, is probably the most important contribution of the project, as well as of the clients who supported it to the end.

Hellmuth Obata Kassabaum
LEVI'S PLAZA
San Francisco, California
1977–82

© Hellmuth Obata Kassabaum

(Left) Urban setting

(Below) Balconies

(Bottom) Site plan

© Hellmuth Obata Kassabaum

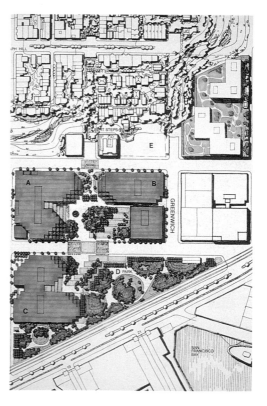

By 1974, Levi Strauss & Company, the original maker of jeans, had outgrown the small wood-frame structure that had been its home since the 1906 earthquake and fire. As befitted the rapidly expanding business, they moved into 12 floors of a fashionable high-rise tower for their new headquarters. What the management and employees soon discovered, was how their trademark sense of family was curtailed by the reduced contact between floors. No casual interactions occurred between staff, and the isolation between departments led to rumors and a sense of loss. Their decision was to build a new complex no higher than the trees, which would reflect a return to the company's tradition of informality.

The result is a campus-like cluster of low-rise buildings, incorporating parks, plazas, and fountains by landscape architect, Lawrence Halprin. The three separate buildings maintain the order of the city's grid pattern, and step down from the base of Telegraph Hill to the Bay with terraced balconies, preserving the views to the waterfront for the surrounding residences. While the complex conveys a coherent image, each of the buildings has singular elements to maintain its identity. The atrium of the main building is a continuation of the landscaped plaza, providing a public indoor space for visitors and employees, and allowing for visual connections between the offices.

And while the red-brick facades recall the site's historic warehouses, modern codes in earthquake-prone San Francisco prohibit much construction in brick. The solution arrived at by the architects was to have bricks half the normal thickness embedded in huge concrete panels, which were then bolted to the steel frame of the building. This skin of brick wraps around the columns and enters into the atrium. While the skin-tight brick cladding is somewhat curious when appearing as columns and rounded corners, HOK's project designer, Bill Valentine, likened the image to being as soft as a pair of well-worn jeans.

The resulting complex both respects its environment and conveys the image of community associated with the workplace of the family-owned company. Employees meet informally in the mini-lounges provided throughout the circulation network of the complex. One finds similar consideration for the communal use of space in the design of the plaza landscaped by Halprin. In fine weather, it is used for brown-bag lunches, where the workers and the tourists intermix. It is this intricate relationship between building and public outdoor space, work, and social interaction that makes the design unique. Levi's Plaza was one of the first examples of the workplace as campus, where work was viewed less in division-of-labor compartmentalization, but as a learning community of workers, acknowledging the increasing importance of communication, and at the same time taking full advantage of its spectacular urban setting.

(Top) Facade

(Above) Public space

(Right) Public space

AT&T HEADQUARTERS BUILDING
New York City, New York
1978–83

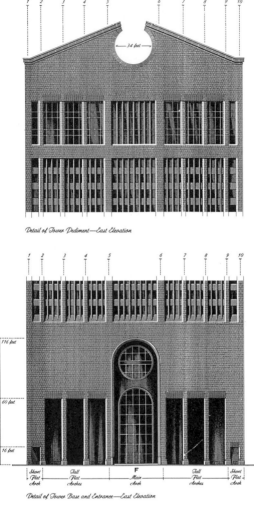

Detail of Tower Pediment—East Elevation

Detail of Tower Base and Entrance—East Elevation

(Left) Round oculus at top of building

(Top) Detail of the tower pediment, east elevation

(Above) Detail of lower base and entrance

© Norman McGrath

AT&T Headquarters is a gigantic, 647-foot skyscraper for 1500 employees, with a retail arcade in the rear, a science museum, and a loggia on the ground floor. Although other buildings had been built in the postmodernist manner before it, Johnson and Burgee's AT&T became, more than any other, the flagship of postmodernism in the 1980s, catapulted on to the cover of *Time* magazine and made into the most talked about building of the decade.

The building was intended as a strong formal statement. This statement was simple. The AT&T client, if the claim of *Progressive Architecture* (July 1994) is correct, wanted it as direct as a painting in the style of Norman Rockwell, which led to what the same publication would call a "pompous essay in pre-war corporate majesty." From a more architectural point of view, Johnson conceived his scheme as a negation of the one building, the Seagram

Tower in New York, that had for twenty-five years come to symbolize, rightly or wrongly, modernism—a building on which Johnson had collaborated with Mies van der Rohe. Both Seagram and AT&T were office towers, similar in plan, steel construction, and overall shape. But whereas the Seagram Building clearly expressed its construction logic in the most rigorous terms, AT&T hid the structure away under pink granite cladding. Moreover, while the Seagram

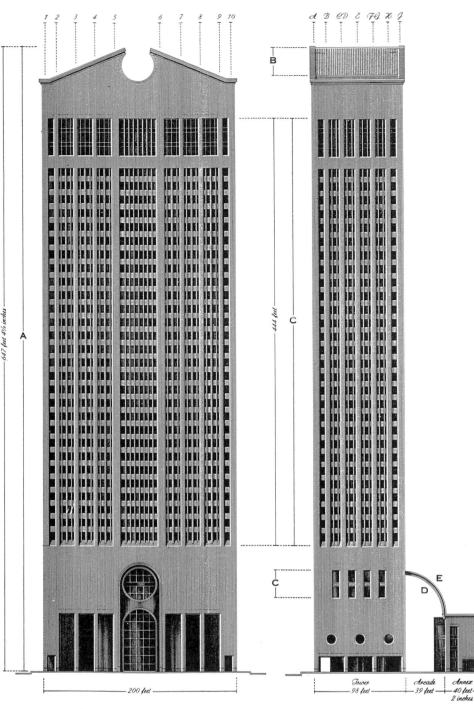

East Building Elevation at Madison Avenue

North Building Elevation at East 56th Street

Building distanced itself from pastiche historicism, although in constant subtle dialogue with historical precedent, AT&T was overtly an almost cartoon-like reinstatement of it. Hence the stone piers and archways of the curiously temple-like loggia on street level, and the pediment on the roof which soon came to be known as the "Chippendale Top."

The building elicited as much praise as censure. Paul Goldberger, the critic of the *New York Times*, waxed lyrical. He saluted it as the "Harbinger of a New Era," as "a strange combination of the noble and the institutional" which "ranked as the beginning of the withdrawal" of the "acceptance" of modern architecture as a corporate symbol (*New York Times*, September 28, 1983). He went so far as to conclude that the building

filled him with "a sense of architectural possibility." At the other end of the spectrum, Ada Louise Huxtable, whom Goldberger succeeded as architectural critic at the *New York Times* just about that time, saw it, on the contrary, as expressing "social and political neo-conservatism" that pushed the admiration for "more conventional and traditional aesthetic values" to a kind of "longing for the traditional social order and practices those values have served." This attitude, according to Huxtable, expressed "a parvenu old-tie, anti-liberal snobbism of the new, and young, far Right." Postmodern is an "odd creature" she concludes, and its practitioners "architectural monarchists, regardless of background or training, with the legendary

preference for cake over bread." (*New Criterion*, November 1982, p. 17.)

As an image, the building was without doubt memorable. But that was only in terms of its innumerable reproductions through the media. As an urban object, it was a failure. Both perceptually and compositionally, it was a misfit for the site. As a contribution to the street, the building was not a success either. Mark Alden Branch points out (*Progressive Architecture*, July 1994) that the arcades soon became notorious for their inhospitability. At a height of 60 feet they managed "to capture almost no sunlight but lots of wind." The galleria, located behind the building, was nothing but "a wind-tunnel" pushing people "through the more pleasant atrium at the IBM Building across the street." (ibid., p. 100.)

Thus, the *New York Times* announced that, due to its many failings, the building's new owners, the Sony Corporation, were prompted to hire the firm of Gwathmey and Siegel to enclose and air-condition the galleria and turn the arcade into Sony retail outfits. Indeed the result is, as the newspaper noted, an increased commercial exploitation of the site, which in turn decreased the amount of public space in the city. But then, the original building had added "neither dignity nor life to the cityscape" (March 28, 1983).

Yet there is a turn to the story. The products displayed in the galleria are dedicated to interactive information technology, robotic equipment for adults and younger people to experiment with. "Sony is about communication, dealing with people: music, movies, video," the new architect said. "They wanted to dispel the elitist image, and engage the building with the ground and make it participatory." (*New York Times*, September 27, 1992.)

The renovation was an immediate success. Yet one has to agree with *Progressive Architecture* that "the bill of rights doesn't accompany the flanneur." In other words, there is still a certain freedom lost in the very end, even if it has to do with "a small part of the population of Manhattan and a small part of their activities, without which however the city cannot maintain its place as the world capital."

Edward Larrabee Barnes/John M. Y. Lee, Architects
IBM BUILDING
New York City, New York
1973–83

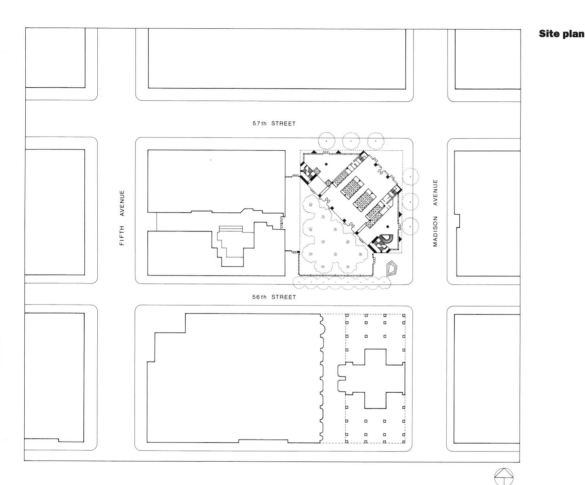

As Mildred Schmertz remarked (*Architectural Record*, May 1984), in the mid-1970s, the financial community in New York feared the city would go bankrupt because of a slump in development, and, in order to lure big employers to stay in or to move to Manhattan, the city administration granted "special permit" buildings. This meant that the 1961 "incentive zoning" ordinance, regulating the height, setback, and site-occupation regulations, was considerably relaxed.

Motivated by the new zoning regulations that offered bonuses in the form of additional floor area for the building in exchange for amenities that benefit the public, IBM, who in 1964 had relocated its headquarters from Manhattan to a bucolic suburb 40 miles north in Westchester County, moved to the corner of Madison Avenue and East 57th Street, one of the most densely packed areas in midtown Manhattan. Adjoining it was the Trump Tower (1979–83, pp. 218–19) and one

block over was AT&T (1978–83, pp. 212–13).

As a result of trade-offs negotiated under the new ordinance, the building was built to an unprecedented height of 604 feet, without setbacks from the sidewalk line. In exchange, IBM offered 8500 square feet of plaza-like conservatory space covering approximately half of the entire site, with retail shops, and exhibition areas. The task to "accommodate the impossible and the undesirable," to quote Ada Louise Huxtable's "The Tall Building Artistically Reconsidered" (*New Criterion*, November 1982, p. 24), fell to Edward Larrabee Barnes.

Barnes's stated aim was to integrate the building to the urban context as much as possible. From this point of view, his approach was highly contrasted to that of Philip Johnson, who conceived his tower as a vacuum. The shape of the tower was chosen to be a 5-sided, green prismatic form with gray–green glass and gray–green polished granite in sleek flush planes.

The advantages of this configuration over the orthogonal glass box is that the bulk of the building is reduced illusionistically when viewed from different vantage points. Sometimes it is a slab-like wall, sometimes a slender shaft, sometimes a tower. In addition, at the corner of 57th Street and Madison Avenue, the building steps back under an astonishingly immense cantilever, freeing an open area at the entrance to the building for pedestrians at this highly congested point of Manhattan—at tremendous expense to the client.

But the most celebrated part of the project is the glass-encased garden, planted with a grove of wispy, 45-foot-high bamboo trees, serving as a plaza and a pedestrian arcade leading from 57th to 56th Street. The garden plaza compares favorably with both AT&T and Trump Tower in the immediate vicinity, all the result of the same "special permit" regulations. The difference resides mainly in that Barnes's idea of a garden was a much more fitting concept than the historicist

© Cervin Robinson

(Left) Cantilever at the corner of 57th Street and Madison Avenue

(Below) Typical office floor

arcade of Philip Johnson, given the context of the site. Further attesting to Barnes's sensitivity to the site, the mass of the building is placed on the wide streets, Madison and 57th, thus keeping to a lower-scaled garden structure, just 68 feet tall, for the more narrow 56th Street.

Although the *New York Times* architectural critic, Paul Goldberger, considered it "the biggest disappointment of the current wave of high-rise construction" (*New York Times,* March 28, 1983), the building received wide acclaim. Its minimalist, understated form contrasts not only with the bombastic glitz of Trump Tower, but also with the mock monumentality of AT&T.

The complex provides a quiet haven of serenity, away from the hustle that surrounds it, and has shown how much highly focussed intentions, combined with craftsmanship, make change possible in the interstices between the slabs, bringing a human scale to Pharaonic surroundings.

© Cervin Robinson

(Below) The sleek flush planes of the shaft

(Opposite) Enclosed garden

© Cervin Robinson

Der Scutt Architect
TRUMP TOWER
New York City, New York
1979–83

(Below left) Interior

(Below) Exterior

Donald Trump, the most famous developer of the 1980s, decided to give his name to this reflective bronze glass and aluminum tower, which, at 68 floors and 664 feet in height, was the tallest residential building and tallest concrete structure in New York when it was built.

Its six-story atrium retail area, accessible through a four-story high bronze portal and with floor-to-ceiling display windows framed in bronze and decorative metals, boasted 41 of the world's most prestigious and fashionable boutiques, restaurants, and shops. Crowned by a transparent skylight in a bronze frame, it contained, besides terraced walkways and hanging gardens, the tallest indoor waterfall, a spectacular 80 feet high, which cascaded into a series of pools on the garden level. The walls and ceilings of the atrium, constructed of more than a thousand pieces of sculptured marble, depleted an entire Italian quarry of brecchia perniche.

The 263 condominium apartments were among the most expensive in the world, ranging in price from $500,000 to "many millions of dollars," in the words of the developer, Donald Trump. Again, in his words, they featured the most spacious rooms in any modern New York residential building, the highest views from any New York City residential building, floor-to-ceiling windows, marble bathrooms with whirlpool baths, heating lamps, and an unprecedented view of Central Park.

Trump Tower's 756,000 square feet was also one of the most complicated zoning packages ever negotiated in New York City. Derived from the 1961 New York City Zoning resolution, the initial area calculations were based upon the footprint of the Bonwit Teller site which consisted of 20,000 square feet. The site permitted an initial development of 300,000 square feet, to which Trump added a lot 50 feet wide and 100 feet deep that connected to the Bonwit site and surrounded

Tiffany's, granting him an additional 375,000 feet. Then he acquired Tiffany's air rights, adding another 35,000 square feet. By devoting a substantial portion of the building to residential use and a covered pedestrian space for use seven days a week between 8 A.M. and 10 P.M., he acquired the rest. Small wonder that Trump's autobiography, *The Art of the Deal*, became a national bestseller.

It is perhaps only fitting that, at the entrance to this building, which more than any other enshrines the almost delirious cult of hyperbole and excess of the 1980s, one passes by a polished bronze plaque that reads "The World's Most Extraordinary Shopping Experience," attended by 6-foot tall bouncers, decked out in Beefeater suits complete with red plumes, after which one is greeted by a tuxedoed pianist in the foyer playing cocktail music on a gleaming white grand piano.

No other space in the United States since Rockefeller Center succeeded in combining

(Below left) Street level plan

(Bottom left) Street level

(Below) Interior

© Norman McGrath

© Norman McGrath

commercialism with the spectacle of space. Despite its flashy lights, colors, and materials, there is a craftsmanship in the detailing and arrangement of space that demonstrates respect for the public. Certainly, the building falls short of Rockefeller Center. Not only is genuine art absent here, but the building is severed from the public transit system. More importantly, the building offers a highly reductive vision of public life—a vision that, to borrow the expression of Edward Luttwak, endangers rather than nurtures the American Dream.

Michael Graves Architect
SAN JUAN CAPISTRANO LIBRARY
San Juan Capistrano, California
1981–83

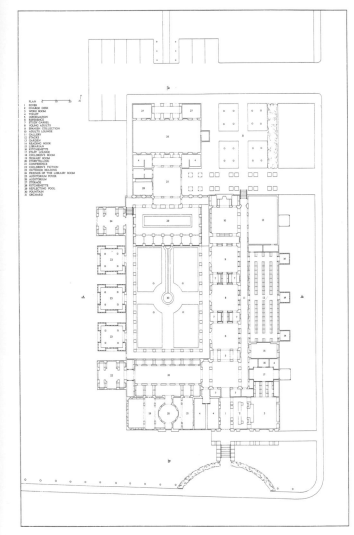

Plan

View from the mission

Michael Graves won the San Juan Capistrano Library commission in a competition whose other finalists were Robert Stern and Moore Ruble Yudell. San Juan Capistrano is a southern California city whose explicit aim was to resist the dissolution of place and community. This was reflected in their choice of Moore Ruble Yudell to set up architectural guidelines that favored conserving the indigenous Spanish Mission style. For Graves, an architect fascinated with tradition and citation, to work within guidelines produced by such a sensitive team of advisors was a challenge rather than a constraint.

The 10,000-foot-square building provides space for book stacks, reading, and administration areas, as well as facilities for special collections and a children's reading area. A 6000-foot-square courtyard includes a reflecting pool spilling into a grotto and leading further down into another cypress-guarded pool with a fountain.

As befits a Mediterranean-derived architecture and a building dedicated to reading, light played an important role in the design of many of the details, as well as in the overall concept of the building—the use of walls as controlers of light, light monitors, clerestories, and the choice of the courtyard plan type. "Traditional" lighting fixtures, designed by Graves himself, were applied to achieve spatial, mood, or iconographic effects, avoiding the purely functionalist solutions so characteristic of many "modernist" institutions of the 1960s. Rather than employing a standard lighting level throughout the project, another institutional cliché, Graves aimed at achieving variety and coziness through the illumination.

The building appears traditional and conservative. In the spirit of much of the 1980s, reaction against modernism, it is a free-wheeling assemblage of design citations, references, and precedent cases with no reference to the immediate context. This encyclopedic approach could have led to a knowledge-based, powerfully integrated composition, but it did not. Nevertheless, the project was one of twelve that won a 1985 honor award of the American Institute of Architects, which saw in it a "delightful experience" and a "masterful transformation of the Spanish mission style."

A decade after its reception as a valid way of "blending new techniques with historic structures," it appears as a highly idiosyncratic scheme. Its fit into the site and its interpretation of the program are far from perfect: rather than integrating the new with the old, the toy-like design of the library makes it seem out of scale with, if not discordant to, the grandeur and nobility of the nearby 1751 Mission church. It is clear now that the design features themselves were less the result of contextual search than a mechano-like standardization of elements: "pointed roofs ... heavy columns ... tomblike ... blocky columns topped by a helmet of lattice," as critic Jane Holtz Kay summed them up (*Christian Science Monitor*, April 17, 1984). These were repeated by the architect in other projects, far removed from the context of San Juan Capistrano, such as the Liberty State Park, a 750-acre site overlooking New York Harbor. Similarly, the over-articulated room divisions, which characterize the Capistrano library scheme, were more an ideological manifesto against the open plan layout than a better functional solution for a facility such as a regional library.

(Above) Courtyard

(Left) Aerial view, as drawn by the architect

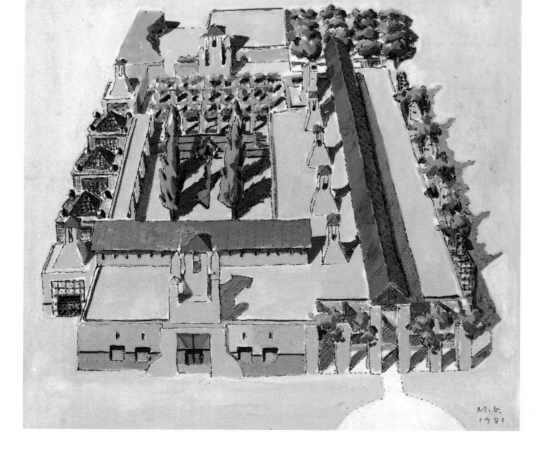

The project appears to have been part of the playful, nostalgic polemics of the architect against modernist architecture, which created major animosity among many of the participants in the 1983 American Institute of Architects convention, who wore buttons that read "I Don't Dig Graves" (*Wall Street Journal*, April 10, 1984). Today it is doubtful how much such polemics, even when applied in the seductively sweet manner of the San Juan Capistrano Library, can help bridge the gap between the community-based place of pre-industrial societies and today's multi-focus, multi-media social aggregates, which Graves justifiably reacted against.

Kelbaugh + Lee
ROOSEVELT SOLAR VILLAGE
Roosevelt, New Jersey
1981–83

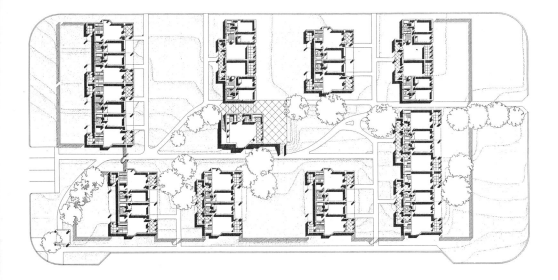

Site plan

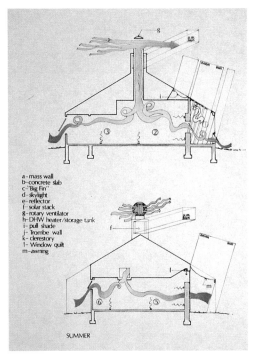

① Solarium
② Living/Dining
③ Kitchen
④ Back Porch/Air Lock
⑤ Bedroom
⑥ Bathroom

WINTER

a – mass wall
b – concrete slab
c – "Big Fin"
d – skylight
e – reflector
f – solar stack
g – rotary ventilator
h – DHW heater/storage tank
i – pull shade
j – Trombe wall
k – clerestory
l – Window quilt
m – awning

SUMMER

Microclimatic control systems

Kelbaugh and Lee's 21-unit Roosevelt Solar Village for the elderly is one of the first examples of low-rise, high-density, passive solar heating in North America. Funded by the Farmers' Home Administration, and built for roughly $50 per square foot, the project deserves recognition for its modest yet successful integration of social, environmental, and historical concerns.

The residents requested housing that would be a continuation of the existing neighborhood, but with an architectural style "new and completely different" from the original town. Almost all wanted one-story, one-bedroom units, and they unanimously did not want flat roofs. True to their community's heritage, they did not want fences around individual yards, favoring instead "only a common lawn."

The Roosevelt Solar Village attempts to learn from nature and to tap the *genius loci* of its site and the essence of its program. It does not look naturalistic, but rather combines some familiar architectural vocabulary of the region in new, more energy-efficient ways. The shed roofs, cupolas, shingle siding, trellises, fences, awnings, and archways are drawn from both vernacular and shingle-style architecture—albeit with certain distortions in scale and materials.

What makes it new is its conscientious attitude to the microclimate, particularly in its orientation to the sun: the east–west linearity, the abundance of south-facing glass, its masonry Trombe walls, and the attached greenhouses. The houses have

© Otto Baitz

© Otto Baitz

awnings to protect from the summer sun, and wind-driven natural ventilation stacks for passive cooling.

The conception of the architectural space is finite: the buildings have middles and ends, fronts and backs, tops and bottoms. The site has a central focus: the community center. Space is sequential, and marked by thresholds, contraction, expansion, and with visual release to the fields beyond. The operation of the buildings requires some participation of the occupants, which is intended to heighten their awareness of diurnal and seasonal cycles.

Unfortunately, federal assistance for low- and moderate-income housing was phased out at the time this project was reaching completion. The broad political support for federally aided housing, which prevailed from the 1930s through to the 1960s, diminished in the 1980s, resulting in increased pressure for such housing with little federal support. Nevertheless, the design experience and the ideals of environment and community consciousness to be found in this project will serve as an example of successful housing, once more enlightened housing policies re-emerge.

Esherick Homsey Dodge and Davis
MONTEREY BAY AQUARIUM
Monterey, California
1978–84

© Dodge

(Above) View from the land

(Left) Plan

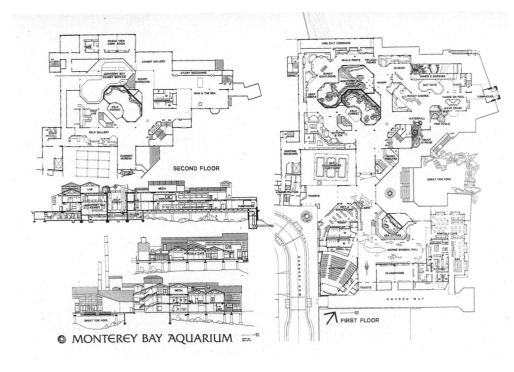

SECOND FLOOR

FIRST FLOOR

MONTEREY AQUARIUM

© Peter Aaron/Esto

The site of the Monterey Bay Aquarium on Cannery Row was heir to a rich and singular historic and emotional legacy. Esherick quotes John Steinbeck on the identity of the place:

> "... A poem, a stink, a grating noise, a quality of light, a tone, a habit, a nostalgia, a dream. Cannery Row is the gathered and scattered, tin and iron and rust and splintered wood, chipped pavements and weedy lots and junk heaps, sardine canneries of corrugated iron, honky-tonks, restaurants ... How can the poem and the stink and the grating noise—the quality of the light, the tone, the habit and the dream—be set down alive?" (*Cannery Row.*)

With this cue, an *ad hoc* industrial vocabulary evolved for the aquarium, using portions of the site's dilapidated Hovden Cannery—the warehouse, boilerhouse, pumphouse, and street facades. By following the footprint of the old cannery, and recalling its massing, proportions, roof pitches, building materials, and structure, architects Linda Rhodes and Charles Davis re-created the presence of the old sardine plant while meeting the needs of the high-tech program for the aquarium.

The building extends out over the water of Monterey Bay supported by concrete piers and pre-cast pre-stressed girders and tee beams. Portions behind the seawall are supported on spread footings. The superstructure consists of reinforced concrete columns and waffle slabs, except for heavy timber roof trusses, reminiscent of old cannery construction. The exterior walls are formed of concrete shear walls and corrugated cement industrial siding over treated wood studs. Windows are steel factory sash, with special corrosion-resistant paint. All reinforcing steel is epoxy-coated, a relatively new technique to ensure long-term performance.

Because of the site's salt-laden environment, extensive research was

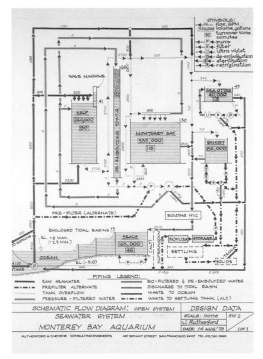

Interior, with tank

© Peter Aaron/Esto

(Opposite above) Night view

(Opposite below) Interior

undertaken to protect not only the tanks and seawater distribution system, but also the building as a whole from corrosion. The result was the use of special protective coatings, as well as fiberglass air ducts and non-metallic piping and valves.

Several technical innovations have been achieved in the design of the Monterey Bay Aquarium, including a 335,000 gallon kelp tank, where kelp is grown in a captive, artificial environment for the first time. Computer sensors monitor the vital life support functions of each tank, and the combined raw and filtered seawater systems allow open-mode functioning to bring nutrient-rich seawater into the system, or closed-mode functioning to increase water clarity for viewing the exhibits.

Advanced technology, however necessary to the project, is not allowed to overwhelm the building, which is conceived as a monument to Steinbeck's populist vision of humaneness in a world of homelessness and poverty. The principal-in-charge, Charles M. Davis, tells how the building evolved, not from a written program, but one that "just happened." The result of this flexible, site-bound approach is that the aquarium visitor, rather than being locked into a single path through the building, is presented with several options for exploring at leisure the marine environments offered by this unique aquarium, a bit like the original Cannery Row, out of "the gathered and the scattered." As such, it is also a reminder that the lyrical can also be about the small and the seemingly insignificant, and that not so long ago poverty was not as hard-edged as it is now. This is not a nostalgic project, but one that applies architecture as a process that integrates past, present, and future.

© Peter Aaron/Esto

© Peter Aaron/Esto

Gatje Papachristou Smith
RICHARD B. RUSSELL POWERHOUSE
Savannah River, Georgia and South Carolina
1978–85

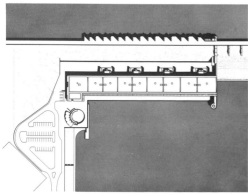

(Top) View from the land

(Above) Site plan

A gigantic machine, a tourist attraction, a monument to the technology of electric power, a landscape sculpture and a modern abstract drama all come together into this rare type of architectural object, the Richard B. Russell Powerhouse. Named after Georgia's late U.S. Senator, located at the border between South Carolina and Georgia, this is the third Savannah River dam built by the U.S. Corps of Engineers, who acted here both as client and consulting engineers.

Hamilton Smith was Marcel Breuer's collaborator in the design of the Whitney Museum (1963–66, pp. 106–09), a building very much preoccupied with sculpture. It comes as no surprise therefore that this project should be so sculptural, both inside the structure and without. Like the Whitney Museum, the powerhouse interweaves,

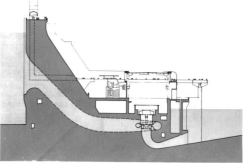

Site section

Theater

inside the shell of the hydroelectric dam, a succession of places offering a sequence of changing views of the formidable powerhouse technology, and the moving water and landscape that surround it.

The visit starts from the road, with a turn-off location providing a vista point for the approaching spectator sufficiently far from the project to allow views of the entire powerhouse structure, extending in front of the dam, from bank to bank. First seen by the visitor is the concrete shell, enclosing eight 75,000 kilowatt power generators, which emerges out of the water, only two fifths of its total height—a similar proportion to that of an iceberg at sea. A series of arched openings dominates the downstream elevation corresponding to the eight generators behind them. A terrace leads to the visitors' entrance and a new viewing point, a gathering and an exhibition place, with an elevated walkway along the length of the downstream face of the powerhouse; they offer commanding views into the structure as well as over the waterscape downstream. Upstream the site is framed by the static breadth of the dam and downstream the river reflects the variable moods of weather and season.

The series of the arched openings, as well as the repeated circular pattern, recall the venerated ancestor of the project, the Roman aqueduct. The well-formed masses of concrete offer a unique, plastic quality. Yet the sublime esthetic impact of the dam is not the outcome of historical associations or sculptural effects. It results from the embedding of the gigantic machine complex in the natural landscape, and the insertion within it of a path along which the mechanical and topographical are constantly confronted by each other. It turns this tourist's tour into a contemplative ritual, forcing the visitor into a reflection on the tragic tension between the human and the natural, power and purpose, destruction and *ingenium*.

(Above left) Belvedere and view on to the water

(Above) Path inserted into the powerhouse

© Paul Warchol

View from the land

The house sits on a large waterfront parcel on the south-east side of the island, Martha's Vineyard, overlooking the Atlantic Ocean as it meets Vineyard Sound. In its location, the building followed the strict planning code which set it back from the marshland as well as from a no-build zone on a hill. The setback, the one-story elevation when viewed from the beach, and the use of natural-weathered, gray-colored wood derived from the code, gives to the structure a strong character of placeness.

Within this framework, Holl writes that he took as his point of departure the locally inspired novel, *Moby Dick*, in which Melville describes an Indian tribe that made a unique type of dwelling on the island. Finding a beached whale skeleton, they would pull it up to dry land and stretch skins or bark over it, transforming it into a house.

Holl conceived the structure of this weekend house as an inside-out balloon frame. Within the whale metaphor, these "wooden bones of the frame carry an encircling verandah, which affords several ocean views." In a surrealistic vision, Holl pictured the bones of the sea, the plants of the waterfront, and the man-made balloon-frame merging into one. "Along this porch, wood members are designed to receive the natural vines of the island." The ground vine tendrils transform the straight linear

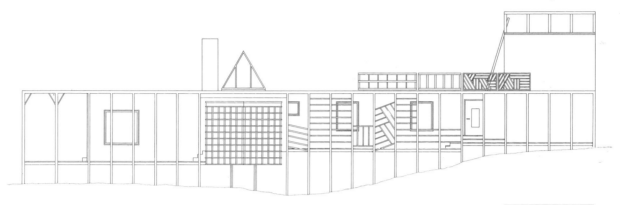

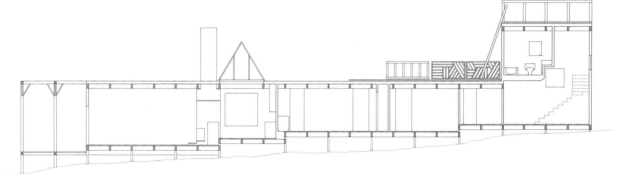

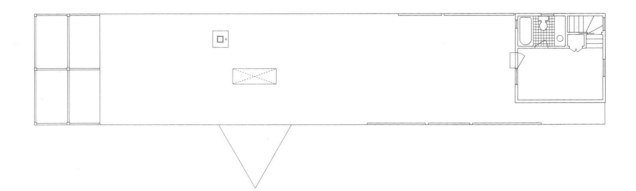

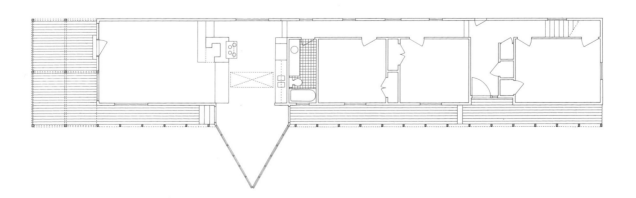

mode of the architecture. Within the smoothness of the curves of the earth, the anarchy of the growth that covers it, and the fluidity of the air and the constant changes of the light which characterize the site, Holl uses a strict proportional system in laying out the rooms, and often sacrifices comfort and function to this ordering grid.

The clarity of the plan is marked by the simple set of rooms positioned perpendicular to the view. Beginning with a mud room off the entry, there are two bedrooms, a kitchen, and a dining room in a protective bay. The living room drops down following the contours of the site. The master bedroom on the second level has a special view to the ocean across an exercise and sun deck on top of the main house—an updated version of the vernacular widow's walk (the upstairs gallery where sea captains' wives would watch for their husbands' return).

Holl works here in an uncomplicated way. He uses wood in a way that allows him the variety of texture, weathering, and scale. The house is framed with 6" x 6" vertical members that are treated and exposed to the weather. The 2" x 2" wood members of the guard railings, as well as the board siding, are all weathered wood; windows are insulated glass in painted wooden frames; the fireplace is of locally gathered stones set in concrete; and the roofing is a rubber membrane unrolled over the frame, analogous to the skins over the whale skeleton. It is in the selection and innovative use of these materials that Holl balances the austerity of his plan.

Praised for its simplicity, the house reportedly falls short on comfort, with an absence of shade on the porch, and lack of cross ventilation (due to its orientation to the shore breezes). Holl responds that in terms of shade, the house was designed to have had canvas awnings added to it. But Thomas Fisher speculates (*Progressive Architecture*, December 1988) on the philosophical appropriateness of a weekend house, not unlike life aboard a ship in a Melville novel, in which we experience smallness, fragility, and

(Above) View from the beach

(Right) Side of the building

occasional discomfort in having to confront the ocean and the sun.

The building's integration with its surroundings—its regionalist character—is achieved through the use of the vernacular tradition, to apply naval architectural experience to houses on the shore. There is a boat-like character to the building in its overall geometry and layout. Holl, however, transcends these precedents of type and technology into poetic metaphor. The building is a point of departure of endless lyrical stories which the viewer can generate as she or he comes into contact with it throughout the hours of the day and seasons of the year. This is one of the most lyrical works of the decade.

(Above left) View towards the sea

(Top) Window

(Above) Play of sun and shadow on the textured walls and details of the interior

Clark & Menefee Architects
MIDDLETON INN
Charleston, South Carolina
1978–85

(Left) Facade

(Below) External view

(Bottom) Site plan

© Tom Crane

© Richard Ingersoll

Potential guests have been known to flee Middleton Inn directly upon arrival because it "doesn't look like Tara" (*Progressive Architecture*, April 1994, p. 95).

The Inn is a hotel and conference center located on the grounds of Middleton Place, one of the 32 plantations that once lined the Ashley River outside Charleston, South Carolina. It was once the home both of one of the signers of the Declaration of Independence, and of a signer of the Ordinance of Secession. In 1865 it was burned by Union troops. Of the three main buildings—a manor house, a library, and a gentlemen's guest wing—only the latter still stands. What do remain in the 6500-acre grounds are the gardens, the ruins, and farm buildings, which are open to the public. The 18th-century gardens are a National Historic landmark and are among America's most celebrated. Known as an American Versailles, the garden is magnificently laid out in an axial manner, organized along a center line that extends from the entrance gate through the manor house's original great hall, down the symmetrical lawn with formal parterres and paired butterfly pools, straight out to the Ashley River. (*Progressive Architecture*, May 1986.)

Clark and Menefee—who teach architecture at the University of Virginia—deliberately made the choice not to yield under the weight of such tradition-laden surroundings. Charles Duell, as developer and patron, and as a descendant of the original builders of Middleton Place, fully supported this view, saying "the Middleton Inn should be of this century, not merely mimic the past." (*Architecture*, May 1987.) The building refuses to perform what Clark

terms "the Colonial Williamsburg number." (ibid.)

The visitor will find no columns, capitals, mullions, mouldings, pediments, and colonnades. The composition, however, inherits basic elements of spatial arrangement from classical architecture. A slender stylobate runs along the base of the facade, a stark copper "cornice" along its top, with minimal concrete "lintels" above some of the openings.

© Tom Crane

(Left) External view

(Below left) Detail of site plan

(Below) Foyer

© Tom Crane

As opposed to the classical spatial partitioning of the formal garden of Middleton Place, the Inn is ruptured into four free-standing fragments, interspersed on a bluff overlooking the banks of the Ashley River. The biggest building contains 25 rooms surrounding a clearing, with 30 other rooms in the three separate pavilions, and another pavilion housing conference facilities. Where the formal garden imposed itself on the land, the Middleton Inn yields respectfully to the existing natural wooded landscape in order to create vistas, mostly out on to the river. The architects went so far as to build the structures around existing trees. *Progressive Architecture* (May 1994) remarked that although many of the trees were uprooted in a hurricane a couple of years ago, this did not affect the harmonious relation of the project to the landscape.

Finally, instead of the imposing grandeur of Middleton Place, Middleton Inn is a world of crafted details that delight and engage with its incorporation of regional architectural elements, such as its "Charleston green" painted wood and custom-made drawers for hiding precious objects in the headboard of the bed, and floor-to-ceiling walls of adjustable pine blinds. The building makes use of local natural materials, such as in the wood-lined bedrooms and reception area, with oak floors, ash and pine furniture, and cypress paneling.

Considering the relation between old and new, local and global, natural and mechanical, the design fulfills the definition of a genuine critical regionalist building as defined in the germinal study by Lewis Mumford, *The South in Architecture*, in 1941.

Murphy/Jahn Architects
STATE OF ILLINOIS CENTER
Chicago, Illinois
1979–85

Aerial view

© Murphy/Jahn

Occupying a whole block of Chicago's North Loop, the State of Illinois Center is a glass and steel box distended to gigantic proportions, then squashed into a squat, sloped, set-back cylindrical hulk, decked out in a turquoise reflective and clear glass pinstripe pattern, propped up on slender, two-dimensional "mock" pink and gray columns, indented with patches of mixed salmon and white marble and, finally, crowned with a glass and steel top truncated to project a rakishly tilted profile.

The loud esthetics of the outside trappings of the building drew not-so-flattering comments. To the *New York Times* architectural critic, Paul Goldberger,

the building appeared as a "glittering and gargantuan object" whose "often gimmicky detailing" and "determined flashiness" called to mind "cheap commercial buildings of the 1950s" (*New York Times*, July 22, 1985). While its "sense of pizzazz" appealed to *Architecture*'s Nora Richter Greer (November 1985, p. 40), Goldberger, remarking on its populist image, stated that Chicagoans likened it to a spaceship built for *Star Wars*.

The building is a widely acknowledged, successful urban experiment, however. The program was dictated by Governor James Thomson of Illinois: to combine a notoriously dreary building type—a government building housing 3000 state employees—with

commercial activity. Offices occupy the top 15 stories, and shops are located mainly on the first two floors; restaurants are below on the concourse level. The rotunda has been praised for its exuberance and open views. Two exposed elevator shafts, each with six glass enclosed chambers, add an element of movement to the soaring space. From the elevators, clip-on walkways lead to circular balconies which overlook the ground floor.

Another fundamental factor in the success of the State of Illinois Building as genuine public space, is its strategic location in relation to public transportation lines, such as the elevated train track line running along the south side of the building and subway

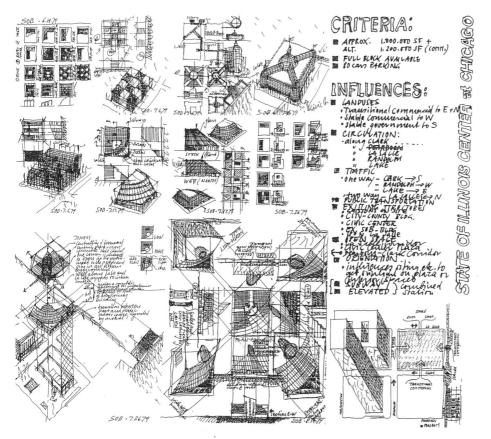

© Murphy/Jahn

(Left) Conceptual drawing by the architect

(Below) View of the court from the top of the rotunda

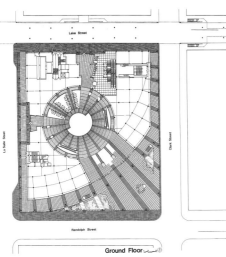

Ground Floor

(Above) Street level plan

(Right) View of the roof from the base of the rotunda

station nearby. In addition to the criticism of its esthetics, the building has been criticized for its environmental and functional inadequacies. Yet it remains a unique achievement. It succeeded in employing a building type that had been applied up to that moment only to private buildings, to a public one. It finally succeeded in breaking the taboo that public buildings had to be approached with awe rather than with a sense of enjoyment, as is due in a democratic society.

© Murphy/Jahn

© Murphy/Jahn

(Above) Aerial view

(Above right) Interior

(Right) Ground plan

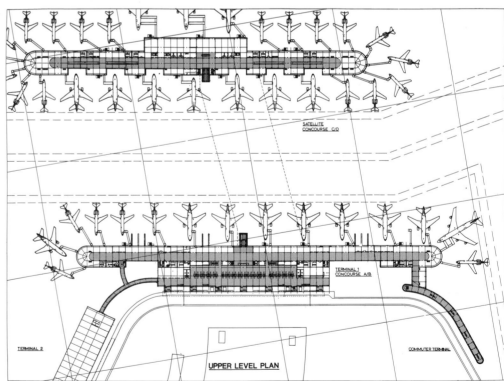

SATELLITE
CONCOURSE C/D

TERMINAL 1
CONCOURSE A/B

TERMINAL 2

COMMUTER TERMINAL

UPPER LEVEL PLAN

At their worst, airports are viewed by modern travelers as holding-pens for interminable delays, and at Chicago's O'Hare airport—one of the world's busiest—the handling of people and baggage often recalls the stockyards of an earlier era. The success of Helmut Jahn's United Airlines terminal is the development of a spatial sequence that lifts the spirits of the traveler, a building that reflects not only the technology and wizardry of flight, but the elation and joy of travel.

The structure is steel and glass, but rather than reconstructing the image of 19th-century railroad stations, the United Terminal looks towards the sophistication of 21st-century travel. The vaulted concourse is of fritted and clear glass units and aluminum panels, anchored to a steel purlin substructure and set on curved steel beams. The overall sense of lightness is due not only to the pervasive abundance of natural light, but also to the detailing of the structure itself. The curved steel beams are painted white and punched with round holes. These are supported on 8-inch steel pipes, bundled into columns, their number determined by the load that each supports. The meticulous

Concourse

detailing of the steel is high-tech, but because of the transparency of the material, the effect is one of art deco. Jahn has taken a Mies skyscraper technological dream and turned it on its side.

Not since Dulles Airport (1958–63, pp. 78–81) has the experience of the visitor been so carefully choreographed to capture the spirit of being on the move and the romance of travel, as it emerges at the end of this century. Mundane and awkward security walk-throughs are replaced here with stations carefully integrated into the overall design. The architectural experience of flight (or escape?) is perhaps best captured in the underground passageway connecting the two concourses. Into this dark subterranean tunnel, 52 feet wide and 815 feet long, the visitor steps on to a moving sidewalk that passes by undulating glass walls, with back-lit, rainbow-painted walls. Meanwhile,

overhead, the sculpture by Michael Hayden pulses neon lights to music by William Kraft, computer-generated in a never-repeating sequence. The senses are literally bombarded from all sides, and the effect is not unlike the experience of the space travelers in Stanley Kubrick's movie, *2001*.

Does all this technological wizardry add up to more than special effects? Indeed, the universally acknowledged success of the terminal occurs because everything works so well, and in this technology plays a supporting role. This is exemplified in the integration of service and served, traveler and staff, techniques and art. The pattern of ceramic frit on the glass panels not only relieves the eye, but admits natural daylight during the day, and reflects the interior lighting at night. And for the weary traveler, the terminal brings the ingenuity of air travel successfully down to earth.

Many fundamental problems still remain. Is this explosion of sensuous experience the appropriate prelude or epilogue to an exhilarating event which is air travel itself? The 19th-century designers of train stations have already answered this in the strongly affirmative. But for the 21st-century commuter, including the air-commuter, overloaded with the unprecedented bombardment of information, and for whom traveling is increasingly a routine convenience rather than a unique event, there might be a good reason for a more tranquil, serene environment. Yet this question poses a problem rather than a criticism of Jahn's project. Its contribution remains as unique as its enlightened clients, who allowed and invited a serious consideration of quality design for an infrastructure service facility.

Center for Maximum Potential Building Systems
LAREDO DEMONSTRATION BLUEPRINT FARM
Laredo, Texas
1987–

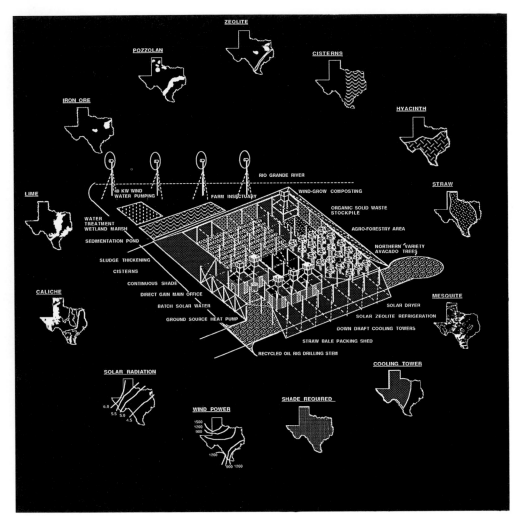

ZEOLITE
POZZOLAN
CISTERNS
IRON ORE
HYACINTH
RIO GRANDE RIVER
STRAW
LIME
40 KW WIND WATER PUMPING
WIND-GROW COMPOSTING
FARM INSECTUARY
WATER TREATMENT WETLAND MARSH
ORGANIC SOLID WASTE STOCKPILE
SEDIMENTATION POND
AGRO-FORESTRY AREA
NORTHERN VARIETY AVACADO TREES
SLUDGE THICKENING
CISTERNS
CONTINUOUS SHADE
CALICHE
DIRECT GAIN MAIN OFFICE
BATCH SOLAR WATER
MESQUITE
SOLAR DRYER
SOLAR ZEOLITE REFRIGERATION
GROUND SOURCE HEAT PUMP
DOWN DRAFT COOLING TOWERS
STRAW BALE PACKING SHED
RECYCLED OIL RIG DRILLING STEM
SOLAR RADIATION
COOLING TOWER
SHADE REQUIRED
6.0
5.5 5.0
4.5
WIND POWER
1500
1200
900
1200
900 1200

Ecological factors forming the basis
of the project

On the outskirts of Laredo, Texas, along the U.S.–Mexican border, and directly adjacent to the Rio Grande River, a group of architectural and ecological pioneers are building the blueprint for a new building typology. The Laredo Blueprint Demonstration Farm is one of a series of ambitious building and research projects undertaken by the Center for Maximum Potential Building Systems and its two co-directors, Pliny Fisk III and Gail Vittori.

For them, architecture is viewed more as a "metabolic process" akin to how living organisms relate to each other and to their region. They approach their work by identifying a series of interweaving networks representing the land, resources, people, and institutions. They characterize the material and energy flows not only by where materials come from, but by where they go. Their palette for the Laredo Farm includes recycled oil-well drilling stems, local

materials, such as straw, lime, pozzolan, caliche, mesquite, and innovative technologies for ordinary activities.

The building system, designed as a grid, enables the interior and exterior spaces to be partially or fully transformed, from closed-in, barn-type structures with roofs that can be raised or lowered, to continuous shade systems for prolonging the growing season. Cisterns collect rainwater for use in the bathroom facilities and the evaporative cooling system. The entire farm is operated by sustainable technologies powered by sun and wind.

The five buildings at the center of the farm house the offices, classrooms, and storage. Built from stacked straw bales, they are finished with either sprayed-on cement supplied by a local swimming-pool builder, or hand-stuccoed. The roofs are locally fabricated steel trusses and decking.

Underlying Fisk's experimental designs is an architectural sensibility shaped by the teachings of Louis Kahn and Ian McHarg at the University of Pennsylvania. Fisk acknowledges a personal concern for architects to conserve resources, promote local economies, and to integrate buildings back into their surroundings. And unlike many of his contemporaries, Fisk puts his ecological beliefs to the test.

Local designer and writer, Ray Don Tilley, has written about their work (*Progressive Architecture*, May 1991), arguing that, embodying a "Kahn-like inevitability," Laredo Farm's "humble sheds take shape from the way they harness the elements and from the straw, steel and wood used to build them." Echoing the sentiment of Fisk himself, he goes on to add that regionalism "never had a more profound model than Blueprint Farm."

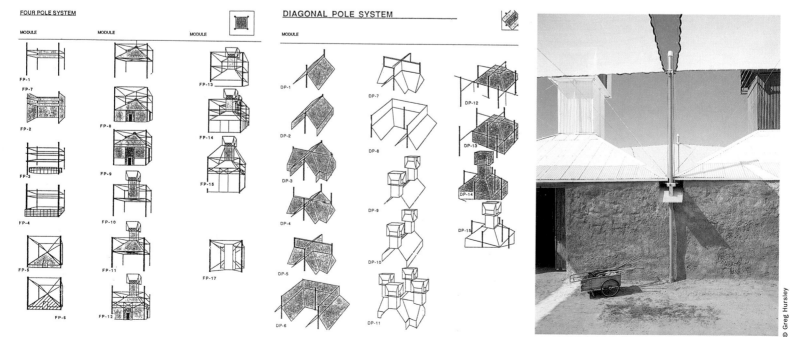

FOUR POLE SYSTEM

MODULE MODULE MODULE

FP-1
FP-7
FP-13

FP-2
FP-8
FP-14

FP-3
FP-9
FP-15

FP-4
FP-10

FP-5
FP-11
FP-17

FP-6
FP-12

DIAGONAL POLE SYSTEM

MODULE

DP-1
DP-7
DP-12

DP-2
DP-8
DP-13

DP-3
DP-9
DP-14

DP-4
DP-10
DP-15

DP-5

DP-6
DP-11

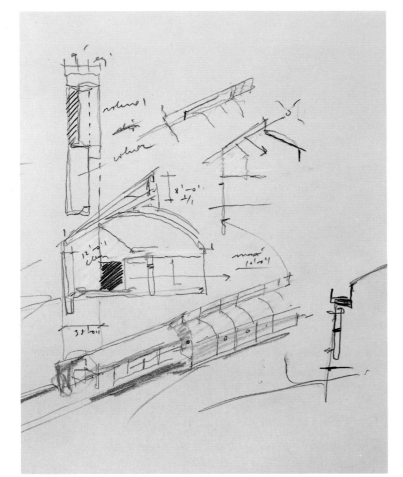
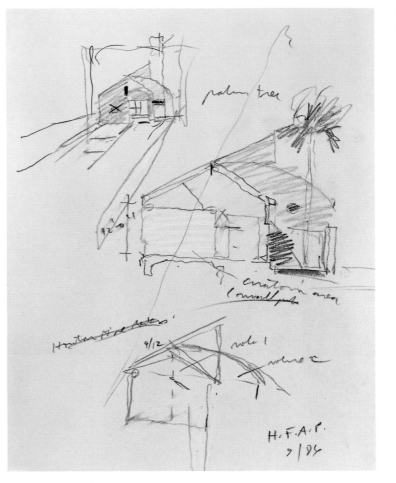

Concept drawings

About 10 miles south-west of Houston's downtown, just west of Loop 610, lies one of the flat, dreary areas, typical of the city's outlying zones, an almost endless, motley, gray horizon punctuated with sad, seedy, dusty apartments, warehouses, and tilt-up concrete containers. In these ramshackle surroundings one comes across the impeccably neat, imperturbably serene Houston Fine Arts Press. With its crisp pitched roof and its stuccoed walls in a hue of magenta, archly stretched out against a patch of green lawn, the effect is surprising.

The surprise only heightens as one approaches the lawn, rounds the agile swoop of the translucent corner, and enters the pristine, hushed interior bathed in a mysterious light. The aim of the architect, as described in his brief, was to create a "sanctuary" for the making of art books and the structure of the Press has all the characteristics of a protective enveloping shelter.

Jiménez brings to the building a love of light and a masterly capturing of its effects, both on the inside and the outside. He also brings geometrical rigor. Both qualities are reminiscent of an approach predominant among Iberian modern architects—the early Josep Lluis Sert, Alejandro de la Sota, and Alvaro Siza.

But the building is not only a formal exercise. The detailing of its all-white environment is impeccable. So is the functional organization of space and the lighting, dictated by the exigencies of art book publishing. The roof of the building, reminiscent of a 19th-century gable-ended industrial shed or loft, is double pitched at the front. At the rear, it is ruptured and asymmetric, with one plane intersecting with a bulging barrel vault. Light shafts for clerestory lighting have been placed at this intersection. The resulting northern natural light fills the entire length of the building interior with the even lighting

(Below) Sections

(Bottom) View from the road

© Paul Hester

(Above) Facade

(Above right) Entrance

conditions required for printing tasks throughout the day.

The interior is designed as a series of reflecting surfaces. Light enters from the clerestory shaft and bounces into the vault, and from the vault on to the white walls below. The tops of closets and partition walls are subtly sloped, causing even more light to rebound. A steel-frame structural system with a roof, simple plywood decking on steel purlins, and a corrugated metal roof dispensed with

the use of shadowy trusses employed in similar sheds.

The Houston Fine Arts Press radiates a calm serenity and an aura of litotes that contrasts with many of the projects of the mid-1980s. This prompted the critic Richard Ingersoll to say it was like "discovering a pearl in a gulf coast oyster." (*A+U*, January 1990.)

© Paul Hester

Concept drawings

The county wanted their new library to be a K-Mart for information, a place that would be totally accessible, and where everyone would be welcome. Jonesboro, Georgia, the project's location, is wedged in between the south-east end of Hartsfield International Airport, one of the busiest airports in the world, and Tara, the mythical home of Scarlet O'Hara, from *Gone with the Wind*.

Between these two locations—the mythical and the real—the site, and by extension the building, is described by architect Merrill Elam as "folksy, hand painted (not all mass-produced), a place where one is apt to pull alongside a pick-up with a rack and ZZ Top coming at you through the open windows. It is a place where information is sought for practical reasons, and history is personal. Scholars will not seek out obscure dissertation-supporting materials here. This library is more a filling-station for information for living life. A puppet show, a cooking class, a seed catalog ... Easy parking. Come on in ..."

The site proper is bounded on the north by Battlecreek Road, on the east by Jester's

Creek and its associated flood plain, a wooded area lush with hardwoods and pine; and on the south and west by other county facilities. The building is located on the south portion of the site at an elevation higher than the parking lot, which is directly in front of the building. The entrance elevation is at the eye level of a seated driver traveling along Battlecreek Road.

The building is organized functionally into two areas: the administration facilities and the public areas. The public areas occupy a large, open room which is oriented to the woods and creek. A stylish monitor divides the space and emphasizes the line of travel towards, and the position of, the genealogy collection. The roofs of this space spring towards the east and the woods. They are arranged so that they fan up towards the south. This allows north light to enter at each "step."

Despite the intricate geometry of the building, which superficially recalls the so-called deconstructive idiom, the approach of the designers is fundamentally populist. David Dillon writes that, thanks to their

non-ideological way of working, "instead of serving up canned solutions to thorny design problems," the firm carries on a "spirited dialogue with itself about the demands of its own making, courting diversity and surprise instead of canonical purity." (*Harvard Graduate School of Design News*, Spring 1994, p. 52.)

The general materials of the building are modest and industrial grade. In an anti-elitist vein, the corrugated metal skin was stenciled with the black and white "library box" pattern. The intent is clearly to make the library an accessible, appealing place for everyone. Mack Scogin tells that the Daughters of the American Revolution hold their meetings here and the seniors from the local high school hang out there as well (lecture at the Harvard Graduate School of Design, June 1994). In response to criticism, partner Lloyd Bray has said: "Architects read the culture and their work manifests what their reading of the culture is. We find a lot of interest in roadside attractions, and this is another roadside attraction."

© Timothy Hursley

(Above) Facade

(Left) Plan

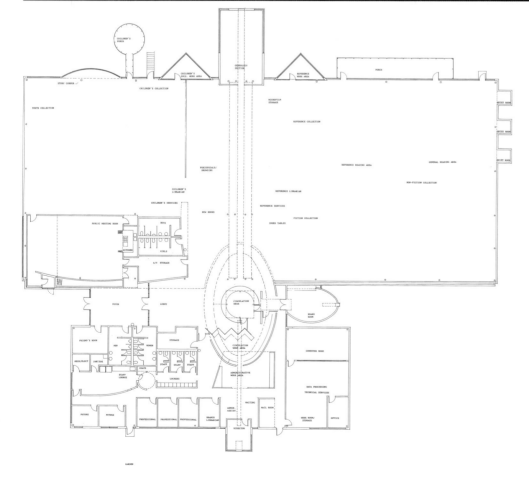

Cesar Pelli & Associates
WORLD FINANCIAL CENTER
New York City, New York
1980–88

View from the river

© Peter Aaron/Esto

The World Financial Center consists of four office towers ranging in height from 34 to 51 stories, the public winter garden, the glass-roofed courtyard, two nine-story octagonal gateway buildings and a 3½-acre landscaped public plaza.

Cesar Pelli was commissioned because of the success of his Pacific Design Center, which was seen as a prototypical way of illusionistically reducing the visual mass of a building of enormous scale. At the World Financial Center, Pelli's device was to give each tower a different silhouette and top— an intentional contrast with Yamasaki's nearby World Trade Center's flat-topped shafts, as Andrea Oppenheimer Dean and Allen Freeman note (*American Architecture of the 1980s*, 1990).

Because the proportion of granite to glass is greater at the base of the towers than at the top, and the towers were truncated at various intervals, the buildings look increasingly lighter as they rise. In addition, Pelli enlarged and elongated the windows with each setback, overlaying the last one with finely drawn mullions and tautly stretching them against a granite of similar

color. The effect was intended, in Pelli's words, to give the impression that "at the base these are skins of stone with windows in them; at the top they are skins of glass with a tracery of stone marking the modular system." (ibid.)

Given Pelli's expertise in glass structures, it is natural that he decided to build a glass Winter Garden adjacent to the great public plaza at the center of the buildings. The space serves as the main connector to all the buildings within the World Financial Center and the World Trade Center. Pedestrian traffic often reaches 35,000 people per hour. The Garden's glass walls are lined with shops and restaurants.

But the amenities are not merely utilitarian and commercial. The Winter Garden creates a great Public Room under a glass vault 125 feet high, 120 feet wide, and 200 feet long. It was designed as a grand glass hall with a huge bay window facing the Hudson River. To complete the project's large scale, yet also to allow for circulation demands, the Winter Garden was planted with *Washingtonia robusta*, a native American palm with a narrow trunk and lush foliage.

This palm is rugged enough to withstand a dry environment and the large temperature swings of the Winter Garden. Sixteen palms are planted in a rectangular grove, with the floor around them paved in diagonal patterns of marble.

A meeting-place for the entire complex, the Winter Garden accommodates activities of individuals as well as large public events. It was intended for the general public as well as for those working in the financial district. Performing arts programs are regularly scheduled and extremely popular, even on weekends during lunch hours.

Through his spatial imagination and deep knowledge of design craftsmanship, Pelli succeeds with this project in giving back to the public some of the joy and celebration that the gigantic productive machines usually take away.

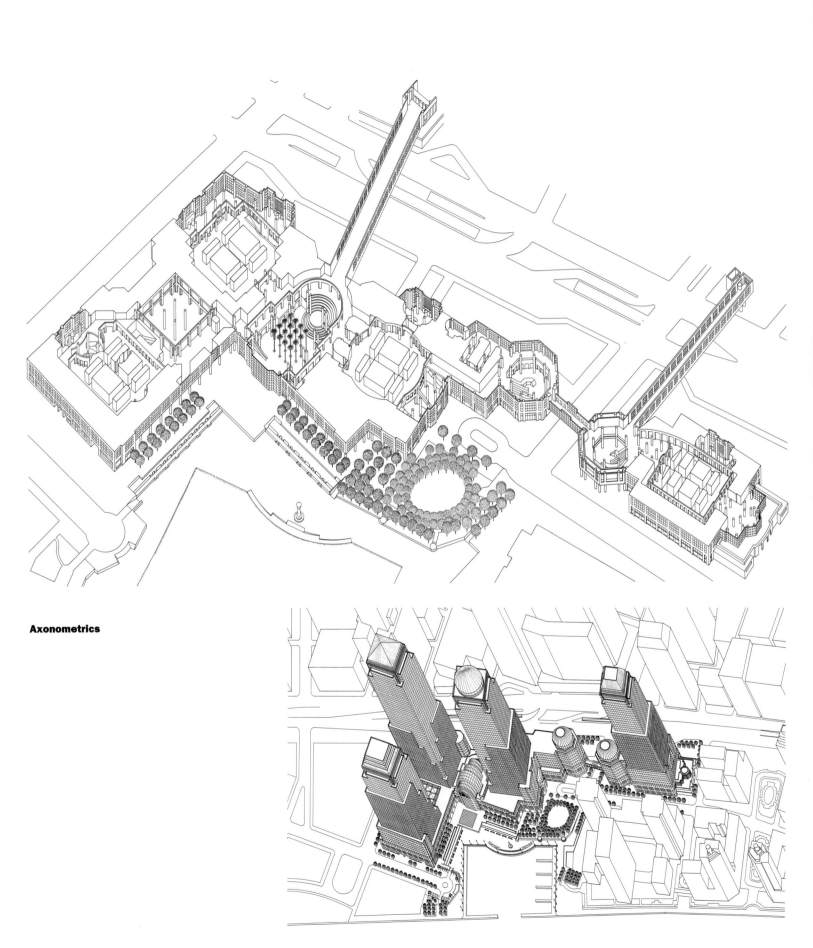

Axonometrics

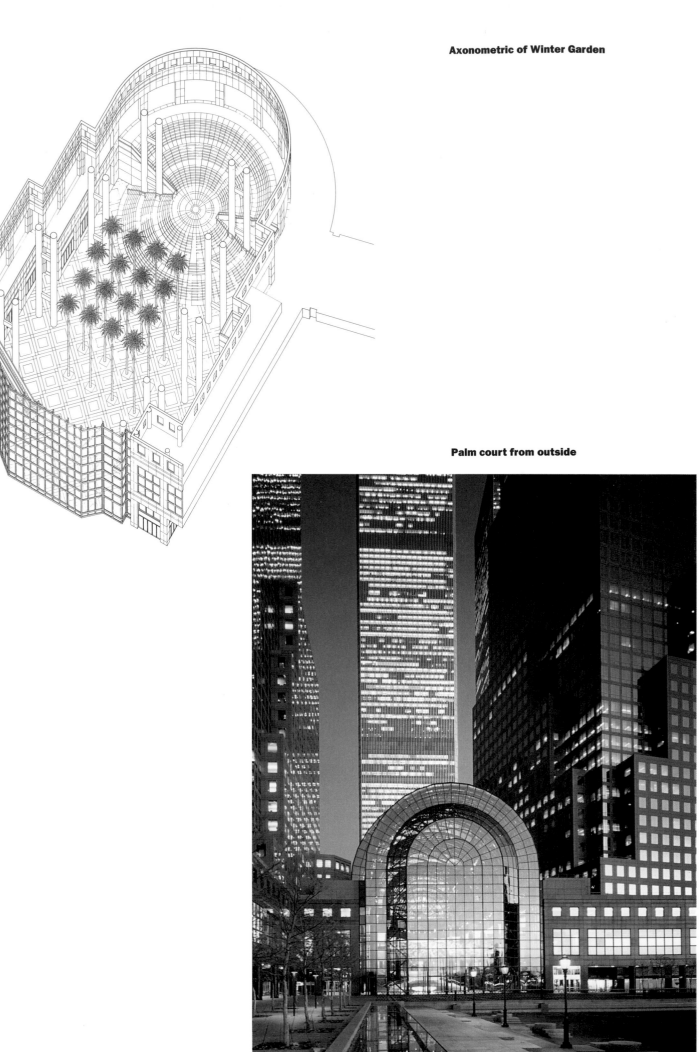

Palm court from outside

© Timothy Hursley

Palm court interior

© Peter Mauss/Esto

Roof axonometric

Douglas Cardinal Architects Ltd.
MUSEUM OF CIVILIZATION
Hull, Canada
1982–89

(Above) View from the hillside

(Right) Site plan

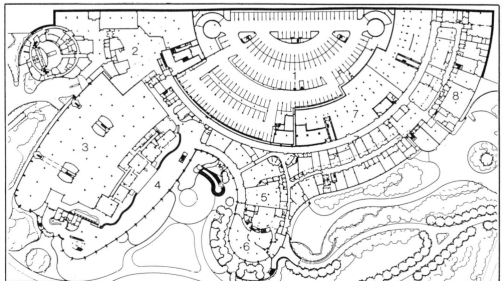

Aerial view of model

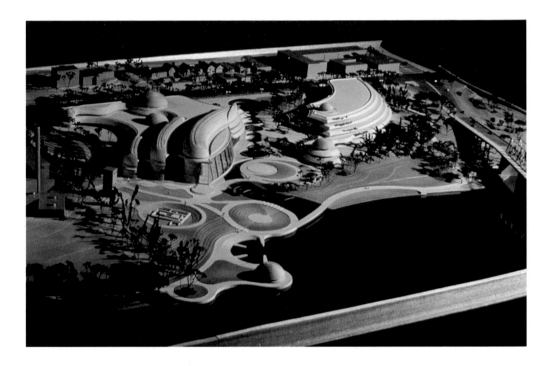

At the personal behest of Prime Minister Pierre Eliott Trudeau, the Canadian Government gave the mandate for a new museum that was to display "the products of nature and the works of man, with special but not exclusive reference to Canada." The building was to house the nation's collection of 3.5 million artifacts representing the history, lore, and archeology of Canada's native tradition, to exhibit these artifacts to the public in realistic, full-scale reconstructions of historical settings, and to provide a special section devoted to a Children's Museum.

The mandate was particularly significant to the museum's architect, Douglas Cardinal. Of Blackfoot ancestry, he viewed the museum commission as the culmination of a 20-year civil rights campaign, during which he became a shaman himself, often donning full tribal garb. Throughout this period he maintained an active architectural practice in Western Canada, wrote a manifesto-like collection of critical writings, and was the subject of an award-winning biography (Trevor Boddy, *The Architecture of Douglas Cardinal*, 1989).

Douglas Cardinal's architecture springs from a keen sense of purpose, to restore a lost relationship with the land. "We feel a great sorrow for the destruction of the land," he writes, "for life springs from the earth. When the land is destroyed all those living on the land are destroyed too. We, the people of the land, feel a sense of loss of our own destruction."

The Museum is located on a spectacular natural site, in a broad, placid bend of the Ottawa River, dug out of the surrounding dark craggy limestone cliffs which rise to a height of 150 feet above the river. Clad in 100 million-year-old tyndall stone, the building keeps a low silhouette against the horizon, follows the slope of the terrain and is terraced on different levels. Its smooth, sinuous forms, in Cardinal's words, are derived from "the forms of the glaciers that eroded the rocks, moving large masses, cutting deeply and sculpting the rock forms into new patterns as they advanced, then receded and melted." This statement places Cardinal in the organic tradition of architecture with echoes of Viollet-le-Duc's famous studies of the geometry of the Alps. It is, however, not easy to place Cardinal's architectural idiom within any tradition, his forms ultimately being intentionally unprecedented.

Visual contact with the surroundings is maintained throughout the Museum's internal organization, which leads the visitor through a path marked by many glazed openings, providing considerable amounts of natural light, but which filter the ultra-violet rays to protect the artifacts.

Inseparable from the search to re-establish a symbiosis with the natural landscape is a social commitment to restore a sense of dignity to the native peoples of North America as well as for any of its immigrants. "Our task is to preserve our culture not only for our own people but for all people who inhabit the land we love. Our first priority is to preserve our culture, identity, language, folkways and mores." (ibid., p. 122.) Today the museum serves as the nation's central multi-media Resource Centre, storehouse of information in computerized formats, linked via satellite with museums across the country. In addition to providing general information along the information superhighway, its intention is to provide specific data to help protect the ecological system and thus to keep us "in harmony with the environment" in a civilization that, in Cardinal's words, is "programmed for the artificial."

Exterior views

(Right) Tyndall stone cladding

(Below) External view

© Cardinal

© Cardinal

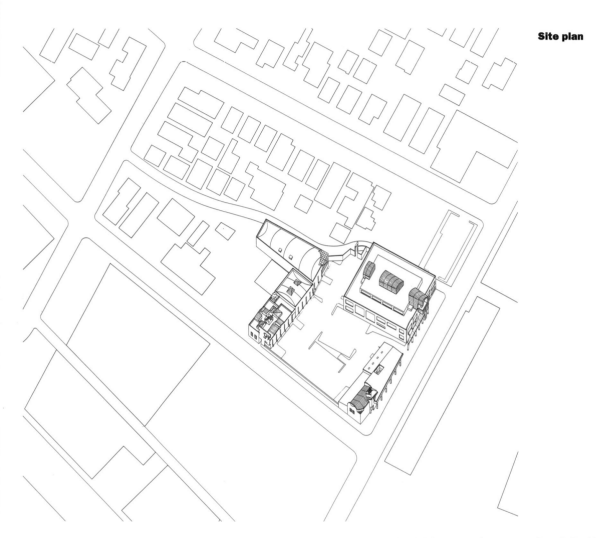

The site is an existing 20,000-square-foot warehouse, built in 1940 to house various industries and support functions required by the military effort, and at the time this project began, in a state of disrepair. This was the case with many of the buildings in Culver City, an industrial wasteland before private developer, Frederick Norton Smith, hired Moss to renovate a number of buildings for use by movie production teams and advertising firms.

The expansion and renovation of Paramount Laundry, which is now occupied by a major Los Angeles graphic design firm, involved the extension of the second floor and the addition of a new, two-part third floor. The original building had two essential organizational components: an open, double-height volume centrally positioned in plan, with clerestory windows and spanned by wooden trusses, and a 2-story perimeter band. Parking requirements limited the expansion to a maximum addition of 6000 square feet. Starting from this configuration and these constraints, Eric Owen Moss disassembled the existing spaces and then reassembled them through the addition of new structures and volumes.

The building is approached from the north, via the Santa Monica Freeway, from which it can be clearly seen. The new central lobby is positioned on this elevation, and was adjusted in plan towards the direction of the freeway view and traffic flow. This lobby is capped with a simple vault that extends above the old roof and identifies the new components of the building below. Where the vault intersects the roof, the existing roof sheathing is removed and the vault and supporting walls are visible from the floors below. Throughout this process, Moss was explicit about the results of adding new

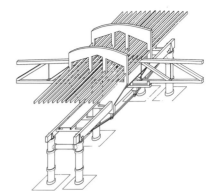

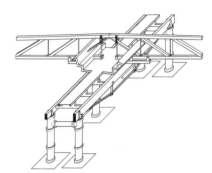

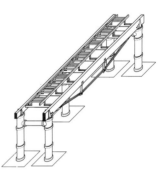

Construction details

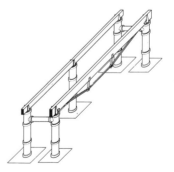

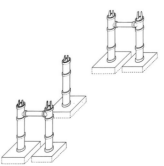

structures to the old. The colliding of geometries is perceived not as grids in plan, but as three-dimensional volumes in space.

The new second floor projects into the central space and is supported by columns which also support the bridge. The new third floor consists of separate areas placed at opposite ends of the central volume. This two-part addition on the third floor occurs just below the bottom chord of the existing wood trusses. Where a bridge connects the two parts, a 4-foot portion of the truss has been removed to allow for vertical clearance, and then restructured with a steel tube below and two new vertical chords.

At the center of this bridge are two benches, one on each side, to enhance informal gatherings. The bridge is aligned

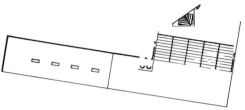

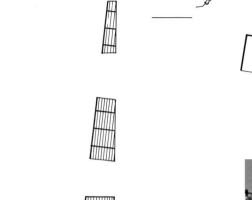

© Alex Vertikoff

(Above) Detail

(Right) Facade

(Below) Elevations

with the new vaulted roof which brings natural light through new clerestory windows to the north. The columns supporting the bridge and the entry canopy outside are vitrified clay pipes, filled with reinforced concrete. A tilted column at the corner of the building seems to be reeling from the shock.

What is going on here? Why the obsession with crashing structural elements, the calling out of parts, the creation of phantom spaces and bridges? Why are clay pipes, made of a weak material, used to prop up the structure? Are these the private explorations of an architect who has called schizophrenia "a cure not a disease," or is it a functional solution to a difficult program in a tight space, or both? Perhaps it is neither. Herbert Muschamp has read the buildings as an allegorical representation of the dislocations and disruptions brought about by "the cracking of the industrial shell" as America shifts from a manufacturing to a post-industrial, service economy (*New York Times*, March 14, 1993, p. 32.) It seems that Moss represents the anxieties generated by such old structures giving way, rather than the pains of rethinking and a change of mind. The building appears to represent not so much the clash between the old and the new within the same organism, as much as the difficulties of the emergence of the new within a surrounding context very much dominated by seediness and the poverty of a paleo-technic past.

Tilted clay "column" at the end of a clay "column" colonnade

© Alex Vertikoff

Eisenman Architects
THE WEXNER CENTER FOR THE VISUAL ARTS AND FINE ARTS LIBRARY
Columbus, Ohio
1983–89

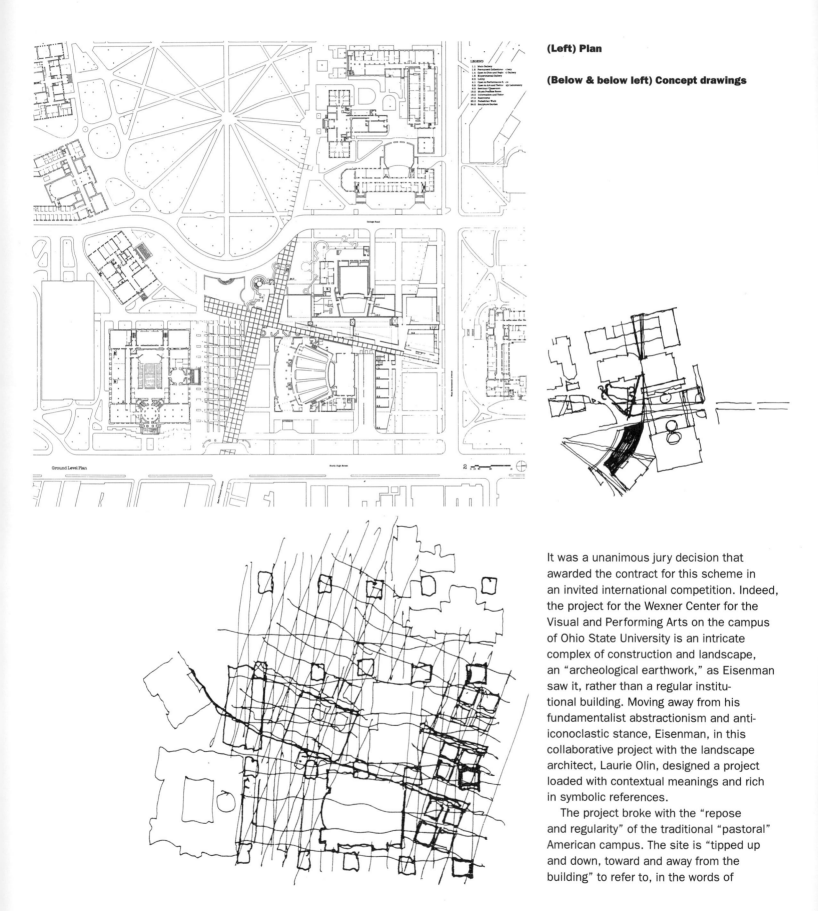

(Left) Plan

(Below & below left) Concept drawings

It was a unanimous jury decision that awarded the contract for this scheme in an invited international competition. Indeed, the project for the Wexner Center for the Visual and Performing Arts on the campus of Ohio State University is an intricate complex of construction and landscape, an "archeological earthwork," as Eisenman saw it, rather than a regular institutional building. Moving away from his fundamentalist abstractionism and anti-iconoclastic stance, Eisenman, in this collaborative project with the landscape architect, Laurie Olin, designed a project loaded with contextual meanings and rich in symbolic references.

The project broke with the "repose and regularity" of the traditional "pastoral" American campus. The site is "tipped up and down, toward and away from the building" to refer to, in the words of

© Jeff Goldberg/Esto

Aerial view

Laurie Olin, "the geological processes of the earth, faulting and uplifting."

The space between the gate and the campus oval is filled in by a "bosque." In a manner similar to that of Rafael Moneo's Merida Museum, with its synthesis of two history-inherited grid systems, the designers of the Wexner Center brought together in this location two historical institutional site contexts—the Jeffersonian grid of the city and of the university. This symbolic act was viewed as connecting the Columbus community with the University academic community. Physical materials used for the synthesis are lines of color-coded granite cobbles that run across integrally colored, pre-cast concrete red pavers. Ginko and linden trees underline the slightly banked intersections of the grids.

Flowers, shrubs, large tilted, red sandstone plinths that contain ornamental grasses are employed in the project not as abstract or decorative landscape elements, but as design objects to produce "an abstract representation of the prairie."

The 140,000-foot-square building houses the experimental arts of computers, lasers, performance, and video. There are permanent, temporary, and experimental exhibition galleries, a Black Box Theater, a Graphics Library, a Film center, studio spaces, music practice rooms, a choral hall, exhibition space, storage, a cafe, a bookstore, and administration spaces.

Without doubt, the project owes much to the three-dimensional sculptural grids of Sol Lewitt, who was extremely influential on Eisenman, from the beginning of his career. Here, however, as it functions in relation to existing urban and architectural grid systems, it achieves a concreteness rather than an abstractness. With its preoccupation with geometry and iconography, the Wexner Center's most memorable image is of its rigorous coupling of architecture with landscape, in a manner that revives the formal geometric integration of garden and building of 17th-century European palaces.

© Jeff Goldberg/Esto

© Jeff Goldberg/Esto

(Above) Elevation

(Right) Detail

© Jeff Goldberg/Esto

(Opposite) Aerial view

© Ricardo Legorreta

Integration of the building and landscape

(Above) Site plan

© David Walker

Westlake and Southlake were once part of the immense, almost scaleless rural farmland, criss-crossed by the national highway system, between Dallas and the Dallas Fort Worth Airport. Then IBM decided to implant a 1900-acre "edge city" there, to borrow Joel Garreau's term (*Edge City. The New Frontier*, New York, 1992) and call it Solana, meaning "place in the sun" in Spanish. The project includes two office buildings, a shopping and office compound, a hotel, conference center, and health and sports club. Within 10 years, this 900-acre lot is expected to contain a dozen corporate headquarters, mainly electronics and communications firms. As many as 20,000 inhabitants might eventually live there (David Dillon, *Architecture*, May 1989).

Ricardo Legorreta was joined by a team of two other architectural firms, Mitchell/Giurgola, and Barton Myers, and one landscape design firm, Peter Walker/Martha Schwartz. In collaboration with them, he developed a scheme that incorporated the landscape, the highway and even the underpass, to resolve the contradictions of the setting in an innovative way.

In contrast to most edge cities, such as Las Colinas, Walnut Creek, or Tysons Corner, as described by Joel Garreau, the site is far from nondescript. Legorreta has taken a "real-maravilloso," or magic realist, approach. The project appears as a series of gigantic, starkly geometric planes in bold color, conceived on the scale of earthworks, carving a clearly demarcated precinct out of this implacably monotonous rural Texan landscape.

Motorists headed for Solana are in for a surprise. As they approach the site on Highway 114, the first things they encounter are a gigantic magenta pylon and a cadmium yellow tower looming on the horizon. Instead of taking the usual off-ramp with traffic lamp and stop sign, they leave the freeway interchange through two great red stucco walls placed parallel to the overpass, which, in an exceptional gesture, the Texas Highway Department permitted Legorreta to design. From there, they enter a series of dramatic, almost surreal, oversize outdoor rooms enclosed by brightly colored walls, with plazas, fountains, and sculptures.

The architectural technique is as old as the Picturesque Movement. The emphasis is on scenographic public space where functional aspects are out of sight. Two long, low parking garages, with arcades and double rows of trees, create a forecourt for the office complex. The colored parking garages have been used to make public spaces, instead of being appended to the backs of buildings, and contain up to almost

Views of the complex

© Jim Hedrich

75 percent of the total parking area, an unusually high ratio for an edge city. Moreover, the garages have been used to create theatrical alternatives to the more common, bland functional parking lots which usually dominate this kind of development.

The most remarkable building at Solana is Legorreta's marketing and technical support center, a low, multi-jointed structure with small mullionless windows, with interior courtyards.

But it is the series of oversize outdoor rooms, starting with the entrance, that are the most striking architectural elements of the site. Their wall elements must be read as a tribute to Luis Barragan, from whose private residential buildings and public sculpture—created with Mathias Goeritz for Ciudad Satelite (1957)—the themes are clearly derived. But they also spring from Legorreta's own passionate "mexicanidad." As Legorreta has written, "we live and see Mexico in its walls; tragedy, strength, joy, romance, light and color, all of these qualities are in Mexican walls." (*The Architecture of Ricardo Legorreta*, 1990.)

The planting of Solana, consisting of Southwestern wildflowers, prairie grasses and fruit trees, complements the brightly colored walls and towers. Connecting these scattered pieces is a network of lakes, streams, ponds, and pathways that harmonize with the architectural elements.

The use of brilliant color on such a large scale was so radical that protests came from the local residents, who, during the planning stages, threatened to sue IBM over the design, claiming that the structures were "loud and Mexican" (Dillon, op. cit.). Ironically, Solana now appears as an illustration of how traditional, vernacular-inspired forms can be used magically to transfigure a utilitarian, workaday world into something bright and vibrant—like the sun.

Antoine Predock Architect
LAS VEGAS CENTRAL LIBRARY AND CHILDREN'S DISCOVERY MUSEUM
Las Vegas, Nevada
1987–90

Axonometric

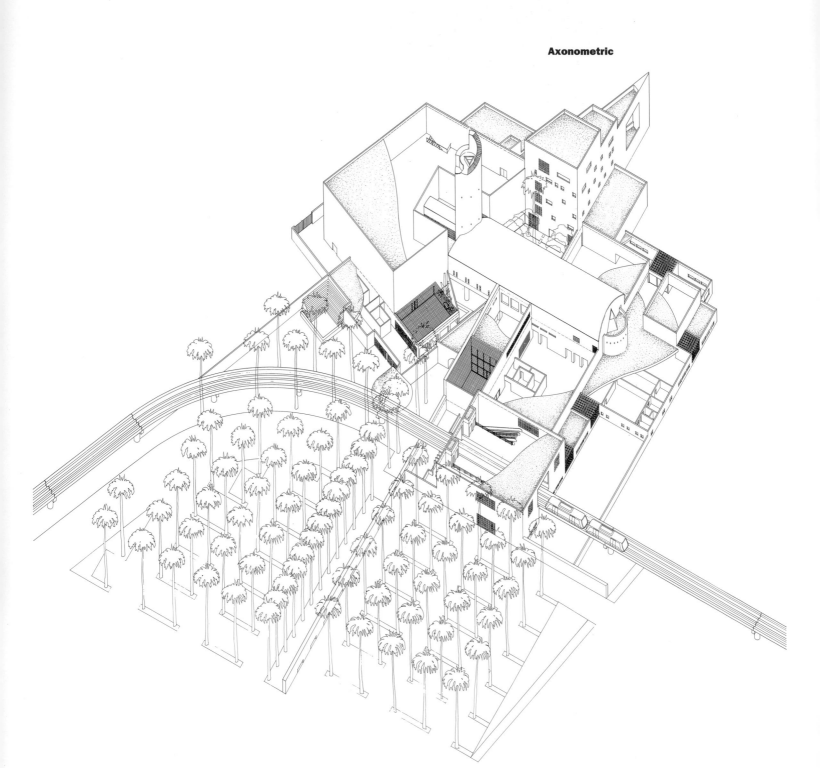

"The fragility of the desert and the communities which colonize it is apparent when one views Las Vegas, Nevada from the air. The Strip, Glitter Gulch, and the city form a thin permeable membrane which keeps the desert marginally at bay. Where the desert relents, rectilinear grids of grass and asphalt prevail." So begins Antoine Predock's narrative brief for this project.

The location of the Las Vegas Library and Children's Discovery Museum is the cultural center of the city, where its original inhabitants, the Paiute, and later Anglo-American settlements were first sited. The architect intended the visitor to experience the library and children's museum "both as desert buildings and as civic monuments." The intersection of these two first appears in the Palm Court, an oasis signaling shelter as well as a place marked by convenient automobile access. From the oasis, the visitor proceeds along the

water course and sandstone wall towards the entry.

The building forecourt is dominated by what Predock calls ceremonial elements: the conical Birthday Room, the Science Tower, and the Meeting Room. Access to these mythopoeic pieces is through a fissure in the lobby, which leads to the two major components of the building, the museum to the west and the library to the east. The intention of the architect is to find a bridge

Main level plan

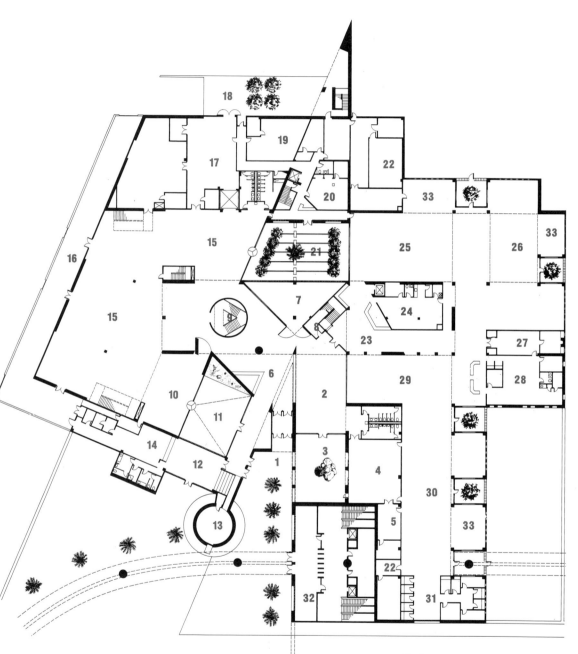

1 Main entry
2 Library/Museum Lobby
3 Mountain Courtyard
4 Multi-Purpose Room
5 Audio Visual Room
6 Museum Information and Ticketing
7 Museum Sales Shop
8 Security Office
9 Science Tower with Stair
10 Traditional Gallery
11 Desert Courtyard
12 Dining Facility
13 Birthday Party Room
14 Kitchen and Catering
15 Museum Gallery
16 Outdoor Exhibit and Work Yard
17 Museum Workshop and Storage
18 Service and Loading
19 Graphic Arts/Framing and Darkroom
20 Library/Museum Volunteers
21 Water Themed Exhibit (Oasis) Courtyard
22 Mechanical/Electrical Rooms
23 Library Foyer with Stair to Young People's
    Library
24 Circulation Desk and Workroom
25 Periodicals
26 Fiction Collection
27 Special Collections
28 Reference Desk and Workroom
29 Reference Collection
30 Non-Fiction Collection
31 Quiet Rooms
32 Rapid Transit System Station Entry
33 Reading Alcoves

0'-0"

between these two "architectural and conceptual" components.

Bridging these two elements is the Children's Library, with its sky-blue metal vault spanning from the massive landform of the two-level exhibition areas to the aggregated village form of the library below. The cast-in-place concrete tower was designed to accommodate science experiments for the children's museum, which includes an oversized kaleidoscope

which uses street activity for a changing demonstration. The sandstone wedge, located at the north end of the building, houses the administrative areas for both the museum and the library district. Predock retained leftover bleachers from the site and located them along the parking lot, which he hoped would encourage more spontaneous community use of the facility.

Throughout the complex, Predock has placed windows in a seemingly random

(Left) View from the desert

(Below) Upper level plans

1 Museum Gallery
2 Connection to Main Level of Museum
3 Outdoor Exhibit Deck
4 Museum Administration
5 Library Administration
6 Library Administration
7 Library/Museum Board Room
8 Outdoor Decks
9 Science Tower with Stair
10 Fabric Shade Tent over Desert Courtyard
11 Lattice Structure over Mountain Courtyard
12 Rapid Transit System Platform

© Timothy Hursley

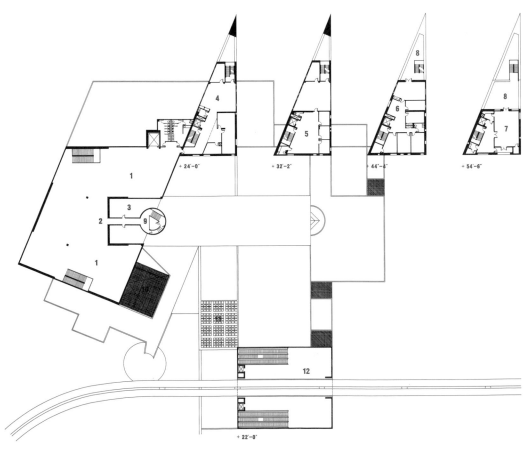

© Timothy Hursley

View on to the desert

pattern to frame views, and to rediscover the world outside. In the lower-level reading room, the windows are raised to capture views of the mountains, while in the children's library above, the low-sill height windows allow the young readers to look down on the adults below. From the top level, where one finds the shared boardroom, the visitors view a panorama of "fragments of mountain, desert, casinos, neighborhoods, and technology (which) come into focus from perimeter openings." Predock sees "this confluence of nature, fantasy, urbanization, and science underscor(ing) the complexities of the desert environment and the task of making architecture responsive to its many faces."

Predock's approach to architecture is deeply rooted in the end of the 18th-century techniques of the Romantic Movement—the Picturesque—hence the reliance on the idea of the promenade as a generator of the composition. There is a moment, however, when the power of the landscape and the local desert culture take over and a genuine discovery takes place.

Holt Hinshaw Pfau Jones
PARAMOUNT PICTURES FILM AND TAPE ARCHIVES
Los Angeles, California
1989–91

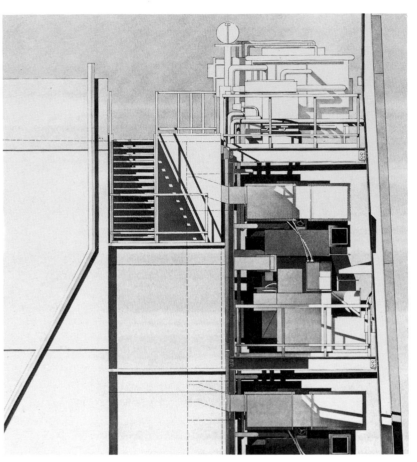

© Holt Hinshaw Pfau Jones

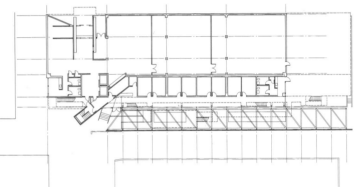

(Top) Model

(Above) First floor plan

**(Above right) Construction detail
of cooling system**

One would be hard pressed to find a technological optimist among architects in the U.S. and Canada today. Whereas Buckminster Fuller and Fazlur Khan displayed an optimistic confidence in the potentials of engineering ingenuity, and SOM's Myron Goldsmith and Hamilton Smith of Gatje, Papachristou and Smith had a deep respect for advanced technology, the overall mood today among the younger generation of practicing architects is a widespread Heideggerian-inspired technophobia.

The Paramount Pictures Film and Tape Archive is designed for the middle-term storage of material and archival or long-term storage of film and tapes. 9-foot-high mechanically assisted, high-density mobile shelving is organized on both sides of a central 5-foot corridor to accommodate the projected inventory, along with routine on- and off-lot distribution activities, barter syndication, and reference cassette library, including a lock-up area for high security

items, the script repository, the film evaluation center, an employee lounge, and an executive office suite. A telecommunications room houses all the technical controls.

The building is more of a critical statement about technology than an inventive technological work proper. In the way it leaves the structural elements uncovered, it is consistent with chief designer Wes Jones's fatalistic stand. "Heidegger," as he pointed out in a recent issue of *Progressive Architecture* (July 1991), "realized that what we must fear is not technology's dangers, but our own desire to disguise them, to keep them hidden." The structure is simply intended as a kind of unmasking of "the technology—ducts, wires, and pipes—that often lies hidden within the walls of buildings."

However, the project is not totally pessimistic. There is an element of ambivalence here. In the cellar of the

Side of the building facing the parking lot, with the artifical sky

old building on the site, where a scene painter used to work, the architects found an artificial sky that had been used as a background in a movie. They repaired it and placed it on the completely sealed concrete box that houses the archives, as a means of saying that without the infrastructure of technology, "our own existence in building would be impossible—and without (it) the sky would fall." (ibid., p.84.)

Structure holding up the artificial sky

Morphosis
CEDARS-SINAI COMPREHENSIVE CANCER CENTER
Los Angeles, California
1991

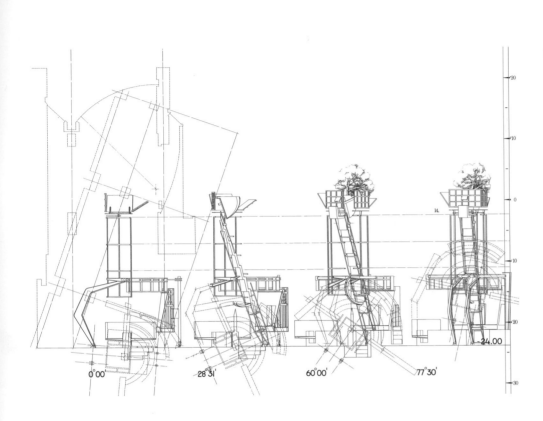

Morphosis's kinetic sculpture in movement

This specialized cancer center, combining diagnosis, therapy, and counseling facilities, was conceived and founded by Dr. Bernard Salick. The Los Angeles kidney specialist had already pioneered the idea of a series of 24-hour kidney dialysis centers in Southern California. But he realized that a similar need existed for cancer patients after one of his daughters was stricken with the condition. She was treated successfully on an outpatient basis, but the direct experience of the emotionally and physically trying circumstances, and of the special needs of the patients, prompted him to approach the celebrated Cedars-Sinai Medical Center with the Comprehensive Cancer Center project (Pilar Viladas, *Progressive Architecture*, July 1988).

Dr. Salick could have opted either for a traditionally neutral or more current "homey" kind of medical facility design. Instead, he was interested in an alternative both to currently available treatment facilities and accepted notions of therapy. He had already commissioned the highly non-conventional, hard-edged, so-called "deconstructivist" architectural firm of Morphosis to carry out one of his dialysis

centers, and when his CCC project was accepted, he turned to them once again.

Designing for a cancer center, where a patient's visit can last up to 20 hours, was a difficult challenge for the youthful team of Thom Mayne and Michael Rotondi. The building had to be at once highly functional and, to quote Dr. Salick, "dramatic and warm" (ibid., p. 68).

Compounding the problem was the building's location—one level below the basement of the Cedars-Sinai Medical Center. The largely underground project's chief aim was to provide pleasant lighting conditions, both natural and artificial. For this purpose, the two main spaces of the building—the lobby and the chemotherapy atrium—were conceived as quasi-exterior places. The chemotherapy atrium is a long space topped by a barrel-vault skylight, flanked by individual cubicles where patients can have as much privacy as they wish, while nurses are stationed at either end of the room. The 45-foot-high waiting room is illuminated by a half-barrel vault skylight. The use of indirect lighting and daylighting is expertly handled and makes users forget that they are underground, according to Pilar Viladas (ibid.).

In accordance with what George Rand, a clinical psychologist and professor at the Graduate School of Architecture and Urban Planning at UCLA, called a "tough" philosophy of therapy (ibid., p. 72), the building does have a symbolically hard clinical edge, with its steel frame benches, custom-made metallic wall and ceiling fixtures, and gray granite floors. These elements were intended to provoke the patient's ability to face the harsh realities of mechanized medical treatment and actively to fight the condition. And among the building's features, the one that most clearly expresses the unsentimental but supportive, humane spirit of the Center is Morphosis's kinetic sculpture, located in the waiting room: the overwhelming mechanical, metallic structure, caught up in a slow but perpetual motion of rising and falling, folding and unfolding, tenaciously bringing forth and nurturing a delicate young tree.

© Grant Mudford

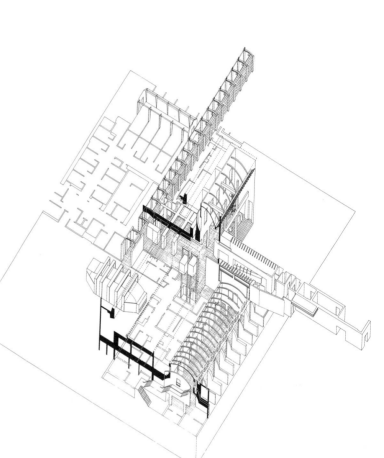

(Above) Interior view, with sculpture

(Above right) View of the complex

(Right) Hall

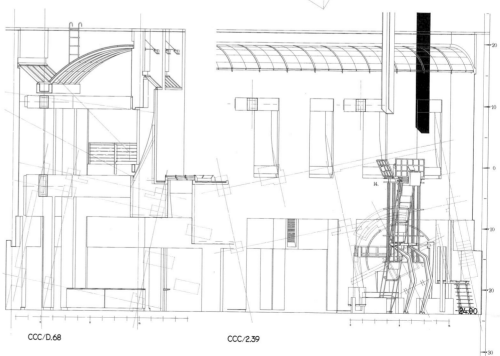

CCC/D.68

CCC/2.39

Patkau Architects, Inc.
SEABIRD ISLAND SCHOOL
Agassiz, British Columbia
1988–91

(Below) Tensile, tilting loggia

(Bottom) Model

The Seabird Island School, located on the Seabird Island Reserve approximately 74 miles east of Vancouver, is the first of a school construction program by the Canadian Bureau of Indian and Northern Affairs in British Columbia.

The extraordinary building is the outcome of a fairly conventional school program, providing an area of 23,564 square feet, which includes 10 elementary and secondary classrooms, a kindergarten, administrative areas, and a gymnasium/community hall. The one distinguishing feature of the brief, and one of the reasons for the design, was that the conception of the project included a participatory approach, in order to make native bands feel that "the schools are their own." (Donald Canty, *Progressive Architecture*, May 1992.)

The Seabird School followed four months of intense meetings between architects, school staff, and students (ibid.). As a result of prolonged dialogue, the architects gradually became immersed in the social and cultural values of the community, values which the architects intentionally incorporated into their design. "Our approach to design is conditioned by an emphasis on the particular," John Patkau writes. "We have adopted this emphasis in an attempt to balance the tendency towards generalization which is becoming an increasingly dominant characteristic of Western culture. We begin with a search for the 'found potential' of a project—a search for those aspects of the site, climate, building context, program, or local culture, etc. that will facilitate the development of an architectural order which is specific to circumstance."

One would look in vain for a single object prototype of Salish culture. Like Arthur Erickson's Museum of Anthropology at the University of British Columbia (1971–76, pp. 160–63)—John Patkau worked in Erickson's office and the Patkaus' firm is located in an Erickson-designed building—the architects incorporated elements from the immediate geographical and cultural context, then recombined them in an unprecedented way.

The outcome is a new architectural hybrid. The extremely complex structure, with eight highly contrasting sides and a roof broken

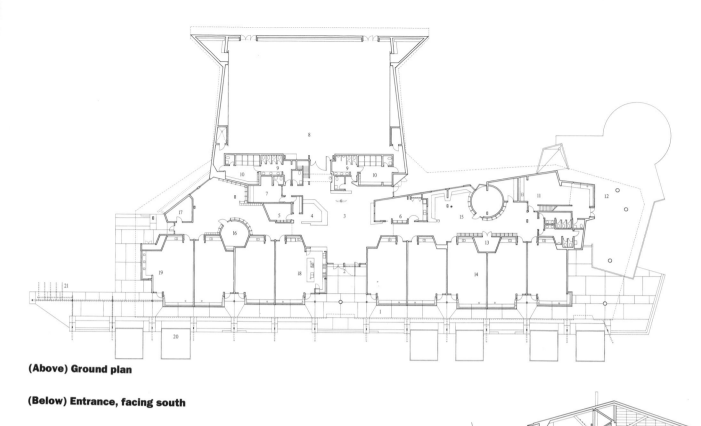

(Above) Ground plan

(Below) Entrance, facing south

(Below right) Sections

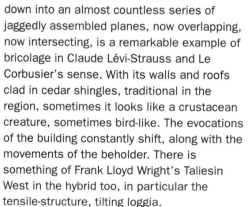

down into an almost countless series of jaggedly assembled planes, now overlapping, now intersecting, is a remarkable example of bricolage in Claude Lévi-Strauss and Le Corbusier's sense. With its walls and roofs clad in cedar shingles, traditional in the region, sometimes it looks like a crustacean creature, sometimes bird-like. The evocations of the building constantly shift, along with the movements of the beholder. There is something of Frank Lloyd Wright's Taliesin West in the hybrid too, in particular the tensile-structure, tilting loggia.

In the harmonious way its forms fit into the landscape, the building recalls the Sea Ranch work by Charles Moore (1963–65, pp. 90–93), with whom Patricia Patkau studied at Yale. In this delta land, where two ranges of the Rockies converge, the cracked morphology of its roof, made up of flat surfaces, responds to the geological

structure of the range nearby. And it does seem to capture the Ruskinian "truth" of the broken crags and crests of mountain ranges and of the clouds overhead as propounded in his *Modern Painters*.

Functional concerns also played a role in the configuration of the building. The southern sides of the building, where the architects have placed classrooms, as well as the main entrance, each opening to a collective porch and the play areas beyond, seem to be stretching upwards to catch the warmth of the sun in a vaguely zoomorphic way, creating a permeable and active edge along the village green. Under the broad eaves to the south and east, walls are clad in translucent white-stained plywood panels to increase luminosity. On the northern side, the building seems to turn its protective, weathered back as a protection against the prairie winds.

Social factors were important in the integral design of the building. Consistent with the educational philosophy of the Band, few distinctions have been made between areas specifically designed for staff and those for students, allowing a significant overlap to occur in the commons and the resource areas. Finally, the wood used in the project, is a modern "engineered" wood, comprised of paralam columns and beams with steel connections on a reinforced concrete grade-beam and pile foundation. This was an ecologically conscious decision in this region of the Pacific Northwest, which produces one third of the supply of Douglas Firs, for decades a reliable source of big, clear-grained wood, but now off-limits to preserve the habitat of the gray spotted owl.

As a measure of how successful this experiment was, many of the members of the

© Patkau and Patkau

Tilting loggia

Band felt the project to be "their own," and they undertook all the construction work. Because it was a complex structure, the architects had to build a model of the work instead of blueprints. According to John Patkau, the architects believe the Band did a better job than a contractor would have done because "they were not intimidated by the complexities." (*Progressive Architecture*, May 1992.) Clearly the Seabird Island School is also indicative of the importance a responsible, creative architectural solution is in creating a sense of place and community.

The project succeeds not only as a single project in response to a specific program, but also as a prototype of a process and an attitude to architecture appropriate for the limitations and potentials of our time.

© Patkau and Patkau

Wood construction

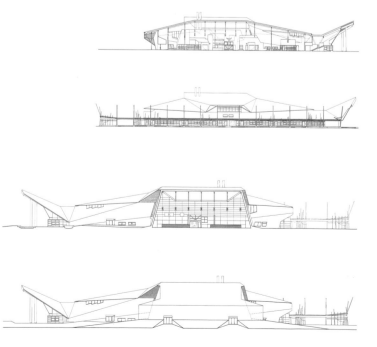

Venturi, Scott Brown and Associates, Inc.
SEATTLE ART MUSEUM
Seattle, Washington
1984–91

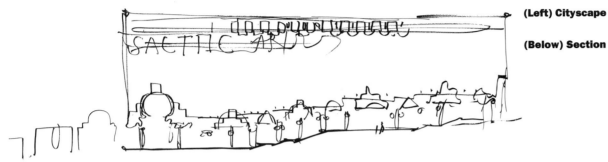

(Left) Cityscape

(Below) Section

The same year that the architects, VSBA, saw the completion of their addition to the National Gallery in London, in 1991, the construction on the Seattle Art Museum's new building in downtown Seattle, came to completion. Despite certain formal similarities in treating the corner and the entrance to the building, the differences between the two museums is striking. The London project was, from the beginning, fraught with contradiction and complexity, including prohibitive constraints of site, program, and budget. The Seattle Museum proceeded much more smoothly, and while the site and program posed challenges, these were addressed in as straightforward a manner as possible.

The site is a half block bounded by the city's non-hierarchical grid. The 150,000-square-foot building has main entrances on the east and west, and is set back on the south 30 feet from the street to preserve the view corridor to the water. Because of the slope of the hilly site, this setback allowed for the creation of a terraced outdoor stair which, with landscaping, sculpture, and low walls for seating, attracts passersby, as well as museum visitors.

The architects, going back to their early use of super-graphics, decided to work with large-scale visual elements to emphasize the building's presence. The decision was due to the projection that the Museum would be surrounded by tall skyscrapers sometime in the future.

The south facade is constructed of limestone that has been scored with vertical fluting, and incised with large letters across the top that announces the museum's name. The west end of this facade pulls back from the hillside terrace to create an entry plaza, and to accommodate the prerequisite large-scale sculpture.

The designers saw the formality of the fluted limestone to be in contrast with the ground level's granites, marbles, and brightly colored terra cotta. They have inserted large windows between groups of piers to reflect "the rhythmic progression of the terraced stair and enhance the continuity between inside and outside." Alternating pediments and arches were assembled in a continuous band of granite juxtaposed to the pattern, foregrounding the pattern formed by the sequence of windows and piers.

A wide stone stair running parallel to the terraced stair of the outside connects the entrances at First and Second Avenues. The architects see this interior stair, "rising gradually with Chinese sculpture displayed on its landings," as a "room on many levels, as well as a means to climb to the galleries." Continuing this idea of the stair as a room rather than a functional service, the restaurant is located at its mid-level, which broadens on to a landing. In this manner, the restaurant area merges with the landing, which can be utilized for banquets and receptions.

Similarly, an ambiguity emerges with the treatment of the facade, which continues inside the building—not literally, but in the way in which the inside stair parallels exactly the outside stair, and how at their midpoints they touch and connect, allowing an inflection of the inside on to the public sidewalk. The wall is no longer a barrier, the stair no longer a circulation device. These elements have become the artifacts of the museum itself. Further unifying the presence of the outdoors inside the main stair hall is the presence of natural light, which in this gray northern city is avidly sought after.

A large flexible gallery for traveling exhibitions is located at the second-floor level, while the third and fourth floors accommodate the museum's substantial holdings of modern ethnic and Asian art. A combination of small rooms linked en suite and larger loft-like galleries to the north recall the variety of spaces offered by traditional museum buildings. Classrooms are located at each floor to be used by art students. The administration offices, the

© Wargo and VSBA

(Left) Corner of the building

(Below) Elevation

(Bottom) Stone stair

© Wargo and VSBA

library, and the conservation laboratory are located on the fifth floor. A two-level parking garage is provided for the museum visitors at the north of the building.

The Seattle Art Museum is a pragmatic solution to a series of overlapping issues, dealing with function as well as urban society, always opting for a "both" rather than an "either/or" strategy when conflicts arise. In the memorable opening of *Anna Karenin*, Tolstoy says that happy families have no history. In contrast to the masterpiece extension to the National Gallery of London, where the struggles associated with the conception and production of the project left a tragic scar on the building for the benefit of art and posterity, the esthetics of the Seattle Art Museum express much more congenial conditions of creation, leading to a much happier—but lower profile—esthetic accomplishment.

Hellmuth Obata Kassabaum
CAMDEN YARDS AT ORIOLE FIELDS
Baltimore, Maryland
1988–92

Aerial view

The site is 85 acres in Baltimore's inner city. The program included a baseball field, a linear plaza between older buildings on the site and outdoor parking for 5000 cars. The result was hailed as "arguably the most significant urban intervention in America of the last decade" (Donald Prowler, *Progressive Architecture*, June 1992, p. 26.)

After a period dominated by the high-tech, standardized, covered, astro-turfed models of the Astrodome of Houston and the Sky Dome of Toronto, Oriole Fields marks a return to the traditional open-air, natural grass ballparks. Here spectators are brought as close as possible to the grass playing field, and a vintage scoreboard hovers above the seats. As if to distinguish itself from the standardized interiors of most other new stadiums, this one boasts an irregular shaped ground plan.

Oriole Fields displays a uniquely careful treatment of small details, such as the color of the dark green slatted seats that bear the 1890s Baltimore Baseball Club logo at the end of each row, and the custom-made handrails. On a larger scale, the structure is a direct response to a particular historic urban site. The attempt to integrate the new baseball field with the city is dramatically brought home to any one of its 48,000 seats with views of such landmarks as the castellated 1911 Bromo Seltzer Tower and

Concourse and warehouse

© Jeff Goldberg/Esto

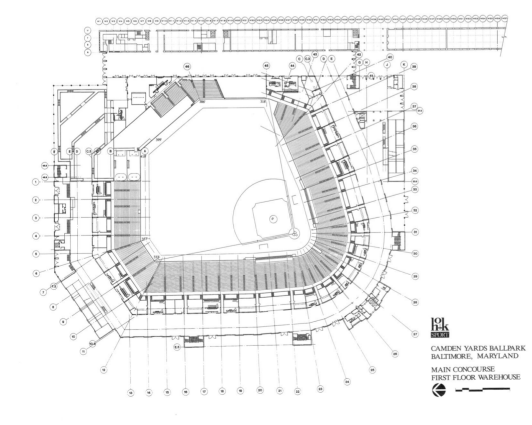

lol
h•k
SPORT

CAMDEN YARDS BALLPARK
BALTIMORE, MARYLAND

MAIN CONCOURSE
FIRST FLOOR WAREHOUSE

the recent skyscrapers of Inner Harbor serving as a backdrop for the games, as Edward Gunts observed (*Architecture*, July 1992).

The plan called for the preservation of the Baltimore and Ohio Railroad's 1898 freight-warehouse to the east and Camden Station, an 1857 railroad terminal, to the north-east. The architects chose to use them as the source of inspiration for the materials, details, and scale of the new park. In deference to the adjacent brick warehouse and train station, the building is clad in red brick and stone. The outdoor walls of the park have arched windows and ornate brick with cornice work, but with grander openings. This shift in scale is meant, according to the firm, to reinforce the juxtaposition of the old and the new, and also allows a great deal of visibility into the park from the outside, so that motorists and passers-by can sense the activity of a game in progress.

In order to make the building seem less massive to pedestrians, the playing field is depressed 16 feet below street level and the upper deck is set back from the street, resulting in a facade that appears as five stories, rather than its true nine. The firm

Views of the ball park

used steel structure for the upper deck, making those elements appear less oppressive and more transparent (*Architecture*, July 1992, p. 69).

The baseball field satisfies larger urban design requirements. Pedestrian circulation patterns have been taken into account. The master plan recommended that the curved seating bowl conform to the existing street grid. Eutaw Street, the 60-foot-deep corridor between Oriole Fields and the warehouse, was designed to be part of the ballpark's lower concourse, where fans are free to roam during the games. On a day-to-day basis, this corridor, a 10-minute walk from the heart of Baltimore's Inner harbor and downtown, is turned into a pedestrian mall adjacent to the 1,116-foot-long warehouse (*Progressive*

© Jeff Goldberg/Esto

© Jeff Goldberg/Esto

Architecture, June 1992, p. 26), which has been restored to accommodate the Orioles' administrative offices, banquet and meeting facilities, retail activities, and a restaurant.

Camden Yards at Oriole Fields has been very popular with the public and it has found a place in the hall of fame of America's sports fields. George Will, a political commentator for the *Washington Post*, classified it enthusiastically in the same league as the "classics," such as Chicago's Wrigley Field and Boston's Fenway Park (ibid.).

This is a very significant experiment in urban revitalization, renewing in a wasteland of abandoned city fabric, the public enjoyment of grassy fields, hot dogs, and the traditional national sport.

Pei Cobb Freed & Partners
THE UNITED STATES HOLOCAUST MEMORIAL MUSEUM
Washington, D.C.
1986–93

(Below left) First main floor

(Bottom left) Facade

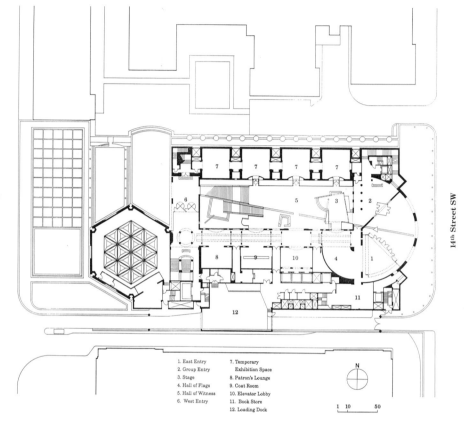

1. East Entry
2. Group Entry
3. Stage
4. Hall of Flags
5. Hall of Witness
6. West Entry
7. Temporary Exhibition Space
8. Patron's Lounge
9. Coat Room
10. Elevator Lobby
11. Book Store
12. Loading Dock

1 10   50

The United States Holocaust Memorial Museum, serving the dual function of a memorial to the Holocaust and a museum to its history, opened 48 years after the liberation of the Nazi concentration camps of Europe. The client was an organization established by the U.S. Congress with the task to create the memorial, the United States Holocaust Memorial Council, together with the Federal Fine Arts Commission. Elie Wiesel was head of the council when, in 1986, the architect was commissioned.

This architect, James Ingo Freed, arrived in America in 1939, a refugee from Nazi Germany. Freed became a student of Mies and worked with him on the Seagram building. His work, as a partner since 1956 of Pei Cobb Freed & Partners, has been recognised as an architecture of high quality, one that employed the conventions of modernism as a received truth. Freed's architecture had been therefore mostly abstract and faithful to technology, not only as a means to endure but also as a goal to celebrate. The design of the Holocaust Museum is a dramatic rethinking of these ideas.

The site is located just off the Washington Mall. Overlooking the Tidal Basin, it lies near the center of the U.S. Government and, in the words of Freed, "right in the nexus of (Washington's) national monuments." The location had been previously considered as a site for a memorial to Franklin D. Roosevelt and also for a memorial to the Vietnam War. To the immediate south is the neoclassical Bureau of Engravings and Printing. The 1879 Auditor's Building is to the north. Both the Washington Monument and the Jefferson Memorial are within walking distance of the site.

The building is entered on Fourteenth Street. A lobby area accommodates individual visitors and groups. From here the visitor passes into the Hall of Witness, a 3-story atrium dominated by an eccentrically pitched trussed skylight, skewed 13 degrees from the plan. As Stephanie Williams wrote, at this point one is confronted by a pattern of disorder, "an angle that is way out of angle," "receding perspectives," "skewing lines," "a floor that drops away before it reaches the wall," giving the impression of "a universe

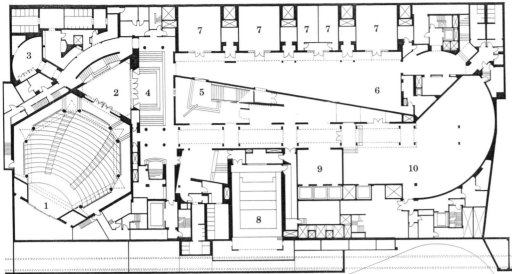

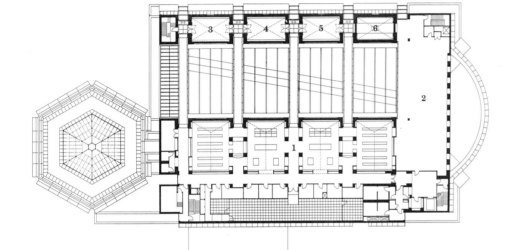

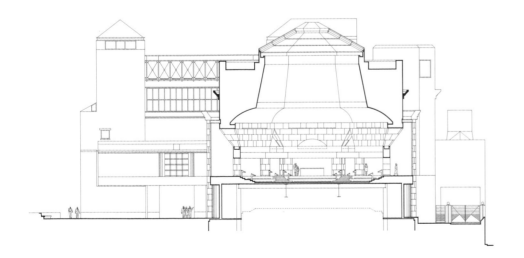

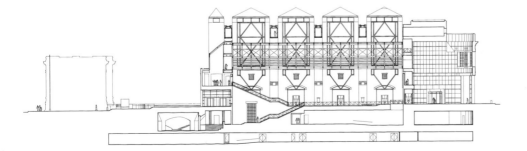

out of joint." ("A Somber Reminder of the Mechanics of Genocide," *The Independent*, June 30, 1993.) And as one proceeds inside the imposing space, one might have an experience as in a camp, as Freed commented, a feeling or a suspicion of being surveyed from above by hidden observers who are, in this case, the other visitors walking across a series of bridges.

From the Hall of Witness one has the choice to ascend by elevator or stairs to the three floors of the permanent collection. Ralph Applebaum Associates designed the exhibition, which includes hundreds of documents, objects, photographs, manuscripts, films, sound tracks, and interviews. Here the visitor encounters the Walls of Nations, which consist, in the words of the architect, of a raw steel structure, without cover or enclosing planes, except that the walls have transparent witnesses: every nation that suffered is identified by a panel of glass.

From the third floor, one descends "under a slot of light" along a path the architect has called the "death march." The "experience . . . of circulating . . . becomes more brutal; the stairs are steel, the slot is very narrow, movement is very restricted." The hexagonal, 6000-foot-square limestone Hall of Remembrance, a place for contemplation, where all physical movement is temporarily suspended, marks the end of the main path through the Memorial.

At the concourse level of the building are an amphitheater, the Meyerhoff theater, a cinema, classrooms, an educational center, and a conference center. On the fifth floor are research facilities, a conference room, photo and survivors' archives, and a library.

The design of a museum dedicated as a memorial to the Holocaust is one of the most difficult problems an architect can be asked to solve. Freed enumerated the possible design strategies as follows: (1) use an existing building; (2) design a "perfectly neutral building"; (3) design a "black box," letting the exhibits be the exclusive subject; and (4) deal "very directly with the emotions." Freed chose this last, and most difficult, strategy.

The building became an "exposition of emotion." The movement through the

© Norman McGrath

Basement level, with sculpture by Richard Serra

building is not an "architectural walk," as in a museum by Richard Meier or I. M. Pei. Freed saw this visit to the Museum to be a "walk through memory." This implied an associational narrative approach, an 18th-century technique for which Freed used appropriately an 18th-century term—"an architecture of sensibility." The right object cues, "images in the memory," had to be identified, recruited, and structured to arouse emotions of "horror and sadness" to the visitor. Once more, the description of the intentions of the designer are strongly reminiscent of the esthetics of the sublime.

Freed was very aware that this could have easily led to scenographic effects. Hence his efforts to make the building "abstractly symbolic." It was at this moment, he tells us, that he gave up all hope of doing a modern building. Modern architecture, however, was not totally eliminated. It reappeared in the iconography of the building, not as a set of principles, but as an icon, an icon of evil, represented by what modern architecture implied—a technology of rationality and functionality. This realization must have been

a painful dilemma for the ex-student and ex-collaborator of Mies, but it was certainly not the only painful experience in this project for Freed, who had to relive the "terror and sadness" of his childhood. "All my life I've done rational stuff," he confessed, "but reason doesn't work here."

Could this horrifying discovery be expressed through the iconographic use of 19th-century industrial and functionalist buildings? Could this make it easier to comprehend the incomprehensible? Would it be effective to put almost side-by-side the schematic representation of the Meunier factory facade with the actual presentation of the wooden doorway of a Polish synagogue? Can we employ the framework of associative esthetics which, as we have seen above, appears to be the following: an idea of art, so much a part of the end of the Enlightenment era, applied to this event, so much of our times? The *New York Times* architecture editor, Herbert Muschamp, (April 11, 1993) asked, even more specifically, the hard question which the use of associative esthetics poses today:

"Does the Holocaust Museum cross the line into kitsch?"

Muschamp responded by pointing out that "in a century of shifting, elastic morality," in times when architecture appears to have severed esthetics from morality, and art from politics, Freed's stance to keep both united, even by resorting to such associative means, is justified. Bringing together building and exhibited objects, refusing to see a difference between the work of the architect and the exhibited documents, shows that when confronted by an incomprehensible criminal act, the division between subject and object, the separation between viewer and viewed, not to mention the acceptance of many points of view as the definition of truth, are not permitted. All this was the commitment of the architect in designing this building, and a call for us to respond in kind.

More questions remain unanswered. While the building succeeds in presenting what it has chosen to, it represents only part of the Holocaust. The Final Solution remains to a great extent a suspended, and often one-dimensional, phenomenon. Thus the

(Right) Hall of Memory

(Below) Main Hall

(Bottom right) View from covered walkays, with names of the Holocaust victims etched on the glass panes

© Norman McGrath

© Norman McGrath

"demonic side of technology" is demonstrated forcefully, and this is based on the presupposition that without technology, the Holocaust would have been technically impossible. Yet, perhaps, an even more fundamental factor of the Holocaust—anti-Semitism—is absent in the architecture. But can one make an architectural reference to this phenomenon, as one does to technology?

The building—as opposed to the exhibits—acknowledges only part of what preceded the Holocaust. Similarly, it acknowledges only part of what emerged out of it. The narrative fabric of the Memorial is occupied by the image of death and destruction of that particular time and place. But the true legacy of the Holocaust, as Shlomo Riskin has commented (*Jerusalem Post*, June 18, 1994), "is not the crematoria; it is rather the nation resuscitated" and the defeat of Nazism. "The vision of the dry bones returning to life," identified as "the whole house" in Ezekiel (37: 11–12), is, as Rabbi Riskin wrote, "one of the strongest promises of the entire Torah."

© Norman McGrath

Frank O. Gehry & Associates
THE FREDERICK R. WEISMAN ART MUSEUM
Minneapolis, Minnesota
1992–94

(Below left) Technical parking level plan and ground storage level plan

(Below) Administration level plan and main museum level plan

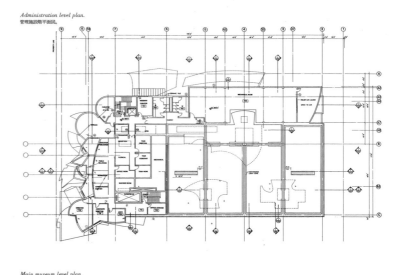

Technical parking level plan.
技術施設・駐車場階平面図。

Administration level plan.
管理施設階平面図。

Ground/Storage level plan.
1階/収蔵庫階平面図。

Main museum level plan.
美術館階平面図。

With this building Gehry addresses a problem which is one of the most pervasive today: how to relate architecture to the implacably rigid, staid, boring ordinariness that seems to have encroached on so much of the built environment, especially since the Second World War.

There are arguably two schools of thought. One is to adopt an Apollonian stance, to create a haven, a separate precinct, a temenos, whose boundaries set up an alternative counterworld, devoid of context. The other approach is actively to engage the site in a Dionysian manner.

For this project, Frank Gehry chose the second approach. And, as opposed to some other recent designs which tend toward a de-contextualized, arbitrary, extravagant "imagineering" zaniness, this work, with its modest budget, and relatively low-cost brick and stainless steel cladding, is intimately

involved with its surroundings. Despite the radical formal dissimilarities, the design method used in the Weisman Museum has deep affinities with that which Venturi and Scott Brown applied to the National Gallery in London, where the kaleidoscopic changes of the facade resulted from a critical, reflective engagement of the building with its context, and of the present with the past.

The result is a building that acts as a kind of extraordinary, pirouetting mirror. It captures elements of the existing context and creates something original yet familiar with them. Gehry brings everything together here in a new way—almost as a cyclone would.

To the south of the site are institutional brick "boxes" that make up the University of Minnesota's West Bank campus, a post-war outgrowth of the original, classical, 19th-century East Bank campus. To these, Gehry

responds with two facades of plain, deep-red brick.

Turning the corner to the west is the Mississippi River, where Gehry creates a facade of wavy, undulating brush-finished shiny stainless steel that wraps around the wall of the building, here 4 stories high, "reflecting" the movement of the river below. With the setting sun it becomes a brilliant fiery-red wall. On a cloudy day, a choppy silvery surface. Under a brilliant wintry sky, it glints and flashes like a frozen splash or a sheet of ice.

The North facade faces the ungainly, clunky, two-decker vehicular and pedestrian Washington Avenue Bridge. Here a long metallic arm in the same industrial vernacular as the bridge swoops out towards it and connects to it like a nozzle, almost seeming to lift pedestrians off their normal course and into the building. The entrance to

the museum is marked by a tilting metallic canopy that looks strangely like a great snow shovel that has cleared the way for visitors, and that might just swallow them at any moment.

For all this posturing, functional constraints were not violated. The architect took advantage of the hillside site to create underground parking, an important asset, given Minnesota's winters. Vehicular access to parking and the Museum's loading dock are at the lowest of the building's 4 levels, which also contain art storage, a frame shop, non-art storage, and mechanical and electrical rooms. The next level has a carpentry shop, non-art storage, and additional parking. The gallery level has a book store, a print-study room, and a 1500-foot-square auditorium with movable partitions that enable its west wall to open into the lobby, for special events.

Since he designed the Vitra Museum in Alphen-an-Rhein in Germany, Gehry has been interested in representing movement in his architectural designs. This also applies to the interior, where light, introduced through skylights, is handled not only as a sculptural element, as in the sculpture of James Turrell at the National Museum in Jerusalem, but as a kinetic sculptural element. Herbert Muschamp has praised the effects of the modulated, airily abstract light dissolving into air, as creating "five of the most gorgeous

galleries on earth." (*New York Times*, December 12, 1993, p. 44.)

With the Weisman Museum, Gehry tries—and succeeds—to release us, creatures of habit that we are, from the dreary effects of the over-familiar. In so doing, he at least raises the awareness of the possibility that things may never be the same again.

(Top) Facade of brush-finished stainless steel

(Above) Close-up of the undulating side of the building

James Stewart Polshek and Partners
MASHANTUCKET PEQUOT MUSEUM AND RESEARCH CENTER
Mashantucket Pequot Reservation, Connecticut
(Begun 1993. Expected completion early 1997)

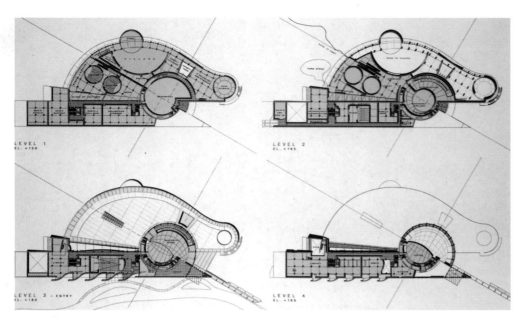

Other museums have been devoted to native North American culture. But this is the first to be directly commissioned by one of the Indian nations. In recent years, the Mashantucket Pequot people have operated a highly profitable casino on their reservation. Out of the proceeds, the elders decided to open a Museum and Research Center devoted to the dissemination of the culture—not only of their own nation, but of all the Native American nations of North America.

The architect they approached with the commission was James Polshek, former Dean of the architecture school at Columbia University. His previous work had emphasized contextualism, preservation of the historic heritage, complex urban situations, and adaptive re-use in a variety of projects including housing, schools, laboratories, and industrial buildings—all works that had served, in his words, "a larger social purpose." The landscape architect selected was the renowned Dan Kiley, whose ecological, Thoreau-inspired work constitutes an intriguing, if surprising, complement to Polshek's more sociological concerns.

The site for the Museum and Research Center was the original location of the Mashantucket and Pequot 17th-century tribal settlement. Polshek has broken the project down into three very different units, which in their overall configuration recall some of the late projects of Frank Lloyd Wright, in

particular his Florida Southern College in Lakeland, Florida.

The first, the Research Center, houses what promises to be the world's largest archive of printed materials on native American topics. The plan is to couple the archaic roots of the Pequot culture with the most sophisticated electronic media for storing, organizing, and communicating this memory. Thus, the programmatic elements include a Media Center that will be the nucleus of a Native American television and radio broadcast network. Also included are a theater for live performances of Native American dance, music, storytelling, and poetry; a public education department; administrative offices; an archeology laboratory; and a collection, storage, and retrieval facility for Native American arts and crafts. To the east, the building terminates in a 175-foot-high, stone-clad tower, which provides access to a viewing platform from which a visitor or tribal member can see the entire reservation.

The second building, the Gathering Space, is for formal celebrations, and serves as the focal point of the complex, unifying the Research Center and the Museum, both formally and symbolically. It is reached by a public lobby in the easternmost portion of the linear bar building, where visitor services are located. Its double semi-circular plan follows the plan of the original Mystic Fort,

the site of the 1637 massacre, and is used here as a symbol of the rebirth of the Mashantucket Pequot nation. Its "basket-like" steel structure was inspired by native American structures. The semi-circle facing the woods offers views of the forest and the sky, emphasizing the essential unity of nature. From the Gathering Space, a wide and very gentle ramp descends to the exhibition spaces below, while a monumental stair ascends to the café balcony above.

The third structure in the complex is to be a museum for permanent exhibitions describing the history of the site and of the Mashantucket Pequots. The exhibits, arranged on two levels, are contained by an undulating glass wall, whose mostly transparent surface allows for views of the swamp and forest from within the exhibit and reflections of the natural landscape from without.

The Museum's roof is landscaped by Kiley and conceived as a meeting-point between architecture and the land, a symbiosis between the human and the natural. Kiley writes: "The Mashantucket Pequot tribe, as all native peoples, led a daily existence that was inexorably tied to the natural systems of the land. The Mashantucket Pequot lived symbiotically with Nature by intervening in a peaceful manner, affecting yet not destroying their environment. They used existing materials—the waterways, flora and fauna,

rich soil, amenable climate, glacial topography—yet created their own functional relationships—hunting and gathering; clearing, planting, harvesting and burning fields; ceremonial traditions—through methods that manifested their people's presence on and with the land."

Kiley believes that "the entire landscape design is an exploration of man's, in particular the Mashantucket Pequot culture, integration with nature." This relationship is examined throughout a variety of gardens which will create a mosaic of man/ecology/history spread across the site. All plantings will be of native species,

including densely planted copses of quaking aspen, canoe birch rising out of beds of maidenhair fern, hay-scented fern, cinnamon fern, dogtooth, and violet.

Polshek, with the collaboration of Kiley, has succeeded in conceiving a new building type which writes up a new building program. He strove after this goal instead of simply satisfying a given brief's requirements and adding to it some eccentric formal adjuncts as a spice to the routine character of the project. In his vision, the conservation of nature and community do not have a conservative or nostalgic aura. Coupled with the most advanced technological inventions,

it is the stuff of which sustainability and evolution are made.

The Mashantucket Pequot Center is an expression of the combination of an organic understanding of the natural landscape with a Mumfordian embracing of the neo-technic "machine." Having survived massacres of their people, the loss of their land, and the marginalization of their culture, the Mashantucket Pequots will be using the Center to convey their collective vision—one directed to the survival and dissemination of their cultural heritage, and, indeed, the survival and dissemination of all peoples and cultures.

(Opposite) Close-up of model

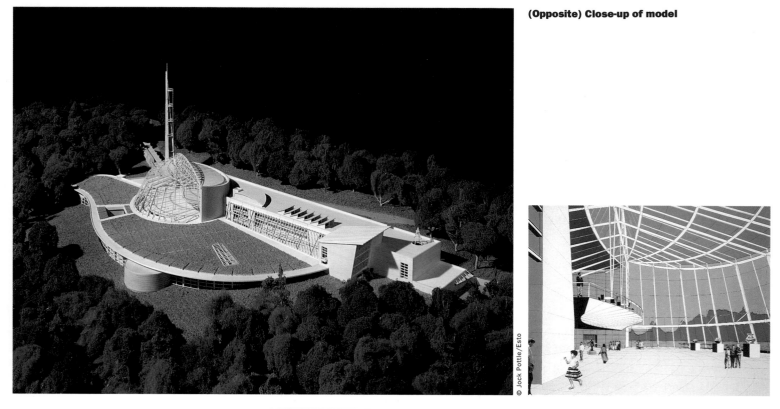

© Jock Pottle/Esto

(Above) Model

(Above right & right) Architects' rendering of the gathering space

© Jock Pottle/Esto

Arranged alphabetically by firm

AFFLECK, DESBARATS, DIMAKOPOULOS, LEBENSOLD, SISE

(now The Arcop Group) 1440 Ste. Catherine Street West, Suite 400, Montreal, Quebec H3G 1R8 Canada

Raymond Tait Affleck: b. Penticton, British Columbia, 1922. Educated at McGill University, Montreal (1941–47), B. Arch. and Eidgenossische Technische Hochschule, Zurich (1948). Principal, R. T. Affleck, Montreal (1952–55); President of Affleck, Desbarats, Dimakopoulos, Lebensold, Sise, Montreal (1955–69). Principal, Arcop Assoc. (1969–89). Assistant Professor, McGill University (1954– 58). Visiting Professor at McGill (1965–75). Died 1989.

Project specifications

Place Bonaventure (Montreal, Quebec), 1964–67, pp. 120–23

Client: Concordia Estates Development Company.

Built area: approx. 3,500,000 ft.².

Design team: Raymond T. Affleck, Ramesh Khosla, Eva Vecsei, Daniel Lazosky.

Construction company: Concordia Construction Inc.

Key materials: poured-in-place reinforced concrete, with surface textures achieved through varied formworks, special aggregates, and different finishing techniques.

Technology of interest: complete integration of architectural, structural, mechanical, and electrical systems in the Exhibition Hall.

Budget: Canadian $80,000,000.

Site characteristics: the site uses the air rights above the railway approach to Montreal's Central Station in the heart of the downtown. It is an important node in the system of pedestrian passageways, both weather-protected and above ground, which presently link most of downtown Montreal. The building occupies almost the entire site.

Bibliography

Architectural Record (December 1967): pp. 139–48.

ANDRES DUANY, ELIZABETH PLATER-ZYBERK, ARCHITECTS, INC.

1023 SW 25th Avenue, Miami, FL 33135

Andres Duany: B. A. Architecture and Urban Planning, Princeton University (1971); Ecole des Beaux-Arts, Paris, Ancien Elève (1972); M. Arch., Yale University School of Architecture (1974). Adjunct Professor, University of Miami School of Architecture (1979–present). Various Visiting Professorships since 1980. Founder and Partner, Arquitectonica, 1976–80.

Elizabeth Plater-Zyberk: B. A. Architecture and Urban Planning, Princeton University (1972); M. Arch., Yale University School of Architecture (1974). Professor with Tenure, University of Miami School of Architecture (1979–present). Various Visiting Professorships since 1978. Founder and Partner, Arquitectonica, 1976–80.

Project specifications

Seaside Plan (Seaside, Florida), 1980–, pp.94–95.

Client: Robert Davis.

Design team: Daniel Broggi, Ernesto Buch, Victoria Casasco, Robert Davis, Andres Duany, Elizabeth Plater-Zyberk, Luis Trelles, and Teofilo Victoria; Douglas Duany (landscape architect); Robert A. M. Stern, Leon Krier (planning consultants).

Construction company: various.

Key materials: primarily traditional wood frame, metal roofs, wood picket fences.

Technology of interest: traditional passive cooling strategies prevalent in the Southeast U.S. architecture of coastal towns (pitched roofs, broad overhangs, porches, undercrofts, cross-ventilated spaces, high ceilings, etc.).

Budget: site acquisition cost, $1,000,000. Site improvement cost, $2,8000,000. Construction cost, $80–120 per sq. ft.

Site characteristics: the town occupies an 80-acre site on a barrier island off the coast of the Florida Panhandle. The buildings include public buildings, civic spaces, houses, apartments, offices, and retail spaces. A 70-foot right-of-way runs parallel to 2,800 feet of beach and 30-foot tall sand dunes, with two pedestrian accesses to the beach.

Bibliography

Dunlop, Beth. "Coming of Age [Seaside, Florida]." *Architectural Record* (July 1989): pp. 96–103.

Santi, Carlo. "Seaside la piccola città." *Abitare* 276 (July–August 1989): pp. 174–93.

"Seaside, Florida, USA." *GA Houses* 27 (November 1989): pp. 90–123.

ANTOINE PREDOCK ARCHITECT

300 12th Street, Northwest Albuquerque, NM 87102

Antoine Predock: Columbia University, New York (1962), B. Arch. University of New Mexico, Albuquerque (1957–61). Principal and sole proprietor since 1967. Numerous awards, exhibits, and Visiting Professorships.

Project specifications

Rio Grande Nature Center (Albuquerque, New Mexico), 1982, pp. 200–03

Client: New Mexico State Park and Recreation Division.

Built area: 5000 ft.².

Design team: Antoine Predock, Ron Jacobs, Geoffrey Beebe.

Construction company: John R. Davis, Contractor.

Key materials: cast-in-place concrete walls, exposed inside and out. Colored concrete floors, wood ceilings, galvanized corrugated steel culvert, galvanized steel doors and windows.

Technology of interest: utilized river front technology for basic building materials, i.e., entrance is through 8-ft-diameter culvert. Building is a bird "blind" located on the pond shore and the edge of a cottonwood grove.

Budget: $500,000.

Site characteristics: flat wooded site of 27 acres with man-made pond. Located in one of the last agricultural areas adjacent to the Rio Grande in Albuquerque city limits.

Bibliography

"Antoine Predock." *L'Architecture D'Aujourd'hui* (October 1990): pp. 177–87.

"Antoine Predock." *A & U* (November 1988): pp. 75–130.

Papademetriou, Peter. "Blind Trust: Rio Grande Nature Center and Preserve." *Progressive Architecture* (March 1984).

"Nature center stands in the water like a sculpted dam." *Architecture* (December 1984): pp. 72–3.

Las Vegas Central Library and Children's Discovery Museum (Las Vegas, Nevada), 1990, pp. 268–71

Client: Clark County Library District.

Built area: 100,400 ft.².

Design team: Antoine Predock, Jon Anderson, Ron Jacob, Kevin Spence, David Hrabal.

Construction company: Argee Corporation.

Key materials: steel frame, studs with 1¼-inch Indian sandstone veneer and stucco, metal vault roof, pre-cast concrete stone, slip-formed, cast-in-place concrete tower.

Technology of interest: tower designed to accommodate science experiments for the children's museum. Over-size kaleidoscope in children's library uses street activity for changing demonstration.

Budget: $13,135,000.

Site characteristics: sloping site in redeveloping area of north Las Vegas on the Strip.

Bibliography

"Antoine Predock." *A & U* (November 1988): pp. 75–130.

Stein, Karen O. "Down the Strip: Las Vegas Library/Discovery Museum." *Architectural Record* (October 1990): pp. 68–75.

"Las Vegas Library—Dicovery Museum." *GA Document* 30 (August 1991): pp. 108–17.

ARCOSANTI

HC 74,Box 4136, Mayer, AZ 86333

Paolo Soleri: b. Turin, Italy, 1919. Ph.D. with highest honors in architecture, Torino Politecnico (1946). Fellowship at Taliesin East and West (1947–49). Ceramica Artistica Solimene commissioned in Italy, 1950. Founded Cosanti Foundation, Scottsdale, Arizona (1956). Received one Graham and two Guggenheim Fellowships. AIA Gold Medal for craftsmanship (1963). Distinguished Visiting Lecturer, Arizona State University.

Project specifications

Arcosanti (Mayer, Arizona), 1970–, pp. 136–37

Client: Cosanti Foundation.

Built area: 4,000,000 ft.².

Design team: Paolo Soleri.

Construction company: Cosanti Foundation.

Key materials: concrete, steel, glass, drywall, wood. Special techniques: 1) pre-cast concrete panels using silt-cast method; 2) dry-pack concrete for vaults; 3) radiant floor heating system via heat-duct tunnel, hot water, radiant floor, and passive solar.

Technology of interest: 1) apse-formed, open-air buildings to allow for passive solar heating; 2) heat-duct tunnel for infrastructure and energy transfer; 3) future use of passive solar pre-heat system for radiant floor heating; 4) Energy Apron—passive solar heating through greenhouses, using chimney effect; and 5) garment architecture—plastic or cloth membranes, or tarps to cover buildings in areas where it can more efficiently cool or heat the space.

Budget: $500,000,000.

Site characteristics: built on the side of a mesa in a high desert climate. Dense urban configuration on 25 acres. Over 800 acres left in natural state around town. There will also be 20–25 acres outside the town for agriculture and recreational areas.

Bibliography

Soleri, P. *Arcology: City in the Image of Man*. Cambridge: MIT Press, 1969.

Moholy-Nagy, Sibyl. *Forum* (May 1970).

Soleri, P. *The Sketchbooks of Paolo Soleri*. Cambridge: MIT Press, 1971.

ARQUITECTONICA

2151 LeJeune Road, Suite 300, Coral Gables, FL 33134

Bernardo Fort-Brescia and Laurinda Spear formed with three others the partnership of Arquitectonica in 1977. Fort-Brescia was educated at Princeton and Harvard, Spear at Columbia. Arquitectonica has headquarters in Miami, with offices in Houston and New York.

Project specifications

Atlantis Building (Miami, Florida), 1982, pp. 204–07

Client: original client, Hugo Zamorano, American Realequities.

Design team: Bernardo Fort-Brescia, Hervin Romney, Laurinda Spear (project designers).

Key materials: reinforced concrete columns and concrete slab. Glass wall with blue-masonry grid acting as a *brise soleil* and hiding the balconies.

Budget: not available.

Site characteristics: edge of Biscayne Bay on former estate of Mary Tiffany Bingham whose mansion is restored as a clubhouse. Sited perpendicular to the waterfront to be easily seen from approaching streets.

Bibliography

Viladis, Pilar. "Rich and Famous: Atlantis and Babylon, Miami, Florida." *Progressive Architecture* vol. 64, no. 2 (February 1983): pp. 99–107.

"The Atlantis, Miami, Florida." *GA Document* 7 (August 1983): pp. 22–7.

"Romantic Modernism: Arquitectonica." (ed. Shinichi Ogawa.) *Process: Architecture* 65 (February 1986): pp. 40–4.

ARTHUR ERICKSON ARCHITECTS

1672 West First Ave., Vancouver, BC V6J 1G1, Canada

Arthur Erickson: b. Vancouver, British Columbia, 1924. Educated at University of British Columbia, Vancouver (1942–45); McGill University, Montreal (1946– 50), B. Arch. (1950). McLennan Travelling Scholarship (1950–53). Canadian Army (1943–45); Captain Canadian Intelligence Corps, India, Ceylon, and Malaysia (1945). Private practice, Vancouver (1953–62). Partner with Geoffrey Massey, Erickson/ Massey Architects, Vancouver (1963–72). Principal, Arthur Erickson Archs., Vancouver, Los Angeles, and Toronto since 1972. President, Arthur Erickson Assoc., Vancouver, Toronto, Kuwait, and Jeddah since 1977. Has taught at University of Oregon and University of British Columbia. Has won numerous awards, including Gold Medals from Royal Architectural Institute of Canada (1984), the French Academy of Architecture (1984), and the AIA (1986).

Project specifications

Museum of Anthropology, University of British Columbia (Vancouver, British Columbia), 1971–76, pp. 160–63

Client: Department of Anthropology, University of British Columbia.

Built area: 66,000 ft.^{2}.

Design team: Arthur Erickson, Ron Bain, Alex Kee, Freeman Chan, Barry Simpson, Nick Milkovich; Bogue Babicki and Assoc. (structural); Mechanical Consultants Western (mechanical); W. T. Haggert and Company (electrical); Cornelia Hahn Oberlander (landscape); Hopping Kovach Grinell (exhibits).

Construction company: Grimwood Construction.

Key materials: *in situ* concrete, pre-cast concrete channels, tempered glass, Pilkington glass suspension system.

Technology of interest: first application anywhere of "visible storage." Entire storage area is designed to be accessible to the public through secured cabinets and drawers.

Budget: Canadian $3,000,000.

Site characteristics: wooded slope on the edge of cliffs over the sea, cleared during World War II for gun emplacements. Museum is set between 3 gun emplacements with 12-foot-deep foundations. Site is conceived as a recreation of a native village from several cultures, including plant life.

Bibliography

Canadian Architect (May 1977): pp. 346–53.

Architectural Review (May 1980).

Douglas and McIntyre. *The Architecture of Arthur Erickson*. New York: Harper & Row. London: Thames and Hudson, 1988.

Robson Square and Provincial Law Courts (Vancouver, British Columbia), 1973–79, pp. 186–87

Client: Government of British Columbia.

Built area: 400,000 ft.^{2}.

Design team: Arthur Erickson, Bing Thom, Janes Wright, Rainer Fassler, Junichi Hashimoto, Randolf Jefferson, Eva Matsuzaki, Yasuo Muramatsu, James Cheng, Arthur Yesaki, Bob Bida, Tom Robertson, Shanti Ghose, Ron Beaton, Barry Simpson, Nick Milkovich, Rodger Morris, Allen Cheng, Eddie Maifredi, Kirat Anand; Bogue Babicki and Assoc. (structural); Reid Crowther and Partners (mechanical); W. T. Haggert and Company (electrical); William Lam and Assoc. (lighting); Cornelia Hahn Oberlander, Ken Morris, Robert Zinser, Raoul Robillard (landscape); Dennis Christianson, Alan Bell (urban design).

Key materials: *in situ* reinforced concrete of special gray-brown mix, channel beams incorporating lighting throughout floor plates. Laminated glass roof panels and pool bottoms.

Technology of interest: Great Hall cooled by convection, letting air in at the bottom of glass roof and out at the top, warmed by solar radiation and localized heat on balconies. 30,000-gallon storage tank stores heat from lighting.

Budget: (U.S.) $95,000,000 target, (U.S.) $80,000,000 actual, plus Art Gallery renovation costs.

Site characteristics: 3 blocks in the center of the city with a central plaza and gardens on top of the 3-story government office building.

Bibliography

Nairn, Janet. *Architectural Record* vol. 168, no. 8 (December 1980): pp. 65–75.

Stephens, Suzanne. "Law Courts and Robson Square Complex." *Progressive Architecture* vol. 62, no. 3 (March 1981): pp. 82–7.

BOND RYDER JAMES

Max Bond, now at Davis, Brody and Associates, 100 East 42nd Street, New York, NY 10017

J. Max Bond, Jr.: Harvard College, B. A. (1955), Harvard GSD, M. Arch. (1958). Designer-Draftsman, Andre Wogenscky (and M. Wogenscky in association with M. Le Corbusier), Paris (1959–60). Designer, Pederson and Tilney, New York (1961–64). Architect, Ghana National Construction Corp., Accra, Ghana (1964–66). Instructor, University of Science and Technology, Kumasi, Ghana (1965–67). Executive Director, Architect's Renewal Committee in Harlem (1967–68). Partner, Davis, Brody and Assoc. Principal, Bond Ryder and Assoc. (1968–90). Chairman, Graduate School of Architecture and Planning, Columbia University, New York, 1980–84 (Assistant and Associate Professor, 1969–80; Professor, 1980–85). Dean, School of Architecture and Environmental Studies, City College of New York, 1985–92 (Professor since 1985).

Donald P. Ryder: University of Illinois (1944–45, 1947–51); B. S. Arch. (1951). Currently Chairman and Professor at the City College of New York, and has taught at Pratt Institute.

Project specifications

Martin Luther King, Jr. Center for Non-Violent Social Change (Atlanta, Georgia), 1976–81, pp. 196–99

Client: Martin Luther King, Jr. Center for Non-Violent Social Change.

Built area: 55,000 ft.^{2}.

Design team: J. Max Bond, Jr. (partner in charge of design); Don Ryder (associated partner); John Rivers (project manager); Steven Gifford, Lloyd de Suze (staff).

Construction company: Holder in asssociation with H. J. Russell.

Key materials: local brick (single-wythe vaults, ground assembled as curved wall), pre-cast and poured-in-place concrete, West African sapele wood, Southern U.S. pine, and white oak. The only expensive material present is that of Dr. King's marble crypt, in order to represent Dr. King's unadorned life.

Budget: $8,000,000.

Site characteristics: urban site, located between Ebenezer Baptist Church (to the west) and Dr. King's birthplace (to the east). Across the street are recreational and community service buildings. Location was chosen to provide a connection between the Church, home, and community facilities.

Bibliography

Holtz Kay, Jane. "Invisible architects: minority firms struggle to achieve recognition in a white-dominated profession." *Architecture* vol. 80, no. 4 (April 1991): pp. 106–13.

Architecture vol. 82, no. 1 (January 1993): pp. 24–5.

CAMBRIDGE SEVEN ASSOCIATES, INC.

1050 Massachusetts Avenue, Cambridge, MA 02138

Founding partners: Louis J. Bakanowsky, Peter Chermayeff, Alden B. Christie, Paul E. Dietrich, and Terry Rankine, and the graphic designers, Ivan Chermayeff and Thomas H. Geismar. Current partners: Louis J. Bakanowsky, Ivan Chermayeff, Peter Chermayeff, Paul E. Dietrich, Thomas H. Geismar, Terry Rankine, Charles Redmon, John W. Stebbins, Richard L. Tuve (senior partners); Ronald D. Baker, Gary C. Johnson, Peter G. Kuttner, Bobby C. Poole, and Peter Sollogub (junior partners).

Project specifications

US Pavillion at Expo 67 (Montreal, Quebec, Canada), 1964–67, pp. 110–13

Client: U.S. Information Agency.

Built area: 146,000 ft.^{2}.

Design team: R. Buckminster Fuller, Fuller/Sadao, Inc. and Geometrics, Inc. (architects/enclosing structure); Cambridge Seven Assoc., Inc. (interior architects/exhibit design); Carol R. Johnson & Assoc. (landscape architect); Goerge F. Eber & Assoc. (associate Canadian architect); Simpson, Gumpertz & Hager, Inc. (structural engineers);

Paul Londe & Assoc. (mechanical engineers); Edison Price (lighting design).

Construction company: George A. Fuller Company, Boston, MA.

Key materials: framework of the geodesic dome was fabricated from tube steel infilled with clear acrylic panels. The platforms, stair towers, and escalator supports were of structural steel framing clad in gypsum wall-board.

Technology of interest: air-handling equipment housed on main floor, using ground form and theater to lessen scale impact. Computerized sun screens.

Budget: $4,500,000.

Site characteristics: dome straddles an area of filled land and the Ile St. Hélène. A station of the Montreal Metro system, specially built for Expo, was located immediately in front of the pavilion.

Bibliography

Life (April 28, 1967).

Time (May 5, 1967).

Architectural Forum (June 1967).

Clasen, Wolfgang. *Expositions, Exhibits, Industrial and Trade Fairs.* New York: Frederick A. Praeger, 1968.

New England Aquarium (Boston, Massachusetts), 1962–69, pp. 132–35

Client: New England Aquarium.

Design team: Cambridge Seven Assoc. (architect and exhibit designer) in joint venture with LeMessurier Assoc. (structural engineer).

Key materials: poured-in-place, board-formed concrete on grade beams with pile foundations. Steel trusses. Pre-cast concrete columns in Great Tank are held together by compression rings. Glass fiber piping.

Technology of interest: large windows in Great Tank are nearly 4 ins. thick at base, to resist pressure from 200,000 gallons of salt water. Advanced salt water and fresh water pumping system.

Budget: not available.

Site characteristics: building sits on a wharf in Boston Harbor.

Bibliography

Progressive Architecture (December 1969).

"Composition of Oceanic Architecture." *Process: Architecture* 96 (June 1991).

CARLOS JIMÉNEZ ARCHITECTURAL DESIGN STUDIO

1116 Willard Street, Houston, TX 77006

Carlos Jiménez: b. San José, Costa Rica, 1959. University of Houston School of Architecture, professional degree, 1981. Co-founded Bowley-Jiménez Studio (1982) and started own design studio (1983). Visiting Instructor, Rice University, Texas, A & M University, UCLA, and University of Texas, Arlington (1987–90). Has also been Visiting Instructor at Southern California Institute of Architecture and University of Houston.

Project specifications

Houston Fine Arts Press (Houston, Texas), 1985–87, pp. 242–45

Client: Richard Newlin, director and owner, Houston Fine Arts Press.

Built area: 8000 ft.^{2}.

Design team: Carlos Jiménez (at the time the sole practitioner).

Construction company: Richard Newlin and Carlos Jiménez.

Key materials: plastered concrete block infill of steel frame, steel studs, and pre-painted steel roof.

Technology of interest: full-length clerestory.

Budget: $375,000 ($40 per sq. ft. for the building, the remainder spent on fencing, concrete masonry perimeter walls, steel gates, etc.).

Site characteristics: 39 x 300 ft. in an industrial area. The long directions of the site face north and south, structuring the north-facing windows and lightwells. The parking lot and courtyard are surrounded by a wall which connects the building to its site and forms an enclave from the surrounding context.

Bibliography

Anderton, Frances. "Cool Work by Jiménez." *Architectural Review* 1105 (March 1989, London): pp. 64–9.

Barriere, Philippe. "Maison d'édition à Houston." *L'architecture D'Aujourd'hui* 263 (June 1989, Paris): pp. 112–13.

Jiménez, Carlos. *Carlos Jiménez.* Introduction by Aldo Rossi. Barcelona: G. Gili, 1991.

CENTER FOR MAXIMUM POTENTIAL BUILDING SYSTEMS

8604 F.M. 969, Austin, TX 78724

Pliny Fisk III: studied under Ian McHarg at University of Pennsylvania (early 1970s) and has degrees in architecture and landscape architecture. Co-founded the company with Gail Vittori.

Project specifications

Laredo Demonstration Blueprint Farm (Laredo, Texas), 1987–, pp. 240–41

Client: The Meadows Foundation (funder), The Texas Department of Agriculture, The Governor's Energy Office, and Laredo Junior College.

Built area: 86,000 ft.^{2}.

Design team: Pliny Fisk III; Ronald Nigh, David Bainbridge (agricultural systems); The Environmental Research Lab (climatic); Sean Hoey (mechanical); Tony Ramirez (plant ecology); Joseph Farbiarz (structural/material mixes); Howard Reichmuth (thermodynamics); Bergy Wind (wind energy).

Construction company: overseen by Center for Maximum Potential Building Systems; Tom Glassford, Tom Morris, Tony Ramirez (contractors/site managers).

Key materials: various indigenous and recycled materials, including: straw bales, fly ash cement (from coal burning plants) for stucco, recycled drilling stems from oil rigs, corrugated metal roofing (80% recycled).

Technology of interest: entire farm is operated by sustainable technologies powered by sun and wind. The gridded building system enables the interior and exterior spaces to be partially or fully transformed, from closed-in, barn-type structures with roofs that can be raised or lowered, to continuous shade systems to prolong the growing season, to a greenhouse for winter use. Up-draft and down-draft cooling towers provide the building's ventilation. Cisterns collect rainwater for use by bathroom facilities and down-draft cooling pads, and are used as a thermal sink for a straw-insulated refrigeration room. The wind systems (40 kW) pump water from the Rio Grande through a wetland marsh (proposed) in order to treat the polluted water before it is used on organically produced crops.

Budget: $372,000 plus $110,00 for 40 kW wind system.

Site characteristics: on U.S.–Mexico border, directly adjacent to the Rio Grande River, within the City of Laredo. A steady, favorable wind regime makes the site well suited for wind generation, while the relatively low humidity, coupled with high temperature, makes the down-draft wind towers cost effective. The region is in a desertification zone, providing an incentive to minimize the use of virgin wood materials, while the shade system provides an extra season of growing during the harsh summer months.

Bibliography

Tilley, Ray Don. "Blueprint for Survival." *Architecture* (May 1991): pp. 65–70.

CESAR PELLI & ASSOCIATES

1056 Chapel Street, New Haven, CT 06510

Cesar Pelli, FAIA: b. Tucumán, Argentina, 1926. Emigrated to U.S., 1952, naturalized, 1964. University of Tucumán (1944–49), Dip. Arch. University of Illinois, Urbana-Champaign (1952–54), M. S. Arch. Associate Architect, Eero Saarinen and Assoc. (1954–64); Project Designer for TWA Terminal at JFK Airport in New York, and Morse and Stiles Colleges at Yale University. Director of Design, Daniel, Mann, Johnson, & Mendenhall, Los Angeles (1964–68). Partner for Design, Gruen Assoc., Los Angeles (1968–76). Projects include San Bernardino City Hall, Pacific Design Center in Los Angeles, and U.S. Embassy in Tokyo. Founder, Cesar Pelli & Assoc., 1977. Dean, Yale University School of Architecture (1977–84); continues to lecture on architecture. AIA Firm Award, 1989. AIA Top 10 most influential living American architects (1991).

Project specifications

Pacific Design Center (Los Angeles, California), Phase I, 1971–75; Phase II, 1984–88, pp. 156–59

Client: Sequoia Pacific, a division of Southern Pacific Company.

Built area: Phase I, 750,000 ft.^{2}.; Phase II, 470,000 ft.^{2}.

Design team: Phase I, Cesar Pelli at Gruen Assoc. (design principal); Edgardo Contini, Allen Rubinstein (project principals); Miloyko Lazovich (designer). Phase II, Cesar Pelli (design principal); Mac Ball, Doug Denis (design team members); Lily del Carmen Berrios (project manager); Philip Koether, Susan Papadakis, Roger Schickedantz (designers); Gruen Assoc. (associate architect).

Construction company: HCB.

Key materials: Phase I, opaque blue ceramic glass. Phase II, opaque green ceramic glass. Phase III, opaque red ceramic glass.

Budget: not available.

Site characteristics: in the heart of the city's well-established trade center.

Bibliography

A+U 7 (July 1990).

McCoy, Esther. "The Blue Bombshell." *Progressive Architecture* (October 1976): pp. 78–83.

Pastier, John. "Evaluation: Utility and Fantasy in Los Angeles." *AIA Journal* (May 1978): pp. 38–45.

Frampton, Kenneth. *Cesar Pelli/Gruen Associates.* (ed. Yukio Futagawa) GA 59 (Tokyo, 1981).

Dixon, John Morris. "Green Phase." *Progressive Architecture* (March 1989): pp. 82–5.

World Financial Center and Winter Garden (New York City, New York), 1980–88, pp. 248–51

Client: Olympia & York Equity Corporation.

Built area: 8,600,000 ft.^{2}.; Leasable office space, 6,000,000 ft.^{2}. Site, 13½ acres/5½ hectares. Floorplate, 8,500,000 ft.^{2}.

Design team: Cesar Pelli & Assoc. (design architect); Cesar Pelli (design principal); Fred Clarke (project principal); Diana Balmori (landscape principal); Thomas Morton, Jeff Paine (project managers); Jon Pickard (design team leader); Mark Shoemaker, Turan Duda, Greg Jones (senior designers); Mitchell Hirsch, Ann Marie Baranowski, Robert Pulito, Lily Del Carmen Berrios, Cassie York, Walter Miller, Bradford Fiske, Douglas Denes, Cheryl Flota, Thomas Soyster, Julann Meyers, Chris Williams, David Leonard, Lawrence Ng, Eric Liebmann (designers). Adamson Assoc., Toronto and Haines Lundberg and Waehler, New York (architects-of-record); Lev Zetlin Assoc., M. S. Yolles & Partners (structural engineers); Flack & Kurtz (consulting engineers), The Mitchell Partnership (mechanical engineers); Mueser, Rutledge, Johnson & Desimone (foundations).

Construction company: Olympia & York Battery Park Company.

Key materials: steel frame, polished and flamed sagami

granite; reflective, clear, and spandrel glass; aluminum and bronze mullions; standing seam copper roofing.

Technology of interest: (client acted as the developer and construction manager, responsible for cost and schedule control, set parameters for cost, budget, and schedule, and was responsible for bid resolution). Winter Garden: receiving platform relieves load over the water and PATH (subway) tubes. 60–80-foot-long painted steel arches were fabricated in Canada and erected in single segments. A horseshoe-shaped stiffening ring was designed and installed on the mechanical room floor to resist the thrust of the arches, enabling the arches to be lighter in weight. A latticed, folded plate (tilted truss) was designed into the front wall of the Winter Garden hidden in the plane of the skin of the wall (110 x 138 feet at apex). To avoid requiring the front wall to be fire-rated, a slip connection (consisting of teflon-coated, lubricated, bronze bearing pin connections) was designed to allow the front wall to be braced against the wind load. The floor and front wall opening was designed to accept a Condor Crane and outriggers for maintainance of the palms (*Washingtonia robusta*) and structure. A series of mechanized pulleys raises and lowers the stage of the Winter Garden.

Budget: $1 billion.

Site characteristics: 4 office towers, a public Winter Garden, two 9-story octagonal gateway buildings and a 3½-acre landscaped public plaza. Location, Battery Park City, bordered by the Hudson River, West Side Highway, Vessey Street, and Liberty Street.

Bibliography

"World Financial Center & Battery Park City Plaza." *Architectural Record* (July 1983): pp. 176–99.

Oppenheimer Dean, Andrea and Allen Freeman. "The Rockefeller Center of the 80s." *Architecture* (December 1986): pp. 36–43.

Pelli, Cesar, *Cesar Pelli, buildings and projects 1965–1990*. Introduction by Paul Goldberger. New York: Rizzoli, 1990.

CLARK & MENEFEE ARCHITECTS

404B East Main Street, Charlottesville, VA 22902

W. G. Clark: b. Louisa, Virginia, 1942. B. Arch., University of Virginia (1965). Architectural practice, Charleston, South Carolina (1974). Formed Clark & Menefee Architects (1985). Professor and Chairman of Architecture, University of Virginia, 1988–90 (Professor since 1990). Has taught and lectured at schools including Harvard GSD, University of Pennsylvania, Ohio State, Yale, Georgia Tech. Rice, RISD, and University of Florida.

Charles Menefee: b. Charleston, South Carolina, 1954. B. Arch. Carnegie-Mellon University (1977). Principal, Charleston Architectural Group (1981 –85). Formed Clark & Menefee Architects (1985). Lecturer, University of Virginia (1991– present).

Project specifications

Middleton Inn (Charleston, South Carolina), 1978–85, pp. 234–35.

Client: Charles Duell.

Built area: 34,000 ft.².

Design team: W. G. Clark, Charles Menefee, William Riesberg, Steven Thompson, Huston Eubank, Dian Boone.

Construction company: Stier, Kent & Co.

Key materials: stucco over brick at "armature," painted wood at guest room "cabinets."

Budget: $80 per sq. ft.

Site characteristics: former mine site; terrace between live oak forest and cliff overlooking Ashley River and marshlands; adjacent to 18th-century gardens of Middleton Place, a National Historic Landmark.

Bibliography

Boles, Daralice, D. "A Place Apart." *Progressive Architecture* (May 1986): pp. 83–91.

Ivy, Jr., Robert A. "Modern Presence in Historic Gardens." *Architecture* (May 1987): pp. 166–9.

Clark, W. G. "Middleton Inn, Charleston, South Carolina." *A+U* (February 1989): pp. 80–6.

Czech, Herman. "On Rigour," *9H*, no. 8, (London, 1989).

CRAIG ZEIDLER & STRONG

(now Zeidler Roberts Architects)

315 Queen Street West, Toronto, Ontario, Canada M5V 2X2

Eberard Zeidler: b. Braunsdorf, Germany, 1926. Educated at Bauhaus, Weimar (1945–48). Dip. Ing. (1949) from the Universität Fridericiana, Karlsruhe Technische Hochschule. Worked in office of Eiermann and Lindner, Karlsruhe and Osnabruck (1949–51). Partner at Zeidler Roberts Partnership/Architects (formerly Blackwell and Craig) since 1951. Has been adjunct Professor of Design at University of Toronto since 1984.

Project specifications

McMaster University Health Sciences Centre (Hamilton, Ontario), 1967–72, pp. 154–55

Client: McMaster University Health Sciences Centre.

Built area: 1,761,500 ft.².

Design team: Eberhard H. Zeidler, A. Banelis, R. H. Jacobs, F. Kulcsar, A. Roberts.

Construction company: Doyle-Hinton Contract Services Ltd.

Key materials: space frame structural steel system for areas requiring flexible planning; reinforced concrete in fixed function areas; smooth form pre-cast concrete wall cladding on main walls; clear single glazing on tower and penthouse skirting; pre-finished galvanized steel insulated panels at elevator; mechanical and electrical penthouse. Entrances and courts glazed with insulating glass in clear anodized aluminum framing.

Technology of interest: the "Bulkveyor," a horizontal handling system, similar to a forklift truck, is capable of handling 3 standard hospital carts. Transportation of smaller quantities of items are handled by "mini-lift," a system similar to a model-railroad set, with briefcase-sized containers, each with its own motor. Mechanical and electrical services: the Sub-Servo Laboratory System is a standardized energy unit that allows total flexibility in the independent arrangement of lab benches.

Budget: Canadian $61,424,500.

Site characteristics: located on 13 acres of the campus of McMaster University.

The project received Award of Excellence from Canadian Architect Yearbook, 1969.

Bibliography:

Zeidler, Eberhard. *Healing the Hospital—McMaster Health Sciences Centre: Its Conception and Evolution*. Toronto: Zeidler Partnership, 1974.

Thomsen, Christian W. *Eberhard Zeidler: In Search of Human Space*. Berlin: Ernst & Sohn, 1992.

DER SCUTT ARCHITECT

44 West 28th Street, New York, NY 10001

Der Scutt: b. Reading, Pennsylvania, 1934. Wyomissing Polytechnic Institute, Pennsylvania (1952–55); Pennsylvania State University, University Park (1957–59); B. Arch. (1959). Yale University (1959–61); M. Arch. (1961). Architectural apprentice, Eastern Engineering Company, Reading, Pennsylvania (1952–55). Assistant Architect, Jochen Weinert, Hagen, West Germany (1955–56); Philip Johnson, New York (1957); Vincent G. Kling, Philadelphia (1958); Edward Durell Stone, New York (1961–62); and

Paul Rudolph, New York (1962–65). Architect (1965–67), Associate (1967–75), Ely Jacques Kahn, and Robert Allan Jacobs, Kahn, and Jacobs Architects, New York. Associate (1975–76), Partner (1976–79), Poor, Swanke, Hayden and Connell Architects, New York. Partner, Swanke, Hayden, Connell and Partners Architects, New York (1979–81). In private practice since 1981, New York. Guest Critic in Architecture (1967), and Visiting Critic in Architectural Design, Yale University (1982, 1983).

Project specifications

Trump Tower (New York City, New York), 1979–83, pp. 218–19

Client: The Trump Organization and The Equitable Life Assurance Society of the United States.

Built area: 756,000 ft.².

Design team: office of Irwin G. Cantor P. C. (structural engineer); W. A. DiGiacomo Assoc. P.C. (mechanical/electrical engineer).

Construction company: HRH Construction.

Key materials: concrete structural frame; exterior aluminum and insulating glass curtain wall (to reduce weight of exterior cladding); atrium clad in Italian brecchia perniche marble (entire quarry was used).

Technology of interest: original potential development of 356,000 ft.² was increased to 756,000 ft.² by obtaining the air rights to the adjacent Tiffany building. This fixes the height of the Tiffany building forever, thus guaranteeing unprecedented and unobstructed views of Central Park, the George Washington Bridge, and the Hudson River.

Budget: not available.

Site characteristics: 115 x 175 feet adjacent to the 11-story Tiffany and Company building.

Bibliography

Rubin, Sy. *Trump Tower*. Secaucus, New Jersey: L. Stuart, 1984.

DOUGLAS CARDINAL ARCHITECTS LTD.

55 Murray Street, 6th Floor, Ottawa, Ontario, Canada

Douglas Cardinal: b. Calgary, Alberta, 1934. University of British Columbia, Vancouver (1953–54). University of Texas, Austin (1956–63), B. Arch., 1963. Design Architect, Bissell and Holman, Red Deer, Alberta (1963–67). Principal, Douglas J. Cardinal Architect, Red Deer (1964–76), Edmonton, Alberta (1967–76), and Douglas J. Cardinal Architect Ltd., Edmonton, since 1976. Fellow, Royal Architectural Institute of Canada, 1983.

Project specifications

Museum of Civilization (Hull, Quebec), 1982–89, pp. 252–55

Client: Government of Canada.

Built area: 1,000,000 ft.².

Design team: Douglas J. Cardinal Architect Ltd. and Tétreault, Parent, Languedoc et Associés Inc. (architects); Asselin, Benot, Boucher, Ducharme, Lapointe Inc. (structural engineers); Bouthillette, Parizeau et Associés (mechanical engineers); Les Consultants Dessau Inc. (electrical engineers); EDA Collaborative Inc./Parent Latreille Associés (landscape architects); Concordia Management Company Limited (construction managers).

Construction company: Concordia Construction Management Company.

Key materials: Manitoba tyndall limestone, copper, triple-glazing.

Technology of interest: world's first combined IMAX/OMNIMAX theater with a 23-meter-diameter hemispherical screen.

Budget: Canadian $1590 per sq. m.

Site characteristics: located in Hull, on the banks of the Ottawa River. Surrounded by grassy parkland and directly across from the buildings of Parliament.

Bibliography

Boddy, Trevor. *The Architecture of Douglas Cardinal.* Edmonton: NeWest Press, 1989.

A+U vol. 7, no. 228 (July 1990): pp: 7–39.

EDWARD LARRABEE BARNES/JOHN M. Y. LEE, ARCHITECTS

320 West 13th Street, New York, NY 10014

Edward Larrabee Barnes: b. Chicago, 1915. Received B. S. (1938) and M. Arch. (1942) from Harvard University. Served in U.S. Naval Reserve (1942–47). Awarded Brunner Prize (1959) and Architectural League of New York's Citation in Landscape for Haystack Mountain School of Arts and Crafts (1965). Has taught at Pratt Institute, Yale University, Harvard University, and University of Virginia. Has been in private practice since 1949.

Project specifications

Haystack Mountain School of Arts and Crafts (Deer Isle, Maine), 1959–61, pp. 66–69

Client: Haystack Mountain School of Arts and Crafts.

Design team: Edward Larrabee Barnes; Severud-Elstaad-Drueger (structural engineers).

Key materials: wood frame structure, cedar shingle siding.

Budget: $104,000.

Site characteristics: steep, rocky, spruce-covered slope on the tip of Deer Isle with views of the ocean.

Bibliography

"Quiet Architecture of Edward Larrabee Barnes." *Architectural Record* (October 1961): pp. 126–7.

"Architect Ed Barnes: Toward Simpler Details, Simpler Forms, and Greater Unity." *Architectural Forum* (August 1963): pp. 74–8.

Campbell, Robert. "Evaluation: A Classic that Retains its Appeal." *Architecture* (February 1989): pp. 61–2.

IBM Building (New York, New York), 1973–83, pp. 214–17

Client: IBM Real Estate and Construction Division.

Built area: 1,000,000 ft.².

Design team: Edward Larrabee Barnes, John M. Y. Lee, Armand Avakian, Richard Klibschon.

Construction company: Turner Construction Company.

Key materials: steel frame, polished Atlantic green granite cladding, gray–green glass.

Technology of interest: building's exhaust is used to heat and cool the public garden.

Budget: not available.

Site characteristics: dense urban site in midtown Manhattan.

Bibliography

Schmertz, Mildred. "A Skyscraper in Context." *Architectural Record* (May 1984): pp. 148–55.

"Edward Larrabee Barnes." *GA Document* (January 1985): pp. 34–9.

EERO SAARINEN AND ASSOCIATES

Eero Saarinen: b. Kirkonummi, Finland, 1910. Son of architect, Eliel Saarinen and the sculptor/weaver, Louise (Loja) Geselius Saarinen. Emigrated to U.S., 1923, naturalized, 1940. Studied at Académie de la Grand Chaumière, Paris (1929–30). B. F. A. in architecture, Yale University (1934). M. A., Yale (1949). Practiced with father in Ann Arbor, Michigan (1936–41), as Saarinen-Swanson-Saarinen (with J. Robert Swanson, 1941–47), and as Saarinen, Saarinen and Assoc., Ann Arbor (1947–50). Principal, Eero Saarinen and Assoc. in Birmingham, Michigan (1950) until death in 1961. Gold Medal, American Institute of Architects, 1962.

Project specifications

Dulles International Airport Terminal (Chantilly, Virginia), 1958–63, pp. 78–81

Client: Federal Aviation Agency.

Design team: Eero Saarinen & Assoc. (architect); Ammann & Whitney (structural engineers); Burns & McDonnell (mechanical engineers); Charles Landrum (airport consultant); Dan Kiley (landscape architect).

Key materials: reinforced concrete columns, steel cable, concrete slab, and roof decking.

Technology of interest: mobile lounges transport passengers between terminal and plane, and double as part of the terminal itself.

Budget: not available.

Site characteristics: 23 miles west of Washington, D.C.

Bibliography

Architectural Record (March 1960).

Progressive Architecture (August 1963).

EISENMAN ARCHITECTS

40 West 25th Street, New York, NY 10010

Peter Eisenman: b. 1932. B. Arch., Cornell University (1955). M. S. in Architecture, Columbia University (1960). M. A. and Ph.D., Cambridge University (1962 and 1963). Architectural Designer, Percival Goodman, FAIA, New York (1958–59). Architectural Designer, The Architects Collaborative, Cambridge, Massachusetts (1959). Principal, Peter D. Eisenman, Architect, New York (1963–80). Partner, Eisenman/Robertson Architects, Design Development Resources, New York (1980–87). Eisenman Architects, New York (1987–present). Has taught at many schools of architecture, including Princeton, Cambridge University, Maryland, University of Illinois at Chicago, and Yale. Eliot Noyes Visiting Design Critic, Harvard University (1993). Irwin S. Chanin Professor of Architecture, The Cooper Union for Arts and Sciences (1986–present). Distinguished Professor of Architecture, The Ohio State University (1984–present). Founder, Director, The Institute for Architecture and Urban Studies, New York (1967–82). Editor, Oppositions Books, IAUS (Rizzoli International), 1975–82. Editor, *Oppositions Magazine*, IAUS (MIT Press), 1967–82.

Project specifications

House II (Hardwick, Vermont), 1969–71, pp. 142–43

Client: Mr. and Mrs. Richard Falk.

Built area: 2,000 ft.².

Design team: Gregory A. Gale, Robinson O. Brown (assistants); Gregory A. Gale, Judith Turner, Christopher Chimera (drawings); Geiger-Berger (structural engineer).

Construction company: Dutton Smith, Middlebury, Vermont.

Budget: $80,000.

Site characteristics: the second house for an academic couple, it is situated on top of a 100-acre site with broad panoramic views on 3 sides which extend for 20 miles.

Bibliography

Eisenman, Peter. "House II, 1969." *Five Architects.* New York: George Wittenborn & Company, 1972.

Eisenman, Peter. *House of Cards.* New York: Oxford University Press, 1987.

The Wexner Center for the Visual Arts (Columbus, Ohio), 1983–89, pp. 260–63

Client: Ohio State University. Richard Eschilman (university architect); Jim Swiatek (university project architect); Tom Heretta (university project manager).

Built area: 140,000 ft.².

Design team: Eisenman Architects, Richard Trott & Partners Architects (architect); Peter Eisenman, FAIA, Richard Trott, FAIA (partners-in-charge); George Kewin, AIA, Michael Burdey, AIA (directing architects); Arthur Baker, Andrew Buchsbaum, Thomas Leeser, Richard Morris, James Rudy, Faruk Yorgancioglu (project architects); Andrea Brown, Edward Carroll, Robert Choeff, David Clark, Clark Crawford, Tim Decker, Ellen Dunham, John Durschinger, Frank Hsu, Wes Jones, Jim Linke, Michael McInturf, Hiroshi Maruyama, Mark Mascheroni, Alex Moser, Harry Ours, Joe Rosa, Scott Sickeler, Madison Spencer, Mark Wamble (project team). Consultants: Hanna Olin, Ltd. (landscape architect), Laurie Olin (partner-in-charge); Lantz, Jones, & Nebraska, Inc. (structural engineer), Tom Jones (partner-in-charge); H. A. Williams and Assoc. (mechanical engineer); Jules Fischer & Paul Marantz, Inc. (lighting design); C. F. Bird & P. J. Bull, Ltd. (civil engineer); Chapman & Ducibella, Inc. (security and fire); Robert Slutzky (graphics and color); Dunbar Geotechnical (soils engineer); Boyce Nemec (audio/ visual); Jaffe Acoustics (acoustics); George Van Neil (specifics).

Construction company: Dugan and Meyers (general contractor); Jim Smith (project manager); A. T. F. Mechanical, Inc. (mechanical contractor); Bob Weiland (project manager); Romanoff Electric (electrical contractor); Sib Goetz (project superintendent); Radico, Inc. (plumbing contractor); Frank Czako (project manager); J. T. Edwards (steel subcontractor); Jack Edwards (president).

Budget: $43,000,000.

Site characteristics: building connects the Columbus community with the University community by the introduction of a new central axis. The building presents a minimal intervention between two existing and adjacent campus buildings; the central circulation spine of the new building resolves the 2 existing geometries with two grids 12.5 degrees askew.

Bibliography

Fisher, Thomas and John Morris Dixon. "Wexner Center for the Visual Arts." *Progressive Architecture* (October 1989): pp. 67–85.

Eisenman, Peter, with Anthony Vidler and Raphael Moneo. *The Wexner Center for the Visual Arts: Ohio State University.* New York: Rizzoli, 1989.

ERIC OWEN MOSS ARCHITECT

8557 Higuera Street, Culver City, CA 90232

Eric Owen Moss: b. Los Angeles, California, 1943. B. A., University of California at Los Angeles (1965); M. Arch. (with honors), University of California at Berkeley, College of Environmental Design (1968). M. Arch., Harvard University GSD (1972). Professor of Design and Member of Board of Directors, Southern California Institute of Architecture (1974–present). Established Eric Owen Moss Architects, 1976.

Project specifications

Paramount Laundry Office Building (Culver City, California), 1987–89, pp. 256–59

Client: Frederick Norton Smith.

Built area: 45,000 ft.².

Design team: Eric Owen Moss (architect); Jay Vanos (project associate); Dennis Ige, Scott M. Nakao (project architects); Greg Baker (tenant improvements); Todd Conversano, Jerry Sullivan, Alan Binn, Dana Swinsky Cantelmo, Carol Hove, Craig Schultz, Isabelle Duvivier (project team). Consultants: Joe Kurily, Kurily Szymanski Tchirkow (structural engineer); Paul Antieri, I & N Consulting Engineers (mechanical engineer); Michael Cullen, California Associated Power (electrical engineer); Steven Ormenyi, Steven Ormenyi & Assoc. (landscape architect).

Construction company: Scott Gates Construction Company, Inc.

Key materials: wood, steel, reinforced concrete, galvanized steel vault, vitrified clay pipe.

Technology of interest: concrete-filled vitrified clay pipes serve as structural columns. A 2-part third floor is connected by a bridge with re-bar railings; to make room for the bridge, a 4-foot portion of the bottom chord of the existing trusses is removed, and restructured with a steel tube below and two new steel vertical chords.

Budget: not available.

Site characteristics: existing 20,000 ft.^{2} warehouse, built in 1940, with poured concrete walls and wood truss supported roof located in a Culver City neighborhood of studio production facilities. The adjacent site is occupied by another Eric Owen Moss/Frederick Norton Smith adaptive re-use building, known as Lindblade Tower.

Bibliography

Murphy, Jim. "A different drummer." *Progressive Architecture* vol. 70, no. 12 (November 1989): pp. 74–83.

Lotti, Luca. "Maniera di due interni losangelini." *Domus* (December 1989): pp. 52–63.

Moss, Eric Owen. *Eric Owen Moss, buildings and projects.* New York: Rizzoli, 1991.

Moss, Eric Owen. "Colpi di grazia a Culver City." *Lotus international* 77 (1993): pp. 92–105.

ESHERICK HOMSEY DODGE AND DAVIS

2789 25th Street, San Francisco, CA 94110

Joseph Esherick: b. Philadelphia, Pennsylvania, 1914. Received B. Arch. from University of Pennsylvania (1937). Has been in private practice since 1946, after serving 2 years in U.S. Navy. Has been honored with the AIA's Gold Medal for Lifetime Achievement

Project specifications

Monterey Bay Aquarium (Monterey, California), 1978–84, pp. 224–27

Client: Monterey Bay Aquarium Foundation.

Built area: 130,000 ft.^{2}.

Design team: Charles M. Davis (principal in charge); James Hastings (project manager).

Construction company: Rudolph and Sletten.

Key materials: concrete, wood studs, timber roof trusses, cement, and bituminous roofing shingles

Technology of interest: sea water system of intakes, pumps, filters, chillers, distribution piping and monitoring devices to provide the exhibits with varying qualities of water; corrosive-resistant exterior coatings, such as epoxy-coated reinforcing steel; fiberglass air ducts and non-metallic piping and valves.

Budget: $35,800,000.

Site characteristics: extends over the waters of Monterey Bay and incorporates portions of the Hovden Cannery: the warehouse, boilerhouse, pumphouse, and street facades.

The project won the AIA Honor Award, 1988.

Bibliography

Schmertz, Mildred. "A New Aquarium for Cannery Row: Monterey Bay Aquarium, Monterey Bay California." *Architectural Record* (February 1985): pp. 114–23.

Davis, Charles M. "Monterey Bay Aquarium." *Process: Architecture* (June 1991): pp. 128–33.

FAY JONES & MAURICE JENNINGS ARCHITECTS

619 West Dickson, Fayetteville, AR 72701

E. Fay Jones: b. Arkansas, 1921. Received B. Arch. (1950) from University of Arkansas and M. Arch. (1951) from Rice University. Apprenticed with Frank Lloyd Wright at Taliesin (1953). Served in U.S. Naval Reserve (1942–45). In private practice since 1953. Has taught at Rice University, University of Oklahoma, and University of Arkansas. Fellow of American Academy in Rome; Awarded AIA Gold Medal, 1990.

Project specifications

Thorncrown Chapel (Eureka Springs, Arkansas) 1979–80, pp. 192–93

Client: Jim Reed.

Built area: 1440 ft.^{2}.

Design team: Fay Jones, Maurice Jennings, John Womack, Fred Derwin, John Wollack, Tim Wollack, David Buergler, Tri Vu.

Construction company: Labounty Construction.

Key materials: Southern yellow pine, glass, fieldstone.

Budget: not available.

Site characteristics: between a stone bluff and a sloping wooded area.

The project received the AIA Honor Award, 1981.

Bibliography

Grandee, Charles K. "Thorncrown Chapel, Eureka Springs, Arkansas." *Architectural Record* (March 1981): pp. 88–93.

Abercrombie, Stanley. "A Building of Great Integrity." *AIA Journal* (May 1981): pp. 140–7.

Ivy, Robert Adams. *Fay Jones: the architecture of E. Fay Jones, FAIA.* Washington, D.C.: AIA Press, 1992.

FRANK O. GEHRY & ASSOCIATES

1520-B Cloverfield Boulevard, Santa Monica, CA 90404

Frank O. Gehry: b. Toronto, Ontario, Canada, 1929. Undergraduate degree from University of Southern California, Los Angeles (1954) and M. Arch. from Harvard University (1957). Before establishing own firm (1962), worked as designer for Victor Gruen (1953–54 and 1958–61), Robert and Company (1955–56), Hideo Sasaki (1957), William Pereira (1957–58), and André Remondet (1961). Has taught at University of Southern California, University of California at Los Angeles, and Harvard University. Recipient of Brunner Prize (1983), Pritzker Architectural Prize (1989), and other national and regional awards.

Project specifications

Frank Gehry House (Santa Monica, California), 1979, pp. 180–83

Design team: Frank O. Gehry.

Key materials: corrugated iron, chain link fencing, plywood.

Budget: not available.

Site characteristics: suburban Santa Monica neighborhood.

Bibliography

"Gehry Residence in Santa Monica." *GA Houses* 6 (1979): pp. 180–3.

"Frank O. Gehry & Associates." *Progressive Architecture* (March 1980): pp. 81–5.

Diamonstein, Barbaralee. *American Architecture Now.* New York: Rizzoli, 1980.

"Frank Gehry's House." *De Architect* (March 1981, The Hague).

Arnell, Peter, Ted Bickford (eds.). *Frank Gehry, buildings and projects.* New York: Rizzoli, 1985.

Pastier, John. *American Architecture of the 1980s.* Washington, D.C.: AIA, 1990.

Frederick R. Weisman Art Museum (Minneapolis, Minnesota), 1992–94, pp. 290–91

Client: University of Minnesota.

Built area: 90,000 ft.^{2}.

Design team: Frank Gehry; Meyer, Scherer & Rockcastle (associated architects).

Key materials: brick, stainless steel cladding.

Budget: $14,000,000.

Site characteristics: located on East Bank campus of University of Minnesota campus, above Mississippi River.

Bibliography

Gerloff, Robert. "Weisman Art Museum opens in Minneapolis." *Architecture* vol. 83, no. 1 (January 1994): p. 24.

"Frank O'Gehry [sic]: Musée Weisman à Minneapolis." *Architecture D'Aujourd'hui* 290 (April 1994): pp. 70–3.

Sack, Manfred. "Weisman Museum of Art in Minneapolis." *Baumeister* vol. 91, no. 9 (September 1994): pp. 40–6.

GATJE PAPACHRISTOU SMITH

(no longer in practice together)

Hamilton Smith, FAIA: b. New York. Received B. A. in Architecture from Princeton University and M. Arch. from Yale University, 1950. During World War II, served as officer in U.S. Naval Reserve. Was apprenticed in office of Eero Saarinen, then worked for Marcel Breuer (1953), becoming partner, (1964). Was partner in the successor firm following Marcel Breuer's retirement (1976). Firm name changed to Gatje Papachristou Smith. Was awarded New York AIA's Distinguished Architecture Award, 1994.

Project specifications

Richard B. Russell Powerhouse (Savannah River, Georgia and South Carolina), 1978–85, pp. 228–29

Client: U.S. Army Corps of Engineers, Savannah District.

Built area: 84,000 ft.^{2}.

Design team: Hamilton Smith, Margaret Helfand.

Construction company: U.S. Army Corps of Engineers (construction management); Republic-Crowder (contractor); Peter G. Roland (landscape design); Claude Engle (lighting design).

Key materials: wood-textured and bush-hammered, poured-in-place concrete, tinted double glazing, granite pavers.

Technology of interest: powerhouse forms the envelope enclosing the eight 75,000 kW power generator units and responds to demanding technical and environmental requirements associated with the equipment and with the operating personnel. A bridge crane capable of hoisting a generating unit from its concrete "barrel" travels the length of the building on rails supported on steel bents designed in composite structure with the concrete walls.

Budget: not available.

Site characteristics: adjacent to the dam located on the Savannah River near Elberta, Georgia, and Calhoun Falls, South Carolina. It is sited three-fifths below water and two fifths above.

GUNNAR BIRKERTS AND ASSOCIATES, INC.

292 Harmon Street, Birmingham, MI 48009

Gunnar Birkerts: b. Latvia. Studied at Technische Hochschule in Stuttgart and received his Dipl. Arch. in 1949. Immediately after, moved to U.S. to work in office of Eero Saarinen, later establishing own firm. Has taught at Lawrence Technological University and University of Michigan. Was Architect in Residence at the American Academy in Rome. Has won 52 major awards, including Brunner Memorial Prize in Architecture (1981) and AIA's Gold Medal, Detroit Chapter (1975).

Project specifications

Federal Reserve Bank of Minneapolis (Minneapolis, Minnesota), 1967–72, pp. 146–47

Client: Federal Reserve Bank of Minneapolis.

Built area: 550,000 ft.^{2}.

Design team: Gunnar Birkerts and Associates, Inc. (architect); Skilling, Hells, Christiansen, Robertson (structural engineer); Jaros, Baum & Bolles (mechanical/electrical engineers).

Construction company: Knutson Construction Company.

Key materials: structural steel trusses and weldments, galvanized wire cable catenaries, granite and steel cladding, reinforced concrete, gray insulated glass.

Technology of interest: catenary construction allowing for 275 x 60 ft. of column-free areas on each floor of the office building.

Budget: $30,900,000 (construction cost).

Site characteristics: located on a 2½-acre plaza in the Gateway Center redevelopment area of Minneapolis, which slopes from street level at the Nicolet Mall, to 20 feet above street level at Marquette Avenue, with 60% of the building area underground.

Bibliography

A & U (July 1972): pp. 17–20.

Architectural Record (November 1973): pp. 105–9.

A & U (September 1974): pp. 35–66.

Moore, Charles and Gerald Allen. *Dimensions*. New York: Architectural Record Books, 1976.

GWATHMEY SIEGEL & ASSOCIATES ARCHITECTS

475 Tenth Avenue, New York, NY 10018

Charles Gwathmey: b. North Carolina, 1938. Received undergraduate degree in architecture from University of Pennsylvania (1959) and M. Arch. from Yale University (1962). Worked for Edward Larrabee Barnes for 3 years, and has been in private practice since. Has taught at Pratt Institute, Cooper Union, Princeton University, Columbia University, University of Texas, University of California at Los Angeles, and Harvard University. Received Firm Award from AIA (1982), AIA New York Chapter's Medal of Honor (1983), and Lifetime Achievement Award from the New York Society of Architects (1990).

Project specifications

Gwathmey Residence and Studio (Amagansett, New York), 1963–65, pp. 102–05

Client: Rosalie and Robert Gwathmey.

Built area: 1,200 ft.².

Design team: Charles Gwathmey.

Construction company: Charles Gwathmey.

Key materials: wood frame, interior and exterior tongue and groove clear cedar siding, aluminum sliding doors, dexotex floors, painted cabinetwork.

Budget: $35 per sq. ft.

Site characteristics: located on one acre of flat field with undeveloped adjacent land at the time of the design, with views to the dunes and ocean to the south.

Bibliography

Abercrombie, Stanley. *Gwathmey Siegel. Monographs on Contemporary Architecture*. New York: Whitney Library of Design, 1981. London: Granada, 1981.

Arnell, Peter and Ted Buckford (eds.). *Charles Gwathmey and Robert Siegel: buildings and projects 1964–1984*. New York: Harper and Row, 1984.

HELLMUTH OBATA KASSABAUM, INC.

71 Stevenson Street, Suite 2200, San Francisco, CA 94105

Gyo Obata: b. San Francisco, 1923. Educated at University of California, Berkeley, and Washington University, St. Louis, B. Arch. (1945) and M. Arch. from Cranbrook Academy of Art (1946). Senior Designer, SOM, Chicago (1947–50); founding member and Principal, HOK (1955–78), and Chairman and President since 1982. Affiliate Professor of Architecture, Washington University, St. Louis, since 1971.

Joseph E. Spear: received B. Arch. from Kansas State University (1976).

Project Specification

Levi's Plaza (San Francisco, California) 1977–82, pp. 210–11

Client: Levi Strauss & Co.

Built area: 832,000 ft.².

Design team: Gyo Obata (principal-in-charge), Ted Davalos (project architect), Bill Valentine (project designer).

Construction company: Dinwiddie Construction Co., Swinerton & Walberg Co.

Key materials: pre-cast, brick-faced concrete panels.

Technology of interest: brick and concrete panels designed to be seismically safe.

Budget: $130,000,000.

Site characteristics: 4 city blocks on San Francisco's north waterfront, at foot of Telegraph Hill and adjacent to San Francisco Bay. Maximum zoning height for site is 84 feet.

Bibliography

Fortune (March 22, 1982).

"Levi's Plaza." *Architectural Record* (May 1982): pp. 114–19.

"Levi's Plaza." *A & U* (October 1982): pp. 111–14.

Camden Yards at Oriole Fields (Baltimore, Maryland), 1988–92, pp. 282–85

Client: Maryland Stadium Authority.

Design team: Joseph E. Spear, Ben Barnert, Steve Evans, David Alexander, Craig Meyer, Brad Burgoon, Susan Carter, Stewart Ervie, Marilyn Feris, Tom Usher.

Construction company: Barton Malow/Sverdrup.

Key materials: pre-cast concrete, brick, and steel.

Budget: $106,000,000.

Site characteristics: 80 acres in downtown Baltimore west of Inner Harbor, adjacent to a restored B & O railroad warehouse (which now houses stadium-related functions) and the Camden Railroad Station.

The project has won a number of design awards, among them AIA's Urban Design Award of Excellence (1992), and American Society of Landscape Architects Honor Award the same year.

Bibliography

Prowler, Donald. "Baltimore hits home with new baseball park." *Progressive Architecture* vol. 73, no. 6 (June 1992): p. 26.

Edward Gunts. "Grand Stand." *Architecture* (July, 1992): pp. 64–71.

HOLT HINSHAW PFAU JONES

(now Holt Hinshaw Jones)

36 Perry Street, San Francisco, CA 94107

Wesley Jones: received A. B. degree from University of California, Berkeley (1980), and M. Arch. (1983) from Harvard University GSD. Prior to establishment of Holt & Hinshaw in 1986, worked with the ELS Design Group and Eisenman/Robertson, Architects. Was awarded Rome Prize in Architecture, and has lectured and served as visiting critic at Harvard, Rice, University of California, Los Angeles, and Columbia.

Project specifications

Paramount Pictures Film and Tape Archives, (Los Angeles, California): 1989–91, pp. 272–73

Client: Paramount Pictures Corporation.

Built area: 39,000 ft.².

Design team: Paul Holt, March Hinshaw, Peter Pfau, Wes Jones, Tom Goffigon, Scott Laidlaw, Craig Schultz, Chris Tanden, Dana Barbera, David Gadarian, Lourdes Garcia, Robert Yue. Ove Arup & Assoc. (consulting engineers).

Construction company: Turner Construction.

Key materials: concrete pile foundation, braced structural steel frame for mechanical, electrical, and fire protection systems, pre-cast concrete "T" beams, poured-in-place and pre-cast concrete shear walls, poured-in-place and pre-cast concrete exterior panels, steel wall system.

Technology of interest: paired storage vaults provided for storage of black and white and color film, each requiring independent temperature and humidity controls, and each vault area provided with a transitional acclimatization area.

Budget: not available.

Site characteristics: 17 acres east of the Paramount water tower, Los Angeles.

Bibliography

Hogben, Gavin and Jeffrey Kipnis. "Paramount Pictures." *Progressive Architecture* (July 1991): pp. 82–4.

"Un cielo de cine: archivos de Paramount Pictures, Los Angeles." *A & V* 32 (1991): pp. 50–3.

JAMES STEWART POLSHEK AND PARTNERS ARCHITECTS

320 West 13th Street, New York, NY 10014

James Stewart Polshek: b. 1930. Received B. S. from

Case Western Reserve (1951); M. Arch. from Yale University (1955). Fulbright Fellow at the Royal Academy of Fine Arts in Copenhagen, Denmark (1956–57). Founded James Stewart Polshek and Partners, 1963. Dean of Columbia University Graduate School of Architecture, Planning and Preservation (1972–87) and currently (since 1972) Professor of Architecture at Columbia. Among many awards, has received Medal of Honor from the New York AIA (1986), and four Honor Awards from the National AIA.

Project specifications:

Mashantucket Pequot Museum and Research Center (Mashantucket Pequot Reservation, Connecticut), begun 1993, expected completion, 1997, pp. 292–95

Client: Mashantucket Pequot Tribe.

Built area: 305,000 ft.².

Design team: James Stewart Polshek, Susan T. Rodriguez (principal designers); Timothy Hartung (partner-in-charge); Charles Griffith (project architect); Jihyon Kim (technical associate); Crystal Anderson, Minsuk Cho, Alexis Kraft, Craig McIlhenny, Amanda Martocchio, Larry Turner, Don Weinreich, Larry Zeroth; Dan Kiley (landscape architecture).

Construction company: C. R. Klewin, Inc., Construction Manager.

Key materials: stone cladding on tower, steel frame on Museum and Research Center.

Budget: not available.

Site characteristics: on a north-facing slope by a cedar swamp to the north, and surrounded by a maple forest.

Bibliography

Polshek, James Stewart. *James Stewart Polshek. Context and responsibility: buildings and projects, 1957–1987*. New York: Rizzoli, 1988.

JERSEY DEVIL

Jersey Devil Homebase, Box 280, Stockton, NJ 08559

Steve Badanes: received B. A. in Art from Wesleyan University (1967); M. Arch. from Princeton University (1971). Founded (with John Ringel) Jersey Devil Design/Build, 1972. Has taught at University of Washington, University of California, Carnegie Mellon, and several other schools. Exhibits and lectures internationally.

Jim Adamson: received M. Arch. from Princeton (1970) and has been member of Jersey Devil since 1975.

Project specifications

Hill House (La Honda, California), 1977–79, pp. 178–79

Client: George and Adele Norton.

Built area: 2,250 ft.².

Design team: Steve Badanes, Jim Adamson.

Construction company: Jersey Devil.

Key materials: sod roof, lenticular trusses, Kalwall glazing with redwood battens, concrete trombe walls.

Technology of interest: passive solar heating and cooling, solar hot water, wind-powered water pumping, earth integration, thermal mass construction.

Budget: $100 per sq. ft.

Site characteristics: in the crest of a steep hilltop with views of the Pacific Ocean and the Bay area, a place subject to rapid weather changes.

Bibliography

"Jersey Devil's Hill House." *Fine Homebuilding* (October/November 1985).

Crosbie, Michael J. *The Jersey Devil Design/Build Book*. Layton, Utah: Peregrine Smith Books, 1985.

JOHANSEN AND BHAVNANI

821 Broadway, New York, NY 10003

John M. Johansen: b. New York City, 1916. Graduated from Harvard University with B. S. (1939), B. Arch. (1942), and M. Arch. (1943). Has taught at Yale University and

Columbia University and currently teaches at Pratt Institute. Has been a visiting critic at MIT, Harvard University, Carnegie Tech., Rhode Island School of Design and University of Pennsylvania. Before establishing own practice (1950), worked as draftsman for Marcel Breuer, and as designer for Skidmore, Owings, and Merrill. Was recipient of Brunner Award (1968) and AIA New York Chapter's Medal of Honor (1976).

Project specifications
Mummers Theater (Oklahoma City, Oklahoma), 1964–70, pp. 138–41
(The theater was later named the Oklahoma Theater Center, now the Stage Center Building.)
Client: Mummers Theater Company.
Built area: 64, 400 ft.².
Design team: John M. Johansen (design principal); David Hays (stage designer); Charles Ahlstrom (project captain); Rudolph Besier (structural engineer); John Altieri (mechanical engineer).
Construction company: Harmon Construction Company.
Key materials: steel frame and sheet steel siding; reinforced concrete.
Technology of interest: air-conditioning systems for theaters are exposed as essential part of the building design.
Budget: $2,500,000.
Site characteristics: located in a business district, adjacent to a public park.
The project won AIA National Honor Award, 1972.

Bibliography
Architectural Forum (March 1971): pp. 31–7.
Architecture (August 1981): pp. 40–6.
Architecture (November 1992): pp. 62–9.

JOHN BURGEE ARCHITECTS WITH PHILIP JOHNSON
(Now Philip Johnson Architect)
885 3rd Avenue, 12th floor, New York, NY 10022
John Burgee: b. 1933. Received B. Arch. from University of Notre Dame, 1956. Before forming partnership with Philip Johnson, worked for a number of firms: Holabard and Root; Naess and Murphy; and C. F. Murphy Assoc. Received AIA Honor Award (1975 and 1976) and Chicago Architecture Award, 1984.
Philip Johnson: b. 1906. Received A. B. and B. Arch. from Harvard University. Director of Department of Architecture for the Museum of Modern Art, New York (1930–36 and 1946–54). Practiced architecture in Cambridge, MA. Worked in partnership with Richard Foster (1964–67) and established Johnson/Burgee Architects, 1967. Recipient of Pritzker Architectural Prize (1979), and has been honored with many other awards, including Gold Medal of Honor (1960) and *Architectural Record* Award of Excellence in both 1957 and 1962.

Project specifications
Garden Grove Community Church (Garden Grove, California), 1980, pp. 188–89
(Johnson Burgee Architects)
Client: Garden Grove Community Church.
Built area: 35,000 ft.².
Design team: Johnson Burgee Architects; Albert C. Martin and Assoc. (consulting architects).
Construction company: C. L. Peck (general contractor).
Key materials: reinforced concrete foundation, reflective glass over white steel space frame truss, bush-hammered concrete. Terrazzo flooring, oak, and granite furnishings.
Technology of interest: passive heating and cooling systems, the open cathedral space designed as a solar chimney, mirror glass panels to filter heat and light.
Budget: $16,000,000.
Site characteristics: 19½ acres in a residential area of Garden Grove.

Bibliography
Tafuri, Manfredo. "Subaqueous Cathedral." *Domus* (July 1980): pp. 8–15.
Goldstein, Barbara. "New Crystal Palace." *Progressive Architecture* (December 1980): pp. 76–85.
Philip Johnson/John Burgee: architecture 1979–1985. Introduction by Carleton Knight III. New York: Rizzoli, 1985.
AT&T Headquarters Building (New York City, New York), 1978–83, pp. 212–13
(Johnson/Burgee Architects)
Client: 195 Broadway Corporation.
Design team: Johnson/Burgee Architects; Alan Ritchie (associate), Rolf Hedlund (field representative), Robertson & Fowler Associates (structural engineers).
Construction company: HRH Construction Company.
Key materials: stony creek granite exterior cladding and lobby walls. Brecchia strazzema marble floors and walls. Teak doors and paneling.
Technology of interest: steel frame made up of a series of tubes, with steel plate shear walls from foundation to sky-lobby.
Budget: not available.
Site characteristics: midtown Manhattan.

Bibliography
Doubilet, Susan. "Not enough said: AT&T Headquarters, New York, N.Y." *Progressive Architecture* vol. 74, no. 2 (February 1984): pp. 70–5.
"Philip Johnson & John Burgee: AT&T Corporate Headquarters, NYC." *Architectural Design* vol. 65, no. 2 (February 1984): pp. 70–5
Banham, Reyner. "AT&T Offices, New York: The post post-deco skyscraper." *Architectural Review* vol. 176, no. 1050 (August 1984): pp, 22–7.
Canty, Donald. "AT&T: The tower, the skyline, and the street." *Architecture* vol. 74, no. 2 (February 1985): pp. 46–55.

JOHN PORTMAN & ASSOCIATES
231 Peachtree Street, N.E., Suite 200, Atlanta, GA 30303
John C. Portman: b. South Carolina, 1924. B. Arch., Georgia Institute of Technology (1950). Before starting private practice (1953) worked for Ketchum Gina and Sharpe, and H. M. Heatley Assoc.; co-founded Edwards and Portman (1956) and since 1968 has been President of John Portman & Assoc. Among numerous design awards are AIA Medal for Innovation in Hotel Design (1978) and AIA Silver Medal for Innovative design (1981).

Project specifications
Hyatt Regency Atlanta (Atlanta, Georgia), 1964–67, pp. 114–15
Client: Peachtree-Baker Corporation.
Built area: 817,800 ft.².
Design team: John C. Portman (design architect); John. R. Street (project architect); R. Don Starr (architect).
Construction company: J. A. Jones Construction Company.
Key materials: pre-cast and poured-in-place reinforced concrete, tile, acrylic dome.
Technology of interest: fire-safety provisions pertaining to the atrium design and construction.
Budget: $13.09 per sq. ft.
Site characteristics: located on an urban city block in downtown Atlanta.

Bibliography
"Hyatt Regency, Atlanta." *Architectural Record* (January 1966): pp. 134–6.
"Hyatt Regency, Atlanta." *Interiors* (November 1968): pp. 122–35.

KALLMANN MCKINNELL & WOOD
(formerly Kallmann McKinnell & Knowles)
939 Boylston Street, Boston, MA 02108
Gerhard Kallmann: b. Berlin, 1915. Received Dip. A. A. from Architectural Association, London. Worked as Assistant Editor for *Architectural Review* (1945–49). Co-founded Kallman, McKinnell & Knowles (1962). Has taught at Institute of Design in Chicago, Columbia University, and Harvard University.
Noel McKinnell: b. Lancashire, England, 1935. Received B. A. from the Manchester School of Architecture (1958); and M. S. Arch. from Columbia University (1960). Has taught at Columbia University, Yale University, and Harvard University. In 1984, KMW won AIA's Firm of the Year Award, and another AIA Honor Award, 1982.

Project specifications
Boston City Hall (Boston, Massachusetts), 1962–68, pp. 124–27
Client: Government Center Commission of the City of Boston.
Design team: Gerhard Kallmann, Noel McKinnell; Robert C. Abrahamson, Henry A. Wood, Gordon F. Tully (project managers).
Built area: 513,000 ft.².
Construction company: J. W. Bateson Company.
Key materials: pre-cast and cast-in-place concrete, and water-struck brick.
Budget: $20,000,000.
Site characteristics: sloping site, formerly Scollay and Dock Squares in downtown Boston.
The project won the AIA Honor Award in 1969.

Bibliography
Kallmann, Gerhard M. *Architectural Forum* (October 1959).
"Boston City Hall: Chandigargh on Scollay Square." *Progressive Architecture* 43 (July 1962): p. 65.
Schmertz, M. F. "The New Boston City Hall." *Architectural Record* 45 (February 1969), pp. 133–44.
Fitch, James Marston. "City Hall, Boston." *Architectural Review* 147 (June 1970): pp. 398–411.

KELBAUGH + LEE
(now Kelbaugh, Calthorpe and Assoc.)
2809 10th Avenue East, Seattle, WA 98102
Douglas Kelbaugh: received undergraduate degree (1968) and M. Arch. (1972) from Princeton University. Before founding Kelbaugh + Lee (1977), worked as planner and architect for City of Trenton, NJ. Notable among national and regional awards honoring Kelbaugh + Lee are AIA Honor Award for Roosevelt Solar Village, and regional AIA Honor Award for Milford Reservation Environmental Center. Since 1985, has taught at and chaired Department of Architecture at University of Washington, and has taught and lectured at numerous other universities. With Peter Calthorpe, founded Kelbaugh, Calthorpe and Assoc. in 1989.

Project specifications
Roosevelt Solar Village (Roosevelt, New Jersey), 1981–83. pp. 222–23
Client: Roosevelt Senior Citizen's Housing Corporation.
Design team: Douglas Kelbaugh (partner-in-charge of design); Sang Lee (partner-in-charge of construction); Ron Ellis, Tom Swartz, Leigh Olsen, Alan Goodheart (landscape architect); Robert Hubbard (mechanical engineer); Jay Woo (structural engineer).
Construction company: Arctic Corners, Inc.
Key materials: wood frame, concrete block foundation, cedar shingle siding, asphalt shingle roof.
Technology of interest: passive solar heating and ventilating systems: solariums, Trombe walls, direct gain windows. Solar chimneys, solar heated domestic hot water.
Budget: $53 per sq. ft. (total $900,000).
Site characteristics: 2 acres, gently sloping, adjacent to a

potato field. The site is part of a planned community built in the 1930s under Roosevelt's WPA projects.

Bibliography

Fisher, Thomas. "Subsidized Housing." *Progressive Architecture* (July 1984): pp. 65–8.

KEVIN ROCHE JOHN DINKELOO AND ASSOCIATES

20 Davis Street, Hamden, CT 06517

Kevin Roche: b. Dublin, Ireland, 1922. Studied at University College, Dublin, receiving B. Arch., 1945. Studied at IIT with Mies van der Rohe (1948–49). Between undergraduate and graduate studies, worked as apprentice in offices of Michael Scott, Dublin, and Maxwell Fry, London. Worked with Eero Saarinen (1950–61); after Saarinen's death (1961), worked on completion of many of Saarinen's projects until 1966, when he established Kevin Roche John Dinkeloo and Assoc., which won AIA's Architectural Firm Award (1974). Among numerous regional, national, and international honors awarded Roche are Pritzker Architecture Prize (1982); American Academy and Institute of Arts and Letters Gold Medal Award for Architecture (1990), and AIA Gold Medal Award (1993).

John Dinkeloo: b. Michigan, 1918. Studied at University of Michigan. Worked as Chief of Production for SOM (1946–50), before joining Saarinen's office (1950) as production chief and technologist. Recipient Medal of Honor, New York Chapter of the AIA. Died 1981.

Daniel Urban Kiley: b. Massachusetts, 1912. Received M. Arch. Harvard University (1938). Received Residential Design Award from National Landscape Association (1973) and Collaborative Achievement in Architecture Award (1972).

Project specifications

Oakland Museum (Oakland, California), 1961–68, pp. 128–29

Client: The City of Oakland.

Design team: Kevin Roche; Dan Kiley (landscape).

Key materials: sand-blasted concrete, oak.

Technology of interest: artificial soil and irrigation system for the roof gardens.

Budget: not available.

Site characteristics: adjacent to the Alameda County Courthouse, overlooking Lake Merritt.

Bibliography:

Progressive Architecture (December 1969): pp. 92–5.
Architectural Record (April 1970): pp. 115–22.
Domus (October 1970): pp. 491–2.

Ford Foundation Headquarters (New York, New York) 1963–68, pp. 130–31

Client: Ford Foundation.

Built area: 287,400 ft.².

Key materials: concrete, weathering steel, granite, glass.

Budget: not available.

Site characteristics: urban setting on New York's 42nd Street.

The project won the AIA's Twenty-Five-Year Merit Award in 1994.

Bibliography

Progressive Architecture (February 1968): pp. 90–105.
Interiors (March 1968): pp. 95–109.
Global Architecture Details 4 (1977): pp. 1–59.
Roche, Kevin. *Kevin Roche*. New York: Rizzoli, 1985.

Deere & Company Headquarters West Office Building (Moline, Illinois) 1975–78, pp. 184–85

Client: Deere & Company.

Built area: 200,000 ft.².

Key materials: weathering steel, polished aluminum ceiling slats.

Budget: not available.

Bibliography

Architectural Record (February 1979): pp. 85–92.
A & U (June 1979): pp. 19–34.
Roche, Kevin. *Kevin Roche*. New York: Rizzoli, 1985.

LEGORRETA ARQUITECTOS

Palacio de Versailles 285-A, Palacio de Lomas de Reforma, 11020, Mexico

Ricardo Legorreta: b. Mexico City, 1931. Educated at Universidad Nacional Autonoma de Mexico, Mexico City, and received Dip. Arch., 1953. Worked as draftsman for Jose Villagran Garcia, later becoming partner. In 1963, established Legorreta Arquitectos with partners, Noe Castro, Emilio Guerrero, Michel Leautaud, and Gerard Alonso.

Project specifications

Solana, IBM Southlake and Village Center West (Dallas, Texas), 1988–90, pp. 264–67

(Legorreta Arquitectos with Mitchell/Giurgola)

Client: IBM Corporation; MacGuire Thomas Partners.

Built area: 39,204,000 ft.². (374,857 ft.² in Phase 1-A.)

Design team: Ricardo Legorreta, Noe Castro, Gerardo Alonso, Max Betancourt, Jorge Suarez, Peter Walker, and Martha Schwartz (landscape design). Mitchell/Giurgola and Barton Meyers were also part of the team.

Construction company: HCB.

Key materials: concrete columns and joists with concrete and steel sheet.

Technology of interest: incorporation of a highway and underpass.

Site characteristics: semi-urban rural landscape.

Bibliography

Barna, Joel W. "Solana in the Sun." *Progressive Architecture* (April 1989): pp. 65–74.
Dillon, David. "IBM's Colorful Place in the Sun." *Architecture* (May 1989): pp. 100–7.
"IBM Southlake and Village Center, Solana, Westlake, Southlake, Texas. Architects: Legorreta Arquitectos." *GA Document* 24 (August 1989): pp. 20–41.
Atto, Wayne (ed.), assisted by Sydney H. Brisher. "How I Design." *The Architecture of Ricardo Legorreta*. University of Texas Press, 1990.

LOUIS I. KAHN

b. Estonia, 1901. Emigrated to Philadelphia, 1906, becoming naturalized U.S. citizen, 1915. Graduated from University of Pennsylvania, 1924. Established independent practice (1935) after working as designer for John Molitor (1924–27), William H. Lee (1927–28), Paul P. Cret (1929–30), Zantzinger, Borie, and Medary (1930–32), and the City Planning Commission of Philadelphia, (1933–35). In 1929, traveled throughout Europe, and on return exhibited travel sketches at Pennsylvania Academy of Fine Arts. Was resident architect at American Academy in Rome (1950–51); was recipient of AIA's Gold Medal (1971), Royal Institute of British Architects Gold Medal (1972), and National Institute of Arts and Letters' Gold Medal (1973). From 1955, until death (1974), taught at University of Pennsylvania.

Project specifications

Alfred Newton Richards Medical Research Laboratory, University of Pennsylvania (Philadelphia, Pennsylvania), 1957–6, pp. 72–75

Client: University of Pennsylvania.

Construction company: Joseph R. Farrell, Inc., General Contractor.

Key materials: brick, pre-stressed, pre-cast concrete columns and trusses, glass.

Technology of interest: Vierendeel trusses to house utility systems.

Budget: not available.

Bibliography

Architectural Record (August 1960).
Arts and Architecture (August 1961).
Joedicke, Jurgen. *Documents of Modern Architecture*. New York: Universe Books, 1961.
Komendant, August. *18 Years with Architect Louis I. Kahn*. Englewood, New Jersey: Aloray, 1975.
Latour, Alessandra (ed.). *Louis I. Kahn: writings, lectures, interviews*. New York: Rizzoli, 1991.

Salk Institute of Biological Studies (La Jolla, California), 1959–65, pp. 94–97

Client: Jonas Salk.

Built area: 400,000 ft.².

Design team: Louis I. Kahn (architect); Roland S. Hoyt (landscape architect); Dr. August E. Komendant (structural consultant); Fred F. Dubin Assoc. (electrical mechanical engineers).

Key materials: poured-in-place concrete, teak, travertine terrace.

Technology of interest: 9-foot-deep Vierendeel trusses spanning the lab spaces.

Budget: $11,415,000.

Site characteristics: located on a 27-acre site on the Torrey Pines mesa overlooking the Pacific Ocean.

Bibliography

Architectural Forum (May 1965).
Architectural Forum (December 1967).
Komendant, August E. *18 Years with Louis I. Kahn*. Englewood, New Jersey: Aloray, 1975.
Kahn, Louis I. *The Louis I. Kahn archive: personal drawings. The completely illustrated catalogue of the drawings in the Louis I. Kahn Collection*. Garland Architectural Archives. New York: Garland, 1988.
Progressive Architecture (October 1993).

Kimbell Art Museum (Fort Worth, Texas), 1966–72, pp. 148–51.

Client: Kimbell Art Foundation.

Built area: 120,000 ft.².

Design team: Louis Kahn, Marshall D. Meyers.

Construction company: Thomas S. Byrne, Inc.

Key materials: reinforced concrete, travertine, lead roofing, double insulating glass, acrylic sheeting at skylights, oak interior cabinetwork.

Budget: $6,500,000.

Site characteristics: 9½-acre trapezoid of land, gently sloping eastward, in Amon Carter Square Park, which houses other museums, theaters, and an auditorium.

Bibliography

Komendant, August. *18 Years with Architect Louis I. Kahn*. Englewood: Aloray, 1975.
Ronner, Heinz. *Louis I. Kahn: complete work, 1935–1974*. Boston: Birkhäuser Verlag, 1987. (2nd edition, Basel.)
Brawne, Michael. *Kimbell Art Museum*. London: Phaidon Press, 1992.
Benedikt, Michael. *Deconstructing the Kimbell*. New York: Sites Books, 1991.

MARCEL BREUER AND ASSOCIATES

Marcel Breuer: b. Pécs, Hungary, 1902. Immigrated to U.S. (1937), and became U.S. citizen, 1944. Was student at Weimar Bauhaus (1920–24) and Bauhaus Master (1925–28). Subsequently formed partnership with F.R.S. York. Upon immigrating, taught at Harvard University GSD, the same year establishing Marcel Breuer and Assoc. Was honored with AIA Gold Medal, Medal of Honor, and numerous other awards. Died 1981.

Project specifications

Whitney Museum of American Art (New York, New York), 1963–66, pp. 106–09

Built area: 76,830 ft.².

Design team: Marcel Breuer and Hamilton Smith; Michael H. Irving (consulting architect).

Construction company: HRH Construction Co.

Key materials: flame-marked granite, bush-hammered and wood-marked concrete, glass.

Technology of interest: flexible panel system for galleries which lock into suspended ceiling grid of pre-cast concrete panels.

Budget: $4,000,000.

Site characteristics: 13,000 sq. ft. in midtown Manhattan, Madison Avenue.

Bibliography

Breuer, Marcel. *Sun and Shadow, the philosophy of an architect*. New York: Dodd Mead, 1955.

Progressive Architecture (October 1966).

Architectural Forum (September 1966).

Interiors (October 1966).

Papachristou, Tician. *Marcel Breuer: new buildings and projects*. New York: Praeger, 1970.

MARQUIS & STOLLER

(now Marquis Associates) 243 Vallejo Street, San Francisco, CA 94111

Robert Marquis: b. Stuttgart, Germany, 1927. Immigrated to the U.S. (1937) and became citizen. Attended University of Southern California (1946–49) and Accademia delle Belle Arti in Florence (1949–50). Established own practice, Robert B. Marquis Assoc. (1953), co-founding Marquis and Stoller with Claude Stoller (1956). Has been honored with over 70 awards for design, including California Council AIA 25-Year Award (1989), Brunner Award (1987), and AIA Firm Award (1984). Died 1994.

Claude Stoller: Educated at Black Mountain College, received M. Arch. from Harvard University, and studied for a year in Florence. Was both Professor and Chair of Graduate Studies in Department of Architecture at University of California, Berkeley.

Project specifications

St. Francis Square Cooperative Apartments (San Francisco, California) 1960–61, pp. 70–71

Client: Pension Fund of the International Longshoreman's and Warehouseman's Union and Pacific Maritime Association.

Built area: approximately 300,000 ft.².

Design team: Claude Stoller, Robert Marquis, Peter Winkelstein.

Construction company: Jack Baskin.

Key materials: wood frame construction, stucco exterior walls.

Technology of interest: 2 vacated city streets within the project have lawn areas with steel mesh below the surface for fire engine access.

Budget: $11.50 per sq. ft.

Site characteristics: generally flat urban site, gently sloping north to south.

The project won numerous awards, among them the AIA National Honor Award of Merit, 1964, and the California Governor's Design Award, 1966.

Bibliography

House and Home (February 1964).

AIA Journal (December 1971).

Cooper, Clare. *AIA Journal* (1971).

MICHAEL GRAVES ARCHITECT

341 Nassau Street, Princeton, NJ 08540

Michael Graves: b. 1934. Received B. Arch. from University of Cincinnati (1958), M. Arch. from Harvard University (1959). Won Rome Prize (1960) and studied at American Academy in Rome (1960–62). Has had own practice since 1964. Has taught at Princeton University (since 1962,

Professor since 1972); Institute for Architecture and Urban Studies, New York (1971–72); University of Texas at Austin (1973–74); University of Houston (1974 and 1978); New School for Social Research (1975), and University of California, Los Angeles (1977). Has won 15 Progressive Architecture awards, and received AIA Award for Excellence in Architecture, 1992.

Project specifications

The Portland Building (Portland, Oregon), 1980–82, pp. 208–09

Client: City of Portland.

Built area: 365,000 ft.².

Design team: Michael Graves.

Construction company: Pavarini Construction Company, Inc.

Budget: $22,420,000.

Site characteristics: urban setting adjacent to Portland's City Hall and County Courthouse.

Bibliography

"The Portland Building, Portland, Oregon." *Architectural Record* 170 (November 1982): pp. 90–9.

Graves, Michael. *Michael Graves: buildings and projects 1966–1981*. New York: Rizzoli International, 1982.

"Conversation with Graves: The Portland Building, Portland, Oregon." *Progressive Architecture* 64 (February 1983): pp. 108–15.

San Juan Capistrano Library (San Juan Capistrano, California), 1981–83, pp. 220–21

Client: Jose Aponte, San Juan Capistrano Regional Library.

Built area: 16,000 ft.².

Design team: Michael Graves (design architect); Nicholas Gonser (job captain); David Teeters, Gavin Hogben (project managers).

Construction company: Newport Harbor Construction Co.

Key materials: wood frame with exposed timber trusses, stucco, built-up roofing, mission clay roof tiles, gypsum board, quarry tiles.

Technology of interest: use of light monitors and clerestories to filter natural light into the building.

Budget: $1,500,000.

Site characteristics: adjacent to the site of the reconstructed Mission San Juan Capistrano.

Bibliography

"San Juan Capistrano Public Library Design Competition." *Architectural Record* 169 (March 1981): pp. 46–9.

Viladas, Pilar. "Ex Libris." *Progressive Architecture* 65 (June 1984): pp. 69–79.

MLTW (MOORE LYNDON TURBULL WHITAKER)

(c/o William Turnbull Associates), Pier 1 1/2, The Embarcadero, San Francisco, CA 94111

Charles Willard Moore: b. Michigan, 1925. Received undergraduate degree in architecture from University of Michigan, Ann Arbor (1947) and M. F. A. (1956) and Ph.D. (1957) from Princeton University. Was co-founder of MLTW (1962), founding own firm, Charles W. Moore Assoc. (1970). Principal in the firm, Moore, Ruble, Yudell, in Los Angeles (1979–93). Has taught at University of Utah, Princeton University, University of California, Berkeley, Yale University, University of California, Los Angeles. Was Chairman of Department of Architecture at University of California, Berkeley, and Yale University (1962–69); Chairman of School of Architecture at University of Texas, Austin (1984–93). Won AIA Gold Medal, 1991. Died 1993.

Donlyn Lyndon: educated at Princeton University, receiving A. B. (1957), and M. F. A. (1959). After 2 years as associate architect for Maynard Lyndon (1960–62), with partners formed MLTW. Has taught at University of Oregon, University of California, Berkeley, University of Texas, Austin, University of Maryland, University College, London,

and Massachusetts Institute of Technology. Was head of Department of Architecture at University of Oregon (1964–67) and Head of Department of Architecture at MIT (1967–75). Studied at American Academy in Rome (1977) and returned in 1986. Was awarded Fulbright scholarship, which he used for study in India (1959–60). Has been teaching at University of California, Berkeley, since 1978.

William Turnbull, Jr.: received B. A. (1956) and M. F. A. (1959) from Princeton University. Worked for Skidmore Owings & Merrill (1960–63). Co-founder of MLTW (1962). Has taught and lectured at Yale University, University of California, Berkeley, and University of California, Santa Cruz. Was Fellow at American Academy in Rome (1980). Recipient of the Maybeck Award (1993).

Richard Whitaker: b. 1929. Educated at University of California, Berkeley. Currently Professor of Architecture at University of Chicago.

MLTW won Firm of the Year Award from the California Council in 1986.

Project specifications

Sea Ranch Condominium I (Sea Ranch, California), 1963–65, pp. 90–93

Client: Oceanic Properties, California.

Built area: 9,341 ft.².

Design team: Charles W. Moore, Donlyn Lyndon, William Turnbull, Jr., Richard Whitaker, Edward Allen, Marvin Buchanan; Patrick Moreau, Ove Arup & Partners (structural engineer).

Construction company: Matthew D. Sylvia.

Key materials: heavy timber-frame structural system, redwood siding, aluminum window frames, copper flashing.

Budget: not available.

Site characteristics: former sheep ranch along the Pacific Coast, 90 miles north of San Francisco Bay.

The project won the architects the *Progressive Architecture* Citation in 1965, the California Governor's Design Award in 1966, the AIA Honor Award in 1967, and the AIA Twenty-Five-Year Award in 1991.

Bibliography

William Turnbull, Jr. *Global Architecture Detail* 3 (1976).

Moore, Charles Willard. *Charles Moore: buildings and projects 1949–1986*. New York: Rizzoli, 1986.

Donald Canty. "Sea Ranch." *Progressive Architecture* (February 1993): pp. 86–99.

Kresge College, University of California (Santa Cruz, California), 1970–73, pp. 152–53

Client: Regents of the University of California, Santa Cruz.

Built area: 101,416 ft.².

Design team: Charles W. Moore, William Turnbull, Jr., Robert T. Simpson, Robert Calderwood, Karl G. Smith II.

Construction company: Bogard Construction Inc.

Key materials: wood-frame structural system, painted stucco exterior, asphalt shingle roofing, gypsum board interior walls.

Budget: not available.

Site characteristics: wooded hillside overlooking Monterey Bay.

Bibliography

Progressive Architecture (May 1974).

Architectural Review (July 1974).

Moore, Charles Willard. *Charles Moore: buildings and projects 1949–1986*. New York: Rizzoli, 1986.

MORPHOSIS ARCHITECTS

2041 Colorado Avenue, Santa Monica, CA 90404

Thomas Mayne: b. 1944. Received B. Arch. from University of Southern California, and M. Arch. from Harvard University GSD. Has taught at SCI-ARC and Columbia University.

Project specifications

Cedars-Sinai Comprehensive Cancer Center (Los Angeles,

California), 1991, pp. 274–75
Client: Dr. Bernard Salick, Salick Health Care, Inc.
Built area: 53,000 ft.².
Design team: Morphosis: Thom Mayne, with Steve Johnson; Gruen Assoc.: Ki Suh Park, Robert S. Barnett.
Construction company: CAL PAC Construction.
Key materials: pre-cast concrete panels, sandstone, painted steel; ductile steel frame.
Budget: not available.
Site characteristics: on the campus of Cedars-Sinai Medical Center.

Bibliography
"Comprehensive Cancer Center." *Progressive Architecture* 68 (January 1987): pp. 112–14.
Rand, George, and Pilar Viladas. "The Road to Recovery." *Progressive Architecture* 69 (July 1988): pp. 66–75.
"Barroquismos gráficos: Centro Integral del Cáncer, Los Angeles." *A & U* 32 (1991): pp. 54–9.

MOSHE SAFDIE AND ASSOCIATES
100 Properzi Way, Somerville, MA 02143
Moshe Safdie: b. Israel, 1938. Received B. Arch. (1961) from McGill University. Worked with Van Gickel & Assoc. (1961–62), and with Louis Kahn (1961–63). In private practice since 1964. Has taught at McGill University, Yale University, and Harvard University. Was Professor of Architecture and Director of the Desert Architecture and Environment Department at the Desert Research Institute at Ben Gurion University, Beersheva, Negev, Israel (1975–78). Awarded Boston Society of Architects, Art and Architecture Collaboration Award (1993), AIA Medal of Honor (1980), Rechter Prize from Association of Architects and Planners of Israel (1982), AIRA Architect of the Year Award, and the Gold Star Award from the Philadelphia College of Art (1970).

Project specifications
Habitat (Montreal, Quebec), 1964–67, pp. 116–19
Client: Canadian Corporation for the 1967 Centennial World Exposition.
Built area: 242,200 ft.².
Design team: Moshe Safdie, David Rinehart, Jean-Eudes Guy, Dorice Walford, Irwin Cleve.
Construction company: Anglin-Norcross (general contractor); Francon (pre-cast contractor).
Key materials: reinforced pre-cast concrete. Superstructure: pre-cast concrete sections, post-tensioned. Box system: pre-cast concrete and post-tensioned connections.
Technology of interest: three-dimensional prefabricated living units, components of which are loadbearing, and connected to each other by a suspension system of post-tensioned high-tension rods, cables, and welding. Bathrooms are prefabricated gel-coat fiberglass. Window framing systems of reinforced plastic; fountain-cooled air-conditioning system, automatic snow-melting system, and accessible mechanical sub-floor system.
Budget: $13,500,000.
Site characteristics: man-made peninsula in the St. Lawrence River, with river rapids to the east and Montreal Port to the west.

Bibliography
Progressive Architecture (October 1966).
Safdie, Moshe. *Beyond Habitat*. Cambridge: MIT Press, 1970.
"Habitat at 25." *Architectural Record* (July 1992): pp. 40–2.

MURPHY/JAHN ARCHITECTS
35 East Wacker Drive Chicago, IL 60601
Helmut Jahn: b. Nuremburg, Germany, 1940. Graduated from Technische Hochschule, Munich (1965) with Dip. Ing./Arch. Joined C. F. Murphy Assoc., 1967. 7-time winner of AIA National Honor Award and Brunner Memorial Prize, 1982. Has taught at Yale and Harvard Universities. Member of the Chicago 7 since 1977.

Project specifications
State of Illinois Center (Chicago, Ilinois), 1979–85, pp. 236–37
Client: State of Illinois Capital Development Board.
Built area: 1,150,000 ft.².
Design team: Helmut Jahn, (principal-in-charge), James Goettsche (project architect), joint venture with Lester B. Knight and Assoc.
Key materials: vision and spandrel glass with granite base.
Technology of interest: energy efficiency through combination of active and passive energy systems (thermal storage and electric heating system). System has had extensive problems maintaining comfortable conditions.
Budget: $152,000,000.
Site characteristics: urban setting near Chicago's North Loop.

Bibliography
"State of Illinois Center: The Embodiment of Complex Goals." *Architectural Record* (August 1980): pp. 68–71.
"The Changing Skins of Helmut Jahn." *AIA Journal* (October 1981): pp. 62–7.
Miller, Nory. *Helmut Jahn*. New York: Rizzoli, 1986.

United Airlines Terminal, O'Hare International Airport (Chicago, Illinois), 1987, pp. 238–39
Built area: 1,200,000 ft.².
Key materials: steel structural frames on concrete caissons. Folded steel truss roof framing allows for free-span of 120 feet. Glazing in vault insulated fluropon.
Technology of interest: extensive use of skylights with fritted glass for 100% natural daylighting during the day. Undulating glass walls and ceiling, backlit with a spectrum of colors in underground walkway.
Budget: not available.

Bibliography
Murphy, Jim. "A Grand Gateway." *Progressive Architecture* 68 (November 1987): pp. 95–105.
Greer, Nora Richter. "Soaring Space that Celebrates Travel. United Airlines Terminal 1: Murphy/Jahn." *Architecture* 77 (May 1988): pp. 158–65.

PATKAU ARCHITECTS
560 Beatty Street, Suite L110, Vancouver, BC V6B 2L3, Canada
John Patkau: b. Winnipeg, Manitoba, 1947. Received B. A. (1969), Bachelor of Environmental Studies from the University of Manitoba, and M. Arch. (1972). Has acted as visiting critic at University of Calgary, University of British Columbia, University of Waterloo, University of California, Los Angeles, University of British Columbia, Technical University of Nova Scotia, and University of Pennsylvania.
Patricia Patkau: b. Winnipeg, Manitoba, 1950. Received Bachelor of Interior Design from the University of Manitoba (1973), and M. Arch. from Yale University (1978). Visiting Critic at: Harvard, Yale, MIT, UCLA, Southern California Institute of Architecture, University of Toronto, University of Calgary, University of Pennvlania, University of Waterloo. Associate Professor, and University of British Columbia.

Project specifications
Seabird Island School (Agassiz, British Columbia), 1988–91, pp. 276–79
Client: Seabird Island Band.
Built area: 23,573 ft.².
Design team: John Patkau, Patricia Patkau, Greg Johnson, Elizabeth Shottom, Tom Van Driel.
Construction company: New Haven Projects Ltd.

Key materials: plywood-sheathed timber joists on heavy timber "paralam" frames with reinforced concrete grade beams on timber piles.
Budget: Canadian $136 per sq. ft.

Bibliography
Canty, Donald. "Aerodynamic School." *Progressive Architecture* (May 1992): pp. 142–7.
Gruft, Andrew. "Seabird Island Community School." *Canadian Architect* (January 1992): pp. 14–23.
Boddy, Trevor. "Pacific Patkau." *The Architectural Review* vol. CLXXXIX, no. 1134 (August 1991): pp. 32–8.

PAUL RUDOLPH ARCHITECT
23 Beekman Place, New York, NY 10022
Paul Rudolph: b. Elkton, Kentucky, 1918. Graduated from Alabama Polytechnic Institute in 1940 and received his M. Arch. from Harvard University GSD in 1947.

Project specifications
Yale School of Art and Architecture (New Haven, Connecticut), 1958–63, pp. 82–85
Client: Yale University.
Built area: 117,575 ft.².
Design team: Paul Rudolph (architect); Henry Pfisterer (structural engineer); Van Elm, Heywood, and Shadford (mechanical engineer).
Construction company: George B. H. Macomber Company.
Key materials: poured-in-place concrete, both interior and exterior.
Technology of interest: utilization of wood formwork for concrete pours. Formwork used tapered battens 2 in. o.c. (on center) and the leading edge of the concrete was broken manually to expose the aggregate.
Budget: not available.
Site characteristics: small corner site at the boundary of the university campus and New Haven.

Bibliography
"Yale School of Art and Architecture: Paul Rudolph, Architect." *Progressive Architecture* (February 1964): pp. 109–29.
Moholy-Nagy, Sibyl. *The Architecture of Paul Rudolph*. New York: Praeger, 1970.

PEI COBB FREED & ASSOCIATES
(formerly I. M. Pei & Partners)
600 Madison Avenue, 9th floor, New York, NY 10022
Ieoh Ming Pei: b. China, 1917. Received B. Arch. from Massachusetts Institute of Technology (1940), and M. Arch. from Harvard University GSD (1946). Naturalized U.S. citizen (1954). On finishing graduate studies, worked for William Zeckendorf and Webb and Knapp (1948) and established partnership, I. M. Pei & Assoc., 1955. Numerous awards include Japan's *Praemium Imperiale* for lifetime achievement in architecture, France's National Medal of Art (1988), The Pritzker Architecture Prize (1983), AIA Gold Medal (1979), and the Brunner Memorial Prize (1963).
Henry Cobb: b. 1926. Graduated from Harvard College, Harvard University GSD. Chairman of Department of Architecture at Harvard University GSD (1980–1985). Awarded the Brunner Memorial Prize and the New York AIA Medal of Honor.
James Ingo Freed: b. Essen, Germany, 1930. B. Arch. from Illinois Institute of Technology (1953). Joined I. M. Pei and Partners (1956), after working with Mies van der Rohe (1955–56). Professor and Dean of College of Architecture at the Illinois Institute of Technology (1975–78). Has taught at Cooper Union and Yale University. Has been visiting critic at Cornell University, Columbia University, Pratt Institute, University of Miami, Harvard University GSD, Syracuse University, and University of California, Berkeley.

Received AIA Honor Award (1988), Lifetime Achievement Award from New York Society of Architects (1992), and AIA Thomas Jefferson Award for Public Architecture.

Project specifications

National Gallery of Art East Building (Washington, D.C.), 1968–78, pp. 174–75

Client: Trustees of the National Gallery of Art.

Built area: 604,000 ft.². (This includes connecting link, 154,000 ft.².)

Design team: I. M. Pei, Eason H. Leonard, James I. Freed, Leonard Jacobson, Yan Weymouth, William E. Pedersen, F. Thomas Schmitt, C. C. Pei, Stephen Wood, Owren Aftreth, William Jakabek, Michael Flynn, Fritz Sulzer, Richard Cutter (architects), Weiskopf & Pickworth, Syska & Hennesy (engineers).

Construction company: Charles H. Tompkins Company.

Key materials: cast-in-place reinforced concrete with long-span post-tensioned beams and trusses. Facade is Tennessee marble with cast-in-place concrete and marble dust aggregate beams. Interior incorporates a steel space frame and aluminum sunscreen. Paving is gray and pink granite cobblestone.

Budget: $83,000,000.

Site characteristics: 9-acre trapezoidal site adjacent to the National Gallery of Art on the mall in Washington, D.C.

The project won the AIA Honor Award in 1981, in 1986 named by AIA's College of Fellows One of America's Best Ten Buildings, and in 1991, One of America's Top All-Time Works of Architecture (1991).

Bibliography

"Mr. Pei Goes to Washington." *Architectural Record* (August 1978): pp. 79–92.

"P/A on Pei: Roundtable of a Trapezoid: East Building, National Gallery of Art, Washington, D.C." *Progressive Architecture* (October 1978): pp. 49–59.

Canty, Donald. "Building as Event: I. M. Pei and Partners' East Building, National Gallery of Art, Washington." *AIA Journal* 68 (May 1979): pp. 104–13.

The United States Holocaust Memorial Museum (Washington, D.C.) 1986–93, pp. 286–89

Client: United States Holocaust Memorial Council.

Built area: 258,000 ft.².

Design team: James Ingo Freed, Werner Wandelmaier, Michael D. Flynn, Craig Dumas, Beatrice Lehman, Michael Vissichelli, Harry Barone, Wendy Evans Joseph, Marek Zamdmer, Jean-Pierre Mutin, Stephen Ohnemus, Jou Min Lin, Alissa Bucher, Abby Suckle, Deborah Campbell.

Construction company: Blake Construction Company.

Key materials: cast-in-place concrete framing and bearing walls, steel gable-roof framing. Walls are self-supporting molded brick. Facade is Indiana limestone and cedar rose granite, molded brick with concrete lintels.

Budget: not available.

Site characteristics: located on a 1.7-acre block between 14th and 15th Streets, overlooking the Tidal Basin to the west.

Bibliography

Murphy, Jim. "Memorial to Atrocity." *Progressive Architecture* vol. 74, no. 2 (February 1993): pp. 60–72.

"A National Memorial Bears Witness to the Tragedy of the Holocaust." *Smithsonian* (April 1993): pp. 50–61.

Schmertz, Mildred. "In remembrance: U.S. Holocaust Memorial Museum." *Architecture* (July 1993): pp. 54–66.

RICHARD MEIER & PARTNERS

(formerly Richard Meier & Associates Architects)

475 Tenth Avenue, New York, NY 10018

Richard Meier: b. New Jersey, 1935. Graduated from Cornell University; worked for SOM and Marcel Breuer. Founded own firm, 1963. Was awarded Pritzker Architec-

ture Prize (1984), the Royal Gold Medal from Royal Institute of British Architects (1989), and New York AIA medal of Honor, 1980. Has taught at Cooper Union, University of California, Los Angeles, Harvard University and Yale University.

Project specifications

Bronx Development Center (The Bronx, New York), 1970–77, pp. 166–67

Client: Facilities Developmental Corporation of the State of New York.

Design team: Richard Meier; Severud-Perrone-Szegezdy-Sturm (structural consultant); Caretsky and Assoc. (mechanical and electrical consultants); Gangemi & DeBellis (landscape consultants).

Construction company: Starrett Brothers and Eken.

Budget: $2,200,000.

Site characteristics: triangular site bounded by the Hutchinson River Parkway on its east side and railroad tracks to the west.

Bibliography

"The Very Personal Work of Richard Meier and Assoc." *Architectural Forum* (March 1972): pp. 30–7.

"Bronx State School." *A & U* (June 1973): pp. 55–68.

Richard Meier: buildings and projects 1964–1984. Introduction by Joseph Rykwert. New York: Rizzoli, 1984.

Atheneum (New Harmony, Indiana), 1975–79, pp. 176–77

Client: Historic New Harmony, Inc.

Design team: Richard Meier and Assoc. (architects); Severud-Perrone-Szegezdy-Sturm (structural consultants); Flack & Kurtz (mechanical consultants); Kane & Carruth (landscape).

Construction company: Peyronnin Construction Company, Inc.

Budget: $1,800,000.

Site characteristics: located on the banks of the Wabash River

Bibliography:

Richard Meier, buildings and projects: 1966–1976. Introduction by Kenneth Frampton. New York: Oxford University Press, 1976.

Stephens, Suzanne. "Emblematic Edifice: The Atheneum, New Harmony, Indiana." *Progressive Architecture* (February 1980): pp. 67–75.

Rykwert, James. "Edifice: New Harmony Propylaeon." *Domus* (February 1980): pp. 12–17.

ROBERT A. M. STERN ARCHITECTS

211 West 61st Street, New York, NY 10023

Robert A. M. Stern: b. New York, 1939. Graduated from Columbia University with a B. A. (1960) and received M. Arch. from Yale University (1965). Professor at Columbia University.

Project specifications

Points of View (Mount Desert Island, Maine), 1975–76, pp. 164–65

Built area: 5,265 ft.².

Client: withheld.

Design team: Robert A. M. Stern, Daniel L. Colbert.

Construction company: The Herrick Corporation.

Key materials: wood framing with red cedar shingle walls and roof, pine trim, redwood decks. Granite fireplace and surround.

Technology of interest: traditionally constructed single-family residence.

Budget: not available.

Site characteristics: located on a granite bluff in Seal Harbor at the Southern tip of Mount Desert Island.

Bibliography

"Robert A. M. Stern/Points of View, Mount Desert Island, Maine." *Architectural Record* 169 (May 1981).

Rueda, Louis F. (ed.). *Robert A. M. Stern, buildings and projects, 1987–1992.* New York: Rizzoli, 1992.

SCOGIN, ELAM AND BRAY ARCHITECTS

1819 Peachtree Road NE, Suite 700, Atlanta, GA 30309

Mack Scogin: b. Atlanta, Georgia, 1943. Graduated from Georgia Institute of Technology (1966) with B. Arch. Worked at Heery and Heery Architects and Engineers (1967–88) as Senior Design Architect, Vice President and Design Coordinator, and President and Chief Operating Officer. Chairman of the Department of Architecture at Harvard University GSD (1991–95), and has taught at Georgia Institute of Technology and Rice University.

Merrill Elam: b. Nashville, Tennessee, 1943. Graduated from Georgia Institute of Technology in 1971 with B. Arch. Received her M.B.A. from Georgia State University, 1982. Worked at Taylor and Collum Architects (1967–69), at Heery and Heery Architects and Engineers (1969–84), and co-founded Scogin Elam and Bray Architects Inc. (1984). Has taught at Rice University, University of Virginia, Ohio State University, Clemson University, SCI-ARC, Harvard University GSD, Georgia Institute of Technology, Auburn University, and Mississippi State University.

Project specifications

Clayton County Library (Jonesboro, Georgia), 1986–88, pp. 246–47

Client: Clayton County Library Board of Trustees.

Built area: 32,000 ft.².

Design team: Merrill Elam, Mack Scogin, Lloyd Bray, Rick Sellers, Isabelle Millet, Tom Crosby, David Murphree, Dick Spangler, Ennis Parker.

Construction company: M. G. Engineering and Construction.

Key materials: structural steel frame, with long span wood and steel truss joists. Industrial-grade corrugated metal skin, stenciled with black and white "library box" pattern. Technology of interest: lighting is a combination of natural light and artificial, supplied by stadium light fixtures aimed at the ceiling. Heat-generating light ballasts are located on the exterior of the building to minimize cooling load.

Budget: $2,100,000.

Site characteristics: overlooks a natural flood plain.

Bibliography

Murphy, Jim. "K-Mart for Information: Clayton County Headquarters Library." *Progressive Architecture* 69 (November 1988): pp. 82–9.

Freeman, Allen. "Practical, Unpretentious, Open, and Family-Oriented." *Architecture* (May 1989): pp. 158–61.

"Work of Scogin Elam and Bray, The High Museum of Art at Georgia Pacific Center, Clayton County Headquarters Branch Library." *Architectural Record* (June 1989).

Linder, Mark (ed.). *Scogin, Elam and Bray: a critical monograph.* New York: Rizzoli International, 1992.

SERT, JACKSON AND ASSOCIATES, INC.

(formerly Sert Jackson and Gourley)

442 Marrett Road, Suite 10I, Lexington, MA 02173

Josep Lluis Sert: b. Barcelona, Spain, 1902. Received M. Arch. (1929) from Escuela Superior de Arquitectura, Barcelona. Worked as assistant in office of Le Corbusier and Pierre Jeanneret in Paris (1929–31). Practiced in Barcelona (1929–37). Partner of Town Planning Assoc. in New York (1939–57). President of CIAM (1947–56). Had private practice in Cambridge, MA (1957–58). Co-founder of Sert, Jackson and Gourley (1958). Was Dean of Harvard University GSD (1953–69). Died in Barcelona, 1983.

Huson Jackson: B. Arch. Harvard University; M. Arch. Harvard University; Ph.D., University of Chicago. Before 1958, practiced architecture in New York City. Co-founded Sert, Jackson and Assoc. (1963) and is currently President and

Director. Has taught at Pratt Institute, Columbia University, and Harvard University GSD.

Project specifications

Francis Greenwood Peabody Terrace (Cambridge, Massachusetts), 1963–65, pp. 100–01

Client: Harvard University.

Design team: Josep Lluis Sert, Huson Jackson, Ronald Gourley, Joseph Zalewski, William Lindemulder, Robert Kramer.

Technology of interest: skip-stop elevators.

Budget: not available.

Site characteristics: adjacent to the Charles River and the Harvard undergraduate student dormitories.

Bibliography

Progressive Architecture (December 1964).

Architectural Design (August 1965).

Progressive Architecture (October 1974).

Progressive Architecture (June 1994).

SITE

65 Bleecker Street, New York, NY 10012

Alison Sky: b. New York. Studied at Adelphi University. Since 1970, has been Coordinator of the Environmental Arts program at the School of Visual Arts, New York.

James Wines: b. Oak Park, Illinois, 1932. Graduated from Syracuse University School of Art, 1956. Received Rome Prize, 1956. Worked as sculptor (1955–67) and co-founded SITE, 1970. Served as Chairman of the Department of Environmental Design at Parsons School of Design (1984–90). Has taught at New York University, The New School for Social Research, Pratt Institute, Cornell University, Dartmouth College, State University of New York, University of Wisconsin, Cooper Union, The New Jersey School of Architecture, Domun Academy, Politecnico di Milano, and Università di Calabria.

Project specifications

Best Forest Building (Richmond, Virginia), 1978–80, pp. 192–93

Client: Best Products Company, Inc.

Design team: James Wines, Emilio Sousa, Alison Sky.

Construction company: The Whiting-Turner Contracting Co.

Key materials: brick, concrete, masonry block, reinforced concrete slab, trees.

Technology of interest: development of the "terrarium wall," incorporating water, vegetation, sand, earth, and rock.

Budget: $2,000,000.

Site characteristics: densely wooded suburban site which begins to penetrate the building's showroom.

Bibliography

Black, David. "SITE for Sore Eyes." *Next* (May/June 1981): pp. 32–7.

Davis, Douglas. "SITE to PostSITE." *Art Express* (September–October 1981): pp. 19–21.

James Wines. *Amicus Journal* (Summer 1993).

SKIDMORE OWINGS & MERRILL

224 South Michigan Avenue, Suite 1000, Chicago, IL 60604

Myron Goldsmith: b. Chicago, Illinois, 1918. Graduated from Armour Institute of Technology (1939). Received M. S. Arch. from Illinois Institute of Technology (1953), studying under Mies van der Rohe. Studied in Rome (1953–55) under Fulbright Grant. Received 1975 AIA Honor Award, and *Progressive Architecture* Award, 1979. Was Professor of Architecture at IIT (1961–80). Has also taught at Harvard University GSD and Huazhong University of Science and Technology, Wuhan, China.

Fazlur Khan: b. Dacca, India, 1929. Graduated from University of Dacca, Bangladesh (1950), and immigrated to

the U.S., 1952. Ph.D. in structural engineering from University of Illinois (1955). Worked at SOM, Chicago, from 1955 until his death. General Partner from 1970 and Adjunct Professor of Architecture at Illinois Institute of Technology. Died 1982.

Project specifications

Robert R. McMath Solar Telescope (Tucson, Arizona), 1962, pp. 76–77

Client: Association of Universities for Research in Astronomy (AURA).

Design team: William Dunlap (partner-in-charge and project manager); Myron Goldsmith (design partner).

Construction company: Western Knapp Engineering Co.

Key materials: structural steel; internal concrete tower, white painted copper exterior tube-and-strip panels (containing chilled circulating mixture of glycol and water), and interior aluminum-covered insulating panels. Windscreen on dome is polyurethane-insulated metal panel within hexahedral structure of metal tubing.

Technology of interest: structurally independent telescope required a structural tolerance of approximately one thousandth of an inch, located 100 feet above grade within a structure designed to minimize the effects of wind and temperature fluctuations of the air and the earth's surface.

Budget: not available.

Site characteristics: Kitt Peak National Observatory.

Bibliography

"Mighty Telescope for 'The Long Eyes'." *Life* (June 7, 1963): pp. 53–4, 56.

"Unusual Buildings Win in AISC Award Program." *Progressive Architecture* (July 1963): p. 48.

John Hancock Center (Chicago, Illinois), 1965–70, pp. 144–45

Client: John Hancock Mutual Life Insurance Company.

Built area: 2,800,000 ft.².

Design team: Al Lockett (partner-in-charge); Dick Lenke (project manager); Bruce Graham (chief designer); Robert Diamont (senior designer); Fazlur Khan (project structural engineer); Dick Warfel/Al Cho (project mechanical engineer); Paul Kwong (electrical engineer).

Construction company: Tishman Realty and Construction Company.

Key materials: structural steel frame, black aluminum cladding, tinted bronze glare-reducing glass; bronze-colored aluminum window frames. First floor base: travertine marble. Paving: dark granite.

Budget: not available.

Bibliography

Kahn, Fazlur R. "The John Hancock Center." *Civil Engineering* (October 1967).

"Fazlur R. Khan, general partner of Skidmore Owings and Merrill." *Architectural Record* (May 1982).

Bush-Brown, Albert. *Skidmore Owings and Merrill: architecture and urbanism, 1973–1983.* New York: Van Nostrand Reinhold, 1983.

STANLEY TIGERMAN AND ASSOCIATES

444 North Wells #206, Chicago, IL 60610

Stanley Tigerman: b. Chicago, Illinois, 1930. B. Arch. (1960) and M. Arch. (1961) from Yale. Before establishing own firm with Norman Koglin (1962), worked as designer for Skidmore, Owings & Merrill, Chicago (1957–59) and Paul Rudolph (1959–61). Has held numerous teaching posts across the country, including University of Illinois at Chicago Circle, Washington University, St. Louis; University of Houston, Northwestern University, Cornell University Cooper Union, University of Notre Dame, and University of California, Berkeley. Received AIA Award of Merit (1970) and *Progressive Architecture* Award (1980).

Project specifications

Illinois Regional Library for the Blind and Physically Handicapped (Chicago, Illinois), 1975–78, pp. 168–71

Client: Chicago Public Library System.

Built area: 32,000 ft.².

Design team: Jerome Butler (city architect); Stanley Tigerman, Robert Fugman, Daniel Sutherland, Richard Taransky, and Rafique Islam; Ray Beebe (structural engineer); Wallace and Migdal (mechanical and electrical engineer).

Construction company: Walsh Construction Company.

Key materials: concrete, cold-rolled carbon steel plate; finished with baked enamel on metal panels.

Technology of interest: linear plan with built-in elements for easy memorization, and tactile clues to organization.

Budget: $1,900,000 (includes built-in furniture and furnishings).

Site characteristics: triangular site located on the southwest corner of the University of Illinois at Chicago campus.

Bibliography

Miller, Nory. "Tigerman shapes a fresh new library for the blind." *Inland Architect* (1976).

Tigerman, Stanley. *Stanley Tigerman: Buildings and Projects, 1966–1989.* (ed. Sarah Mollman Underhill.) New York: Rizzoli, 1989.

STEVEN HOLL ARCHITECTS

435 Hudson Street, 4th floor, New York, NY 10014

Steven Holl: b. 1947. Graduated from University of Washington (1971), and did post-graduate work at the Architectural Association in London (1976). Has taught at Columbia University since 1981; has also held teaching positions at Syracuse University, University of Washington, Pratt Institute, Parsons School of Design, and University of Pennsylvania. Established Steven Holl Architects, 1976.

Project specifications

Berkowitz Odgis House (Martha's Vineyard, Massachusetts), 1984, pp. 230–33

Client: Steven Berkowitz, Janet Odgis.

Built area: 2800 ft.².

Design team: Steven Holl with Peter Lynch; Peter Shinoda and Stephen Cassell (assistants).

Construction company: Doyle Construction.

Key materials: wood frame.

Technology of interest: exposed exterior balloon frame, to convey the idea of skeletal bones, inspired by a passage from Melville's *Moby Dick*.

Budget: $275,000.

Site characteristics: on the hilly waterfront of the southeast side of Martha's Vineyard.

Bibliography

"The Berkowitz Odgis House." *Progressive Architecture* (January 1986): pp. 104–6.

Holl, Steven. *Anchoring: Selected Projects, 1975–1988.* New York: Princeton Architectural Press, 1989.

THE STUBBINS ASSOCIATES, INC.

(formerly Hugh Stubbins & Associates, Inc.)

1033 Massachusetts Avenue, Cambridge, MA 02138

Hugh Asher Stubbins, Jr.: b. 1912. Received B.S. in architecture from Georgia Institute of Technology (1933); M. Arch. from Harvard University (1935). Served in U.S. Naval Reserve (1933–35). Worked for 2 years as designer for R. B. Wills, establishing own firm, Peter and Stubbins, in 1937 (now The Stubbins Assoc., Inc.). Has taught at Harvard University, Yale University, University of Oregon, and University of Virginia, and was Chairman of Department of Architecture at Harvard (1953). Received R. S. Reynolds Memorial Award (1981) and AIA's National Honor Award (1979).

Project specifications

Citicorp (New York City, New York), 1970–77, pp. 172–73

Client: First National City Corporation.

Built area: 1,715,850 ft.² (tower); 56,420 ft.² (church).

Design team: Hugh Stubbins, Peter Woytuk, Richard Green, W. Easley Hamner, Howard E. Goldstein, Robert Fager; Emery Roth and Sons (associated architects); William Le Messurier (structural design).

Construction company: HRH Construction Corporation.

Key materials: structural steel frame, aluminum spandrel panels, double-glazed, insulated reflective glass; concrete tuned-mass damper. The 24-foot square supporting columns contain ductwork and stairs.

Technology of interest: structural design incorporates diagonal bracing, clear-span floors, and a tuned-mass damper to moderate building motion. Energy-conserving features, such as low-brightness lighting, a heat reclamation system, a computer-based building management system, and double-decker elevators were incorporated into the building's design.

Budget: $82,000,000 (tower); $4,700,000 (church).

Site characteristics: midtown Manhattan block. The raised tower allows for a sunken plaza below its base, and St. Peter's Lutheran Church at the upper plaza level.

Bibliography

Mehlman, Robert. "Skyscrapers for people: New York's Citicorp Complex." *Contract Interiors* (May 1978): pp. 127–39.

"Citicorp Center: If you don't like its crown look at its base." *Architectural Record* (June 1978): pp. 107–16.

VENTURI, SCOTT BROWN AND ASSOCIATES, INC.

4236 Main Street, Philadelphia, PA 19127-1696

Robert Venturi: b. Philadelphia, 1925. A. B. degree (1947) and M. F. A. (1950) from Princeton University. Rome Prize Fellow at American Academy in Rome (1954–56). Before establishing own company (1961), worked as designer in firms of Louis Kahn and Eero Saarinen. Taught at the University of Pennsylvania, University of California at Los Angeles, Rice University, Yale University, Princeton University, and Harvard University. Received The Pritzker Architectural Prize (1991) and AIA Medal of Distinction, Pennsylvania Society of Architects, 1990.

Denise Scott Brown: educated at University of Witwatersrand, Johannesburg (1948–52); Architectural Association in London (1955); University of Pennsylvania, M. C. P. (1960) and M. Arch. (1965). Has taught at University of Pennsylvania, University of California at Berkeley and Los Angeles, Rice University, Yale University, and Harvard University. With partner, Robert Venturi, was awarded National Medal of the Arts, 1992. Awarded the Chicago Architecture Award, 1987.

Project specifications

Vanna Venturi House (Chestnut Hill, Philadelphia, Pennsylvania), 1961–63, pp. 86–89

(Venturi and Short)

Client: Vanna Venturi.

Design team: Robert Venturi, with the assistance of Arthur Jones.

Key materials: block and stucco with wood joists.

Budget: not available.

Bibliography

Schwartz, Frederic. *Mother's House: The Evolution of Vanna Venturi's House in Chestnut Hill*. New York: Rizzoli, 1992.

Robert Venturi. "A Postscript on my Mother's House." *Architectural Record* (June 1982): pp. 114–15.

Guild House, (Philadelphia, Pennsylvania), 1961– 65, pp. 98–99

(Venturi and Rauch)

Client: Friends Neighborhood Guild.

Design team: Robert Venturi (partner-in-charge); Gerod Clark, with Frank Kawasaki (project managers).

Key materials: flat plate concrete structure with brick and block walls.

Budget: not available.

Site characteristics: small urban site adjacent to a warehouse.

Bibliography

Progressive Architecture (May 1967): pp. 133–7.

Lotus 4 (1967–68): pp. 98–105.

Moos, Stanislaus von. *Venturi Rauch & Scott Brown: buildings and projects*. New York: Rizzoli, 1987.

Seattle Art Museum (Seattle, Washington), 1984–91, pp. 280–81

(Venturi, Scott Brown and Associates, Inc.)

Client: Seattle Art Museum.

Built area: 150,000 ft.².

Design team: Robert Venturi (partner-in-charge); John Pringle, James C. Bredberry (project managers); John Bastian (project architect); Daniel C. Borden, Gary Griggs, Brian LaBau, John Forney, Matthew J. Schottelkotte, Douglas E. Seiler, Mark Stankard, Mary Wieand, James G. Winkler (project team). With the assistance of: Denise Scott Brown, Steven Izenour, Ann Trowbridge, David Vaughan.

Construction company: Howard S. Wright.

Key materials: steel frame with fluted limestone, granite, terra cotta cladding.

Technology of interest: lighting, mechanical, and security systems.

Budget: not available.

Site characteristics: urban Seattle hillside.

Bibliography

"Venturi, Rauch, Scott Brown: Seattle Art Museum." *Domus* 699 (November 1988): p. 40.

Canty, Donald. "New VSBA Museum Opens in Seattle." *Progressive Architecture* vol. 73, no. 2 (February 1992): pp. 19–20.

Belluzzi, Amadeo. "Seattle Art Museum." *Abitare* 306 (April 1992): pp. 182–7.

Acknowledgments

Key: *t*=top, *c*=center, *b*=bottom, *l*=left, *r*=right. References are to page numbers.

© Peter Aaron/Esto 211*t*, 211*bl*, 225*t*, 226, 227*t*, 227*b*, 248; © Joe C. Aker 156, 159*b*; photo Glen Allison 52*t*; © Arcosanti 136*r*, 137; © Atlantic Filmworks 157*b*; © S. Badanes 179*t*, 179*bl*; © Morley Baer 91*t*, 91*c*, 92*tl*, 93; © Otto Baitz 223*l*, 223*r*; © Edward Larrabee Barnes 68*t*; Gunnar Birkerts 47*b*; © Bond 197*t*; © Tom Bonner 54, 55*t*, 55*c*, 55*b*; Buckminster Fuller Archive 28; © Cambridge Seven 110*b*, 111*b*, 112*t*, 112*b*, 113, 134*t*, 135; © Cardinal 254*t*, 254*b*, 255*l*, 255*r*; © Tom Crane 234*l*, 235*t*, 235*br*; © Mark Darley/Esto 152*l*, 153*tr*, 273*t*, 273*b*; © P. Dodge 224*t*; © Michael Drummond 122*b*, 123*t*; © Duany/Plater-Zyberk 194*r*, 195*t*, 195*bl*, 195*br*; photo Ron Ellis 222*bl*; © Erickson 160*b*, 161*t*, 162, 163*b*, 187*l*, 187*tr*, 187*cr*, 187*br*; © Christopher Erickson 163*t*; © Esto 193*tl*; © GPS 228*t*, 229*tl*, 229*bl*,

229*r*, © Gatje Papachristou Smith 106–07, 228*t*, 229*tl*, 229*bl*, 229*r*; © Jeff Goldberg/Esto 261, 262, 263*t*, 263*b*, 283*t*, 284–5*t*, 284–5*b*; © Graetz 117; © Michael Graves 38*t*, 38*c*, 209*l*, 209*r*, 220*r* (photo Paschall/Taylor), 221*t* (photo Paschall/Taylor); © Gwathmey Associates 40*b*, 103*l*, 104*tl*, 105; © Jim Hedrich 266*tl*, 266*tr*, 266*b*, 267*t*; John Hejduk 39, 40*b*; © Hellmuth, Obata & Kassabaum Inc 210*tl*, 210*tr*, 211*br*; © Paul Hester 243*b*, 244*l*, 244*r*, 245; © David Hirsch 23*b*; © Holt Hinshaw Pfau Jones 56*t*, 272*tl*; © Holt, Rinehart and Winston 33; © Greg Hursley 241*t*, 241*br*; © Timothy Hursley 118*br*, 201*t*, 202–3, 247*t*, 250*b*, 270*t*, 271*t*; © Richard Ingersoll 234*r*; Carlos Jiménez 53; Johnson/Burgee Architects 45, 46; © Fay Jones 191*tl*, 191*tr*, Kahn Archive 20, 72–4, 75*br*, 94–5, 148; © Kallman, McKinnell & Knowles 127; © Phokion Karas 101*t*, 101*bl*, 101*br*; photo Douglas Kelbaugh 222*br*; © Balthazar Korab 47*t*, 139*t*, 140*t*,

141, 146*r*, 147*tl*, 147*bl*, 154*b*, 157*t*, 158*t*; © Rollin R. La France 88*l*; © Ricardo Legorreta 264*l*; © Lars Lerup 56*b*; Kevin Lynch 25*t*, 25*c*, 25*b*, 34*t*; © Peter Mauss/Esto 251*t*; © Norman McGrath 142*tl*, 143*tr*, 172, 173*tl*, 205, 206*l*, 207, 212*l*, 218*l*, 218*r*, 219*bl*, 219*r*, 286*b*, 288, 289*tl*, 289*tr*, 289*b*, 291*t*, 291*bl*; © Peter Millard 23*b*; © MIT Press 25*t*, 25*c*, 25*b*, 32, 34*t*, 35*t*; © Joseph Molitor 2, 68*b*, 69; © Bob Moore 178*t*; Charles Moore 16, 17, 18; © Michael Moran 52*c*; © Grant Mudford 275*tl*; © Murphy/Jahn 236, 237*tr*, 237*br*, 238*tl*, 238 *tr*, 239; © Mary Otis Stevens 28*t*, 28*c*; © Patkau and Patkau 278*t*, 278*b*, 279*t*, 279*bl*; © George Pohl 86*t*, 87*tr*, 87*br*, 89*tl*, 89*r*; © Portman 115*tl*, 115*tr*; © Jock Pottle/Esto 294*tl*, 295; *Progressive Architecture* 10; Proto Acme Photo 209*l*, 209*r*; © Michel Proulx 123*b*; © Karl Riek 71*br*; © James V. Righter 165*t*; © Cervin Robinson 215*t*, 216, 217; © Roche Dinkeloo and Associates 78, 79*t*, 80*t*, 129*t*,

130*b*, 131*t*, 184*tr*, 185*bl*, 185*br*; © Paul Rudolph 23*t*, 23*c* 24*bl*, 24*br*, 82–3, 84*t*, 84*br*; Eero Saarinen 24*t*; © Safdie 118*tl*, 118*tr*, 119*t*, 119*bl*, 119*br*; © Gordon Schenk 188*t*, 189*l*, 189*r*, 197*b*, 198*t*, 199; © Malcolm Smith 75*tl*; © Ezra Stoller/Esto 22, 24*c*, 76*tl*, 76*tr*, 77*l*, 77*r*, 79*b*, 80*bl*, 80*br*, 81*l*, 81*r*, 84*bl*, 85*cl*, 85*bl*, 85*br*, 96*t*, 96*b*, 97, 108, 109, 125*b*, 144*l*, 145*br*, 149, 150, 151, 166*r*, 167*t*, 167*b*, 175*t*, 175*cl*, 175*br*, 176*tr*, 176*b*, 177*tl*, 177*b*; © Stoller Partners 71*t*, 71*bl*; © Tim Street-Porter/Esto 182, 183; © Wayne Thom 186*tl*; © Tigerman (photos Philip Turner) 169, 170, 171; © Alexander Tzonis 31*t*, 31*b*; © Vanderwarker 126*tl*; photo John Veltri 67*b*; © Venturi, Scott Brown and Associates 32, 35*t*, 34*c*, 35*b*, 98*b*, 99*b*; © Alex Vertikoff 258*cr*, 259; © David Walker 265; © Paul Warchol 232*t*, 232*b*, 233*l*, 233*tr*, 233*br*; © Wargo and VSBA 281*l*, 281*br*; © William Watkins 99*t*; © ZRP/A 155*b*

Index

Aalto, Alvar 54, 88

Abstract Expressionism 33

Action Architecture 21, 33, 43, 124, 138

aedicular structure (see also Moore, Charles) 92

Affleck, Desbarats, Dimakopoulos, Sise 15, 27, 32, 58, 120–3, 296

Alexander, Christopher 15, 28, 37, 42, 61, 62, 63

Algarotti, Francesco 19

Alinsky, Saul David 33

American Renaissance 15–17, 19–23, 60

anti-city 55, 64

aquaria 132, 200, 224

Arcosanti 136–7, 296–7

Arquitectonica 52, 204–7, 297

atria 82, 124, 130, 184, 186, 218, 236, 286

Banfield, Edward 25

Banham, Reyner 34, 303

Barnes, Edward Larrabee 15, 17–18, 48–9, 50, 52, 58, 61, 66–9, 92, 214–17, 300, 302

Barnett, Jonathan 114

Belluschi, Pietro 11

Berlin, Isaiah 42

Birkerts, Gunnar 47, 49, 146–7

Black Mountain 18, 66

Bond Ryder James and Associates 37, 96–9, 297

Breuer, Marcel 106–9, 228, 301, 304–5, 307

Brolin, Brent 36

Bruner, Simeon 58, 64

Buford, Bill 31, 55, 63

Bunshaft, Gordon 106

Burgee, John (see also Philip Johnson) 45–7, 48–9, 188–9, 212–13, 214, 303

Cambridge Seven Associates 15, 27, 36, 110–13, 132–5, 297–8

Cardinal, Douglas 53, 252–5, 299–300

Carlin and Pozzi 24

Carson, Rachel 12, 13, 61

Center for Maximum Potential Building Systems 18, 53, 136, 240–1

Cézanne 180

Chafee, Judith 52, 53

Chandler, Raymond 34

chaos 10–11, 42, 57, 58, 60, 140, 180, 256

Chaoticism 10, 12, 14, 58, 140

Chermayeff, Serge 11, 15, 26, 28, 54, 61, 62

Chimacoff, Alan 38

Chomskean linguistics 142

churches 188, 190

City Beautiful 23

cityscape 23–4, 25, 26, 46, 50, 82

civic presence 22–5, 82, 98, 124, 147

civic purpose 22–5, 98, 124, 147

Clark & Menafee Architects 54, 234–5, 299

Classicism 43, 45, 126, 148, 174, 184, 261, 286

cognitive mapping 23–4, 58, 167

Collage City 41–3, 63

color 156, 168, 204, 208, 239, 242, 267

Columbia University 39, 40, 292

commercial facilities 120, 156, 192, 212, 218, 248

community 13–14, 15, 17–18, 19, 21, 22, 23, 26–8, 37, 39, 44, 45, 48, 49, 51, 53–4, 56, 57, 58, 59, 60, 90–2, 94, 98, 115, 117, 127, 136, 152, 176, 188, 194, 196, 210, 222, 224, 252, 276, 286, 292, 293

Community Action Program 33

complexity and contradiction 86–9

Cooper, Claire 29, 305

Craig Zeidler Strong 154–5, 299

Creighton, Thomas H. 10–12, 61

critical architecture 31, 42, 55–9, 180, 193, 286

Critical Regionalism 17–19, 51–4, 57, 66, 90, 190, 191, 202, 224–8, 230, 234, 235, 242–8, 252, 255, 264–72, 276

Cullen, Gordon 33, 34

Davidoff, Paul 37

Davis, Mike 55–6, 64

De Kooning, Willem 180

De l'Orme, Philibert 98

Der Scutt Architect 49, 214, 218–19, 299

Deutsch, Karl 25, 26, 62

Dewey, John 60, 64

Diamonstein, Barbaralee 180

Dirty Realism 55–9, 80, 256, 272

disability 168

Disneyland 34

Doxiadis, Constantine 177

Drexler, Arthur 43, 63

Duany, Andres and Elizabeth Plater-
Zyberk 52, 194–5, 296

Duchamp, Marcel 55, 181

Dyckman, John 25, 26, 36

Ecole des Beaux-Arts 43, 45, 74, 174, 193

ecology 12, 16, 25, 28, 51, 53, 55, 137, 193, 200, 226, 228, 240, 276, 293

Economic Opportunity Act 32, 33

Edwards, Trystan 23, 62

Eisenman, Peter 39, 40–1, 59, 142–3, 260–3, 300, 302

energy 17, 21, 38, 50, 178, 222, 228, 236, 240

environment, natural 16, 18, 23, 133, 136, 160, 190, 200, 276

Erickson, Arthur 18, 58, 160–3, 186–7, 208, 276, 297

Esherik Homsey Dodge Davis 52, 224–7, 301

Expo 67 27, 36, 110, 116, 117, 120, 133

Fernau and Hartman 54

FHA and FNMA 70

Fisk, Pliny (see Center for Maximum Potential Building Systems)

Fleisher, Aaron 25

Foley, Donald 20, 62

Ford, Gerald 45

Formalism 38, 40–44, 59, 142

Frampton, Kenneth 44

Fuller, Buckminster 11, 15, 27, 28, 58, 110–13, 146, 272, 297

Functionalism 15, 16, 19–20, 21, 23, 25, 29, 39, 57, 58, 60, 77, 138, 164

Galbraith, John Kenneth 12, 13, 22, 27, 61, 187

Gandelsonas, Mario 39, 142, 208

Gatje Papachristou Smith 53, 228–9, 272, 301

Gehry, Frank O. 25, 31, 55–6, 59, 180–3, 290–1, 301

geodesic dome 27, 28, 110–13

Gilded Age 114

Gitlin, Tod 32, 63

Giurgola, Romaldo 40, 264–7

Goethe, Wolfgang 47

Goldberger, Paul 48, 50, 213, 215, 236

Goldsmith, Myron 15, 22, 76, 77, 308

Graves, Michael 38, 39, 40, 41, 42, 43, 208–9, 220–1, 305

Greenberg, Alan 40

Greenhough, Horatio 16, 18, 19, 22, 47, 60, 62, 77

Griswold, A. Whitney 82, 84

Gropius, Walter 33, 43, 84, 106

Gwathmey Siegel & Associates 39–40, 50–1, 102–5, 213, 302

Halprin, Lawrence 18, 36, 70, 90, 210

Harrington, Michael 12, 13, 61

Harrison and Abramovitch 20

Hartman, Chester 36, 135

Harvard Graduate School of Design 11, 26, 36, 100, 246

Haskell, Douglas 20, 33–4, 62

health facilities 154, 166, 274

Heimatsarchitektur 16

Hejduk, John 39, 40, 41, 170

Hellmuth Obata Kassabaum 36, 45, 57, 58, 210–11, 282–5, 302

historicism 10, 24, 43, 45, 51, 86, 164, 194, 212, 220

Hitchcock, Henry Russell 16

Holl, Steven 52, 59, 194, 230–3, 308

Holt, Hinshaw, Pfau, Jones 56–7, 59, 302, 272–3

Holtz Kay, Jane 100, 221, 297

hotels 114, 120, 138

Housing and Urban Affairs Department 12

Huxtable, Ada Louise 50, 127, 213, 214

imageability 23, 24, 26, 46, 127, 158, 236

industrialized construction 29, 116

Jacobs, Jane 15, 29, 42, 61, 124

jazz 20

Jersey Devil 18, 53, 178–9, 302

Jiménez, Carlos 53, 54, 58, 242–5, 298

Johansen and Bahvani 11, 126, 138–41, 302–3

Johns, Jasper 99

Johnson, Lyndon 32–3, 37–8, 42

Johnson, Philip 11, 16, 20, 22, 31, 45, 46–7, 48–9, 50, 64, 188–9, 208, 212–13, 214, 215, 299, 303

Joint Center, Harvard-MIT 23, 25

Jones, Fay and Maurice Jennings 53, 190–1, 301